FATHERS
AND
FAMILIES

Other Works by Henry B. Biller

Father, Child and Sex Role: Paternal Determinants of Personality Development (1971)

Paternal Deprivation: Family, School, Sexuality and Society (1974)

Father Power, with Dennis L. Meredith (1974)

The Other Helpers: Paraprofessionals and Nonprofessionals in Mental Health, with Michael Gershon (1977)

Paternal Death and Psychological Development, with Ellen B. Berlinsky (1982)

Child Maltreatment and Paternal Deprivation: A Manifesto for Research, Prevention and Treatment, with Richard S. Solomon (1986)

Stature and Stigma: The Biopsychosocial Development of Short Males, with Leslie F. Martel (1987)

FATHERS
AND
FAMILIES
PATERNAL FACTORS IN CHILD DEVELOPMENT

HENRY B. BILLER

AUBURN HOUSE

Westport, Connecticut • London

Library of Congress Cataloging-in-Publication Data

Biller, Henry B.
    Fathers and families : paternal factors in child development /
Henry B. Biller.
        p.   cm.
    Includes bibliographical references and index.
    ISBN 0–86569–208–4 (alk. paper). — ISBN 0–86569–227–0 (pbk.: alk paper)
    1. Father and child—United States.   2. Child development—United
States.   3. Family—United States.   I. Title.
    HQ755.85.B54   1993
    306.874′2—dc20   92–18361

British Library Cataloguing in Publication Data is available.

Library of Congress Catalog Card Number: 92–18361
ISBN: 0–86569–208–4
ISBN: 0–86569–227–0 (pbk.)

First published in 1993

Auburn House, 88 Post Road West, Westport, CT 06881
An imprint of Greenwood Publishing Group, Inc.

Printed in the United States of America

The paper used in this book complies with the
Permanent Paper Standard issued by the National
Information Standards Organization (Z39.48–1984).

10 9 8 7 6 5 4 3 2 1

To the memory of my parents and grandparents

To my wife, children and grandchild

Contents

Preface

Fathers and Familes focuses on the implications of research findings concerning the impact of paternal involvement in child development.

- The capacity of the father to form a close bond with his newborn and his crucial role during the infant's development.
- The importance of the father in helping his son or daughter to develop a positive body image, self-esteem, moral standards and intellectual and social competence.
- The linkage of the early father-child relationship to the son's and daughter's later adjustment in adolescence and adulthood.
- The contributions of the involved father to the mother's marital satisfaction and effective coparenting.
- The benefits of equitably shared child rearing to the personal development of both the father and the mother.
- The advantages of the father's continuing involvement with his child even when the parents are divorced or do not live together.
- The ways that active fathering lessens the risk of serious problems for children and families.
- The negative consequences of paternal neglect and other forms of inadequate fathering.
- The reality that men must make a greater commitment to the welfare of children.
- The recognition that more men should be involved in early childhood education and in other programs serving children and families.

While the significance of the early mother-child relationship has long been acknowledged, the father's contributions to the family received very scant attention from researchers and clinicians before the 1970s. Despite the growing consideration given to paternal behavior in the last two decades, most discussions of parenting do not provide enough emphasis on the role of the father. Taking a life-span perspective, this book elaborates on how variations in paternal involvement affect many different dimensions of child and parent development.

Fathers and Families should be of interest to parents, students, researchers, mental health professionals and others concerned with the welfare of children.

Throughout the book, recognition is given to interconnections among biological, psychological and social influences that impact on the father's role in child development. An attempt is made to integrate research findings from many different sources in a way that suggests practical guidelines for improving the quality of father involvement and family life. Relevant research has been contributed by scholars from various disciplines including cultural anthropology, early childhood education, family sociology, nursing, pediatrics, psychiatry and social work as well as from several areas of psychology.

For those readers interested in more of the details of studies relating to specific topics, pertinent references can be found in the Further Reading sections that conclude each chapter. Given the methodological limitations of any single research project, I have tried to make generalizations on the basis of the overall pattern of findings from a variety of investigations. There is a definite need for more research following families over time, with greater consideration being given to the reciprocal influences that parents and children have on one another.

Since the 1960s, a major goal of my research and writing endeavors, including most of my previous books, has been to encourage more systematic investigations of the father-child relationship. My teaching, clinical activities and consulting have also involved efforts to understand better the role of the father in individual and family development. I have learned much from students, parents and therapy clients as well as from the hundreds of individuals who have participated in research projects conducted by me and my associates. Without such shared experience this book could not have been written. However, aside from references to public figures and members of my own family, the names of parents and children whose situations are described here have been changed to protect their privacy.

In addition to scholarly and professional influences on my work, there is a definite link between my family history and career interests. My introduction into graduate school and clinical training coincided with being a first-time father. I was amazed that so little attention had been given to the father's role in either the child development or therapy literature. At that time, I had difficulty locating more than a handful of published research articles concerning paternal influence, and these dealt primarily with the father's absence rather than his role within the family.

In the early 1960s little theoretical discussion of paternal behavior took place. Clinical work with children was generally built on a model of maternal determinism with information about the father usually sought only indirectly by interviewing the mother. I encountered considerable skepticism regarding my interest in investigating fathering from many other researchers and clinicians. I was even chided for being concerned with "sociological rather than psychological issues" and for being "unrealistic" in wanting to include fathers as active participants in therapy with young children. Given my own family background, this prevailing lack of consideration for paternal influence was particularly disconcerting.

I was born into a household that included my maternal grandparents and an uncle in addition to my father, mother and sister, almost eight years my senior. As a young child, I was in the unusual situation of having three adult males to interact with on a regular basis, and I developed especially strong attachments to both my father and my grandfather. However, our family subsequently suffered a series of wrenching changes. My uncle was drafted into the army and, even more significant, first my grandfather and then my father died within less than two years after my fourth birthday. By the age of six I was the only one left of the original four male family members in the household. Throughout middle childhood and adolescence, I struggled to provide a vital sense of paternal influence for myself, based in large part on memories of the early relationships I had with my father and grandfather.

But just as significant, my experiences as a father have profoundly influenced my views about parenting. Jonathan, Kenneth, Cameron, Michael and Benjamin have each greatly enriched my life and knowledge. My wife Margery Salter Biller, herself a clinical psychologist, has helped me to understand better the importance of sensitively balancing marital and child-rearing responsibilities.

I want to acknowledge some others whose personal interest and encouragement helped me over these last several years to persevere with this project: Ann and Stephen Broomfield, Euda and Harvey Fellman, Debbie and Marvin Gordon, Julie and Gerry Goulet, Linda and David Haskell, Edythe and Gershon Salter, Beth and Richard Salter, Ruthie and Robert Salter, Bill Sullivan and Peter and Rose Merenda.

Debbie Carroll expertly typed several drafts of the manuscript, and her kindness and patience facilitated my dealing with many writing-format challenges. The efforts of Diane Sipe, Anne Marie Famiglietti, and Catherine Lee also contributed to the completion of the manuscript. Brenda Hanning served as copyeditor and Julie LeGallee carefully shepherded the book through production. Special thanks are due to John Harney for his expert and incisive editorial guidance.

FATHERS
AND
FAMILIES

1

The Two-Parent Advantage

During the past twenty years, an increasing number of researchers and clinicians have begun to give more recognition to the father's impact on individual and family development. Nevertheless, a great discrepancy remains between current knowledge and concrete applications to parenting practices. Meaningful guidelines acknowledging the importance of the father in child development must be provided in order to help families work out effective patterns of parenting that fit their particular circumstances. Serving as an introduction, the first half of this chapter outlines some of the general advantages of shared parenting while the second half provides a brief preview of the major issues discussed in the rest of the book.

BASIC PERSPECTIVES

The book's emphasis is on the special contribution of the father in the context of his sharing of parenting responsibilities with the mother. Within a life-span perspective, fathers and mothers should be sensitized not just to the immediate consequences of their parenting practices but also to the longer-term implications for their children and for themselves. Consideration must be given to the continuing development of parents as well as children.

Sharing Responsibilities

Discussions of parenting have been too exclusively directed toward the mother's role in responding to the child's basic needs. The father is extremely important for the child's intellectual, emotional and social development. Both the father's and the mother's individual development and the quality of their relationship with one another need to be considered in understanding the parenting process. Immense cultural variations occur, but the father-mother-child connection is the foundation for the family, each member benefiting and learning from the other. A tendency toward a strong attachment to the infant is not just the preserve of the mother. The father, too, possesses a predisposition for nurturing his child.

Compared to the fathering role, the mothering role is more consistent from society to society, as well as from family to family. Because men are more variable in their involvement with children, the quality of family relationships is especially apt to be linked to differences in the level of father connectedness. There is a strong association between variations in fathering and the resultant personality adaptations of males and females in a society. Cross-cultural research points to the benefits of the active participation of fathers in the parenting process. Societies with a clear expectation of paternal involvement with infants generally also have more positive attitudes relating to the rights of women and children. Low father availability tends to be associated with an emphasis on boys and girls being compliant, whereas children in societies with high paternal involvement are more likely to receive encouragement for assertive behavior.

In societies where fathers are excluded from infant care, young children tend to be more restricted and overly dependent on their mothers. However, males who are father deprived early in life are likely to engage later in rigidly over-compensatory masculine behaviors. The incidence of crimes against property and people, including child abuse and family violence, is relatively high in societies where the rearing of young children is considered to be an exclusively female endeavor. Girls and boys develop best when they have the benefit of two positively involved parents. This is not to say that a single parent cannot be very effective in child rearing. In fact, many of the parenting guidelines suggested in this book are applicable to either single-parent or two-parent families.

In any case, a major way to improve family effectiveness is to increase the amount of constructive father influence. This includes educating and sensitizing both females and males to the importance of the father becoming a full-fledged partner in parenting. Both parents benefit when they cooperatively share child-rearing responsibilities. A frequent roadblock to positive family functioning is that the father is not an actively involved parent. The father should have confidence in his ability to contribute to his child's development. He needs to feel secure that effective fatherhood is a basic part of being masculine and is important to his own continuing development.

Men as well as women need to experience a sense of emotional connectedness to their children. If the father increases his involvement, it does not diminish the significance of the mother's role. Constructive paternal involvement can actually aid the mother in becoming a better parent and person. Too many mothers in two-parent as well as one-parent families suffer great restriction in their personal development because of the widespread noninvolvement of fathers. Employed mothers often find themselves doing the equivalent of two full-time jobs because their husbands take relatively little responsibility in child rearing. Both the husband and the wife need to realize the advantages of positive paternal involvement. The husband-father's motivation to share parenting responsibilities can benefit the marital relationship as well as the child's development. However, a key issue is that both parents are supportive of the father's role in child rearing.

If the father is not motivated to be an active participant in parenting, or if the mother is unwilling to support his involvement, it is unlikely that the child will be the beneficiary of constructive paternal influence.

The "husband factor" is a major ingredient in marital and family adjustment. The husband's, as compared to the wife's, degree of emotional expressiveness and nurturance has been found to be associated more strongly with the level of both partners' perceived marital satisfaction. Most women enter into marriage with at least a moderate ability to communicate their feelings, but a greater proportion of men have difficulty in expressing affection and nurturance. When the husband is able to be emotionally supportive, it bodes well for the couple's adjustment to parenthood, increasing the likelihood that the father will constructively share parenting responsibilities and develop a close relationship with his child. A strong bond with the father, as well as with the mother, helps the child develop greater intellectual and social competence. Closeness with the father can be especially important in fostering the child's sense of self-esteem and confidence. Children and adults in families where both parents are positively involved are more likely to develop their talents and other personal resources.

Parenting Variability

Fathers in two-parent families typically spend about one-third as much time with young children as do mothers, although over the past decade evidence points to a slight average increase in the quantity of paternal involvement. Even more significant, on average fathers spend only about one-quarter as much time in one-to-one endeavors with young children. In two-parent families, relatively few men take on an equitable share of the day-to-day responsibilities involved in child rearing.

I am not arguing that fathers and mothers must spend exactly the same amount of individualized time with their children. How parents divide up child-rearing responsibilities depends on their particular preferences and family circumstances. But what is important is that the couple has a cooperative partnership and that the child perceives a positive emotional commitment from both parents. The child needs to have the opportunity for the development of a high-quality individualized relationship with the father as well as with the mother.

To the extent that a society does not support a constructive child-rearing role for the father, it pays the price in terms of the prevalence of individual maladjustment, the waste of valuable talent and various types of social problems. A vast number of children, in two-parent as well as in single-mother households, are victims of chronic father neglect. Paternal deprivation is often associated with personal insecurity and a poor self-concept. Many individuals with otherwise slight handicaps become psychologically disabled because of paternal neglect while others never develop their talents because of the lack of supportive fathering. In our society, young children who do not have a close relationship with their biological fathers are unlikely to receive consistent attention from any other male adult. Young children generally have frequent opportunities to interact with more than one caring woman, but they may be totally bereft of any committed contact with a man.

Although the styles and the specifics of the relationships are likely to differ, children can be just as emotionally connected and bonded with their father as their mother. Father-child attachment can be especially critical because most young children lack positive and predictable contact with other men. The degree to which the father is effectively integrated into the family and cooperates with the mother is a major predictor of how well the family can cope with problems. The weak link in chronically troubled families is often the father, who is uninvolved or inappropriately relates to his children and their mother.

Certainly great variation occurs from family to family in the quality of mothering that is available to children. But most children grow up experiencing a mother who is accepting and emotionally accessible. They typically have a mother who represents a clear frame of reference to them. And if for some reason their biological mother is incapable of providing adequate parenting, they will probably receive some relatively consistent nurturance from another female adult who may be a family member, neighbor, teacher or paid caretaker.

Compared to mothers, much more variability exists among fathers in different families. Having a father living at home is no guarantee of meaningful paternal involvement. Some fathers are exceptionally committed parents while others are only occasionally involved or are virtual strangers to their children, even though they may reside in the same household. Given the prevalent segregation of young children from adult males, a very serious void in their experience is likely to occur if they do not have an actively involved father.

This is not to say that an individual's level of psychological well-being is just a function of the quality of paternal involvement experienced during childhood. Many different biological and social influences impact on personality development. Some individuals who have been the recipients of attentive fathering still have serious developmental difficulties, while others are extremely well functioning despite having had a history of paternal deprivation. Nevertheless, variations in the quality of fathering generally have a crucial impact on child development. Children who experience positive father involvement are likely to develop their personal resources and social competence whereas those who are paternally deprived are at risk to suffer from psychological problems. Biological predispositions and social circumstances have much to do with the details of how variations in paternal involvement affect particular children. Inadequate fathering may increase the vulnerability of a child to developing a poor self-concept, insecurity in peer relationships and other types of dysfunction depending on the specific intermix of individual predispositions and social circumstances. In contrast, high-quality paternal involvement enhances a child's opportunity to live a satisfying and productive life. Effective fathering increases the child's chances of developing a positive body image, self-esteem, moral strength and intellectual and social competence (see Figure 1).

CHAPTER PREVIEWS

The father's involvement is discussed within the context of the many interacting biological, psychological and social influences on child and family development. In each chapter, for example, consideration is given to how the child's temperamental predispositions, as well as broader cultural expectations, may affect paternal behavior and family relationships. Attention is also paid to the impact of the child's evolving maturity on parents and their marital relationship. Ongoing emphasis is on the dynamic interplay among paternal involvement, child development and family relationships.

Enhancing Competencies

Chapter 2 examines the development of father-mother-infant relationships. Even with the newborn, the father can become an attentive and involved parent. Each parent offers special advantages, and much research underscores how the infant benefits from active fathering.

Chapter 3 elaborates on the importance of the father and mother being partners in parenting. The ability of the husband-father to be nurturant and sensitive is a key factor in marital satisfaction as well as in successful parent-child relationships. Particular recognition is given to specific ways that the father and mother can share parenting responsibilities and enhance their child's development. Relevant preparenting issues, including husband-wife cooperation during pregnancy and childbirth, are discussed.

Chapter 4 emphasizes the impact of both parents on the development of the child's self-concept and gender identity. Self-acceptance in terms of gender identity is promoted by nurturant fathering and is especially important in giving a child a sense of security in dealing with various peer and social pressures. Parents should try to avoid restrictive gender stereotypes in dealing with children.

Chapter 5 underscores the significance of the father's role in the child's development of self-control and moral standards. Child-rearing suggestions are presented in the context of discipline as positive teaching rather than as punishment for misbehavior. Families function much better when both parents are clear about their expectations, behaving in the considerate, caring manner that they wish their child to emulate. A democratic family environment facilitates the positive development of the father, mother and child. The committed father plays an especially important role in helping his child to develop a concern for the rights of others.

Chapter 6 highlights diverse modes of intellectual functioning with attention given to both biological predispositions and parenting factors. Guidelines are provided for stimulating various types of problem solving and creative endeavors, with special attention given to the role of the father in nurturing his child's intellectual competence.

Chapter 7 deals with school and educational issues, emphasizing the importance of effective collaboration among parents, teachers and children. The rel-

FATHER-FAMILY IMPLICATIONS

Need for more family development research considering reciprocal father-mother-child influences within a lifespan biopsychosocial perspective.

Expanded accountability of father with the expectation that he assume a more equitable share of parenting responsibilities even during his child's infancy.

Greater attention to the father's role in parent preparation programs and educational, social service and therapy interventions with increased efforts directed toward preventing paternal deprivation.

Emphasis on the significance of mutual father-mother support for effective parenting, positive family functioning and the rights and welfare of children.

Parenting guidelines acknowledging the crucial role of paternal involvement whether or not the father and mother live together.

CHILD'S INDIVIDUALITY, BIOLOGICAL PREDISPOSITIONS

Genetic/Prenatal Processes, Neurological, Hormonal Functioning.

Temperamental Characteristics, Maturational Level.

Health, Wellness, Resiliency.

Abilities, Talents, Disabilities.

Gender, Body Type, Personal Appearance.

FAMILY SYSTEM, ADEQUACY OF FATHERING/MOTHERING

Each parent's childhood history, developmental level, individual assets/liabilities, temperament, work satisfaction, education and adaptability to changing circumstances.

Family responsibilities/pressures including number and spacing of children, financial and housing resources, grandparent and other intergenerational support.

Quality of marriage or single parent's relationship with adult partner/former spouse, father-mother-child-sibling interactions, contrasting parental styles including gender relevant characteristics.

Degree of parental cooperation, nurturance, attentiveness, accessibility, self-understanding, respect for individuality, modeling of positive behavior, appropriateness of limit setting, encouragement of initiative and competence (continua ranging from optimal parenting to child maltreatment).

SOCIOCULTURAL INFLUENCES

Cultural Values, (Status of Minorities, Women, Children, Gender Roles, Etc.)

Ethnic Background, Socioeconomic Status, Educational and Employment Opportunities.

Neighborhood-Community Networks (Peers, Relatives, Coworkers, Child Care Providers, Social/Health Services).

Institutional Forces (School, Church, Legal, Medical Media, Technology, Military, Political-Governmental.

Historical/Socioenvironmental Events (Peace/War, Economic Fluctuations, Chance Occurrences, etc.)

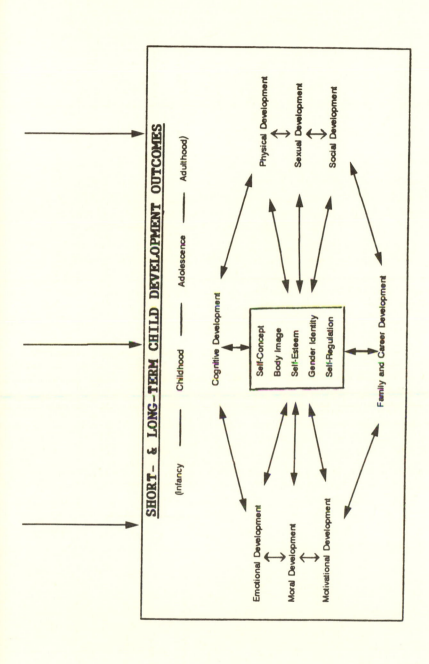

FIGURE 1-1: FATHER, FAMILY AND CHILD DEVELOPMENT: A Biopsychosocial-Interactional Perspective

7

ative lack of adult male involvement in elementary education is a particularly serious problem. Suggestions are also made for the father and child learning together in outside-of-school activities. The continuing impact of paternal involvement along with the increasing influence of peer and school experiences are emphasized.

Chapter 8 analyzes the development of assertiveness and independence. A major goal is to encourage an active sense of self-determination in all family members. The father who demonstrates a sense of personal efficiency while maintaining positive family relationships facilitates his own and his child's development.

Chapter 9 concentrates on the ways that the father can contribute to his child's positive body image and physical fitness. Body-type variations can greatly influence parent-child relationships and personality development. Suggestions are made regarding mutual parent and child benefits derived from fitness and athletic activities.

Chapter 10 provides an overview of evolving social and sexual relationships. The focus is on parents transmitting positive values and social skills to their children. Research discussed in this chapter highlights the impact of the father's influence on his child's social competence and capacity for intimacy.

Preventing Problems

Chapter 11 addresses a variety of circumstances that may make family functioning particularly difficult for parents and children. Many child and family development problems are associated with inadequate father participation and an overburdened mother. The first half of the chapter focuses on divorce and single-parenting, while the second half is directed toward issues concerning troubled and maltreated children. Programs designed to help families and children must recognize the importance of men and women constructively sharing parental responsibilities.

Chapter 12 considers the impact of community factors and social change on parents and children. Throughout our society, greater attention must be paid to the role of the father and shared parenting. Men as well as women need to become engaged in endeavors strengthening supportive connections between various social institutions and the family.

SUMMARY

Insufficient attention has been given to the father's role in child development. Men are very variable in their family relationships, but a clear connection exists between degree of positive paternal involvement and the quality of personality adaptations at both the individual and the social level.

Children and families develop best when fathers and mothers are partners in parenting, giving individualized attention to sons and daughters. Both boys and girls greatly benefit from positive father-child relationships. Young children who receive inadequate fathering are unlikely to encounter other men who will be positively nurturant to them on a regular basis. The father's impact needs to be viewed from a biopsychosocial perspective, with greater attention being given to life span developmental research considering the reciprocal influence that parents and children have on one another. The scope of the book is briefly outlined in chapter previews emphasizing the complex interrelationships between paternal involvement and other dimensions of individual, family and social functioning.

FURTHER READING

Basic Perspectives

Sharing Responsibilities

For cross-cultural perspectives on the father's role and influence, see Biller (1971a, 1974c), Bozett and Hanson (1991), Crano and Aronoff (1978), Katz and Konner (1981), Lamb (1987), Levinson (1988), Lynn (1974), Mackey (1985) and Mackey and Day (1979). On the influence of ethnic, historical, social class, and subcultural factors impacting on paternal behavior, see especially Bozett and Hanson (1991) and Carter and McGoldrick (1988).

With respect to parental sharing of child-rearing responsibilities, see Biller and Meredith (1974, 1982). For reviews of research relating to the father's role in child development, see Biller (1971a, 1974a, 1981b, 1981c, 1982a), Biller and Solomon (1986) and Lamb (1981b, 1982, 1986, 1987). Regarding the impact of husband variability on marital satisfaction, see Barry (1970), Baucon and Aiken (1984), Lamke (1989) and Murstein and Williams (1983).

Parenting Variability

Concerning the variability of fathers relative to mothers and the tremendous costs of paternal deprivation, see Biller (1971a, 1974c, 1982a), Biller and Meredith (1974) and Biller and Solomon (1986). About how social factors and the child's phase of development and individuality influence parenting, see also Brooks (1991), Chess and Thomas (1987), Galinsky (1981), Mattessich and Hill (1987), McGoldrick (1988a, 1988b), Peterson and Rollins (1987) and Rapoport et al. (1977). With respect to sociobiological influences on paternal and maternal behavior in humans and other species, see Draper and Harpending (1989), Nash (1978), Redican and Taub (1981) and Smith (1989).

For discussions concerning the methodological limitations of research on parenting and family development, see Berlinsky and Biller (1982), Biller (1971a, 1974c, 1981b), Bronstein and Cowan (1988), Lamb (1981b, 1986), Larzelere and Klein (1987), Mattessich and Hill (1987), Parke and Beitel (1986), Pedersen (1976) and Peterson and Rollins (1987).

2

Father, Mother and Infant

A common misconception about parenthood is that the father cannot have much influence on his child during infancy. In most societies, it is believed that the mother has to be the primary parent for the baby, with the father playing, at best, a very peripheral role. The father may feel that his infant is too young to interact with, wistfully looking forward to becoming more actively involved when his child is older. Delaying paternal involvement is a loss for both the father and the child.

FORMING RELATIONSHIPS

Studies that other investigators and I conducted during the 1960s suggested that not only did the father have a direct impact on his older child's adjustment but also that he could have much influence on his infant's development. Some data indicated that the early absence of the father was often associated with developmental difficulties for the child whereas active paternal involvement seemed to increase the competence of the preschooler. Such findings stimulated more systematic research aimed at examining father-infant relationships.

Parent Bonding

At least initially, the newborn seems to have no innate preference for one parent over another, or for the natural parent rather than an adoptive or foster parent. Most newborns like to be held and stimulated, but the specific identity of the holder is not that important to them, as long as the individual is sensitive to their needs. However, during their first months of life, infants do begin to develop attachments that can have a profound and lasting significance for them. Most infants usually develop a primary bond to their mothers, but they typically begin to form other attachments during their first year of life. In fact, some infants have just as strong, or even stronger, initial attachments to their fathers as they do to their mothers.

Research by physicians Martin Greenberg and Norman Morris revealed that fathers who have the opportunity to view and react to their newborn infants within twenty-four hours of their birth are very similar to mothers with respect to feelings of bonding and engrossment. Most new fathers upon viewing their newborn infants feel very stimulated and fascinated with even the smallest details of their offspring's appearance and movements. More important, much research indicates that motivated fathers are just as sensitive to infant behavior and as competent in nurturing babies as are mothers. No biological imperative necessarily makes the mother-infant bond more primary than the father-infant bond. In general, however, many more mothers than fathers are regularly involved in interacting with, and caring for, infants. Thus most infants do develop a primary bond with their mother rather than their father.

Because they do not usually take part in most baby-care activities, fathers tend to spend relatively little time with their infants. Developmental psychologists Peggy Ban and Michael Lewis, studying one-year-old infants from middle-class families, found that fathers spent only about fifteen to twenty minutes per day playing with the infants. In another study of fathers, the time spent with the baby averaged about eight hours per week. This time was probably composed of the twenty minutes or so per weekday reported in the Ban and Lewis study, plus a few additional hours on the weekends. Compare this with the enormous amount of time that most mothers spend with their babies. Although the trend in paternal interest has been gradually upward, recent reviews of available data indicate that even relatively involved fathers are likely to spend less than one-third of the time that mothers do with their infants, and only about one-quarter of this time in individualized activities with them.

Infant Attachments

Although the mother is usually the first attachment figure for the baby, many infants react just as much to their father, cooing and smiling and becoming excited at his approach. Some infants become attached primarily to their fathers and thrive at least as well in their development as do infants with initial maternal attachments. Moreover, fathers who are supportive of mothers and are themselves involved parents make it more likely that the infant will develop a secure maternal attachment as well as a secure paternal attachment.

By their second year most infants who are well fathered show approximately equal attachment to both parents. It is important to note that attachment is not an all-or-none phenomenon. The style of the attachment and the details of the relationship vary with each parent and infant. Researchers have presented evidence that even newborns are capable of responding differentially toward their mother and father. The infant can become attached to any individual who is a consistent source of stimulation, attention and comfort, not just to the mother. If both parents are involved, an infant can develop a strong attachment to each of them. Despite such research findings, traditional conceptions of maternal primacy are difficult to change.

An example of how gender stereotypes affect thinking about early childhood is Freud's theory of identification, still viewed by many clinicians and researchers as a sound perspective for understanding early parent-child relationships. Freud theorized that all children first identify with their mother, and boys must later switch their identification to the father for normal masculine development. Since Freud's theory was conceived in a society in which women did almost all of the early child rearing, it is only natural that he would postulate a basic, exclusive psychological identification with the mother for both boys and girls.

Other leading theorists such as sociologist Talcott Parsons and psychiatrist John Bowlby readily incorporated the notion of the primacy of early mother-child identification into their theoretical formulations concerning family development. Bowlby, a pioneer in examining early parent-infant bonding, viewed the father's role as a peripheral one. The father was conceived as significant only to the extent that he helped meet the mother's emotional needs, which in turn would support her in being nurturant toward the infant.

In fact, men have always been capable of directly nurturing babies, and there is no reason that infants cannot attach themselves initially to their fathers as well as to their mothers. Traditionally men have been expected to limit their expression of caring toward children and to show their concern primarily by being economically responsible for their families. However, a great deal of research has accumulated during the past twenty-five years underscoring the important and special roles that fathers as well as mothers can have in infant and child development.

Special Stimulation

Differences between the mother and father can be very stimulating to the infant, even those that might appear quite superficial to the adult. Even if the father and mother behave in generally similar ways, they provide contrasting images for the infant. The father is usually larger than the mother, his voice is deeper, his clothes are not the same and he moves and reacts differently. Furthermore, parents differ in odor and skin texture. The father and mother offer the child two different kinds of persons to learn about as well as providing separate but special sources of love and support. The infant also learns that different people can be expected to fulfill different needs. For example, the infant may prefer the mother when hungry or tired and the father when seeking stimulation or more active play.

The infant who receives verbal as well as physical stimulation from both mother and father profits from the experience. Parents should talk about their activities with their infant. They should not be embarrassed to sing, croon, or make funny noises. Even the newborn responds by movement and attention to human speech. Mothers and fathers, in addition to having distinctive sounding voices, have different verbal styles when communicating to infants and children as well as to other adults. Such differences provide the infant with an important source of stimulation and learning.

Because some of my initial findings suggested that father absence during the first few years of life might inhibit certain aspects of the child's development, I began to observe more closely parent-infant relationships in various types of two-parent families. I discovered that when they are involved with infants, fathers tend to be more physically active with them than mothers are, playing more vigorously. This seems to be not only because fathers may be less concerned with their children's fragility, especially if they have sons, but also because they themselves have more of a need for physically stimulating activities. It was also apparent that infants with involved fathers formed strong paternal attachments and were usually at a developmental advantage compared to those who had close relationships only with their mothers.

Fathers tend to make even mundane activities like holding an infant or pushing a baby stroller more intensely physical endeavors than mothers. The pace and tempo of such activities tends to be faster and more varied for fathers than for mothers. Involved fathers are more likely to stimulate the infant to explore and to investigate new objects whereas mothers tend to engage their infants in relatively prestructured and predictable activities.

Infants who develop positive relationships with both their parents are likely to feel secure in exploring their environment in a relaxed manner and to enjoy being picked up by others. In contrast, among insecure infants some may anxiously cling to their mothers while others seem to ignore them and to avoid eye contact. The quality of parenting that the infant receives certainly has important implications, but other factors including temperamental predispositions also play a major role in the social responsiveness of children to adults inside and outside of the family.

Infants are not passive creatures just waiting to be fed or to have their diapers changed. They are active and striving, gradually increasing their self-motivated competence. Infants have a built-in motivation to explore and influence their environment. During the first month or so, the infant seems to be using many "prewired" responses. The infant has the capacity for orientation with respect to various stimuli including light and sound. Moreover, researchers have found that even the newborn is capable of some basic patterns of social reciprocity and is usually showing variations in responsivity toward different people. Despite marked individual variations, newborns are clearly social beings who can actively learn from their experiences of interacting with their fathers as well as their mothers.

The social capabilities of newborns go far beyond what was described, or even imagined, by most early investigators, including Piaget. Ingenious research procedures in the 1970s and 1980s, for example, established that newborns, during the first day or two of life, can visually respond in a way that indicates differentiation between the face of the mother and that of a stranger. Other research demonstrates the newborn's ability to make gross physical movements that are coordinated with the speech patterns of the caregiver. Furthermore, there is even evidence that newborns can imitate a few of the care giver's gestures such as mouth opening and tongue protrusion.

Differential Responsivity

Although a few other researchers and I had been reporting some naturalistic observations concerning the significance of the father-infant relationship, developmental psychologist Michael Lamb was one of the first investigators to do systematic and controlled data collection. Among his varied studies of the father's role is research assessing the family development of children from the time they were seven months old until they reached two years of age. During the first year of life, lengthy home observations indicated that infants were just as interested in their fathers as they were in their mothers, apparently being similarly attached to both parents. In the second year of life, the boys began to demonstrate more interest in interaction with their fathers, although the girls did not display any consistent preferences. In fact, by the end of the second year, all except one of the boys seemed to have a stronger paternal than maternal attachment. However, when these same infants were observed in the context of stressful laboratory conditions, they were most likely to seek out their mothers, suggesting differential, situationally influenced parental attachments. Comparing paternal and maternal behavior in the home indicated that fathers spent a higher proportion of their time in spontaneous play with their infants while mothers were more involved in soothing and structured caretaking activities with them.

The difference in the daily schedules of the mother and father can also affect the baby. While more mothers of very young children are homebound, fathers are usually away from the household for much longer periods of time. The father's (or mother's) comings and goings can be very stimulating to the infant. Elaborate preparations and good-byes and hellos are frequently a part of family rituals relating to a parent's work schedule.

In many families, the father's work schedule is a major stimulus for the baby's awareness of events being linked in sequence. For instance, the infant may connect a parent's preparations for leaving the house with those that are made when the whole family gets ready to go somewhere. The infant who is attached to the father as well as to the mother is much more likely to demonstrate an interest in such activities. The mother can help the baby realize the regularity of the father's comings and goings and his importance in the family by excitedly declaring, "Daddy's home!" or "Daddy's coming home in just a few minutes!" And, of course, the father can do the same with respect to the mother's comings and goings.

The father and mother need special times to be together and to pursue their own individual interests. Neither parent has to be with the infant around the clock. Leaving the infant with another responsible adult for several hours at a time can indeed be beneficial for all family members as long as regular and abundant quality time is reserved on a daily basis for parent-child interaction. However, the infant's very limited time sense should caution either parent from being away from the family for several days at a time. Children are usually much better able to handle longer separations after the age of two, when their understanding of the permanency and continuity of relationships, although still somewhat primitive, has greatly advanced compared to their functioning at a year or eighteen months. Attachment to both parents generally makes it much easier for the child to accept limited periods of family separation.

Developmental psychologist Milton Kotelchuck and his colleagues studied the adaptations of one-year-olds in situations where they were briefly separated from one or both parents. They studied how the infants reacted when various combinations of the mother, the father, and a stranger entered and left a room in which the child was playing. They assessed the quality of play behavior and the degree to which the child was upset by the comings and goings of various adults. In general, the children cried mainly when left alone with the stranger but usually not at the departure of one or the other parent. This indicated that the children were afraid of the stranger, rather than necessarily missing their mother or father. However, most of the children with highly involved fathers showed little crying, fretting, or disruption of play when left with the stranger. In contrast, most of the children of less-involved fathers were very disturbed when left with the stranger.

Much research underscores the advantages of the positive involvement of both parents. Children with an involved father are exposed to more varied social experiences and are more intellectually advanced than those who only have regular contact with their mother. Infants with two involved parents can cope better with being alone with strangers and also seem to attend more effectively to novel and complex stimuli. Well-fathered children have a greater breadth of positive social experiences than those exclusively reared by their mothers.

Differences between the father's and mother's schedules and activities can also stimulate new learning and adaptation for the child. If the father and mother go to different places in the community, the infant when taken along can learn about a wide variety of situations. The sights and sounds at a service station, the objects at a supermarket, or the activities at a sports event can make for a great learning situation for the infant. The infant may not fully understand what is going on, but seeing, hearing, touching and feeling new things in the company of a trusted and loved parent will nevertheless be a positively stimulating experience.

ADAPTIVE IMPLICATIONS

Infants who have two positively involved parents tend to be more curious and eager to explore than those who do not have a close relationship with their fathers. They generally relate more maturely to strangers and react more competently to complex and novel stimuli. Well-fathered infants are more secure and trusting in branching out in their explorations, and they may be somewhat more advanced in crawling, climbing and manipulating objects. Involved fathers typically initiate more active play and are more tolerant of physical exploration by infants than are mothers.

Cognitive Enrichment

Psychologist Frank Pedersen and his colleagues found that several measures of infant competence were correlated with the degree to which five- and six-month-old babies were involved with their fathers. Frequent interaction with fathers was associated with more advanced functioning for sons. Although girls did not seem to be influenced by family structure, father-absent infant boys were also less cognitively competent than boys from father-present homes. Father-present infant boys demonstrated more social responsiveness and novelty-seeking behavior than those who were father-absent. Having found no discernible differences in the behaviors of married and husbandless mothers, the researchers attributed variations in the infant boys' behavior to the type of interaction they had with their fathers.

Data collected by psychologist Jay Belsky indicates that both maternal and paternal influence are important factors in the development of exploratory competence. The most competent infants had fathers who participated in their physical care, expressed high levels of verbal responsiveness and affection and initiated vigorous motion play with them. Belsky stressed similarities as well as differences in the paternal and maternal factors that influenced infant behavior. In their efforts to encourage infant competence, mothers are generally more concerned with verbal-intellectual teaching, whereas fathers are more oriented toward active, arousing play and fostering autonomy and independence.

Research by pediatrician Michael Yogman and his colleagues supports the facilitative effect that active father participation may have on the developmental competence of infants. Yogman reported a significant relationship between a combined measure of father involvement during the prenatal and postnatal periods and the infant's developmental functioning at nine months. In addition, he described a collaborative study done in Ireland that revealed a positive correlation between level of early father involvement and the cognitive maturity of year-old infants.

Psychiatrist Kyle Pruett's findings from an intensive study of seventeen two-parent families in which fathers were the primary infant caretakers is consistent with the notion that paternal influence can have a special facilitating impact on the child's cognitive and social development. The parents in Pruett's study were a relatively diverse group in terms of socioeconomic status and educational and family background, but they had decided for varying reasons that the father would be the at-home caretaker during the child's infancy while the mother continued her career. During infancy and again when tested two and four years later, the children generally scored several months above age norms on a comprehensive developmental assessment procedure, displaying rather impressive problem-solving abilities, social skills, curiosity and persistence. Since the mothers were regularly involved with their infants after work and on the weekends, Pruett makes the cogent point that the children benefited from having the nurturant involvement of two committed parents rather than being exposed to the more typical family situation where the father's participation is relatively peripheral.

Early Competence

Developmental psychologists Ann Easterbrooks and Wendy Goldberg have also found evidence for the importance of positive paternal influence in the young child's development. Their study with twenty-month-old firstborns and their parents indicated a strong association between the behavior of fathers and toddler competence, especially for boys. Paternal participation in care giving was not a factor in itself, but the overall level of father involvement was a significant variable. Even more important was the father's acceptance of the child and his sensitivity to the needs of his son or daughter.

Paternal more than maternal behavior was associated with the children's functioning. Fathers who encouraged autonomy but also intervened with age-appropriate cues when necessary had toddlers who were particularly competent in problem solving. Positive paternal influence was linked to the child's persistence in completing tasks and secure parental attachment when the child was with either the father or the mother. The work of Easterbrooks and Goldberg highlights the impact of both parents on toddler development.

Easterbrooks and Goldberg have reported additional data supporting the later emotional and social advantages provided by a secure father attachment during early development. Among toddlers, those who had both secure father and secure mother attachments were less likely as five- to six-year-olds to express (maternally reported) negative emotionality, including fear and guilt. Those who had a secure father attachment were better able to modulate their emotions and impulses in an adaptive manner. In contrast, more of those who had insecure father attachments were described by their kindergarten teachers as emotionally overcontrolled, constrained and relatively unresponsive in social situations.

Developmental psychology researcher Norma Radin and her colleagues have collected especially provocative evidence concerning the special significance of paternal involvement for infants and toddlers. They studied grandparent-grandchild relationships in predominantly working-class households in which adolescent unwed mothers were living with one or both of their parents. Overall, young children who had positively involved grandfathers displayed more competent behavior than those with relatively uninvolved or absent grandfathers. Although other researchers have sometimes noted the contribution of the grandmother to the development of the child living in a single-mother family, Radin reported no clear-cut impact, suggesting a redundancy between the two forms of maternal influence. On the other hand, the grandfather's nurturance seemed to contribute in several ways to the young child's adaptability. His observed nurturance was associated with infants being more responsive to maternal requests and with the cognitive competence of two-year-olds. Furthermore, relatively high grandfather involvement in child care was related to observations of less fear, anger and distress being displayed by one-year-olds, especially boys. Overall, evidence also suggested that the grandfather's positive involvement indirectly helped the teenage mother to parent more effectively as well as directly stimulating her child's competence.

Other researchers have presented findings indicating that an early positive relationship with the father is predictive of the child's later social competence. For example, findings support an association between father attachment during infancy and the empathetic capacity of toddlers, and data links paternal involvement experienced during the preschool years with adulthood sensitivity to feelings and emotions in social situations.

Some research, including the provocative work of psychologist Graheme Russell with Australian families, has suggested that highly masculine fathers may be more resistant to becoming involved in infant care than those who are androgynous or not so rigidly sex-typed. But being highly masculine does not necessarily mean a man views child rearing as feminine. For example, most of the fathers in Pruett's study who assumed a primary parenting role for their infants grew up in traditional families and appeared to be relatively masculine.

In counseling parents, I have found considerable variability among men who have been able to share child-rearing responsibilities successfully with their wives. Rather than being an issue of sex typing per se, the father's desire to be an effective parent and to be supportive of his wife seem to be the most crucial factors motivating him to be actively involved with his infant. A variety of investigations, when taken together, indicate that highly active male parents are very diverse with respect to their sex-role functioning and family backgrounds. For example, many of them model their father's positive involvement, whereas others are trying to provide their offspring with a kind of constructive paternal interest that was lacking in their own childhood.

Partner Support

The quality of the husband-wife relationship greatly influences the interactions of both parents with their child. When fathers are supportive and encouraging, mothers are more competent and responsive to their infants and young children. Even before the child's birth, an emotionally supportive husband can contribute to the wife's sense of well-being and is likely to be associated with a relatively problem-free pregnancy, delivery process, and competence in parenting. In the successful family, a balance is required between the needs of the parents and those of the children. The husband and wife who can be supportive of one another in parenting functions are also generally enriching the quality of their marital relationship as well as presenting a positive model of male-female cooperation to their children.

Mothers have been found to be more competent in nursing and caring for their newborn infants when they receive a high level of emotional support from their husbands. The husband's emotional support during pregnancy has been found to be positively related to the mother's responsiveness to her child's needs during infancy and the preschool years. The quality of the husband-wife relationship may be even more predictive of the mother's success in dealing with her infant than the degree to which the father actually participates in child care. Mothers are expected to be highly involved with their infants but social values allow fathers much more latitude. An unsupportive husband-wife relationship tends to be related to a relative lack of paternal involvement with the infant, whereas a positive marriage is likely to be associated with a high level of father-infant interaction.

Fathers are more comfortable parenting their infants when they receive encouragement and emotional support from their wives. Studying fifteen-month-old babies and their parents, Jay Belsky reported that the extent of husband-wife communication about infants was positively related to the amount of the father's interaction with the child. This finding underscores the important role that the husband-wife relationship can have in influencing the father's behavior with the infant and vice versa.

The quality of a marriage is associated with the degree to which the spouses view each other as competent parents. Frank Pedersen found that fathers with good marital relationships and a positive view of their wives were likely to be actively involved in playing with their infant sons. In contrast those husbands who experienced stressful interactions with their wives and perceived them negatively were more apt to engage in only a low level of playful activity with their infant sons. A wife's view of her husband's competence as a father is related to her satisfaction with him as a spouse. Women tend to define good husbands as those who are able to be supportive of them in their roles as both wives and mothers. In turn, the father's affection and warmth toward the mother buttresses her competence to parent. On the other hand, when husbands are aloof and uninvolved in child rearing or are absent from the home, mothers are apt to have much more difficulty in dealing positively with children.

Balanced Commitments

Parents who have a strong cooperative relationship with one another provide a great advantage for the developing infant. Sharing parenting responsibilities with the father can lessen the risk that the mother will become too obsessed with child rearing. When responsibility is shared cooperatively, the mother can be a much happier parent and wife. On the other hand, mothers who compulsively overinvest in parenthood can make it extremely difficult for a father-child bond to develop and put the family system at risk for future developmental problems.

In many two-parent families, the father may be particularly concerned with the child's autonomy and independence. However, the father's expectations may mean very little if he has not been consistently involved with his child. A typical scenario is for a child to get too much mothering in the sense of being overprotected and too little fathering. Some mothers have a need to inhibit their infant's natural drive for autonomy, and their focus may be so intrusive that it interferes with their baby's own attempts at exploration and trying out new behavior patterns.

Consideration needs to be given to the amount and quality of time that each parent should spend with the infant. Every family, of course, is different, and the individual schedules and priorities of both parents must be taken into account.

In more and more families, both parents are working full-time even when the child is an infant. The crucial point is that both the father and the mother have regular, consistent quality contact with each child. An hour or more of daily positive father-infant as well as mother-infant interaction can have a great impact on the child's later development. This does not mean just feeding, changing diapers or being in the same room with the child. It includes some focused one-to-one activities such as playing, going places, and letting the child watch the parent doing chores.

Infant-focused activities can easily be divided into separate time blocks for the working parent's convenience. This might include a little time in the morning playing with the child, a period at noon if the parent comes home for lunch, and a longer period in the evening. If a parent works late or at odd hours, the child's schedule can be adjusted somewhat. Parents can also spend time with their infant in the context of errands or individual outings. They may find that even tedious household chores take on a whole new aura as they watch their child make new discoveries. Most parents are especially intrigued by the infant's efforts to observe and imitate them. A baby can give a parent a whole new, more sensitive outlook on many otherwise mun-dane activities.

Daily caretaking can be a meaningful way for the parent and infant to learn more about each other. In many families, the mother does not feel burdened by changing all the diapers and giving all the baths, while the father may be uncomfortable being responsible for these activities. However, what is important for the child's well-being is that the father, as well as the mother, has some regular daily mode of positively relating to the infant. What is most essential is that both parents recognize each other's significance in the child's development.

Toward the end of their first year, if not before, infants typically have a definite surge of motivated independence from parents. A ten-month-old infant, for example, may struggle to take a spoon away from the parent in a self-feeding effort even though less food may be eaten than ends up on the floor. Awkward as they may seem to parents, infants should be allowed and even encouraged to follow their inclinations for greater independence.

Although the form, sequence and timing of early development is greatly influenced by a biologically programmed unfolding, parental behavior can have a significant impact. Precocious sensorimotor development among infants is more likely to be associated with the active involvement of both parents than just the mother. Similarly, much research indicates that positive fathering is related to increased infant exploration, better ability to adjust to short separations from parents and the security to relate to strangers.

Having two caring, supportive parents is a definite advantage for the infant in various aspects of intellectual, emotional and social development. There is a big difference between pressuring the infant to reach a higher level of functioning and providing an encouraging and secure environment in which the child can develop at a more self-defined pace.

Looking Ahead

Beginning around the age of eighteen months and continuing to approximately three years, the child can be viewed as making the transition from infancy to early childhood. It is often a time when the child is quite defiant and negativistic. In general, the child is attempting to take more control but typically fluctuates between "I'll do it myself" and a rather infantile mode of dependency on the mother or father.

Parents have to begin to deal with issues revolving around their own sense of control with the emerging toddler. The child's burgeoning abilities may greatly challenge parental expectations. The parent must develop more of a style of negotiating with the actively verbal child. No longer is it usually so easy just to move the child from place to place or to tolerate noncompliance. However, toddlers who receive positive attention from both their parents are much more likely to be responsive to adult requests for cooperation than those who are nurtured only by their mother.

Both temperamental and family factors are influential in a child's adjustment to a new sibling. Children vary greatly in their adaptability to changes in their family situations. However, children who have had a relatively exclusive relationship with their mother and a distant, or nonexistent, relationship with their father are more at risk for sustained sibling rivalry. When children have only one nurturant parent, they are much more likely to compete negatively for adult attention.

In England, developmental psychologists Judy Dunn and Carol Kendrick conducted a detailed observational and interview study aimed at assessing young firstborn children's reactions to the addition of a baby brother or sister into their family. Almost all of the children, who ranged in age from about one-and-a-half to three-and-a-half at the time of the baby's birth, showed some initial negative reactions, often involving an increase in disobedience, demandingness and other forms of regressive behavior. Children who had previously been rated as having a difficult temperament, including a tendency toward negative emotional expression and withdrawal in new situations, generally experienced more adjustment problems after their sibling's birth. But Dunn and Kendrick also found that children who had a highly positive relationship with their father were much less likely to have severe and continuing adjustment problems after the birth of a new sibling.

Although older children usually continue to have some mixed feelings, in most families much playful and positive interaction also happens between siblings. For instance, Dunn and Kendrick found that most preschool-age firstborns were, at least occasionally, interested in the care of their infant sibling and were able to demonstrate affection and empathy. Parents cannot completely prevent feelings of anger and jealousy between siblings. However, they can contribute to a positive family atmosphere by responding to each child's individual needs and by appreciating the occasions when siblings do get along well together.

Having more than one child increases the time demands of parenting, especially if there is a commitment to high-quality individualized relationships. Parents should thoroughly discuss potential advantages and disadvantages before making a decision to have an additional child. Major considerations revolve around the quality of parenting each child receives as well as the potential impact on the marital relationship and the family's financial situation.

When children are spaced closely in age, it may be more difficult for parents to treat them as individuals and maintain a special relationship with each of them. From this perspective it could be argued that having children at least four years apart has clear advantages in helping both parents and children to get to know each other without being overwhelmed by diapers and sibling rivalry. Parents should make sure that they can really be committed to each child before they decide to enlarge their family.

Fathers who have several offspring may get particularly defensive about the amount of time they are available to their children. Many fathers insist that they are regularly at home but upon further analysis, it is clear that they seldom interact with their children in a focused, quality manner. If all a child sees of the father is a glimpse in passing, the child may come to develop a very negative view of adult males. Some children in such families do end up describing their fathers quite positively but view themselves as relatively worthless since their so-very-important parent has so little time for them. Children who are truly fatherless usually seek out a substitute male model, sometimes an older brother or teacher. They may achieve a better perspective with regard to the worthiness of men than do those children who live in the same household as their father but are consistently neglected by him.

The quality of the father-child relationship has a great influence on development during the preschool years. The father's nurturance and positive expectations contribute to his young child's gender security, self-esteem and intellectual and social competence. Although the father's impact must be viewed within a context acknowledging individual differences among children, those boys and girls who have the active support of both parents are more likely to develop an enduring sense of self-acceptance and confidence than those who have the consistent interest of only one parent.

SUMMARY

Even with the newborn, the father can become an attentive and involved parent. If given the opportunity, men have just as much capacity as women to become attached to babies and to be sensitive to their needs. However, they are likely to offer the infant different kinds of experiences.

Fathers are apt to be more arousing and stimulating in interacting with their infants, engaging them in active, relatively unstructured play. Infants who are attached to both their parents are generally more socially adaptable and cognitively advanced compared to those who have only maternal attachments. In fact, a strong paternal attachment is also related to a relatively secure relationship with the mother.

Infants who have positive relationships with both their parents appear to be especially advantaged in dealing constructively with new people and situations. It is particularly important for the father and infant to develop an individualized relationship since the young child is unlikely to encounter another nurturing male adult on a regular basis. It is beneficial for future family functioning when the father and mother share in the daily care of the infant.

FURTHER READING

Forming Relationships

Parent Bonding

For basic research on mother-infant attachment, see Ainsworth et al. (1978) and Schaffer and Emerson (1964). Concerning the significance of mother-infant attachment for later child development and social competence with peers, see Easterbrooks and Lamb (1979), Hartup (1989), Main and Cassidy (1988), Pastor (1981) and Rutter (1979). For research relating the quality of the mother-infant attachment to the support of the male partner, see Biller and Solomon (1986) and Egeland and Farber (1984).

On initial father bonding, see Greenberg (1985) and Greenberg and Morris (1974). For relative amounts of time fathers and mothers spend in infant care, see Ban and Lewis (1971), Biller (1974c), Parke (1981), Pedersen (1981), Rebelsky and Hanks (1971) and Yogman (1982). For evidence that men can be just as sensitive and competent in dealing with newborns as women, see Frodi and Lamb (1978), Lamb (1981b), Parke (1981) and Pruett (1987).

Infant Attachments

For reviews of father-infant attachment research, see Biller (1974c), Biller and Solomon (1986), Lamb (1981b), Parke (1981) and Pedersen (1981). For more traditional views of mother primacy during infancy, see Bowlby (1958, 1969) and Parsons (1955). For Freudian-influenced theories of identification, including the emphasis on the early mother-child attachment, see Biller (1971a), Biller and Borstelmann (1967) and Bronfenbrenner (1960).

Special Stimulation

Regarding the special types of stimulation that each parent offers to the infant, see Biller (1974c, 1977b, 1982a), Biller and Meredith (1974), Brachfield-Child (1986), Lamb (1976, 1977, 1981a), Parke (1981, 1985), Pedersen (1980, 1981), Power (1985), Pruett (1987) and Yogman (1981, 1982).

Regarding children's intrinsic motivation to master their environment and be assertive, see Biller and Meredith (1974), Kagan (1984) and White (1960). About the impressive learning and adaptive capacities of the infant, see Bahrick (1988), Field et al. (1984), Gibson and Spelke (1983), Rose and Ruff (1987) and Stern (1985).

For discussions of his conceptions of cognitive development in infancy and childhood, see Piaget (1954, 1967). For applications and limitations of Piaget's theory, see Flavell (1985) and Gelman (1979).

Differential Responsivity

For evidence indicating that father attachment increases children's adaptability to new situations, see Biller (1971a, 1974c), Biller and Solomon (1986), Cohen and Campos (1974), Kotelchuck (1976), Lamb (1976, 1977, 1981a), Pedersen (1981), Ross et al. (1975), Spelke et al. (1973) and Weintraub and Lewis (1977).

Adaptive Implications

Cognitive Enrichment

Regarding specific research studies, see Belsky (1980b), Easterbrooks and Goldberg (1984, 1985), Pedersen, Anderson and Cain (1980), Pedersen, Rubinstein and Yarrow (1979), Pruett (1987), Russell (1983) and Yogman (1981, 1982). For other relevant research linking positive paternal involvement with highly significant intellectual and social development advantages for infants and children, see Biller (1974c) and Biller and Solomon (1986).

For discussions of the special types of stimulation that each parent offers the child, see Biller (1974c), Biller and Meredith (1974), Parke (1981), Parke and Beitel (1986), Pedersen (1981), Pruett (1987) and Yogman (1981, 1982).

Early Competence

With respect to specific studies, see Easterbrooks and Goldberg (1984, 1985, 1990) and Radin, Oyserman and Benn (1991). Concerning data linking early paternal involvement and later empathic capacity, see Koestner, Franz and Weinberger (1990).

Partner Support

For research indicative of the constructive impact of the husband's involvement during pregnancy and childbirth, see Cronenwett and Newmark (1974), Henneborn and Cogan (1975), Parke (1981) and Peterson, Mehl and Leiderman (1979).

About research focusing on the positive association between partner support and effective parenting, see Belsky (1979a, 1979b, 1980b), Belsky and Rovine (1988), Durrett et al. (1986), Genevie and Margolies (1987), Heath (1976), Lamb and Elster (1985) and Pedersen (1976). For the importance of joint parental participation in limit setting and maternal difficulties in dealing with children, especially sons, without paternal participation, see Biller (1971a, 1974c), Biller and Solomon (1986), Hetherington, Cox and Cox (1978a, 1978b, 1982), Hoffman (1989) and Lytton (1976, 1979).

Balanced Commitments

On the difficulties of balancing work, marital and child-rearing commitments during the transition to new parenthood and the problems associated with partner conflicts when a spouse feels unfairly burdened or, on the other hand, feels that the other parent is too much involved with the infant, see Belsky (1985), Berman and Pedersen (1987), Biller and Meredith (1974), Biller and Salter (1985), Clarke-Stewart (1978), Hochschild and Machung (1989), Pruett (1987) and Russell (1983, 1986). For helpful perspectives on balancing work and parenting responsibilities, see Brooks (1991), Grollman and Sweder (1986), Loman (1984) and Olds (1989).

Looking Ahead

About the importance of both mothers and fathers being available to their young children on a daily basis for an hour or two of quality time together, see Biller (1974c), Biller and Solomon (1986), Blanchard and Biller (1971) and Reuter and Biller (1973). For data suggesting that more than forty hours a week of maternal employment can interfere with the quality of the mother-child relationship, see Gottfried, Gottfried and Bathurst (1988) and Hoffman (1989).

For evidence that men feel better about themselves and their relationships with their children when they are actively involved in child rearing, see Baruch and Barnett (1986), Pruett (1987), Russell (1983, 1986) and Russell and Radin (1983). For benefits of shared parenting for mothers as well as children, see Genevie and Margolies (1987), Hoffman (1983, 1989), Pruett (1987) and White (1988).

Concerning the perspective that high father participation does not detract from a positive mother-child relationship, see Biller and Meredith (1974), Genevie and Margolies (1987), Pedersen et al. (1987), Russell (1983, 1986) and Russell and Radin (1983). For potential risks for both adult and child when one parent takes on exclusive child-rearing responsibilities, see Biller (1971a, 1974c) and Biller and Solomon (1986).

Regarding older child's adaptation to a new sibling, see Dunn (1985) and Dunn and Kendrick (1982). For other perspectives pertaining to sibling relationships, see Bank and Kahn (1982), Lamb and Sutton-Smith (1982) and Sutton-Smith and Rosenberg (1970).

Concerning the impact of baby's birth on older sibling-parent relationships, see Brooks (1991), Dunn and Kendrick (1982), and Taylor and Kogan (1973).

For excellent discussions of the importance and availability of maternity and paternity leaves, see Klinman (1986), Olds (1989) and Pleck (1986). With respect to the increasing pressures for father-mother cooperation after the birth of the second child, see Biller and Meredith (1974) and Dunn and Kendrick (1982).

3

Partners in Parenting

This chapter concentrates on the significance of the father and mother having a cooperative parenting relationship. The father and mother can support each other's parenting competence and strengthen their marital relationship while also contributing positively to their child's development. Being able to observe a supportive father-mother relationship provides excellent social learning opportunities for the child. When the father and mother are truly partners in parenting, families are much better able to handle developmental challenges.

BALANCING RESPONSIBILITIES

The focus in this section is on the interconnection of marital and parenting relationships. When the husband and wife have a cooperative partnership, the family atmosphere is conducive to the positive development of each member of the household. Constructive coparenting can greatly enhance the competence of both adults and children. The father's commitment to carry an equitable share of parenting responsibilities is a key factor contributing to the relative success of family relationships.

Sharing Influence

There has been a traditional overemphasis in women's lives on the mother's role and a corresponding underemphasis in men's lives on the father's role. The female, even as a young girl, has the importance of motherhood consistently brought to her attention. On the other hand, the male, even in early adulthood, usually hears little about his potential responsibilities as a father except in terms of being an adequate financial provider. This type of gender double-standard has contributed to the frequent and unfortunate one-sided responsibility of mothers in child rearing. The young female is likely to have a very intense early socialization for being a parent. In contrast, the male all too often has little preparation for a child-rearing role.

In particular, the male may have had little direct contact with his own father whereas the female's mother has likely been a much more consistent frame of reference. In general, females come to parenting situations with more confidence than do males, who may feel an incompatibility between their sense of masculinity and day-to-day child-rearing responsibilities.

The influence the typical father does feel in the family is all too often based primarily on his ability to provide financially for his children. To the extent that he is the primary economic provider, he may determine the family's standard of living yet have little impact on a direct personal level in his child's life. It is better for the father to feel some sense of influence, even if it is restricted to a purely economic function, rather than none at all. However, for fathers to be truly effective parents, they must become emotionally connected to their children in an individualized manner. Fathers need to be more than occasional playmates or periodic enforcers of family rules. A strong sense of positive family involvement can benefit the father as well as the child.

Fathers and mothers should share day-to-day parenting responsibilities. Paternal effectiveness must stem more from the father's profound personal impact on each child than simply from being a function of the size of his paycheck. As Dennis Meredith and I stressed in our book *Father Power*, the traditional notion of the patriarchal father should be replaced with a conception of positive paternal influence based on democratic family relationships.

A preoccupation with a simplistic conception of family dominance is still all too common. This narrow view implies that if one parent is dominant in a particular area, such as the disciplinary or economic role, he or she is decisive in all domains. Conversely, the less dominant parent is viewed as ineffective in influencing the family. According to sociologist Jessie Bernard, each marriage is actually composed of the "husband's marriage" and the "wife's marriage." Each of these marriages is a somewhat different reality according to the varying perspectives of the husband and wife. When couples are asked to answer questionnaires about their relative dominance concerning family decisions, fathers often overestimate their impact while mothers tend to downplay their influence.

Some evidence suggests that in families in which the father is perceived as relatively dominant, children, especially boys, are happy and secure. Conversely, in families in which the father plays a very submissive role, children seem at greater risk for emotional problems. Traditional definitions of dominance may make it difficult to recognize that what often appear to be somewhat father-dominated families are actually more of a healthy balance of cooperative paternal and maternal involvement. Maternal dominance generally is associated with father neglect. A careful examination of available research indicates that excessive mother or father dominance inhibits the child's and spouse's development. Children and adults need to develop their own capacity to make decisions. Autonomy and independence are extremely difficult achievements when either parent is dominant in an overcontrolling and restrictive manner.

The danger exists of either parent being too intrusive and insensitive to the child's needs. Children need to be protected, supervised and stimulated, but only up to a point, and much of this depends on their own temperament and abilities.

Children need parental guidance and stimulation but also the space to make choices appropriately and develop their own interests.

Task Distribution

Each couple has to develop a pattern of cooperation that works for them. They need to have a sense of mutual support and comfort in each other as individuals. A problem in some relationships is that one or both members of the couple feel that they have to conform to some abstract notion of relative or shared dominance. Ironically, so-called liberated views of equality may be just as straitjacketing as more traditional role-sharing arrangements.

Each couple has to discover a meaningful structure and division of responsibilities that works for them and their children. This book offers guidelines and suggestions but not hard-and-fast rigid rules. Many parents discover that when they confront the emotional responsibilities of parenting they are not as liberated or nonsexist as they perceived themselves to be in terms of abstract intellectual values. Both partners may be quite comfortable in what might have earlier seemed to them to be a relatively traditional division of labor. They may be surprised that their images of a cooperative husband-wife relationship before they were married or prior to having a child were quite different from how they now share the realities of parenting. What is most important is that each parent feels appreciated for his or her particular family contributions.

Parents should not view their relationship as a struggle for dominance. Rather, they should try to recognize and accept the fact that each one of them may be more influential in particular areas. At the same time, they may have relatively equal impact in endeavors in which neither one is more interested or competent.

In some facets of family life one partner will assume leadership and responsibility; the other will have more impact in different areas. Because one partner may be more influential in particular situations does not necessarily mean that the other is submissive. It is highly functional for one partner to defer to the other's greater interest or competence in a certain area while retaining the right to express an opinion positively. It is basically a question of a division of labor along the most advantageous lines. Each partner has power. No single blueprint determines the division of child-rearing responsibilities that is ideal for all families. Partners have to explore what best fits for them as a couple.

Moreover, as individuals and families change over time, new patterns of dividing responsibilities will likely emerge. The birth of another child, a shift in working status and other situations may require a reshuffling of the couple's responsibilities. The key issue is that each partner is able to accept the functionality of such changes. The healthy marital relationship is one that responds adaptively to the natural changes and stresses of family life.

Each marriage is composed of two people who have a unique fingerprint of abilities. Parents should not allow their partnership and parenthood to be hemmed in by rigid conceptions of masculinity or femininity or by what other couples do. If a husband does not enjoy the ocean but his wife does, he should encourage her to take their child boating and sailing. If a husband has an interest in sculpture and painting but his wife does not, he should be the one to take their child to art galleries. On the other hand, if both parents are comfortable with traditional sex-role divisions of labor, they should not feel that they have to conform to so-called liberated marriage or parenting styles. The crucial issues in successful family life revolve around love and acceptance, not the particular gender styles of the partners. The individuality and interests of each family member, whether adult or child, should receive positive support.

Mutual Acceptance

The parent's attitudes toward one another can have a big influence on overall family functioning. The mother, for example, can have a great impact on her children's image of their father. Because the mother is typically the parent who spends the most time with the children, she has considerable opportunity to convey her view of the father to them. In all too many families, children's perceptions of elusive fathers are heavily weighted by information provided by mothers. To the extent that the father realizes the significance of his role for his children, he can increase the amount and quality of time he spends with them. As the father becomes more involved with his children, he can become a more explicit frame of reference for them.

An important basis for the mother communicating a favorable view of the father to the children is her high esteem for him as a husband and partner. The happier the marriage, the more likely there will be a positive father-child relationship. This is partly because the mother lets the children know that their father is a valuable asset to the family. A mother's high regard for the father is of benefit to both the male and the female child. Boys feel that they have their mother's approval to identify with their father and use him as a male role model. Girls feel that it is appropriate to value their father as the kind of man with whom they would choose to have a committed relationship when they reach adulthood. When the mother is positive about the father, it supports both boys and girls in learning from his areas of competence. When the couple respects and values one another, it decreases the chance that a child will become involved in destructive competition with one parent for the affection of the other parent.

Perhaps the most significant factor in the child's social development is the opportunity to view the mother and father communicating and cooperating effectively with one another. The parents' mutual respect and their ability to resolve differences of opinion in a constructive manner provide excellent learning opportunities for their children. By observing over time an effective relationship between their parents, sons and daughters are absorbing much that will positively stimulate their own emotional and social functioning.

On the other hand, a parent's negative evaluation of the partner can become a self-fulfilling prophecy. For example, if a mother continually uses derogatory terms in describing the father, the children may come to believe her and begin to withdraw their respect for him. Unless they have an early and strong bond with their father, the children may indeed become less affectionate toward him and less interested in his activities. Fathers who do not spend much day-to-day time with their children are at a particular disadvantage in trying to modify potentially negative attitudes. In families where maternal views of paternal behavior are rather derogatory, many fathers immerse themselves further in their work or other activities outside of the home. They end up hardening the already tarnished image their children have of them.

There are serious implications if either parent blatantly devalues the other to the child. Comments by a father such as "All your mother cares about is herself," or "She never wanted to have children" or "She doesn't know anything about making decisions" can be quite destructive to the child's sense of security. Similarly, the mother's undermining of her partner with statements such as "He doesn't really care about you, just his job," or "He's not smart enough to be successful" or "I'm the only real parent you have" are likely to tarnish not only the father's image but also the child's self-concept and ability to feel comfortable with other men.

Analyzing Expectations

Given the traditional overemphasis on maternal child-rearing responsibilities, most mothers may not realize the significance of the father's role. They may succumb to parenting stereotypes because of limitations in their own socialization. Because many of them were once daughters in homes where paternal effectiveness with children was not appreciated, they are likely to have serious misconceptions concerning the father's role. Mothers who devalue the potential influence of the father may undermine their own development as well as that of their children. Many women simply do not think of their husbands as having clear-cut child-rearing responsibilities. When considering a man as a prospective husband, a woman may not even consciously concern herself with his role as a potential father, except for a brief discussion to find out if he wants to have children.

Men in our society have been stereotyped as the members of the family who are the financial providers, the fixers, the builders and the planners. Women tend to be stereotyped as the primary experts on domestic endeavors and family relations. The mother may feel that the father is quite adept at explaining mechanical principles to the children but does not really know how to understand their moods. The father may also perceive himself in this manner, which further strengthens family stereotypes. The family that relies on the mother for dealing with day-to-day interpersonal issues cuts off potential sources of emotional satisfaction and learning for parents as well as children. Some fathers consistently defer to mothers on all issues relating to the welfare of their children, believing that they have no expertise.

A father's rigid views about motherhood can also interfere greatly with his parenting effectiveness. If a father defers most parenting responsibilities to the mother, he severely limits his impact on his children. The father may even insist that the mother take care of both him and the children because he does not feel any sense of parenting responsibility. Some fathers perceive themselves as in command of the family, simply delegating day-to-day responsibilities for parenting to the mother. However, whatever the intention, fathers who do not share a consistent commitment and emotional connectedness to their children are doing themselves and their families a grave disservice.

Within the two-parent family, mothers can greatly influence the expression of paternal influence. Because of rigid family role expectations, many mothers have come to believe that motherhood is their life and crowning glory. For them, the raising of children is a mission above all others. Such women resent active father involvement because it represents a threat to their exclusive parental relationship with the child. Women who define themselves solely in terms of their motherhood frequently become quite defensive when confronted with the fact that paternal influence can be just as significant as maternal influence. They may also have considerable ambivalence in allowing their children a sense of independence. Such women develop an identity based primarily on mothering dependent individuals, rigidly resisting their children's efforts to gain any autonomy from them.

LIBERATING FAMILIES

During the last few decades, there has been some dimunition of gender stereotypes relating to parenting roles. Two major social developments have helped to lessen the motherhood mystique and have made more room for the father in the family. These related developments are the advent of the full-time working mother and the impact of the women's movement.

Working Parents

In 1960 less than 20 percent of mothers with preschool children were employed, but by 1972 this had risen to over 45 percent and by 1990 to over 50 percent. In 1960 less than 40 percent of mothers with school-aged children had employment outside of the home. By 1972 this rose to almost 50 percent and by 1990 to over 60 percent. A long-standing concern exists in our society about possible problems for young children when their mother works outside of the home.

In general, available evidence indicates that children from families with two employed parents are as a group similar to those with housewife mothers in terms of emotional, intellectual and physical development. Children with two employed parents generally show as much maternal attachment as those whose mothers are full-time housewives. However, maternal employment can, along with other family circumstances, have either positive or negative ramifications for particular children.

Many complex factors are involved in determining the impact of maternal employment including the age of the child, type of day-care arrangements and the amount of time the child is actually separated from the parents. The ways that maternal employment may affect the young child can be influenced greatly by the quality of the father's involvement in parenting. Under some circumstances, maternal employment can have a quite positive influence on both the parents and the child. Maternal employment often defuses an overly intense parent-child relationship, allowing the woman to develop more generalized feelings of competence. On the other hand, if the mother's employment means an already somewhat neglected child receives even less attention, there can be very negative implications for family functioning.

The employed mother can provide the father with an opportunity for a closer one-to-one relationship with his child. In many families before the advent of the employed mother, the father was less likely to be with a young child in individualized situations. More than one-third of all child-care arrangements made to aid employed mothers involve some increased participation by fathers. This can be a great advantage indeed if fathers realize their potential positive influence on children. The child with employed parents may also be able to spend some time, at least occasionally, at each of their workplaces. It can be quite stimulating for even very young children to discover that their mothers and fathers are competent adults outside the home. Unfortunately, most employed mothers in two-parent families still find themselves having much more than their fair share of household and parenting responsibilities.

Role Redefinitions

Wives often balance employment and parenthood better than their husbands do. Employment does not in itself detract from a woman's motherhood. The personal satisfaction derived for the woman who enjoys her career may actually increase her effectiveness as a parent. The fact that the employed mother can be a very competent parent while still spending time away from home should support the contention that more fathers can also combine successful careers with effective child rearing.

Among educated middle-class mothers, evidence suggests that many of those who are employed actually spend more quality one-to-one time with their children than do most of those who have no career. Many mothers who are home much of the day feel that simply being there is enough for their children. In contrast, employed mothers may feel that they must positively make up for being away from their children. Fathers, too, can learn a great deal from such mothers. Working mothers who have highly demanding careers tend to become more focused in their attention to their children when they are at home. Most working mothers realize that their children definitely need a period of close contact with them on a daily basis. They are usually committed to quality after-work time with their children. The child may get even more constructive attention from a working mother than from one who does not have a career. The housewife might not have as much of a need to interact as positively with her child on a one-to-one basis. After all, she may feel that she is always at home anyway.

When a mother has been the primary parent and then decides to pursue a career, especially before her children reach adolescence, much stress may be put on the marital relationship and the family system. In cases where the mother has assumed traditional responsibilities, the transition of going to work or back to school requires role redefinitions affecting both parents and children. Modification of conceptions of marital and parenting responsibilities are necessary but may be difficult to some extent for all family members. The first year in the family's readjustment to the mother's changing status is crucial. Unfortunately many couples cannot adapt in a successful way, and their marriages may deteriorate, sometimes ending in divorce. However, if they stay together during the difficult transition period, most couples actually seem to develop better relationships than when only the husband was an employed parent.

Child Care

During the last three decades, particular social concern has been directed at the quality of day care provided for children when mothers have employment outside of the home. A woman who has had a career may be in a state of indecision about continuing to work after she has had a baby. In most families, availability of day care and economic considerations are the major factors impacting on the family's options. If the couple looks strictly at the economic aspects of work, the situation may seem bleak. The potential income the mother earns may get absorbed by the new expenses of child care. But her job may be a significant source of pride as well as money for her. It is to be hoped that her career provides her with personal satisfaction as well as economic benefits.

In most cases, the father and mother can take at least some parental leave from their jobs. If they decide that neither of them will take any extended period of time off from working, both should be involved in planning day care for the baby. If some responsible adult cannot be found to care for the child in the home, the mother and father should visit several alternative settings and talk to other parents using such facilities before making a decision. They may find a day-care situation close to where they work so that they can visit their child during the day.

Parents should not feel that they have to settle for an institutional day-care center where babies and children may be treated as little more than parts on an assembly line. They can form a small baby-care cooperative with other parents— fathers as well as mothers—so that their child will be cared for with more personalized attention and commitment.

As a general rule, it is best for parents to take primary responsibility for the care of their baby. Ideally, parents should not be reticent about presenting their special needs to their employers. They should explain that they may need some time off or will want to work unconventional hours, or even bring the child to work with them occasionally. Many potential arrangements can be made to minimize the need for day care outside of the family. For example, both parents may work thirty-five hours a week, but if one goes to work two hours earlier than the other and comes home two hours sooner, most of the care of the infant can be managed without including other adults. Also, either or both parents may be able to spend part of their lunch hour with the child.

Another alternative is that parents work full-time but put their hours in during a four-day rather than a five-day week so that nonparental care is required three days a week rather than five. Obviously, one or both parents could work part-time, further reducing the need for outside help. Many couples are able to combine their schedules with those of another family member or couple so that the child is able to have a very stable and individualized social environment.

Partner Equity

Any child-care arrangement should take into account the needs of both parents and children. Regular day-to-day quality interactions with each parent, especially for infants and young children, are very important. However, some parents become so obsessed with caring for their children that they hardly ever have time to be alone with each other, or to pursue their more individualized interests. Parents should avoid making arrangements that preclude having some relaxed time for themselves, away from child rearing and employment responsibilities.

One goal of the women's movement is to lessen mothers' burdens in domestic and child-rearing activities. Many leaders in the movement have focused on changes relating to better financial support and day-care assistance for mothers, especially those who are single parents. At a fundamental family level, the equality of women involves men becoming more responsible parents. Men need to share day-to-day child-rearing responsibilities with women. Positively involved fathers can facilitate their daughters taking advantage of greater career and creative opportunities and their sons being supportive of such social changes. By making a consistent commitment to parenting, men can help women develop more varied career options without creating hardships for the family.

A general consequence of the greater involvement of adult females in positions of social and political leadership is a lessening of the emphasis on women just being mothers. This is beneficial in relieving some of the enormous pressure on women to define themselves solely in terms of their parenting responsibilities. However, this redefinition of adult femininity can be destructive to the quality of family life if fathers are not involved partners in parenting. The father's and mother's attitudes toward the woman's role outside the family are crucial. If the mother wants to work, to continue her education, or to become more involved in endeavors outside of the home, it is important that the father views it as his responsibility to be positively involved with his children.

Greater flexibility for mothers can benefit fathers in many ways. While the mother is gaining an opportunity to broaden her interests outside of the home, the father can have more of a chance for a one-to-one relationship with his child. On a more general level, men must be sensitized to the enormous need for more constructive paternal influence in our society.

The danger of the wife subtly resenting the husband's increased involvement with their child is lessened because she is gaining a greater confidence in herself as a well-rounded person. There is a very low probability that a child will be harmed by spending less time with a previously full-time mother, assuming they still share a regular, ongoing relationship. In fact, the child can be greatly stimulated by periods of time getting to know each parent as an individual as well as by opportunities to function more independently of family influence.

Expanding Opportunities

The father who is an active participant in parenting is one of the principal liberators of both mother and child. Unfortunately, the incredible importance that has been attached to traditional motherhood in our society has made too many women ambivalent about the father's role. These women may believe that children will be harmed if they are not always at home with them. Such a maternal perspective tends to restrict the development of all family members. The mother's involvement in a career may give the father more opportunities to have special times with his child. But the mother's confidence in her husband as a father can also do a great deal for her own liberation. She can pursue goals outside the home guiltlessly, knowing her husband is a responsible parent. And if her husband truly values her activities outside the home, she will be much happier in her career.

Many women, especially those with infants and young children, do not feel any need for pursuing a career or other endeavors outside the home. When children are very young this type of maternal attitude may indeed help to create a positive family atmosphere. However, over an extended period of time, such mothers risk eventually becoming too dependent on having their identity based entirely on being parents and relying on their children to meet all their needs.

Fathers can help mothers avoid this narrow channeling of self by being conscious of their paternal influence. In the process, they may have to overcome some entrenched misconceptions about fatherhood. Helping their wives to realize that fathers have a legitimate and necessary role in child rearing can defuse overbearing mother-child relationships and be a constructive springboard for both men and women to broaden their personal identities. Parents need to support and reassure one another in areas that are new to either one of them. The equality of men and women is too often discussed in mathematical rather than in human terms. Women's liberation should also mean men's liberation.

The crucial issue is the opportunity for the couple to define and work out a comfortable partnership that provides their child with ample support and stimulation from each of them. How they divide up responsibilities depends on their particular family circumstances, values and interests. Complete conformity to abstract standards rarely fits specific families. What is essential, however, is that both parents convey mutual respect for one another to their children. In the complex web of family connections, the quality of the father-mother relationship influences each parent's interaction with the child. For example, the father not only affects his children directly, but also indirectly by the way he relates to their mother. Good fathering is often associated with good husbanding.

Much evidence indicates that, in general, the husband's personality characteristics are more predictive of the couple's overall marital satisfaction than are the wife's. The husband's past history, his relationship with his father and the relative happiness of his parents have been found to be more related to marital adjustment than similar factors for his wife. Men who have experienced positive relationships with their fathers during childhood and whose parents were happily married are especially likely, themselves, to have successful marital relationships.

A major ingredient in marital satisfaction is the husband's ability to be expressive and sensitive. Most women enter into marriage with at least a moderate ability to communicate their feelings, but a far greater proportion of men have difficulty expressing affection and nurturance. In fact, the ability of husbands to be constructively expressive of their feelings is highly related to wives' as well as husbands' marital adjustment. Moreover, the husband's, as compared to the wife's, degree of expressiveness has been found to be more strongly associated with the level of both partners' perceived marital satisfaction. A positive marital relationship also facilitates the development of the husband's expressive behavior. Male expressiveness influences marital adjustment, which reciprocally stimulates further feelings of intimacy among husbands and wives and a relatively satisfying relationship for both partners. This, in turn, bodes well for the couple's adjustment to parenthood, increasing the likelihood that the father will constructively share parenting responsibilities with his wife and develop a close relationship with his child.

MAKING PREPARATIONS

A great need exists to sensitize both males and females to the crucial role of the father prior to their becoming parents. This section concentrates on parenting experiences that can increase the likelihood of the new father and mother constructively sharing child-rearing responsibilities. The discussion highlights factors involved in men and women choosing and preparing to become parents, emphasizing the importance of self-awareness and a life-span perspective. A strong focus is on the importance of husband-wife cooperation during the pregnancy period.

Responsible Decisions

Adults should first decide whether or not they really want to become parents. Being a responsible father or mother requires a long-term commitment, and some individuals decide to remain childless to devote themselves to other pursuits. As their life situations change at different points in adulthood so too may their attitude toward initial entry into parenthood.

Many individuals do not actively and freely choose whether or not to have children. For some becoming a parent is not unwelcome but, at least at the pregnancy stage, is rather a surprise. For others it may be a responsibility that has been clearly forced upon them or at least something that they wished could have been avoided until some later time. The following discussion assumes that both men and women have a very important choice to make before launching themselves into parenthood.

Each person has some limitation on the number of people with whom he or she can have a deep relationship. Any decision regarding childbearing should take this factor into account. Decisions about having a second, third or even a sixth child should continue to be made in a responsible manner. Fathers and mothers who already have one or more young children should give especially serious thought to their resources and responsibilities in contemplating the enlargement of their families.

The quality of a marriage and the partners' ability to parent together are usually interconnected. For most couples, the decision to marry should also involve a consideration of each partner's attitudes about parenting. The courtship process usually does not include thorough enough discussions on how potential partners feel about having and rearing children. The process of deciding whether to have a child can give each partner greater insight into the other's attitudes. Neither a husband nor a wife should let pressure from the other force an unwanted decision to have a child. Factors such as each partner's life stage, educational and career goals as well as family financial resources should be taken into account in deciding to start or add to a family.

There are varied reasons for deciding to become a father or mother. For most adults, if not all, children may represent a link with immortality and a chance to influence society. It is natural to have a dream of future happiness involving a successful and close relationship with a child who fulfills some dimension of one's own striving. But it is also important for the father and mother to have a realistic attitude about child-rearing responsibilities in order for them to accept the difficulties as well as the rewards of the parenting process. They should realize that some aspects of parenting may be stressful and frustrating as well as fulfilling. They should look forward to learning and growing, sometimes painfully, with their child, who needs to develop a strong sense of personal identity to become a happy, successful member of society.

Becoming a parent calls for much more dramatic changes for the couple than getting married. If the husband and wife have already been having great difficulties in dealing cooperatively with each other, it is not a good time for them to become parents, adding even greater stress to the relationship. For most couples, waiting from two to five years after they get married to have a child, and allowing for more stability in the relationship, increases the likelihood that they will both adapt better to the challenging transition to parenthood.

Neither the husband nor the wife should be hesitant about bringing up concerns about the relative stability of their relationship if they are contemplating having a child. It is better that such concerns be discussed early in a marriage. In many cases allowing time to work out differences in a cooperative way contributes to a much more constructive basis for the couple to share parenting responsibilities later. Even if the husband and wife are secure in their relationship, the addition of a child still requires new adaptations for both partners. Children have varying effects on marriages. By putting considerable stress on the marital partners, the presence of children may break up shaky relationships or fuse strong ones into solid, lasting partnerships.

Men and women are often quite different in the way that they approach the decision of whether to have a child. Most men do not get that much of a chance to be around babies before themselves becoming parents. Until they have their own children, or at least until they become expectant parents, men are less likely than women to show a generalized interest toward infants. When men contemplate whether or not to become parents, they may seem to ponder the issues in a much less emotional manner than women in similar circumstances. However, they can become just as excited, euphoric and engrossed upon seeing and holding their own newborn infants as women can.

Prebirth Considerations

Although lack of birth control precautions can lead to relatively instant conception for some couples, becoming pregnant for others may take years or may never happen. In as many as 15 percent of couples, at least one of the partners suffers from some sort of fertility problem. In many cases medical intervention can relieve the difficulty, in others the couple may have to consider other alternatives to a conventional pregnancy including in vitro fertilization, artificial insemination or adoption. Even in cases where neither partner has a fertility problem and both are eager to have a baby, it may take from six months to more than a year to become pregnant. The length of time involved before each pregnancy is achieved may also vary considerably. Despite regular intercourse, it is certainly not atypical for a year or more to pass without the achievement of pregnancy. Furthermore, experiencing a miscarriage is not unusual for couples before the completion of a successful pregnancy.

Couples should seek medical consultation if pregnancy has not occurred after a year of trying to conceive a child. In cases where the wife is over thirty, consultation should probably be sought if she does not become pregnant after six months of the cessation of birth control measures. Couples planning to become parents have a great responsibility, even before pregnancy occurs, to take good care of themselves. Some adults mistakenly feel that, in terms of the well-being of the fetus, a woman need only maintain positive health practices *after* she becomes pregnant. However, a woman's poor prepregnancy health status can put both her and the fetus at risk. Furthermore, the potential father's negative health and self-care habits can also increase the likelihood of future medical complications for the expectant mother and fetus. Abstaining from heavy drinking and cigarette smoking and treating any chronic medical conditions well before planning to conceive a child are highly advisable.

Couples planning to become parents should also be aware of the significance of genetic factors in child development. Assessment can be done to determine if either partner's genetic contribution might put future offspring at some risk. In many cases a thorough family medical history may give a clue as to whether there may be cause for concern; a number of relatively simple blood sample analyses can also be performed for each partner.

Even if little risk is present of a debilitating hereditary-related condition, some awareness of how genetics can influence development is still important in providing parents with a perspective on the significance of biological factors and the reality of individual differences. Such information can help fathers and mothers to realize the limits of their own direct impact in shaping certain dispositions, abilities and interests in their children. For example, parents may be less frustrated and more loving and accepting of a relatively shy child if they are aware of possible underlying genetic as well as environmental influences on social behavior.

Perhaps most important, couples should acknowledge their shared responsibility in contributing to the genetic predispositions of their offspring. Fathers have at least as much genetic influence as mothers and, in particular, chromosomal material (X or Y) transmitted in their sperm is the primary determinant of the child's sex. Either parent's genetic heritage may predispose a child toward certain strengths or deficits but, overall, the complex interactive quality of paternal and maternal genetic contributions needs to be emphasized. Despite the obvious importance of paternal genetic influences, not enough attention has been given to the father's prebirth role in child development. On the other hand, many of those who do acknowledge paternal genetic influences still view the father's impact in a limited fashion. Although it is important to focus on the expectant mother's emotional and physical well-being, the expectant father's influence on the quality of the pregnancy and prenatal environment should not be ignored. Awareness of paternal prebirth factors underscores the interactional nature of genetic and environmental processes during prenatal as well as later development.

Vast amounts of evidence attest to the importance of adequate prenatal care during pregnancy. Expectant parents have a responsibility to ensure as much as possible that the unborn child has the benefit of a positive prenatal environment. Some developmental delays and disabilities are directly attributable to poor prenatal care: millions of children have been adversely affected with problems ranging from profound retardation to more subtle learning disabilities. Many developmental problems could have been prevented if expectant parents did a better job of protecting the health of the pregnant woman and the unborn fetus. Such preventative care includes the pregnant woman abstaining from drinking alcoholic beverages or taking any drugs or medication not prescribed by her gynecologist. It also means appropriate diet, exercise, rest and avoidance, as much as possible, of emotional stress.

The expectant father has an extremely important role to play in supporting the well-being of his pregnant partner. His own abstention from smoking or drinking will make it easier for her to give up such habits. Accompanying the expectant mother for doctor's visits is not only supportive but also will provide the opportunity for him to to be clearly informed about pregnancy issues.

Even if a couple is unmarried and even if they have no intention of sustaining a long-term relationship, the expectant father can have an important role in the pregnancy process as a caring, concerned partner. Cooperation of the father-to-be during pregnancy and into the first year of the child's life often has advantages for mother and child, even if the couple does not have a committed family relationship. In contrast, evidence suggests that the breakup of the partners' relationship or the death of the expectant father during pregnancy may be associated with a greater risk of later developmental problems for the child.

Some expectant parents have to deal with unanticipated family stresses, and their mutual support becomes especially critical. Shortly after I was conceived, my father had a reoccurrence of tuberculosis necessitating his hospitalization during several months of the time my mother was pregnant. As an adult, I discovered some of my parents' correspondence from this time period and was quite moved by their loving concern for one another in the face of having to cope simultaneously with the pregnancy and my father's illness. Fortunately, my father recovered sufficiently to return home before my birth. The presence of an emotionally supportive husband can contribute to his pregnant wife's sense of well-being. His positive involvement is likely to be associated with a relatively problem-free pregnancy and delivery process, as well as later success in parenting the infant. On the other hand, the mother's lack of an emotionally supportive partner during the pregnancy process is often a precursor to a child's later developmental difficulties.

Adoption Implications

Similar to other adults planning to become parents, those who consider adoption may have varied motivations for wanting to add a child to their families. Socially sanctioned reasons for adopting include the desire to enlarge one's family without contributing to the population explosion or the wish to give a needy child a good home. Providing a child who cannot be cared for by the biological parents with a chance to live in a loving family atmosphere is a particularly admirable accomplishment. For the couple who face chronic infertility or serious medical or genetic risks associated with a potential pregnancy, adoption is usually the most viable parenthood option.

The present discussion is not intended to deal in depth with all the complex issues involved in the adoption process. Important factors to consider in the adopted child's development include the genetic contributions of the biological parents, the quality of prenatal care and age at placement. Other significant influences are the motivations for the adoption and the child's temperament and abilities relative to other family members. The adopting couple should be realistic concerning some special stresses and problems that may be experienced by them and the child. For example, typical adolescent-parent conflicts relating to autonomy and independence may be exacerbated by the adoptive child's need to know more about his or her biological heritage. Adoptive parents may have to confront particularly intense feelings of being rejected and unappreciated as their adopted child deals with basic problems in identity. When the child comes from a similar social background and at least superficially resembles one or both parents, the relationship may be less complex. If the child is interracial or markedly different in appearance from other family members, adjustment issues may be more difficult as the child matures. Development may also be especially problematic for the child who has biologically related handicaps or who experiences further major family disruptions such as the adoptive parents' separation or divorce.

Most children who are adopted have relatively successful family and personal adjustments. Adopted children tend to do much better educationally and socially than they would have if they grew up in a household similar to their family of origin. This is especially evident when adopted children reared in middle class homes with a positively involved father and mother are compared to those who have remained with economically disadvantaged single biological parents.

Many adopted children have an advantage that is, ironically, not shared by a large proportion of children brought up by their biological parents. Adopted children usually live in families where both the father and mother are actively committed to their welfare. Most adoptive couples have strengthened their relationships during the often complex process involved in adding a child to their family. Adopted children have a very good chance of growing up in a family with a relatively high level of cooperative parenting.

The risk of later problems is generally less for children adopted in early infancy than it is for those who have begun their lives in inadequate or abusive home situations. The originally minor difficulties of some adopted children can also be compounded if they do not function as well as the other individuals in their adoptive families. No matter how well matched an adoptive child and parents may initially appear, as with any parenting situation there may still be adjustment problems. Even for the child adopted in infancy, some stronger resemblance between certain styles of intellectual functioning and emotional reactivity is likely with the biological parents than with the adoptive father and mother. Furthermore, some infants who are available for adoption have not received adequate prenatal care, which may make them more susceptible to later learning-related problems.

Adopted children may experience special difficulties dealing with their self-concept development, in particular coping with differences with other family members. Adopted children may also be at risk to have an intensely difficult adolescent development while confronting feelings of abandonment by their biological parents. This process can be complicated by their realization that their biological parents were probably adolescents themselves when the adoption took place. On the other hand, many biologically related children and parents face much more frustrating developmental issues than is the case in most adoptive families.

The responsibility of being a parent offers certain challenges, satisfactions and opportunities to grow that transcend the issue of whether the child is adopted or a biological offspring. As is stressed throughout this book, it is crucial for the father and mother to accept the child's individuality. When parents can provide a loving and accepting home environment, the child is likely to be able to deal with differences from other family members and to develop a solid sense of self-worth.

Evolving Perceptions

The pregnancy process can be a very significant developmental phase for expectant fathers and mothers. The expectant-parent period is often marked by reflection upon one's past as a way of preparation for the future. Just as both partners should be involved in the decision to have a child, so they should continue to be mutually supportive during the pregnancy. Some difficult periods occur in most pregnancies, but overall, expectant parenthood is likely to be a very happy time for couples who are able to share their new status and remain sensitive to each other's needs. The expectant-parent period provides the couple with the opportunity for a more sensitive intimacy and sharing of adult roles. It can be an enriching experience of closeness and planning for the future, for constructing vivid images of sharing in the development of another human being.

Expectant parenthood is often a time of reflection and reevaluation in the face of new opportunities and challenges. It is an introspective time. Self-examination is influenced by the particular context surrounding expectant parenthood, including whether the pregnancy was planned and the partners' level of financial security and career development.

Expectant parents generally go through different phases regarding perceptions of their unborn child. During the initial phase, after the expectant mother has missed her period or first found out about her pregnancy, images of the unborn child will probably be somewhat vague. On the other hand, couples who have been trying to become pregnant for a long period of time may have already formed some specific images of their anticipated baby. When the fetus begins to move, expectant parenthood assumes a much more immediate reality. In fact, one of the most profound experiences may occur when each parent can see and feel the developing fetus in its movement against the expectant mother's stomach. When the expectant mother becomes obviously pregnant, the couple's preparations for parenthood become much more active. Most expectant mothers and fathers at this phase of pregnancy increasingly react to children and vicariously practice for approaching parenthood.

The expectant mother is often better prepared for becoming a parent than is the expectant father. However, great individual differences are apparent among both men and women in dealing with anticipated parenthood. At least three general categories seem to represent mens' attitudes toward marriage and pregnancy. Some husbands readily and eagerly accept the responsibilities and fulfillment of being a family man. They consider the pregnancy a gift and become even closer to their wives. A subgroup of these men may have relatively contemporary or nonsexist views toward parenthood, eagerly wanting to share all aspects of the pregnancy and parenting experience with their wives. Other men in this first group have more traditional views of fatherhood but are quite committed to being supportive of their wives and effective models for their children. Great variations occur among men in this group, but they do share a positive expectation as to what fatherhood will bring to their lives.

A second group includes men who are extremely career-oriented, often regarding prospective fatherhood as a burden that interferes with job responsibilities. Such men try hard to reaffirm their independence from other family members and deny the need for any changes in their life-style. For instance, this type of man engages in all his regular activities, including being out with friends or at work, even when the birth is imminent. These men are likely to become even more obsessed with their work as the pregnancy progresses.

A third group is comprised of generally immature men who approach fatherhood without much forethought. This type of man may suddenly become quite frightened at the prospect of having to support a wife and a child, having previously been financially dependent on others. His main problem is making the transition from carefree adolescence to responsible adulthood and the pregnancy is frequently accompanied by marital conflicts.

Individualized Reactions

Although the majority of expectant parents generally adapt positively, the stress of pregnancy may trigger emotional and behavioral difficulties. In reaction to their new status, some expectant fathers are occasionally subject to fits of frenetic physical activity, minor psychosomatic ailments and even deviant social behavior. Some anxious fathers-to-be may strive to reassert their intellectual or physical prowess, because they feel that impending fatherhood is aging them. For example, they may rather suddenly engage in strenuous sports or immerse themselves in demanding new hobbies. A common reaction to expectant parenthood for some husbands is to put more time and effort into their work, especially during the latter phases of pregnancy. Such husbands stay away from home for increasingly long periods of time. Though their apparent motive is better to provide for their expanding families, trying to deny intense personal anxiety about impending fatherhood may actually underly their frenetic work activity.

Coping with the stress accompanying expectant parenthood can magnify concerns relating to career advancement. However, adults who are older and more occupationally settled tend to have a much less ambivalent pregnancy experience than those who feel divided loyalties because of the energy needed to move ahead successfully in their careers.

Approximately 15 to 20 percent of expectant fathers develop some physical symptoms similar to those that may be experienced by their pregnant wives. These symptoms are varied and may include loss of appetite, indigestion, nausea, vomiting and backaches as well as weight gain. Some fathers even become bedridden toward the end of their wife's pregnancy, reminiscent of the custom called *couvade* in many preliterate societies. In couvade, the husband acts out many of the behaviors of giving birth, going to bed himself when his wife begins labor. Moaning and thrashing about, the new father is attended to by family and friends, given gifts, put on a strict diet and told to rest. The curious practice of couvade has stimulated many different possible explanations: envy of women's ability to bear children, assertion of paternity, warding off evil spirits and empathy with the mother are listed among the possible causes.

The custom of couvade is particularly prevalent in preliterate societies in which children do not experience the presence of a strongly involved father during their early development. The practice could stem from the basic identification of men in these societies with the woman's role, leading to an underlying discomfort with their own sexuality. This may also sometimes be the case with couvadelike behavior in Western society, for example when a father feels ill during his wife's pregnancy or has sympathetic labor pains. This type of man may have had little contact with his own father and have to rely totally on his maternal identification to form any image of himself as a parent.

Relatively mature men can usually handle the occasional disruptions in their lives associated with their partner's pregnancy. But for emotionally immature expectant fathers, changes in sexual routines may trigger very inappropriate behavior. Psychologists Arthur Hartman and Robert Nicolay found that sex offenses among first-time expectant fathers were more than twice as high as they were for other married men. These offenses were especially frequent during the last four months of pregnancy, when sexual deprivation was most likely. Fortunately, the vast majority of expectant fathers do not commit sexual offenses. But among maladjusted expectant fathers, sexual acting out may become more of a focal point of their problems. Their socially inappropriate behavior stems from a combination of weak impulse control and immature reactions to impending fatherhood.

Childbirth Education

The expectant father and mother may have been around children all their lives, but not until they have their own baby will they really experience the full impact of parenthood. Having a child involves a profound period of learning for each partner. The more cooperatively involved the expectant parents are with childbirth preparations, the better it will be for their marital relationship. This joint venture adds a new dimension to their development as a family.

Although childbirth education courses are not absolutely necessary, both expectant parents are well advised to take them. During the classes, the expectant father is strongly encouraged to be an active participant in the labor and delivery, and he is usually well prepared for the experience. Being with his wife when their baby is born can be very gratifying for the husband. His presence can also provide a great source of support for his wife and help to strengthen their marital relationship. By his active participation, the expectant father can help to alleviate his partner's anxiety during labor and delivery. During labor, he can give the mother-to-be back rubs, help her to relax and breathe properly and time her contractions. Just by being in the labor room, the husband may calm his wife, make her delivery easier and even reduce the risks of birth-related problems.

Prepared childbirth, with the father coaching, can be a very meaningful experience for both parents. The most widely used method of childbirth is named after one of its originators, French physician Fernand Lamaze. In Lamaze classes attended by the expectant parents, the pregnant woman is taught to dissociate uterine contractions from the experience of pain. The notion is repeatedly reinforced that such contractions are natural and not harmful. A mother learns to relax her abdominal muscles voluntarily so that she does not tense up during the delivery. Her husband or partner goes through childbirth exercises with her and coaches her during the actual birth process. Couples are usually shown films on childbirth and given tours of hospital facilities. Husbands are prepped on where they will change into delivery room garb and what they will do during the birth process.

In addition to structured childbirth education, informal discussion can be very important. Husbands as well as wives can be encouraged to ask questions, even about such traditionally "female" topics as the relative advantages and disadvantages of bottle and breast-feeding, and adjusting after childbirth. Unfortunately, most preparative courses put all the emphasis on pregnancy and the childbirth process without giving the prospective parents guidelines for actually dealing with the infant or with changes in their own relationship.

Programs involving fathers in the childbirth education process have yielded very positive results. When husbands are supportive during labor, wives are less anxious and distressed and are also not as likely to need medication. Both parents usually report a relatively high level of satisfaction with the birth process when fathers are present. Although women typically assume a primary parenting role, fathers can be just as competent caretakers of infants as mothers can. In certain situations, such as subsequent to a cesarean delivery or when the mother is otherwise incapacitated, the father can even take total responsibility for the care of the newborn.

New Adaptations

The presence of a baby makes various family relationships vastly more complex. Not only do the father, mother and infant affect one another, but each is affecting and influenced by the relationship between the other two. If the parents already have other children, many more relationships need to be considered. And, of course, in many families close relationships with grandparents and other extended family members come into play, even if they are not household members.

During the first ten days after giving birth, more than half of all women experience some episodes of sadness and crying. Hormonal changes and the fatigue that accompany the childbirth process can contribute to the mother's feelings of depression. The physical stresses of childbirth, the pressures of being a new mother, having an infant who is difficult to soothe or feeling neglected by her husband can all increase the risk of a woman suffering from postpartum depression. For most mothers feelings of depression may not be severe at all, reflecting only hormonal changes and the normal decline in positive emotion following the dramatic exhilaration and relief of giving birth. The more the couple can support one another in their new roles and the more responsive the infant is to parental attention, the less likely postpartum depression will be severe.

Occasional negative or resentful feelings toward the baby are certainly common for new parents. The mother may feel that she needs more care and support and that the newborn is getting most of the attention. She may be concerned that she is losing her attractiveness, her career or her effectiveness as a marital partner. The father can do a great deal to support the mother's sense of well-being. If he is careful to show commitment to his wife as well as to his new child, she is less likely to feel her individuality is being neglected. He should help her to participate in activities that she enjoys in addition to those revolving around the new baby. The mother needs to know how important she is to her husband beyond her role as a parent to his child. Consideration should also be shown for the new father's needs for support and reassurance from his wife. Both partners are going through a major transition in their lives as they adapt to being new parents.

For many new parents the pregnancy was a relatively idyllic and relaxing period, whereas for others it was intermittently or consistently stressful. The birth of the baby, depending on the circumstances, can be a great relief or a too abrupt change from a period of relative tranquillity. The interplay between change and stability is a fundamental issue throughout development. The birth of a child, especially the family's first one, is a great challenge to existing patterns of relationships. Couples with infants generally struggle to maintain or recapture their level of closeness prior to the birth of the baby. For many couples, this remains an ongoing issue or it may evolve into a rather passive resignation to the new priority of parental responsibility.

Cooperative Support

Women need to be quite comfortable and confident to breast-feed successfully, and the father can contribute a great deal to the mother's security by an encouraging, supportive attitude. If the father is jealous of the baby or if he pressures his wife to resume all her regular activities as soon as possible after giving birth, she may be deterred from breast-feeding. But most fathers are quite supportive when the decision has been made for their wives to nurse their offspring.

If the mother wants to breast-feed, it is usually beneficial for the baby for several reasons. Human milk is the best food for most (but not all) infants. It has an optimal proportion of nutrients and is free of bacteria and other contaminants. Breast-fed babies are less likely to develop colic, diarrhea and constipation, because human milk is so easily digestible. A yellowish fluid called colostrum, secreted from the breast after childbirth, tends to give the breast-fed infant protection against infections and food allergies. And of course, breast-feeding can offer an enormously satisfying emotional experience for the new mother.

Despite the general advantages of human milk, its benefits can be oversold by zealous advocates. Prepared formulas have proved to be quite adequate for the great majority of babies whose mothers may be unable or unwilling to breast-feed. In fact, some infants are actually allergic to human milk and need substitute nourishment. In any case, assuming adequate nourishment, the most critical factor in the baby's early emotional development is the overall quality of parent-child interactions rather than the mode of feeding.

The father of a baby who is breast-fed should not be made to feel left out of the parenting process. The involved father can still interact with his breast-fed infant in many other ways. However, in some families, breast-feeding assumes such a major focus that fathers feel they have no meaningful parenting function. It is advisable to use a breast pump occasionally so that the father has an opportunity to bottle-feed the infant. This type of father-infant involvement can also take some of the pressure off the mother and give her more free time during the day and more sleep during the night when the baby wakes up hungry.

The father and mother can support each other in a variety of ways to make their new parenthood a shared, growing experience. The mother has probably learned many practical tips on baby care that she can share with the father. As long as she realizes that an alternative style may be equally appropriate, having the mother coach the father in baby-care techniques can reinforce his awareness that the new baby is not all her responsibility.

Fathers as well as mothers should be involved in basic child-care activities. An equitable sharing of responsibilities can contribute to the quality of the infant's relationship with both parents. When the father bathes, feeds, changes diapers or dresses the baby another opportunity is presented for them to get to know each other. Given that the father and mother are likely to have different styles even when engaged in the same activity, the infant is exposed to a broader range of stimulation when taken care of by both parents. The parents must work out a cooperative plan of sharing and mutual support. The actual division of responsibilities is not as important as the establishment of a comfortable partnership in infant care. Both parents should have ample opportunities to interact regularly in an individualized fashion with their child.

SUMMARY

The ability of the husband-father to be nurturant and sensitive is a key factor in marital satisfaction as well as in successful parent-child relationships. Particular recognition needs to be given to specific ways that the father and mother can share parenting responsibilities and enhance their child's development. How parents divide up family work depends on their particular circumstances, but it is crucial that children perceive a continuing sense of emotional commitment from their father as well as their mother.

Father-mother cooperation and mutual respect is an important ingredient in the child's development of positive attitudes toward both males and females. It is much easier for working parents to handle changing family circumstances and day-care issues when the father and mother equitably share child-rearing responsibilities. Mothers have a much greater chance of experiencing a sense of pride in their parenting and working outside of the home when fathers are supportive partners.

Preparation for parenthood is important if couples are going to share child-rearing responsibilities effectively. There is a great need to sensitize men and women to the crucial role of the father even before they become parents. Couples should discuss their feelings about future parenthood and feel comfortable and committed to one another before attempting to add a baby to their households. The expectant husband's active support increases the likelihood of a positive pregnancy and birth experience and, moreover, bodes well for the father-mother-infant relationship.

FURTHER READING

Balancing Responsibilities

Sharing Influence

About data underscoring the importance of both parents being positively involved in child and family development, see Biller (1982a), Biller and Meredith (1974, 1982) and Biller and Solomon (1986). For analysis of nontraditional child-rearing arrangements, see Lamb (1982, 1986), Pruett (1987) and Russell (1983, 1986).

For discussion of differences between the views of husbands and wives concerning marriage and family responsibility see Bernard (1982), Blumstein and Schwartz (1983) and Szinovacz (1987). For the common dissatisfaction of mothers that they and/or their children are not receiving enough emotional support from the husband-father, see Biller and Meredith (1974, 1982) and Genevie and Margolies (1987).

On theories and research relating the relative dominance of parents to the sex role and personality development of children, see Biller (1969b, 1971a, 1974c) and Lynn (1974, 1979).

Task Distribution

For data relating to the way couples distribute money, work and child-rearing responsibilities, see Blumstein and Schwartz (1983) and Genevie and Margolies (1987). For helpful guidelines for balancing work and parenting responsibilities, see Grollman and Sweder (1982), Loman (1984) and Olds (1989).

Regarding how fathers in dual wage-earner families are more likely to become involved in child care when mothers have time-consuming jobs outside of the home, see Barnett and Baruch (1987), Hoffman (1989) and Moen and Dempster-McLain (1987). For review of literature indicating differing motivations, styles and levels of satisfaction associated with the father's participation in child care within various family contexts, see Hoffman (1989).

Mutual Acceptance

For review of some of the research relating the quality of marital relationships to quality of child rearing, see Biller and Solomon (1986). For other data underscoring the dynamic interplay between marital and parenting relationships, see Belsky (1979a, 1979b, 1980b, 1985), Doherty and Jacobson (1982), Duvall and Miller (1985), Galinsky (1981), Lerner and Spanier (1978) and Waite, Haggstrom and Kanouse (1985).

Analyzing Expectations

Concerning research relating to marital choice, see Duvall and Miller (1985), Miller (1987) and Murstein (1982). For interrelationship between father-mother cooperation in parenting and marital satisfaction, see Baruch, Barnett and Rivers (1983) and Genevie and Margolies (1987).

On the importance of balanced husband-wife relationships, see Bernard (1982), Nichols (1984) and Scarf (1987). For problems engendered by women defining themselves exclusively as wives and mothers and the related costs to men who may be excluded from the child-rearing process, especially with infants, see Biller (1971a, 1974c), Biller and Meredith (1974), Chodorow (1978), Dinnerstein (1977) and Lott (1981, 1987).

Liberating Families

Working Parents

For research about maternal employment and child and family adjustment, see Hoffman (1984, 1989) and Piotrowski and Crits-Christoph (1982). For data linking father's sharing child-care responsibilities with the employed mother's sense of emotional well-being, see Genevie and Margolies (1987), Hoffman (1989), and Silverstein (1991).

Regarding parenting and marital problems often associated with involuntary job loss and unemployment, see Elder et al. (1985, 1986), McLoyd (1989), Ray and McLoyd (1986) and Voydanoff (1983).

Role Redefinitions

For research relating maternal employment to family system changes, including some gradual lessening of gender stereotypes, see Hoffman (1989) and Pleck (1984). (Many of the problems associated with maternal employment are linked to husbands' rigidly traditional gender stereotypes including an unwillingness to share more directly in parenting responsibilities.)

Child Care

On ways that working parents can constructively make child-care/day-care decisions, see Brooks (1991), Dreskin and Dreskin (1983), Grollman and Sweder (1986) and Olds (1989). For discussion of the impact of various types of day care on children, see Clarke-Stewart (1989), Galinsky and Hooks (1977), Pleck (1986) and Zigler and Gordon (1982).

Partner Equity

About men and women cooperatively working together in child rearing for the sake of their children, themselves and their families, see Biller and Meredith (1974, 1982) and Biller and Solomon (1986). For perspectives on male liberation and their implications for greater father involvement in child rearing, see Bronstein and Cowan (1988), Faber and Mazlish (1974), Farrell (1986), Friedan (1981), Levine (1976), Lewis and O'Brien (1987), Pleck (1981), Pruett (1987) and Russell (1983, 1986).

Expanding Opportunities

Regarding the long-term developmental impact of parental cooperation concerning work and child rearing, see Biller (1982a), Biller and Solomon (1986), Gottfried, Gottfried and Bathurst (1988) and Hoffman (1989).

For the importance of acknowledging individual and gender-related differences but at the same time fostering mutual respect and positive communication and cooperation between the spouses, see Biller and Meredith (1974), Nichols (1984) and Scarf (1987).

Concerning the impact of husband variability on marital satisfaction, see Barry (1970), Baucon and Aiken (1984), Lamke (1989) and Murstein and Williams (1983).

Making Preparations

Responsible Decisions

For research relating to marital choice, see Duvall and Miller (1985) and Murstein (1982). For reasons why adults choose to have children, see Biller and Meredith (1974), Daniels and Weingarten (1982), Hoffman (1987), and Kimbal and McCabe (1981). For reasons why some adults choose to remain childless, temporarily or permanently, see Houseknect (1987), Peck (1971), Robinson and Barrett (1986) and Veevers (1980, 1982).

Regarding the development of child-rearing attitudes prior to parenthood, see Berman and Pedersen (1987), Galinsky (1981), Kimbal and McCabe (1981) and Ross (1982a, 1982b). For the impact of parenthood on marriage, see Belsky (1985) Cowan and Cowan (1992) and Waite, Haggstrom and Kanouse (1985).

About the various ways that financial concerns can influence fertility rates, see Miller (1987). For detailed discussions about various expenses related to parenting, see Benning (1974), Biller and Meredith (1974) and Olds (1989).

For research relating to an interest in babies and having children among young adult men and women, see Barnhill, Rubenstein and Rocklin (1979), Feldman and Nash (1978) and Humphrey (1977). Concerning the impact of the father's participation in child rearing even if the parents are not married, see Furstenberg, Morgan and Allison (1987).

With respect to ways that parents may become more aware of how their childhood family experiences affect their current attitudes toward parenting, see Biller and Meredith (1974), Cowan and Cowan (1992), Bowen (1978) and Galinsky (1981). For perspectives indicating that some men become involved parents by modeling their own fathers' behavior toward them during childhood while other men may become highly involved with their children as a reaction to feelings of earlier paternal deprivation, see Biller and Meredith (1974), Parke and Beitel (1986), Radin (1981), Russell (1986) and Sagi (1982). For support of the notion that mothers who have had a positive relationship with their fathers are more encouraging of their husband's taking an active role in child rearing, see Biller and Meredith (1974), Feldman, Nash and Aschenbrenner (1983), Radin (1982) and Russell (1986).

Prebirth Considerations

For practical advice pertaining to problems in becoming pregnant as well as information about alternative forms of contraception, see Silber (1980). Regarding the probability of infertility in women over thirty, see Menken, Trussell and Larsen (1986) and Menning (1975). For adjustment problems relating to marital stress and infertility, see McEvan, Costello and Taylor (1987).

Concerning genetic counseling, see Chedd (1981) and Vander Zanden (1989). Regarding more detailed discussion of potential genetic influences on personality development, see Daniels and Plomin (1985), Nash (1978), Plomin (1989), Scarr and Kidd (1983) and Wellborn (1987).

For more specific information about prenatal risk factors and the importance of maternal health in a successful pregnancy and delivery, see Holmes, Reich and Pasternak (1983), Osofsky et al. (1985), Stechler and Halton (1982) and Vorhees and Mollnow (1987). Regarding the importance of the expectant parents' relationship during the prenatal period, see Biller (1972), Biller and Solomon (1986) and Bittman and Zalk (1978).

Regarding the importance of receiving supportive medical care during pregnancy, see Bittman and Zalk (1978), Holmes, Reich and Pasternak (1983) and Stechler and Halton (1982).

Adoption Implications

Concerning the varied issues involved in the adoption process and raising an adopted child, see Chess and Thomas (1987), Gilan (1984), Levine (1976), Melina (1986), Schaffer and Lindstrom (1989), Sokoloff (1983) and Wishard and Wishard (1979).

For research relating to the influence of genetic factors among adopted children, see Bouchard et al. (1981), Hutchings and Mednick (1977), Plomin (1987), Scarr and Kidd (1983), Scarr and Weinberg (1976) and Wender et al. (1986).

Evolving Perceptions

For descriptions of the changing perceptions of expectant parents over the course of the pregnancy, see Barnhill, Rubenstein and Rocklin (1979), Galinsky (1981), Gurwitt (1982), Lips (1983) and Robinson and Barrett (1986). For research relating prebirth parent characteristics to family adaptations during the child's first year of life, see Heinicke et al. (1983).

Concerning husbands' and wives' attitudes during the expectant parent period, see Belsky, Lang and Huston (1987), Berman and Pedersen (1987), Biller and Meredith (1974), Cowan and Cowan (1992), Lips (1983) and Robinson and Barrett (1986).

For typical concerns and satisfactions experienced by most expectant parents, see Berman and Pedersen (1987), Biller and Meredith (1974) and Galinsky (1981).

Individualized Reactions

Concerning the varied reactions of expectant fathers during pregnancy, see Arnstein (1972), Biller (1972), Biller and Meredith (1974), Bittman and Zalk (1978), Cowan and Cowan (1992), Gurwitt (1982) and Hartman and Nicolay (1966).

For information about sexual adaptations during pregnancy, see Bittman and Zalk (1978), Cowan and Cowan (1992) and Masters and Johnson (1966).

Regarding guidelines for coping with partner differences, see Biller and Meredith (1974), Bittman and Zalk (1978) and Robinson and Barrett (1986).

Childbirth Education

For discussions of various childbirth education techniques that include a special role for the father, see Bittman and Zalk (1978), Bradley (1965), Lamaze (1970), Leboyer (1975), Robinson and Barrett (1986) and Wente and Crockenberg (1976).

About the potential benefits of childbirth education and husband involvement during labor and delivery, see Biller and Salter (1985), Bittman and Zalk (1978), Cowan and Cowan (1992), Cronenwett and Newmark (1974), Henneborn and Cogan (1975), McHale and Huston (1984), Palkovitz (1985), Parke (1981, 1985), Parke and Beitel (1986), Pawson and Morris (1972), Peterson, Mehl, and Leiderman (1979) and Robinson and Barrett (1986). For perspectives stressing that the father's birth attendance is not necessary for bonding to the infant, see Biller and Meredith (1974), Greenberg (1985), Greenberg and Morris (1974), Palkovitz (1985) and Parke and Beitel (1986).

New Adaptations

With respect to postpartum depression among new parents, see Cowan and Cowan (1992), Field et al. (1985) and Hopkins, Marcus and Campbell (1984). For research relating to the significance of the birth of the first child on the parents and their marital relationship, see Belsky (1985), Belsky, Lang and Huston (1987), Berman and Pedersen (1987), Biller and Meredith (1974), Biller and Salter (1985), Cowan (1988) and Waite, Haggstrom and Kanouse (1985).

For discussions of role transitions involved in the birth of the first child, see Belsky (1985), Belsky, Lang and Huston (1987), Berman and Pedersen (1987), Biller and Meredith (1974), Biller and Salter (1985), Cowan and Cowan (1992) and Cowan (1988).

Cooperative Support

For more detailed discussion of breast-feeding and nutritional issues, see Eiger and Olds (1987), Lozoff (1989) and Pipes (1988). With respect to later eating-related problems and disorders that may be associated with inadequate paternal involvement, see Humphrey (1986) and Klesges et al. (1990).

Concerning the importance of father-mother cooperation in infant and child care, see Biller (1976b, 1986), Biller and Meredith (1974), Biller and Salter (1985), Bozett and Hanson (1985), Clarke-Stewart (1978), Cowan and Cowan (1992), Cowan (1988), Genevie and Margolies (1987), Greenberg (1985), Parke (1986), Parke and Beitel (1986), Pedersen (1980), Pedersen et. al. (1987), Pruett (1987) and Russell (1983, 1986).

Concerning various child rearing advantages middle-aged adults may have in comparison to their younger adult counterparts, see Biller and Meredith (1974), Gilligan (1982), Heath (1976, 1977, 1978), Levinson (1978, 1980, 1986), Sears (1977), Sternberg (1986a), Vaillant (1977) and Vaillant and Vaillant (1981). For discussions of the advantages and disadvantages of becoming a parent at different phases of adulthood, see Daniels and Weingarten (1982), McLaughlin and Micklin (1983), Moreland and Schwebel (1981), Robinson and Barrett (1986) and Wilkie (1981).

4

Gender, Individuality and Identity

Whether a child is male or female, slim or muscular, intellectually brilliant or below average, timid or extremely assertive, he or she needs paternal interest, understanding and support. When both the father and the mother are actively involved, there is a greater likelihood that each child's specialness will get an adequate amount of constructive recognition and stimulation. A crucial parenting goal should involve encouraging the child to develop self-acceptance and a sense of personal effectiveness and competence.

PERSONAL ACCEPTANCE

Children need the opportunity to develop their talents and a sense of self-respect. They should be proud of their individuality but not be crushed by their limitations. Children do not have to be pushed or pressured into expressing their interests and abilities. Parental support and patience is the best formula for encouraging the child to develop a strong sense of competence and confidence.

Biosocial Factors

Biology gives a definite nudge to gender differences in behavior and personality style. Parents should help to prepare the child to cope with those nudges and to accept their individualized consequences. On the other hand, the duty of the father or mother is not to try to force or funnel the child into a narrow social definition of sex-appropriate behavior. To be well rounded, regardless of gender a person must possess some degree of assertiveness, independence and physical competence as well as emotional expressiveness, tenderness and an ability to relate to others. Parents should encourage their children to develop multiple competencies.

In most families, girls and boys are treated differently from birth. However, researchers are generally skeptical concerning the existence of significant behavioral differences between males and females during infancy. The prevailing view among developmentally oriented psychologists is that sex differences in infant behavior are more a function of differential treatment than of innate biological predispositions. On the other hand, just because male and female newborns are generally very similar in their behavior does not mean that all sex differences in later childhood are merely a reflection of parental and social influences. The genetic basis of sexual differentiation is also associated with other physical maturation processes as children grow older. Sex-linked maturational factors can have a significant influence in contributing to some overall differences in male and female personality development and adult parenting styles.

Genetic and prenatal factors may interact with parental behaviors to produce subtle sex-related behavioral differences even in early infancy. For instance, baby girls often seem to be more perceptually mature and responsive to the sounds and sights around them. Male infants, on average, seem to be more vigorous physically and to cry more. Parents may exaggerate relatively minor sex differences by talking to their girls more and handling their boys more vigorously.

Some average gender differences in children are apparent by the end of the first year. Girls tend to learn to talk earlier than boys and, on average, seem to be more attentive to parental cues; boys venture farther from their parents, stay away from them longer and look at them less than do girls. Boys tend to be more aggressive, trying to push around a barrier placed between them and their parent while girls are more likely to remain relatively immobile and cry in frustration.

Differential Treatment

When they are involved in play and caretaking roles with infants, fathers tend to be the parents who differentiate most in the way they treat sons and daughters. Fathers may greatly stimulate infant sons but treat infant daughters as if they are particularly fragile. Even with newborn sons, fathers are generally much more playful and stimulating, mothers more soothing and quieting. It is common to observe involved fathers encouraging their infant sons to move faster, crawl further or reach higher. Fathers are usually less concerned than mothers if a child gets tired or dirty. This generally allows them to tolerate the temporary discomforts that the child may experience in exploring the environment more easily.

Fathers are more likely than mothers to institute a clear-cut double standard in terms of the infant's gender. Even with infants, fathers appear to be more influenced by the sex of the child than mothers are. Fathers are likely to cuddle infant daughters gently but to engage in rough-and-tumble activities with sons. Fathers are more apt to accept a temperamentally difficult male infant but to withdraw from a female infant who presents similar problems. Some fathers consistently encourage their infant sons to achieve competence in the physical environment but inhibit their infant daughters when they stereotypically perceive them as more fragile. Ironically in many such cases the daughters are even more

robust than the sons were at a similar age. An inhibiting sexist attitude is counterproductive to the daughter's development of initiative and assertive behavior.

The infant is not a passive participant in the family system. How the infant
responds to parental overtures influences greatly how a father or mother perceives
the child. For example, it may not simply be a sexist attitude on the part of
some fathers to pay more attention to infant sons than infant daughters. The
child's reaction can be a major factor; in general, infant sons may actually display
more positive emotional reactions than daughters do when fathers engage them
in physically stimulating rough-and-tumble play.

To the extent that gender differences correspond to the particular tendencies
of children, some differential treatment of boys and girls is understandable. The
happiest individuals are the ones who are comfortable with themselves and their
activities because they achieve a good fit with their basic temperament, interests
and abilities. Trying to force a boy or girl into a straitjacket conception of
appropriate sex-role behavior is certainly not in the child's best interests. But
neither is trying to pressure a child into behaving in a so-called nonsexist manner
when he or she naturally appears comfortable with more traditional expectations.

Most young children become rather rigid in what they consider to be sex-
appropriate behavior, but they are capable of developing a broader repertoire of
skills, transcending narrow gender stereotypes as they mature. Young children
who are uncomfortable with their basic biological sexuality are at risk for later
developmental problems. Children are able to expand their interests and skills
once they have clearly established a secure sense of gender identity. Regardless
of their specific beliefs about traditional gender stereotypes, it is important that
both parents convey a positive acceptance of their child's sex and individuality.

Developmental Complexities

Parents cannot avoid having some clear gender-related expectations for their
children. Parents holding rather traditional gender-stereotype views are criticized
for their rigidity by those who are committed to a more liberated perspective.
However, parents who are highly supportive of nonsexist child rearing may be
quite frustrated when their two- or three-year-old (or even younger child) exhibits
traditional gender stereotypes. The female toddler who is extremely attached to
dolls and kitchen activities, or her male counterpart who seems only to want to
roughhouse and play with guns, is apt to create much dismay for avowedly
nonsexist parents.

Judith Kaliski and I found that most young children go through a rather rigid
sex-typing stage even when both of their parents are strong believers in nonsexist
child rearing. Parents can obsessively strive to behave in a nonsexist manner
toward their offspring, but the child still differentiates between mother and father
and forms a gender-related self-image. The child may not differentiate as much
between parental sex roles when the father is relatively uninvolved in the family.
However, paternal deprivation is likely to lead to later gender conflicts rather
than to a more positive flexibility.

Young children have a much more simplistic view of the world than adults or even older boys and girls. Once young children discover that they belong to the category of male or female, they naturally tend to strive to be similar to older, bigger people of the same sex. In fact, the findings of developmental psychologists Lawrence Kohlberg and Edward Zigler suggested that very bright preschoolers were apt to become more sex typed at three or four years of age than their less intellectually gifted peers. In contrast, extremely intelligent children were actually found to exhibit more sex-role flexibility in middle childhood when compared to those with relatively average abilities. Other data also indicate that those children who become comfortably sex typed at an early age are more likely to develop the sense of security and confidence to be more flexible in the expression of their interests by the time that they reach their middle elementary school years.

Even if there were no gender differences in temperamental predispositions, the experience of growing up with a male body as compared to a female body would greatly influence personality and social development. Sex differences become greater as individuals physically mature. Baby boys or girls do not differ nearly so much from each other as do adolescent males and females, or particularly as do adult men and women. After all, adolescents and adults have gone through puberty, and females experience certain additional basic biological changes during menstruation and pregnancy.

Although the average adult male is bigger and stronger than the average adult female, this type of gender difference is not consistent during earlier development. Boys lag behind girls in many areas of physical development prior to adolescence, but they are generally more intensely active and aggressive even during the preschool years. On the other hand, boys continue to grow after girls stop, and they reach their larger mature size three to five years later.

A basic sex difference relates to the biochemical variations between men and women. Much of biological maleness and femaleness is related to delicate balances of two kinds of sex hormones, androgens and estrogens. Though androgens are referred to as male hormones and estrogens as female hormones, both sexes produce both kinds. The predominance of one or the other type of hormones is involved in the development of certain distinctive male or female sex characteristics including genital appearance, body hair, voice quality and breast development. However, hormonal functioning by no means completely predetermines personality differences. Hormones have an important interactive influence on behavior and physical development, but it is a mistake to picture them as rigid chemical straitjackets. Similarly, culturally related gender stereotypes, although generally powerful influences, do not have to limit individual potential severely. Parents can play a major role in facilitating a child's self-acceptance, healthy gender identity and sense of individuality.

Family Patterns

Parents who feel supported by their partners in their child-rearing efforts are more effective in fostering their children's positive gender development. In far too many families, the mother is left to make all the day-to-day decisions involving children while the father focuses on his occupational commitments. When the father constructively shares parenting responsibilities with the mother, children are far more likely to develop a healthy gender identity, self-acceptance and personal competence.

In some of my earlier research, I evaluated the parenting relationships of fathers and mothers by having them discuss various child-rearing situations. Paternal assertiveness in family decision making concerning children was found to be associated with the masculinity of kindergarten-age sons' self-concepts, preferences and interpersonal behavior. Moreover, interviews with the sons revealed that the boys' own perceptions of their fathers' relative family involvement was even more strongly related to their gender development. The boys' behavior was linked to their fathers' relative participation in day-to-day aspects of their lives. Consistent with findings from other studies, boys who were father-absent during their preschool years were especially likely to have relatively unmasculine self-concepts.

However, several boys with relatively unmasculine self-concepts and rather passive personality styles had fathers who had a very dominant role in family interactions. Unfortunately, they had fathers who were controlling and restrictive of their children's behavior. For instance, this type of dominant father punished his son for disagreeing with him and generally demonstrated very rigid and authoritarian attitudes. A positive gender identity and social development are facilitated when the father is a competent model but also allows and encourages the child to be assertive.

In an extensive study with preschool-age children, developmental psychologist Mavis Hetherington and her colleagues found that the behavior of fathers was very important with respect to the gender development of both daughters and sons. The fathers of extremely feminine four- to six-year-old girls were generally highly masculine in their sex-role preferences, liked women and reinforced feminine behaviors in their daughters. These fathers were nurturant and actively involved with their daughters but also somewhat restrictive and controlling. Maternal warmth was also directly related to the girls' femininity but those who displayed more general competence, or what could be conceived as positively androgynous behavior, seemed to be influenced by the behavior of both parents. Their fathers were warm, had positive views toward females and consistently encouraged independence and achievement, while their mothers were likely to be working and also to be supportive of the child's independence. Parental encouragement of independence and achievement and a lack of rigid restrictiveness are especially important if young girls are to develop feelings of competence in intellectual endeavors.

For boys, masculinity with respect to self-concept, sex-role preference and interpersonal behavior was related to their father's warmth, expectations for maturity and involvement in family decision making. Boys who seemed able to combine a positive masculinity with more generally competent patterns of social interaction had fathers who were warm, active in decision making and child care, emotionally expressive and supportive of the mother-child relationship.

Gender Conflicts

A very small proportion of children demonstrate highly atypical sex-role behavior even during infancy and toddlerhood. They may completely deny their
biology, insisting that they are actually trapped in a body of the wrong sex. For
instance, some young boys feel as if they are really females. These "transsexual"
boys represent an extreme in terms of the pervasiveness of their feelings of
femininity, but their development may also provide clues to the origins of homosexuality and other types of sexual adaptations.

Transsexual boys typically have unusually close physical relationships with
their mothers. Analyzing case histories of such boys, psychiatrist Robert Stoller
reported that mother-child body contact during infancy was especially intense,
and much evidence suggested that the mothers reinforced many forms of feminine
behavior. In none of the cases was the father assertive or involved with his child.
Other forms of disturbed sex-role development in males are frequently associated
with a family history of an overly intense mother-son relationship in the context
of paternal deprivation.

Psychiatrist Richard Green reported a high rate of early paternal deprivation
among severely effeminate boys who wished that they were girls and preferred
to dress as females. These boys had exceedingly strong maternal identifications
and were exceptionally feminine in their self-concepts and preferences. More
than a third of these transsexual boys became father-absent before the age of
four. Among the others, father-son relationships were very limited or distant.
The mothers were excessively attached to their sons and had difficulty in per-
ceiving that there was anything deviant in the boys' behavior. Although many
of the fathers were quite upset that their son continued to behave in a feminine
manner at four or five years of age, they had been generally tolerant of the
child's behavior during the infancy and toddler periods. Such data suggest that
these fathers may be different from most men, who would be extremely uncomfortable if their sons deviated greatly from expected sex-role patterns.

Further analyses of data from Green's provocative research program revealed
that during the infancy period fathers spent less time with their feminine-behaving
boys than fathers with conventionally masculine sons did. There was a tendency
for less father-son interaction even in the first year, and significant differences
emerged beginning in the child's second year. Among divorced parents, those
with feminine sons separated earlier than those with masculine sons. In general,
early father deprivation, whether in the context of two-parent or one-parent
families, was much more common for the feminine boys.

Green's work is particularly valuable because he traces the complex interaction
of various factors in the development of unusually feminine boys. He discusses
how, in some cases, sibling and peer group reactions as well as parental behavior
can strongly reinforce an inappropriate gender identity. Perhaps most significant,
his research suggests ways in which the child's characteristics may influence
parental behavior. For example, in several of his cases, the father's lack of

interest seemed to increase because of the young boy's disinclination to participate in masculine activities.

Constitutional predispositions as well as direct parental influence are often
involved in the child's developing a transsexual or otherwise sexually unusual
behavior pattern. Young boys who become transsexual are frequently rather
"pretty" and delicate, typically resembling their mothers much more than their
fathers in various aspects of their outward appearance. This is not to say that
biological factors inevitably cause a transsexual adaptation but that constitutional
predispositions may increase the likelihood that certain children will develop
gender-atypical behavior patterns. Parental expectations are very much influenced
by the child's appearance and temperament.

In some cases biological factors such as genetic anomalies have relatively
more direct impact on the development of transsexualism or other forms of
atypical sex-role development. Rapidly accumulating data also indicate that levels
of prenatal androgenic hormones are connected to the degree to which young
children engage in rough-and-tumble play, are assertive or timid and express
interest in babies and doll play. In addition, children with gender-deviant predispositions may be more at risk to suffer from paternal rejection. Chapter 10
includes further discussion of sexual adaptations that are often embedded within
a history of father deprivation.

Life-span Implications

The quality of early parental attachments is an important factor in the young
child's sex-role and personality development. The first two to three years of life
can be crucial in the formation of an individual's gender identity. Early father
deprivation can interfere with the achievement of a secure gender identity, especially for boys. Father-absence and other forms of paternal inadequacy before
the age of four or five may retard early masculine development. Although sex-
role development in girls is not as directly affected by paternal deprivation as it
is for boys, an early history of inadequate fathering is often associated with the
difficulties that females have in relating to males during adolescence and
adulthood.

Sex-role functioning in young children is very important because of its initial
influence on the child's identity and self-concept. Positive father involvement
helps give a healthy start in the development of self-esteem, whereas paternal
indifference or maltreatment makes the child especially vulnerable in later life
to many different types of gender-related difficulties. With respect to overall
psychological adjustment, a solid gender identity and a happy acceptance of
one's sexuality, not the extent of superficial masculinity or femininity, are most
important. For example, the fact that young father-absent boys tend to score
lower on measures of masculinity than their father-present counterparts is not in
itself a sign of a psychological deficit, but it may indicate a lack of positive
gender identity, which in turn increases the risk of later developmental problems.

Although the degree to which an older child, adolescent or adult conforms to sex-role expectations may in itself reveal little about his or her overall personality integration, the younger child's positive acceptance of basic gender expectations is quite likely to be a function of having constructive relationships with both parents. Even before the age of two, and certainly by three, the active imitation of the same-sex parent is usually much related to a healthy initial gender development. Preferences typically become more flexible at later phases of development, but it is important that the young child achieves a basic foundation of gender security. Young children who are both well fathered and well mothered are likely to have positive self-concepts and security about their biological sexuality. They typically possess a solid gender identity, feel good about themselves and develop a relatively broad range of personal and social competencies as they mature.

DEFUSING STEREOTYPES

Gender identity goes far beyond the recognition of one's reproductive potential. Many of the ways a person feels about the self, how he or she builds a lifestyle and gets along with others are connected to the security of his or her gender identity. Gender-related self-definitions are a major determinant of the quality of marital, career and leisure-time endeavors. If an individual has a secure gender identity, other dimensions of his or her life will more likely fall into place in a positive manner and transcend rigid cultural stereotypes.

Positive Definitions

Possessing a secure gender identity means being comfortably male or female. Maleness and femaleness are biological categories. Masculinity and femininity are psychological concepts, and specific definitions are greatly influenced by cultural factors. Biologically related sex differences in physique and hormonal functioning do influence social relationships, but there needs also to be a careful probing of gender stereotypes. The extent of the fixation on biological sex differences is manifested in the use of terminology implying that males and females are opposite categories of people. In using the term *opposite sex* the implicit assumption is of extreme differences between males and females in all behavior categories, which clearly is not the case.

Gender stereotypes are largely defined by cultural expectations. Such expectations are very rigid, and if taken literally can greatly inhibit the full development of the individual. On a psychological level, masculinity and femininity are not simply contrasts or opposite types of characteristics. In narrow and traditional sex-role conceptions, the masculine individual may be viewed as being aggressive, dominant and independent, the feminine one as timid, nurturant and dependent. Cultural stereotypes also include expectations regarding the association of certain types of physical-appearance characteristics with masculinity or femininity. However, life is not so simple.

The most important dimension of gender functioning relates to the individual's self-definitions.

Unmasculinity is not the same as femininity, nor is being unfeminine equal to being masculine. With respect to basic gender identity, an unmasculine man or an unfeminine woman can be viewed as a person who has basic body-image insecurity and sexual discomfort. Thus, an unmasculine man can appear quite masculine but he may be overcompensating for a feeling of inadequacy and inferiority. On the other hand, a securely masculine man may appear outwardly effeminate.

In terms of personality characteristics, the relationship between masculinity and femininity can be thought of as two overlapping bubbles: In the shared portion are many traits that individuals of both sexes are likely to have if they are self-fulfilled individuals. Many dimensions of assertiveness, sensitivity, independence and nurturance are all in this middle portion.

A well-rounded individual, whether male or female, has many positive characteristics traditionally associated exclusively with masculinity or femininity. The unhappy person may be one who is constricted by a very narrow self-definition of masculinity or femininity or one who has not developed any basic gender-related competencies. From an adaptational perspective, masculinity and femininity are not mutually exclusive domains but rather two closely intertwined facets of humanity. Well-functioning males and females are more similar than different.

Growing Flexibility

Contemporary changes in definitions of masculinity and femininity are occurring principally because more people are realizing that particular personality characteristics are not exclusive to one sex or the other. They are also reacting to the unhappiness that can be associated with rigid self-definitions. Personal definitions can provide the best guide as to how individuals should express their gender identity.

In the context of traditional gender stereotypes, dealing with children is a central dimension of the feminine but not the masculine role. Females are encouraged to be nurturant, sensitive and emotionally expressive, characteristics viewed as important for helping others, especially infants and young children. In contrast, the masculine role is supposed to be focused on achievements outside of the home. The emphasis is on being assertive, adventuresome, independent, dominant and competent with respect to nonfamily issues. However, individuals, whether male or female, are at a definite advantage when they have a wide range of adaptive characteristics that go beyond circumscribed definitions of masculinity or femininity. By being an integral part of the child's socialization, the father as well as the mother can grow as a person, expanding what may have initially been a very limited gender-role self-definition. The father who fits the traditional masculine mold can learn to develop his ability to be nurturant and sensitive by being a caring parent. He can, at the same time, still retain his sense of assertiveness and independence, which are equally important in parenting effective children.

The father needs to sort out his feelings about his masculinity and how it relates to his role as a parent. Thoughtful reflection about his early family development should provide him with more insight into his self-definition of masculine behavior and his attitude toward children. The father should think of himself as a multifaceted person—a parent, a husband, a worker, a citizen and an individual with varied talents and interests. The father's sense of masculinity can play a legitimate part in all of his roles including the expression of his parental effectiveness. Being aware of the masculine nature of fatherhood can make a man more likely to devote a significant amount of his time to being with his children.

All too often the paternal role is defined just in terms of the father's career or economic value to his family. Fathers should resist pressures to define their functions narrowly. Regardless of whether a man's job pays $5,000 or $500,000 per year, whether he is at the lowest rung on a company ladder or the chief executive officer, he should never be satisfied to view his significance as a father solely in terms of his career and financial achievements. Many men are dynamic and active on the job and in the community but are failures as fathers because they feel that being an involved parent is not a proper masculine role. They defer all day-to-day family decisions to their wives and leave their children almost totally bereft of active paternal involvement. Neither parent's life should be devoted exclusively to children. However, both parents should spend sufficient time with their children to provide them with a clear frame of reference as to the multiple dimensions of their lives.

Being an involved father does not mean giving up one's masculine identity. Too many men get caught up in the idea that to be an effective parent they must adopt a more maternal or mothering role. Parents should attempt to become more aware of their sex-role biases, but the fundamental issue is that both the father and the mother provide their children with a solid and loving frame of reference. Children need to learn how to relate positively to both males and females. As is emphasized throughout this book, children are at a particular disadvantage when they are deprived of constructive experiences with their fathers. Infants and young children are unlikely to be provided with other opportunities to form a relationship with a caring and readily available adult male if their father is not emotionally committed to them.

It is not necessary to fit either a narrow gender stereotype or some abstract model of androgyny to be an effective parent, but it is crucial to be actively involved with your child. Mothers and fathers have the opportunity to change, grow and develop into more insightful and sensitive individuals by their active participation in the parenting process. Over time, both fathers and mothers who are positively involved with their children can themselves develop greater self-awareness and social competence.

Conveying Strength

A strong sense of personal efficacy is an important facet of a healthy self-image whether the individual is a male or a female. However, to some individuals, being masculine means using power to manipulate others insensitively according to one's own ends. To these individuals, such power has become an obsession and a central focus of their lives. In contrast, a mature man's or woman's power relates to a sense of being able constructively to make decisions and influence the course of one's life rather than attempting to control the behavior of others rigidly. The parent should realize that the search for personal power in the context of self-efficacy has a legitimate outlet in parenting but that it should be used in a very judicious manner. Compared to their young children, parents are in a position to exert much power, physical and otherwise. Parents have great potential power with respect to restricting the movements of their young children. They can usually intimidate them into temporary submission, whether by use of their greater strength, their louder voices or superior intellectual abilities.

Because of his relative size and strength, the father may convey an even more imposing and powerful image than the mother to the child. If the father is sensitive to the effect that his physical presence may produce, he is much less likely to become the fearsome creature that many men represent to their children. Parents should use their physical competence as a source of support and protection for the child rather than as a threat. Fathers, for example, can convey a sense of their strength to their young children by playful wrestling, hugging and cuddling rather than by intimidation. Physical closeness can help children gain a feeling of sharing their parent's strength.

Children, male and female, possess a natural disposition to give and respond to tenderness. If fathers allow nurturance to be a totally feminine domain in the family, they deprive themselves and their children of important experiences. Rigid, punitive fathers encourage their sons to stifle tender feelings and to become harsh and unloving themselves. These fathers convey to their daughters an image that men are not capable of being tender and affectionate. Rather than seeing such caring behavior as some sort of weakness, the father should adopt the attitude that he is actually demonstrating a positive nurturance consistent with his basic masculinity. He should realize that he is evincing an important kind of competence by nurturing the child. A nurturant father helps produce a caring and empathetic child.

To associate nurturance only with femininity is a common mistake in American society. Indeed, mothering is all too often treated as if it were synonymous with parenting. Parental nurturance can be expressed in many forms. Some fathers may find it difficult to be physically demonstrative or even very verbally expressive, but a man who is initially inhibited in communicating tenderness can grow and change in his role as a parent to become more capable and comfortably affectionate. Nevertheless, the most fundamental type of parental nurturance involves being emotionally supportive, not just being the dispenser of occasional hugs and kisses. Children can still receive much from involved fathers and mothers who have difficulties in certain areas of self-expression as long as they somehow communicate their love and acceptance to them. There is not just one style of effective parenting.

Encouraging Competence

In traditional views of the parenting of young children, the significance of the mother has never been questioned, but the father's role has been viewed as secondary, especially in the development of daughters. The father has been accepted as influential only as the child becomes older, and then typically the focus is on the son's development. However, the quality of fathering a child receives even in infancy can have long-term psychological implications for females as well as males.

Because the relative involvement of the father may not have an obvious and immediate influence on the young female, the tendency has been to overlook his long-term effect on his daughter. Just as the mother is the first woman in her son's life, the father is the first man in his daughter's life. The father acts as a proving ground for his daughter's developing femininity and sense of personal effectiveness. The adult female's potential for developing her talents, career goals and family relationships is likely to be strongly linked to the quality of paternal involvement she received during childhood.

A problem that many fathers face is a feeling that they do not know what to do with their daughters. Fathers as well as mothers should strive to include their infants and young children in many of their own activities. Taking a son or daughter on errands, visits to friends or to work can contribute to a meaningful parent-child relationship. The father's best resource is in the sharing of his interests and himself.

Fathers tend to be more accepting of passivity in their daughters as compared to their sons. Most men have been socialized to treat females as if they are more delicate and fragile than males. Fathers generally have lower expectations of competence for daughters than for sons. Low paternal expectations for independence may undermine the daughter's self-directed motivation for achievement and mastery. Compared to his perception of a son, a father is less likely to emphasize the similarity between himself and a daughter. Because his daughter is of the other sex, he does not usually feel it as necessary to encourage her to live up to his expectations of assertiveness, independence and success. Neither parent should fall into the trap of downplaying the daughter's potential competence. From a life-span perspective, both parents can be vital to the successful development of children of either sex.

Daughters can identify very much with their fathers as people and not just as men. Both parents can influence sons and daughters in developing self-confidence. When consistently positive paternal involvement exists in the family, the daughter learns to understand and empathize with her father. Her close relationship with him facilitates her ability to have successful social experiences with both males and females at various phases in her life. By having an involved father and mother, the daughter can develop a broader range of competencies than if she has only had close contact with one of her parents. She will find that she can be successful in many situations and still feel comfortably feminine. The father can demonstrate to his daughter, for instance, that he believes that a woman can be assertive and independent and still be feminine. In this way, the daughter receives the type of message from her father, a man she loves and respects, that will be relevant throughout her development.

Accepting Individuality

Although usually not as attentive to their children as mothers are, fathers typically spend much more time with sons than they do with daughters. The father's relationship with his son can also be much more stormy than his relationship with his daughter because of greater paternal pressures and expectations for male children. Viewing his son as a young counterpart of himself, he may try too hard to shape the boy in his own image. Rather than supporting his son's individuality, the father may try simply to transfer his own ambitions to his son. If the father and child are very different in temperament and talents, much conflict can ensue. When the father cannot accept his child's individuality, the son may further rebel and reject his father.

Nurturance is a key quality in determining whether or not the parent will have a positive impact on the child. But parental behavior must always be viewed in the context of the child's characteristics. Parents find it much easier to be nurturant, supportive and accepting when the child meets their expectations. It is generally easier for parents to be responsive to the affectionate, outgoing and intellectually precocious child than to one who is shy, unaffectionate and relatively nonverbal. A father or mother can definitely contribute to the child's social competence but it must be remembered that a son's or daughter's temperament and other characteristics can reinforce or discourage the parent's emotional investment. Parents, especially fathers, may withdraw their attention if their child does not perform in a way that makes them feel comfortable. Fathers may have a particularly difficult time relating to a male child who does not fit their stereotype of age-appropriate masculine behavior.

In general, fathers put greater pressure on sons than they do on daughters to conform to what they consider gender-appropriate behaviors. During childhood, girls who are tomboys are not nearly so frowned upon as boys who indicate preferences for engaging in feminine play patterns. Fathers often use words like *horrified* and *furious* when asked how they would react to their sons playing with dolls, wearing dresses or pursuing other traditionally feminine activities.

When the father has a nurturant and active role in the family, boys are more likely to develop a stronger sense of masculine identification. Fathers who are nurturant and involved in family decision making typically have sons with secure and masculine self-concepts. The son's self-esteem and competence are facilitated if he is exposed to effective paternal behavior, but his development can be hindered if either parent is a family tyrant. Many boys and girls who are not secure in their gender identity have fathers or mothers who punish or otherwise criticize their children for disagreeing with them or for acting in an independent manner. Constant parental sarcasm directed at the child's attempts at mastering new skills can harm the boy's or girl's self-concept. Unfortunately, some parents cannot seem to refrain from giving consistently negative feedback focusing on the child's inadequacy in various activities. Domineering parents have an especially difficult time giving encouragement unless they are controlling the child's choices.

Parents who pressure their children to conform to rigid standards, and to be passive in the face of authority, are not preparing them for a happy and successful adulthood. Being a good child should not be defined as conforming to parental expectations in an unthinking manner. Children need to learn how to be assertive and independent while at the same time being sensitive to the rights of others including their parents. Being caring and kind does not mean being timid and passive. Neither boys nor girls, if they are going to develop a solid foundation for effective adult functioning, should be forced into a submissive style of relating to parents and other authority figures. Children should be encouraged to make choices for themselves consistent with their individuality, positive self-acceptance and respect for others.

Transcending Rigidities

Parental support is important in helping a child develop his or her particular pattern of competence. Parents should take a hard look at their stereotypes and be sensitive to each child's individuality. Parents need to develop a life-span perspective concerning their child's behavior.

At any point in development, an individual's adaptation is a function of many factors. Ralph and Jimmy represent two individuals who varied in their high school life-styles but also received very different kinds of parental messages about sex-appropriate behaviors. Ralph had a great time in high school. He was very popular, athletic and an especially accomplished football player. Jimmy had a few close friends but was more interested in debating, the math club, and playing the flute than in athletics.

Ralph and Jimmy had similar grades in high school, and each had a father who was very successful and respected in the community. However, a major difference between them was in their relationships with their parents, particularly their fathers. Ralph's father was proud of his son and often rooted for him at football games but did not have that much other contact with him. He taught his son that men were strong and aggressive but communicated much less about other aspects of the male role. In contrast, Jimmy's father was interested in all his son's activities, going places with him and simply talking with him about diverse subjects. He taught his son that a sense of masculinity was complex and had to be worked out by each person on an individual basis. He encouraged

Jimmy to have confidence in what he felt was masculine and not to worry excessively about peer pressures or the expectations of adults.

Ralph was much more successful socially and athletically in high school than Jimmy. But after these two young men graduated from high school, an abrupt reversal occurred. Ralph took a few semesters of college work before deciding that higher education was not for him. After basking in the glories of high school, he felt ignored in the larger and more competitive context of college. For Ralph, being a man meant being tough and nonintellectual. He began to feel that he would never be able to recapture his high school success and feared that his life was destined to go downhill after age eighteen. In contrast, Jimmy blossomed in his post–high school years. After four years of hard work at college, during which he also played on the junior varsity soccer team, Jimmy went on to become a lawyer specializing in helping minority groups.

Ralph and Jimmy were similar in terms of their basic intellectual abilities. A major difference in their earlier childhoods was in how their parents, and particularly their fathers, had taught them to think about being competent males. Ralph learned to believe that only football playing and partying were particularly masculine. Jimmy learned that masculinity meant mainly confidence in himself and that it did not rule out being a reflective, sensitive person.

The implication from the lives of these two young men is not that football players will be unhappy in later life or that members of math clubs will be happy. The issue is that no matter how outwardly successful an individual may be at a particular juncture in life, he or she should also develop a rather broad perception of personal competence. An individual whose self-definition revolves around a narrow band of perceived masculinity or femininity may find it very difficult to cope with changes in life circumstances that are likely to evolve in adulthood. Ralph was a failure in his own eyes partly because he adopted a crude, rigid caricature of masculinity. Ralph's simplified version of masculinity became rapidly outmoded in the adult world.

Parents can promote their children's sense of self-efficacy by helping them to value and express their individuality. Ralph, for instance, liked to draw pictures of people in his family when he was a first-grader. But after repeated comments by his father that he was afraid Ralph was liable to turn into one of those "faggy artsy types," Ralph lost interest in drawing. Perhaps Ralph's adult adjustment might have been much more favorable if his father had been accepting of his artistic talent or if his mother had been less passive in supporting her son's interests.

Narrow gender stereotypes can have an especially inhibiting impact on self-concept development when parents are not supportive of their child's individuality. All too common examples are the great number of talented young women who define themselves only in terms of very traditional definitions of femininity, greatly restricting their potential educational and career options. Some daughters are so constrained by family and gender stereotypes that they conceive of opportunities for themselves outside of the home only in terms of very subservient work roles.

Because of their own internalized gender stereotypes, many parents overly restrict the child's expression of individual competence. They should not convey to their child that "boys always . . . " or "girls don't . . . ." Each child should be accepted as a unique individual and not simply as belonging to a particular gender category.

Parenting Identity

All adults in the process of development, whether or not they have children, need to nurture the parent within themselves. Adulthood can be viewed as the time at which individuals become capable of being their own parents. This does not mean that they are without occasional needs to be directly parented by other adults, but that they are generally capable of being both self-reliant and nurturant toward others. A sense of accountability for one's own behavior is a critical part of being an adult.

Developing a positive parenting identity can be especially difficult for those adults who have not experienced a nurturing paternal relationship. Psychologist Samuel Osherson found that the majority of the forty-year-old men he interviewed lacked a sense of emotional connectedness to both their fathers and their own sons. In his insightful book, *Finding Our Fathers: The Unfinished Business of Manhood*, Osherson argues that most adult men, especially those in midlife, are struggling to come to grips with elusive images of their fathers. He emphasizes that many of the problems that men have in achieving a positive intimacy with their wives and children are linked to not having experienced a sense of paternal closeness during childhood.

Much of sociologist and therapist Lewis Yablonsky's provocative book, *Fathers and Sons*, also discusses communication problems between adult sons and their fathers. Yablonsky shares his personal and professional experiences in an attempt to help men develop better father-son relationships. He focuses on father-child relationships in terms of three different phases corresponding to the son's childhood, adolescence and adulthood. Problems in earlier phases, including insufficient paternal involvement during childhood or the father's later inability to support his adolescent's autonomy, can stifle the emergence of a positive father–adult son relationship.

The most significant parts of Yablonsky's book involve detailed dialogues relating to the perceptions that adult sons and their fathers have about each other. His work is especially valuable in encouraging men to imagine themselves empathetically in the position of their father or son. He provides illuminating excerpts from in-depth interviews as well as from his therapeutic interventions involving role-playing techniques with fathers and sons.

According to both Osherson and Yablonsky, in order to become effective parents, men have to try to understand the circumstances that may have contributed to their father's difficulties in intimately relating to them. The observations of Osherson and Yablonsky are highly consistent with much of the material I present in this book. A large part of achieving a positive adult identity involves integrating balanced images of one's parents. In preparing for parent-hood, men and women need to deal with perceptions of both their fathers and their mothers.

Most men and women do have a clear frame of reference with regard to their mothers, but their experience with their fathers is likely to have been much more restricted or amorphous. Osherson's thesis certainly could be extended to include women. "Finding our fathers" can also be viewed as being a major part of the "unfinished business" of womanhood. The problems that all too many women and men have in marital and parenting relationships are connected to inadequacies in their childhood relationships with their fathers.

If they are willing to take the time for one-to-one discussions, most adults in their thirties and forties still have much opportunity to get to know their parents better as individuals. In fact, once they have children themselves, adults may find more common ground on which to communicate with their parents. Sharing perspectives about paternal and maternal feelings may indeed give adult children and their parents a stronger sense of mutual understanding than was possible during earlier phases of development. This can particularly be the case with respect to adult children's feelings about their fathers, since they may have previously had relatively little communication of a self-disclosing nature with them.

Reassessing Perspectives

Preparation for being a father or mother is an ongoing process. A parent is faced with various challenges while coping with self, child and family devel-opment. At the same time that the parent is confronted with a new phase of the child's development, memories of his or her own childhood resurface or take on new meaning. The continuing need exists for the parent to reexamine both self and child images in the light of new experiences.

Family life educator Ellen Galinsky argues in *Between Generations* that six stages of parenthood correspond to different phases of the child's development. The six stages that she focuses on relate to pregnancy (image-making), infancy (nurturing), the preschool years (authority), middle childhood (interpretive), adolescence (interdependent) and early adulthood (departure). Galinsky acknowl-edges some overlap in these stages but insists that the self-images of parents are likely to change as their children move through different phases of development. To every stage parents bring certain images and expectations of self, child and family, which are modified by exposure to the realities of their particular son or daughter.

According to Galinsky, each stage has a preparation phase and a reevaluation phase. Each stage may involve difficult challenges in reordering priorities and dealing with emotionally laden issues resurfacing from earlier phases of the parent's own development. The adult is sometimes caught up in sorting out dissonant and simultaneous identifications with a parent and child. Key issues at every stage involve processes of separation and individuation, and acknowledging the reality of similarity and dissimilarity between parent and child. Parents need to deal with the individuality of self and child even under conditions of positive attachment and mutual identification. Growth for both parent and child involves a sense of connectedness but at the same time an increasing sense of individuation.

Every stage of a child's development offers new challenges for the parent. The parent's image of self and child do not change in a vacuum, and relationships with other family members and friends can be quite influential. Developing a more realistic view of self and child is part of each stage of parent growth. A particular adult may be experiencing several stages simultaneously, as with having children of varying ages or when one is suddenly confronted with responsibility for an older child through adoption or stepparenting.

The evolution of family relationships is much influenced by gender-related factors. Although subcultural variations occur, daughters tend to stay in closer contact with their parents, especially their mothers, than sons. More women seem to be trapped in a lifelong dependency on family at the expense of the development of their individual autonomy and self-direction. In contrast, more men become emotionally isolated from their fathers and have difficulty achieving intimacy with their wives and children. During early adulthood, most men are beginning to make strong occupational commitments but many, although married, have much more difficulty participating fully in an emotionally intimate relationship with their wives. Either or both marital partners may be unprepared for a relationship involving sensitivity, empathy and self-disclosure of feelings. In general, however, during early adulthood men seem to be relatively less ready for emotionally intimate relationships than women.

For the young adult couple, the achievement of a continuing sense of mutual marital satisfaction is likely to be very much a function of the husband's level of emotional maturity. The greater variability among men in their ability to participate fully in intimate relationships is also associated with their generally more diverse adaptations to parenthood. This is a major reason why degree of positive paternal involvement is such an important determinant of the quality of family development.

Adults can develop a more positive parenting identity once they have achieved a basic understanding of their fathers as well as their mothers. They can learn to appreciate parental contributions and limitations. From this perspective, they are then in a better position to foster self-esteem and competence, regardless of their child's gender.

Whether or not they deal directly with their own fathers, however, most men and women moving through adulthood still have continuing opportunities to develop a more positive parenting identity while increasing their self-understanding and nurturing ability. Men's and women's styles of dealing with mid-life issues may be different but some of the underlying factors are often quite similar. Many middle-aged women have never effectively separated from their mothers, often remaining enmeshed in highly dependent relationships with them. Many middle-aged men, though superficially freer than their female counterparts, have never resolved their boyhood anxiety about overconnectedness to their mothers, merely trying to distance themselves from other close relationships. Men and women who find themselves in these predicaments at mid-life are likely to have not only been paternally deprived in childhood but to also have been unable to successfully parent their own sons and daughters. In contrast to those individuals who suffer intense self-doubt and depression during mid-life, many others experience optimism and a renewed sense of freedom if they have positively negotiated the challenges of parenthood.

Men and women, especially if they have a supportive partner, can overcome their childhood paternal deprivation in the context of their own parenthood. Fathers and mothers who have constructively encouraged their children's emerging adulthood are likely to have enhanced self-confidence. They feel greater freedom as their sons and daughters become more independent and, if they choose, can shift more of their attention toward both community and leisure time activities. Whatever their particular goals, for many whose family development has progressed in a basically positive way, their middle years can allow a freeing up and redirecting of energies.

SUMMARY

Self-acceptance and a positive gender identity are promoted by nurturant fathering. The father's support can be especially important in giving the child a sense of security in dealing with various peer and cultural pressures. Biological and social factors influence sex-role functioning, but both the father and the mother hold important roles in fostering the child's development of a healthy self-concept.

The father's nurturance and support of competency bodes well for the son's and daughter's gender development. Children with attentive and supportive fathers have much more of a chance to develop a strong sense of self-determination. In contrast, gender difficulties or problems in later family and sexual functioning are much more common among individuals with a childhood history of paternal deprivation.

Parents should be accepting of their child's individuality while avoiding restrictive gender stereotypes. Children of either sex are capable of developing a broad range of competencies if they experience positive paternal involvement. For example, both males and females can be nurturant and sensitive as well as independent and assertive. However, this does not mean that average sex differences between males and females will disappear, since distinct personality dispositions are related to genetic differentiation and other biologically predisposing factors in interaction with cultural influences.

The way that adults relate to their spouses and children has much to do with the quality of paternal involvement they experienced during childhood. Many men and women need to get in greater touch with feelings and images about their fathers if they are going to develop positive personal identities and be more successful in marital and parenting relationships.

FURTHER READING

Personal Acceptance

Biosocial Factors

On the interrelationship of gender acceptance, self-concept and sex-role and personality development, see Biller (1968a, 1971a, 1977c, 1981c), Biller and Borstelmann (1967), Francoeur (1987), Heilbrun (1974, 1976) and Lynn (1974).

Concerning methodological controversies and complexities surrounding the measurement of sex-role related behaviors, see Basow (1986), Baumrind (1982), Bem (1985), Biller (1977c, 1980b), Biller and Borstelmann (1967), Downs and Langlois (1988), Gill et al. (1987) and Lips (1988).

Regarding within-sex and between-sex physical variations, see Katchadourian (1985), Nash (1978) and Money and Erhardt (1972). For the interaction of hormonal, neurological and social factors, see Money (1987).

Differential Treatment

For evidence of early gender differences in children and their possible connection to differential treatment by fathers and mothers, see Biller (1971a, 1974c), Bronstein (1984), Condry and Condry (1976), Fagot (1978), Gilbert, Hanson and Davis (1982), Goldberg and Lewis (1969), Lamb (1988), Maccoby and Jacklin (1973), Pedersen, Anderson and Cain (1980) and Willemsen et al. (1974).

About parental preferences and reactions to infant gender, see Biller (1971a), Feldman and Nash (1972), Osofsky and O'Connell (1972), Parke and Tinsley (1981), Rendina and Dickerscheid (1976) and Rubin, Provenzano and Luria (1974).

Developmental Complexities

For study of sex typing among children of nonsexist parents, see Kaliski and Biller (1978). For other data concerning the children of nonsexist parents, see Baumrind (1982), Pruett (1987), Radin (1982), Russell (1983, 1986), Sagi (1982) and Stein (1983).

For research relating cognitive and sex-role development, see Kohlberg (1966) and Kohlberg and Zigler (1967). For relationship between sex typing and intelligence among retarded children, see Biller and Borstelmann (1965). For more extended discussions of the interaction of cognitive and sex-role factors, see Basow (1986), Biller (1974a, 1974b) and Lips (1988).

About hormonal and other biological factors relating to sex differences in behavior, see Money and Erhardt (1972) and Money and Tucker (1975). For prenatal hormonal factors involved in early childhood sex differences, see Jacklin et al. (1984) and Maccoby et al. (1979).

Family Patterns

For earlier research relating father-mother dominance patterns to children's sex-role development, see Biller (1968a, 1969a), Hetherington (1965) and Hetherington and Frankie (1967). For other data relating to the relative impact of fathers and mothers on son's and daughter's sex-role development, see Biller (1981c), Biller and Barry (1971), Biller and Solomon (1986) and Hetherington, Cox and Cox (1982).

With regard to the complex social factors, in addition to parenting, that impact on the sex-role development of children, see Basow (1986), Biller (1971a, 1974c), Block (1983) and Lips (1988). About sibling effects on sex-role development, see Biller (1968a, 1971a, 1974c), Lamb and Sutton-Smith (1982) and Sutton-Smith and Rosenberg (1970).

Gender Conflicts

For research on transsexual children, see Green (1974, 1987), Green, Williams and Goodman (1985) and Stoller (1968). For comments regarding Green's research, see Biller (1975b). For the influence of prenatal hormones, see Jacklin et al. (1983, 1984) and Maccoby et al. (1979).

Life-span Implications

Concerning research relating to long-term implications of paternal deprivation and gender insecurity, see Biller (1971a, 1973b, 1981c) and Biller and Solomon (1986).

Defusing Stereotypes

Positive Definitions

About different aspects of sex-role development and the importance of parents accepting their child's individuality, see Biller (1971a, 1977c), Biller and Meredith (1974) and Block (1974, 1983).

For especially detailed discussions of the impact of gender stereotypes on individual development, see Basow (1986), Lips (1988) and Lott (1987). For more general discussions of self-concept development, see Blasi (1988), Harter (1983) and Wylie (1979).

Growing Flexibility

On the need for a more flexible conceptualization of parenting and sex roles for men and women, see Biller (1971a, 1974c), Biller and Meredith (1972, 1974), Farrell (1986), Kelly and Worell (1976, 1977), Moreland and Schwebel (1981) and Russell (1978, 1983, 1986). For discussions of the concept of androgyny, see Baumrind (1982), Bem (1985), Gill et al. (1987) and Lips (1988).

Conveying Strength

For reviews of research emphasizing the importance of paternal as well as maternal nurturance for both sons and daughters, see Biller (1971a, 1977c, 1981c), Biller and Solomon (1986) and Lynn (1974, 1979).

Encouraging Competence

Regarding the significance of the early father-daughter relationship for the female's later development, see Biller (1971b), Biller and Weiss (1970), Biller and Solomon (1986) and Lynn (1979). For research relating to stereotyped adult expectations as a function of child gender, see Condry and Condry (1976), Rothbart and Maccoby (1966) and Rubin, Provenzano and Luria (1974).

Accepting Individuality

For reviews of research underscoring the importance of both parents accepting and supporting the child's individuality and competencies, see Biller (1971a, 1974c, 1981c) and Biller and Solomon (1986).

Transcending Rigidities

For parenting perspectives arguing for more positive and flexible definitions of masculinity and femininity, see Biller and Meredith (1972, 1974), Osherson (1986, 1992), Pleck (1981), Pruett (1987) and Russell (1978, 1983).

Parenting Identity

For individualized pathways and patterns of achieving a sense of adulthood, see Aylmer (1988), Biller and Meredith (1974), Erikson (1980, 1982), Field and Widmayer (1982), Fullmer (1988), Gould (1978, 1980), Helson and Moane (1987), Helson and Wink (1987), Levinson (1978, 1980, 1986), McGoldrick (1988a, 1988b), Novak (1981), Sheehy (1976) and Vaillant (1977). For marital choice and satisfaction in early adulthood, see Murstein (1982) and Novak (1981).

For discussions of different "stages" of parenting and how they relate to adult and family development, see Galinsky (1981). For other perspectives on the way that the child's development impacts on the parents' development, see Biller (1982a), Biller and Meredith (1974), Carter and

McGoldrick (1988), Elder (1983), Field and Widmayer (1982), Hill (1986), McCullough and Rutenberg (1988), McGoldrick (1988b), Osherson (1986, 1992), Rapoport et al. (1977), Rubin (1982), Snarey (1992), Snarey et al. (1987) and Yablonsky (1982).

Reassessing Perspectives

Regarding transitions in adult development and marriage associated with becoming an expectant and new parent, see Belsky, Lang and Huston (1987), Biller (1971a, 1976b, 1982a), Biller and Meredith (1972, 1974), Biller and Salter (1985), Bittman and Zalk (1978), Cowan (1988), Field and Widmayer (1982), Galinsky (1981), Gould (1978, 1980), Harriman (1986), Heath (1976, 1978), Levinson (1986), Osherson (1986, 1992) and Waite, Haggstrom and Kanouse (1985).

On differing expectations of adulthood for males and females, see Biller (1971a, 1976b, 1982a), Biller and Meredith (1972, 1974), Helson and Moane (1987), Helson and Wink (1987), Lips (1988), Lott (1981, 1987), Neugarten and Neugarten (1987), Osherson (1986, 1992) and Roberts and Newton (1987). For cultural, ethnic and socioeconomic factors affecting conceptions of adulthood entry, see Fullmer (1988) and McGoldrick (1988a).

On issues often confronting individuals in the later phases of early adulthood, typically in their late twenties and early thirties, see Fullmer (1988), Galinsky (1981), Gould (1978, 1980), Heath (1978), Levinson (1978, 1980, 1986), McGoldrick (1988b), Osherson (1986, 1992) and Vaillant (1977). For emphasis on life events and crises influencing adult development, see Brim and Riff (1980), Chiraboga (1982b) and Stull and Hatch (1984).

About middle adulthood phases of development, see Brim and Kagan (1980), Fullmer (1988), Galinsky (1981), Gould (1978, 1980), Heath (1976, 1977, 1978), Helson and Moane (1987), Helson and Wink (1987), Levinson (1978, 1980, 1986), McCullough and Rutenberg (1988), McGoldrick (1988a, 1988b), Osherson (1986), Rubin (1982), Snarey et al. (1987), Strickland (1987), Vaillant (1977) and Vaillant and Vaillant (1981).

For emphasis on midadulthood issues confronting women, see Baruch, Barnett and Rivers (1983), Gilligan (1982) Helson and Moane (1987), Lott (1987), McCullough and Rutenberg (1988), McGoldrick (1988b), Roberts and Newton (1987) and Strickland (1987). For perspectives arguing against a stage approach to adult development, see Neugarten and Neugarten (1987) and Rosenfield and Stark (1987).

5

Nurturance, Discipline and Morality

This chapter focuses on the significance of parental nurturance in the development of the child's self-control and moral sensitivity. In the context of the parent-child relationship, nurturance can be conveyed in many different ways. The father's nurturance enhances his effectiveness as a role model, limit setter and facilitator of positive moral development.

NURTURING BEHAVIOR

Physical affection and verbal declarations of love relate to only a small portion of the varied ways that a parent can be nurturant. Some parents make their child feel very loved and secure without being especially demonstrative of their affection. Parental nurturance can be communicated primarily through positive attention and support for the child's interests and competence.

Demonstrating Commitment

Much of the problem with traditional definitions of parental nurturance is that they are based on a limited and rather rigid view of gender and family roles. Nurturance should not be equated with permissiveness or passivity. Paternal nurturance, as well as maternal nurturance, should include a wide array of caring behaviors directed toward the child. Fathers and mothers should be able to hug and kiss their children comfortably, take them to many different types of places, patiently demonstrate activities, verbally communicate affection and give credit for achievements. There are adults who believe that frequent demonstrations of affection and caring somehow weaken a child, foster dependency and result in ineffective discipline. Some parents even mistakenly fear that nurturant fathers encourage effeminancy and homosexuality in their sons.

Competent children are likely to have fathers and mothers who are nurturant and positively encouraging of independence. Parents who are overly stern with their offspring in an attempt to produce self-reliant children may have just the opposite effect. Parental nurturance fosters independence and self-reliance because it helps to provide the child with a foundation of self-confidence upon which to build competence. Fostering emotional security in the child is an all-important overall function for parents, and their nurturance is a vital component of the process.

Nurturant caring is a crucial factor in the parent's effectiveness as a limit setter. If the parent has a warm relationship with the child, it will be much easier for both to maintain appropriate and responsible behavior. The child will be much more likely to accept parental limits and to pay attention to adult concerns. In the absence of an emotionally close relationship, the danger increases of the parent resorting to arbitrary disciplinary techniques.

A secure gender identity is facilitated by paternal and maternal nurturance. Having a nurturant father and mother provides children with a broader basis to develop feelings of self-acceptance. The importance of supportive mothering is often emphasized, but enough attention has not been given to the profound significance of paternal nurturance. The son of a nurturant father will strive to be like him. Of particular importance, the boy will also learn to value his own nurturing capacity. The daughter with a nurturant father will have a firm basis to feel accepted as a female. If the father has a warm relationship with his children, they will also be predisposed to respond positively to many dimensions of his behavior such as his moral tenets, achievement motivation and patterns of relating with others.

Children with nurturant fathers will also be more likely to be generous and altruistic, as illustrated by an interesting study conducted by psychologists Eldred Rutherford and Paul Mussen. Candy was passed out to four-year-old boys at a nursery school. The children were given two bags and instructed to disperse candy to the two other boys they liked best. The boys who were the most generous with their candy tended to be those who consistently perceived their fathers as warm, affectionate and comforting.

Other research suggests that the nurturant father can have a long-term impact on his child's ability to be empathetic and caring toward others. Psychologist David McClelland and his colleagues examined possible connections between interview data collected from mothers concerning parenting practices when their children were in kindergarten and the sons' and daughters' adjustment as adults twenty-six years later. They discovered that individuals who were judged to have had involved fathers were much more likely to grow up to be tolerant and understanding than those whose fathers had been relatively uninvolved with them. The investigators concluded that when both the father and the mother are actively involved parents, their child is much more likely to develop into a socially and morally mature adult.

Being Accessible

Being an effectively nurturant parent requires the investment of a significant amount of time. With a very young child it is especially important to provide loving interaction on a daily basis. Making the commitment for regular and direct contact with children has tended to be more problematic for fathers than for mothers.

In fact, mothers tend to be more successful in their child-rearing activities when fathers are also supportive parents. Developmental psychologist Hugh Lytton found that mothers are much more successful and comfortable in setting limits for their two- and three-year-old children when fathers are a visible presence in the household. Children were more likely to comply with their mother's requests for appropriate behavior when the father was present. Furthermore, when the father explicitly supported the mother's requests, the child was especially likely to be cooperative. Mothers seemed much more able to carry through in setting reasonable limits for their young children when fathers were present. For example, the father's presence decreased the number of the mother's demands for control while at the same time increasing the success of limit setting and the positive quality of maternal response to compliance by the child. When the father is present, the mother's limit setting for the child appears to be more appropriate.

Nurturant parenting does not mean that either the father or the mother must spend most of their time with the child. However, it does require regular and positive contact with the young child on a day-to-day basis, especially for the infant and toddler. Traditionally, the mother has been the omnipresent parent with the father there on an occasional basis. It could, in fact, be argued that most children get too much mothering and too little fathering. In general, the amount of direct parental contact a child may need decreases gradually with age. Time estimates are relative and also vary as a function of the child's individuality and the availability of other involved adults. However, two or more hours daily, on average, where each parent (father as well as mother) is accessible is highly advantageous for the child at least through the preschool and early elementary school years. Young children profit from feeling that they have the opportunity for undivided parental attention for at least some significant period of time each day.

This does not mean that the young child will suffer if a parent is occasionally away for a few days. But frequent or extended absences make it more difficult for the child and parent to maintain a secure and meaningful relationship. Preschool-age children whose fathers are nurturant and are regularly available to them two or more hours per day have more positive self-concepts and social adjustments than those whose fathers are much less involved with them.

Mark Reuter and I collected data that also suggests the potential long-term positive effects of paternal availability and nurturance during childhood. We gave personality tests to college men along with a detailed questionnaire to determine how much their fathers were home and how nurturant their fathers had been to them when they were children. The most well-adjusted students had fathers who were at least moderate in both nurturance and availability. Our results suggested that fathers who had consistent and relatively warm contact with their children helped to provide a good foundation for their later adjustment.

However, nothing indicated that more than one or two hours a day of nurturant paternal behavior was necessary during childhood for positive adjustment in late adolescence or early adulthood.

Well-adjusted students were likely to see themselves as dependable, trusting, practical and friendly. Poorly adjusted students were more likely to label themselves as aloof, anxious, inhibited and unfriendly. The most poorly adjusted students included those whose fathers were home very little yet were very nurturant, or were home a great deal but were relatively uninvolved with their children. These students tended to be about as poorly adjusted as those whose fathers were both low in nurturance and low in availability. The frequent adjustment problems of children in two-parent families who have fathers low in availability and nurturance is not surprising. In such a situation the father is likely to be perceived as uncaring and is clearly not a good role model for his child.

When a father is home infrequently but is highly affectionate and caring, the child is apt to feel very frustrated during paternal absences. It is especially difficult for the child when the parent's availability is not only sparse but also inconsistent and unpredictable. Considerable anxiety may arise concerning the parent's real love for the child in the face of his relative unavailability. If the father is home a great deal but is cold and distant, the child is at risk to feel inadequate and insecure. Low self-worth is a likely consequence because the father does not appear to value the child's activities. It might even be better for a child with a cold, distant father to have him be home very little. At least the child would not be so constantly confronted with paternal disinterest.

Active Interest

A supportive attitude vis-à-vis the child's activities can go a long way toward creating a more positive family atmosphere. Whether the achievement is saying a first word, tying a shoelace or writing a term paper, the parent should encourage each accomplishment with respect to the child's phase of development, not in terms of how difficult it might appear at first glance. The more recognition that is given for accomplishments and appropriate behavior, the less likely the child will have to get parental attention by disruptive or otherwise negative conduct.

The emphasis in this book is on taking a positive approach in encouraging the child to develop responsible behavior. Basic to this constructive strategy of dealing with the child is having specific and realistic expectations. A child needs clear feedback. When focusing on incidents of inappropriate behavior parents should not make broad accusations concerning the child's alleged personality defects. They should take care to focus only on the behavior and not make generalizations concerning the child's basic personality. A child should not be told that he or she is bad, stupid, dishonest or vicious. Such generalized parental criticism can undermine the child's self-confidence. Indeed, some children who receive little positive parental involvement take a sort of perverse pleasure in being miscreants, at least partially to fulfill negative family expectations.

Parents should clearly convey their disappointment concerning poor conduct but assure their child that they believe that an act such as taunting a pet, being disrespectful to a grandparent or taking another person's possession without permission was only a temporary failing. The child's misbehavior should not be viewed as a reflection of a deep-seated character flaw. In order to live up to positive parental expectations, the child is then likely to strive to avoid irresponsible or hurtful behavior in the future. But most important, the parent should strive to be an available and effective role model. The child can develop confidence and self-esteem by having the opportunity to become positively involved in some of the parent's activities. Many parents, particularly fathers, have not really been sensitized to the problem of how little their child gets to spend individualized time with them.

A key issue when including a child, especially a young one, in an activity is having the patience to tolerate a reduction in task efficiency. However, if the priority is developing a closer relationship with the child, the joy of mutual participation will usually far outweigh the additional time a particular chore may consume. Parents may need to do a little planning ahead by making sure the child has appropriate "tools" for the intended endeavor. Young children cannot be expected to perform tasks on a par with adults. But parents usually can find some aspect of any chore, hobby or other pursuit that is appropriate for their child. For instance, a parent could not expect a preschooler to help paint a house efficiently, but the child could work on a small predesignated section or assist in carrying supplies. The young child's activities can be scaled-down versions of grown-up jobs.

If a parent has work to do at home, a child can often share in the process. All my children have spent time with me while I have been writing articles and books. Even a two-year-old can get a sense of involvement scribbling on a pad while the parent is performing a task involving paperwork. It is not so much the specific skills or interests that the child is learning but a sense of mutual participation with the parent.

As the child matures, parents can encourage more and more responsibility. When capable of doing arithmetic, the child can check tax-return figures. The child, if interested, can help plan menus and even prepare a family cookout. Even if the young child tires easily and loses interest, some specific opportunity of sharing and involvement with a parent has still taken place. The key is that the child is spending some time working closely with the parent, even if not taking an equal share of the responsibility. Parents may be surprised at what their youngster can accomplish given the chance. Many years ago I handed my then ten-year-old son Jonathan a draft of a research article I was writing while he was sitting with me at my desk. Much to my happy surprise, he not only read and understood the paper fairly well but also discovered some errors in punctuation and spelling. Moreover, he asked some provocative questions about the material discussed in the paper.

Parents should practice responsible impulse control, but this does not mean hiding their feelings. Rather it requires inhibition of hurtful behaviors such as those involved in child or spouse abuse. Parents may want to strive for self-composure even under very stressful conditions, but they can go overboard in hiding or distorting emotions that may later surface in very hurtful ways toward other family members. While it is important for parents not to direct uninhibited rage at their child, sharing feelings about day-to-day problems that are upsetting can be a means of positive family communication. They should not be afraid to let their child know about a particular situation that is bothering them. When my son Benjamin was three, I was taken aback when he blurted out "Why are you frustrated?" after I had slammed our car door and muttered a few choice obscenities. I explained how I could not fit a large box into the car. His comment helped me to relax, and we quickly solved the problem by securing the box on top of the car with some rope.

Children are sensitive to emotional nuances in their parents. They may mis-interpret the meaning of parental mood changes if not given some clear infor-mation. Being relatively egocentric, younger children are especially likely to attribute something they did as causing the parent's anger, sadness or frustration. Some parents are averse to revealing their feelings in front of children because they fear it will damage their image of authority. But children need the direct, personalized support of both their mother and their father. In actuality, the more parents are able to express their feelings of affection positively, the more likely their children will respect their opinions and expectations.

Parental Generosity

A common way for parents to express nurturance is by buying toys and presents for their children. Parents, especially fathers, who have extensive commitments outside of the home may provide frequent gifts in an attempt to compensate for their time away from their children. If the family is affluent, parents may perceive money and presents as an easy way of seemingly ensuring the child's happiness. Some fathers end up defining their relationships with their children primarily in terms of gift giving and other forms of financial support. However, parents are likely to be disillusioned eventually by a focus on giving gifts as an expression of their love; as a substitute for more direct attention and caring, in the long run it is self-defeating.

If, on the other hand, gifts are given with the spirit of stimulating the child's enjoyment and not as a compensation for lack of parental involvement, they likely will achieve much more positive results. Children develop an early aware-ness about the use of gifts in place of true nurturance. In fact, the most precious gift a parent can give a child is consistently loving support, interest and attention. Parents may also give gifts to children to gain a feeling of control, of adequacy or of being needed in the family. For example, a father may perceive that he is an emotional outsider and his only means of achieving a sense of connectedness to his family is through his financial resources. He may try to use his economic power to ingratiate himself to his child.

A major reason that many parents provide gifts for their children is an attempt to satisfy some need in their own lives. It is indeed very natural for parents to purchase something for their child that they would have liked to have had themselves when they were younger. There is usually nothing wrong with this practice of mutual indulgence. However, if done in an insensitive manner, this type of gift giving can be counter productive. It may have a negative effect if an uninterested child feels unduly pressured to use the gift. The parent should try to understand the child's perspective and not expect that he or she will always share the same interests or reactions.

Experiences dealing with the purchase of gifts can also be important in fostering the child's sense of self-control. The two- or three-year-old may find it very difficult to go into any store without getting something. On the other hand, most five-year-olds can grasp the notion that they will not always get a toy when they are shopping with their parents but that they will be allowed to make a purchase at a later time. Children can begin to learn about some of the economic realities of life at a very early age. They need to develop gradually a more mature time perspective. The ability to delay gratification is a valuable trait to encourage in the child. The confident expectation of future rewards is an important characteristic whether practicing a complex athletic endeavor, doing homework, preparing for college, starting a business or writing a book.

CONSTRUCTIVE DISCIPLINE

The perspective put forth in this book is that all members of the family share certain rights. No matter what the individual's age or developmental status, he or she has the right to express feelings and to have a sense of self-determination. Parental responsibility should not translate into children being deprived of their right to make appropriate decisions and to receive respect for their individuality.

Maturational Considerations

Children should not be expected to function at a level that is inconsistent with their maturational status. This is especially the case for very young children. A sixteen-month-old probably cannot grasp why it is unkind to call another family member an "asshole." Punishing the child for such a verbalization is highly inappropriate. The parent should suggest a different word to use, if possible, or simply divert the child's attention from the negative behavior, providing an alternative activity. When the child is more intellectually developed, he or she will have a greater command of alternative words. Moreover, with increased maturity, the child will become more responsive to specific feedback regarding appropriate behavior in various social situations.

Adults must remember that the young child may be limited in many dimensions of development. The parent should take into consideration the child's less articulated rationality and relative immaturity in physical functioning and impulse control. For example, children generally have a less differentiated time sense than adults, so ten minutes to them seems like a very much longer period to wait or be quiet than it does for an adult. Young children are also likely to be clumsier than adults, so allowance must be made for inadvertent accidents. Whenever possible, the child's environment should be altered so that such mishaps will be less likely to occur in the first place. Rather than blame the child, the parent who leaves a delicate piece of crystal on the coffee table should accept the responsibility when it is broken by a boisterous three-year-old.

Some parents would simply grit their teeth, smile and say, "Don't worry about it" if a guest accidently damaged a precious heirloom, but if their child even spills a glass of milk they respond with extreme criticism for the alleged carelessness. In giving the benefit of doubt as to motivation, ironically many parents are much kinder toward relative strangers than with their own young children. Like adults, children differ in the length of time it takes for them to accomplish everyday responsibilities comfortably. In a positive family atmosphere, an allowance is made for individual differences, and varying paces and competencies in completing tasks are accepted.

Parents often have rigid gender stereotypes when it comes to dealing with their children. They are usually more tolerant of traits such as sloppiness and aggressiveness in their sons but they may let their daughters have more leeway in many other areas. In general, both parents expect girls to be more responsible and obedient when it comes to self-care and domestic activities. Parents should be careful not to be disciplinary sexists but consider each child's individuality. Before punishing a certain act, the parent should consider how the child's physical and mental development may be related to the behavior. It is also important to remember that the child is capable of different levels of responsibility at different times. The same child behaves very differently when tired than when well rested. Parents do have an obligation to give children appropriate feedback about their behavior, but this should involve positive teaching and not a punitive approach.

Parental Teaching

Some parents rationalize their responsibility as a manifesto for punitive discipline, depriving the child of basic human rights. Nowhere do parental values vary more than in the area of the proper way of teaching and socializing children. Parents often consider the type of discipline they use to be the major factor in the child's moral and character development. Disciplinary approaches are not static techniques and can, in turn, be much influenced by a particular child's basic temperament and intelligence. When assessing the impact of different modes of discipline it is important to consider not only short-term goals but long-range expectations for children.

Parents need to weigh whether immediate conformity to their expectations is the most important priority or whether the focus should be on the child's future functioning and independence. A toddler or preschooler can usually be intimidated or pressured into compliance if the desired end product is parental control and management. However, if parents are seeking to encourage internalized moral standards and independent thinking then the extent to which they themselves constructively and nurturantly model positive behaviors assumes special significance. Stated in simple direct terms, parents should treat children with respect, kindness, patience and consideration.

The parent's role as an authority figure includes the responsibility of teaching the child appropriate conduct. Nevertheless, discipline does not have to be the only form of teaching, or even the principal one. In fact, for the effective parent, punishment in the traditional sense may not be necessary in socializing the child. The parent can teach the child by being a role model for appropriate behavior. Confidence, independence, empathy and high moral standards can all be encouraged by parental example. By being nurturant and considerate of individuality, the parent can make self-discipline a much more positive force for all family members.

Parental disapproval of specific types of inappropriate behavior by the child can be a very constructive disciplinary technique. If the parent is perceived as being an effective and nurturing individual such critical feedback in itself can have much positive influence on the child's behavior. If the parent is concerned with improving the child's behavior, the focus should be on particular issues rather than expecting immediate overall change. Parental goals should be consistent with the child's level of maturational readiness. Gradual improvements in behavior should be taken into account. For some children, the pace of mastery is much slower than for others. It is very important that the child's constructive efforts be focused upon rather than imperfections. Helping children to build self-confidence is a key to their successful development whether it concerns improving impulse control or intellectual abilities.

At times a simple request for the child to calm down or redirection to another activity may not be effective. If a child loses control, hits out at others or destroys property, the parent should make it clear that such behavior is not appropriate. In any case, power struggles should be avoided and the child should have a chance to calm down without receiving excessive parental attention for acting out. Having a child sit down or go into another room for a few minutes should not be viewed in a punitive context. It can be construed as an opportunity for the child to have a "time out" or cooling-off period. It is a chance to calm down after a frustrating situation rather than to continue to act out in an impulsive manner. With increasing maturity, the child develops a greater capacity to reflect constructively on the consequences of his or her behavior.

If there is a close, nurturant parent-child relationship, thoughtful parental comments concerning the child's specific behavior can have far more long-term significance than traditional methods of rewards or punishments. The parent should provide clear explanations about what it is that the child has done wrong, and how to correct the behavior, if possible. But even more important than giving explanations is providing a model of appropriate behavior. If parents scold their child for something they do themselves, they are not practicing effective parenting. They may produce an abiding cynicism in their child, and it is important that they more closely examine their own conduct. Unfortunately, a common role model is the yelling parent berating the child for not being more polite in talking to other children or adults. Another very blatant example of the "Do what I say, not what I do" syndrome is the parent with a two-pack-a-day habit punishing the teenager for smoking.

Children are more affected by what they observe in family interactions than by what parents simply say is appropriate behavior. The best instruction is carried out in a caring manner. Parents need to demonstrate daily the behavior and values they desire by acting in a kind, considerate and respectful manner toward their child and spouse. Their positive actions toward other family members are especially valuable contributions that they can make to their child's development.

Resisting Maltreatment

The physical punishment of children occurs in many different contexts. For some parents, it is viewed as a structured disciplinary method while for others it is an impulsive reaction to severe stress and frustration. However, even when parents have well-meaning intentions, physically punishing children is not a positive teaching technique for demonstrating appropriate behavior.

While both parents may use some form of physical punishment, a mother may feel a need to resort to it more frequently. Mothers generally spend much more time at home and are more likely to feel overwhelmed sometimes with child-rearing responsibilities. In contrast, fathers, because of their usually more imposing size and strength, may only have to threaten physical punishment in order to achieve at least temporary conformity from the child. A wealth of data indicates that mothers with husbands who are actively involved in the parenting process experience fewer disciplinary problems with their children. When fathers do use physical punishment, however, they tend to hit harder and are more likely to injure the child. In two-parent families, fathers or stepfathers perpetrate nearly two-thirds of all reported incidents of physical abuse, much of it inflicting serious harm to children. Abusive parents were often themselves maltreated when they were children, having been subjected to severe physical punishment by other family members. Abusive parents have difficulty accepting their child's individuality and tend to demand an impossible level of perfection, seemingly unaware of maturationally based limitations. Such parents may possess a feeling of certainty that they are always right and the child is always wrong.

There are many other forms of child maltreatment in addition to inappropriate physical punishment. As is emphasized in chapter 11, paternal neglect can be viewed as the most prevalent type of child maltreatment. Even compared to the serious harm perpetuated by physical abuse, far more children are negatively influenced by chronic emotional neglect or verbal abuse. Maltreatment can come in the form of excessive parental threats of withdrawal of love in response to the child's past transgressions or for failure to obey. "I won't love you if you don't . . . " can greatly threaten the young child's sense of emotional well-being. Much harm can be done by parents claiming that prior misbehavior indicates that the child is innately bad or hateful.

In helping to develop a sense of morality in children, just as in facilitating the development of other positive traits, the key is for parents to model appropriate behavior and to expect competence. Parents need to demonstrate by their own behavior that they have high moral standards. Being nurturant and considerate but at the same time clear when the child's behavior is inappropriate is the best way to achieve positive long-term results in socialization. Though they may inspire temporary conformity in children, intimidation and physical punishment are not effective in internalizing high moral standards.

Avoiding Punitiveness

Physical punishment and threats of retribution are not an effective solution for dealing with a child's misbehavior. The parent's physical intervention may in effect model punitiveness as a desirable way to respond to others. Depending on the level of parental warmth that is present and their own temperamental predispositions, children who are subjected to a pattern of physical discipline are likely to end up as either excessively submissive or unthinkingly rebellious in relating to authority figures.

Physical punishment may undermine confidence and lead to overly dependent behavior because of threats to the child's sense of emotional security. Frequent use of physical punishment, whether it be with a belt, hairbrush or palm of the hand, may also result in a child who is unable to express nurturance adequately. Despite what may appear to be a positive intention, the parent who relies on physical punishment as a means of discipline is not demonstrating appropriate social behavior to the child. Physical punishment may also reinforce the child's feeling that outside forces and not an internal conscience are supposed to govern behavior.

The emotional release afforded by hitting the child may temporarily provide a sense of relief for the frustrated parent. However, if there is a need for some direct physical expression of frustration, it is far better for parents to bang a table or kick a chair rather than to risk injuring their child. Moreover, it is important for children to learn that hitting others is not a mature way to communicate their displeasure.

The aftermath of physical punishment can actually be more disturbing to the parent than to the child. Many parents feel very embarrassed and guilty about what they have done and end up being overly solicitous to the child. This can reinforce a cycle of child misbehavior, physical punishment and parental attentiveness. The child may actually learn that the best way to obtain a reward is to get the parent angry because more attention is eventually received than when no misbehavior has occurred.

Many children sadly receive much more parental attention when they do something wrong and are largely ignored at other times. The following example illustrates some of the potential negative consequences of poor parental impulse control and physical punishment. Victor viewed himself as a loving and generous father but he had a very quick temper. Whenever he became angry at his children he would usually slap them but when he calmed down he would ask their forgiveness, give them money or even go out and buy them toys. His children learned to manipulate their father by getting him angry. At even the slightest cuff they would bawl uncontrollably, knowing that it would mean more presents for them later. Victor began to realize the negative implications of his own behavior when one day he observed his five-year-old son intentionally push a little girl and then try to placate her by handing her a dollar. He recognized his own punishment-bribery pattern mirrored in his son.

A positive parenting approach is the best assurance that the child will cooperate with parents' expectations for appropriate behavior. If the young child is asked to behave in a certain way—to put toys away or wash up—a promised reward may reinforce the behavior, especially if it is administered immediately after the completion of the desired task. But even better than material rewards is positive parental participation with the child in the activity. For example, engaging the preschool child in a cooperative game of putting away toys ("Who can fill up this box with blocks first") or brushing teeth ("Let's see whose teeth can get the whitest") is in the long run much more effective than admonitions, threats or even promised material rewards. The child participating with the nurturant parent in a desired activity is the best way to foster constructive cooperation in learning family values. Parents should encourage their young children in a playful communicative context rather than using intimidation or pressure to ensure conformity.

MORAL DEVELOPMENT

Personality characteristics such as self-esteem, achievement motivation, independence, assertiveness and nurturance can be viewed in the context of moral development. Relationships with friends, the other sex and authority figures are also influenced by standards of morality. Moral development is the process by which the child learns to make decisions according to standards of right and wrong, experiences appropriate guilt for misdeeds and feels the responsibility to strive for integrity. The morally mature individual has principles that encourage a consideration of the rights and welfare of others.

Different Levels

Six relatively distinct levels of moral development were proposed by psychologist Lawrence Kohlberg. He contended that an individual has to go through certain stages to reach full moral maturity. Progressing from stage one through stage six, an individual performs certain acts because he or she:

1. will be punished for disobedience;
2. will directly benefit for good behavior;
3. will be considered a good person and please others;
4. will show respect by following the dictates of authority figures;

5. will honor the rules and laws of society; or

6. will know it is right in his or her own mind.

According to Kohlberg, the individual progressively learns more mature and appropriate guidelines for conduct. New considerations are either incorporated into already existing principles or, as in the case of moving to a more advanced level, modifications are made so that an expanded perspective emerges in making moral decisions.

Some individuals may achieve the highest level of morality by late adolescence, although many adults never reach this phase of development. What actually happens is that many individuals become stuck at a certain level without being able to move toward a more mature moral perspective. Some adults, for example, obsequiously obey police or employers simply in order to please them (stage three) or declare that they do everything by the book (stage five). In contrast, the person at the highest level is the one typified by a well-developed, personalized set of moral principles and standards. Actually, moral functioning is much more complex than this mere outline of somewhat arbitrary stage notions indicates.

Even a person who is capable of a very high level of moral functioning may occasionally do things because he or she wants approval or fears authority. But, in any case, such an individual's life is lived primarily at stage six. Some children can understand stage six morality quite early in adolescence, but this does not mean that they can consistently function at this level. A great many factors in addition to the individual's intellectual sophistication are involved in the moral development process. Also, Kohlberg's emphasis on abstract standards being associated with so-called stage-six functioning does not aptly describe highly moral individuals who are extremely sensitive and empathetic to the special needs of others. The focus on the highest stage in Kohlberg's system, and that of many moral philosophers, is too exclusively impersonal and logical, reflecting a rather traditional masculine bias. Within a humanistic perspective, moral principles based on being considerately attuned to the rights and needs of others represent the highest level of moral development.

Family Influences

Fathers as well as mothers can have a strong impact in supporting their child's moral development. Studying seventh-graders, psychologist Martin Hoffman found that weak father identification was related to less adequate conscience development among boys than in cases of strong father identification. Father identification was determined by responses to questions involving the person to whom the boy felt most similar, whom he most admired, and whom he most wanted to resemble when he grew up. Boys with strong father identifications scored higher on measures of internal moral judgment, moral values and conformity to rules than those with weak feelings of paternal similarity.

Father-absent boys consistently scored lower than those from two-parent families on a variety of moral indexes. They scored lower on measures of internal moral judgment, guilt following transgressions, acceptance of blame, moral values and rule conformity. In addition, they were rated as higher in aggression by their teachers, which may also reflect difficulties in self-control.

Hoffman has summarized other data supporting the father's role as an identification figure in the moral development process for both sons and daughters. He speculated that identification with the father may contribute to the acquisition of observable moral attributes but that the internalization of moral standards and values is a complex process in which the mother, because of her greater availability, usually plays a more primary role. He also discusses evidence suggesting that for fathers and their sons, achievement may become a moral imperative that obscures the learning of important values dealing with interpersonal sensitivity.

The role of both parents in the child's moral development is important. The kinds of moral decisions the mother and father make are often quite different, and each parent is likely to have a special perspective that can positively influence the child. Fathers and mothers have a responsibility to contribute constructively to their children's moral development, especially with respect to the type of standards that are directly reflected in their parenting behavior.

Moral behavior is multidimensional. An individual needs to develop self-control as well as consideration for the rights and feelings of others. The process of developing an increasingly differentiated time perspective is a key factor in the child's reaching progressively higher levels of moral functioning. To become a more responsible individual, it is important to gain the patience to delay gratification, to be able to resist the temptation of the moment. Moral development is also a gradual process. Parents cannot expect their six-year-old to have the same capacity as the typical nine- or ten-year-old to delay gratification, complete homework assignments or remember to follow through on a promise made several months earlier. As with other developmental processes, the interaction of underlying maturational potential and family factors provides the basis for the child's progress toward higher levels of moral functioning.

Learning to deal with schedules facilitates the ability to delay gratification. Paternal deprivation can interfere with the child's learning how to delay gratification. In a pioneering study conducted by psychologist Walter Mischel, children in Trinidad were given a choice between receiving a smaller piece of candy right away or a much larger piece a week later. Mischel found that among the younger children, those who were father-absent were much more likely to choose the smaller immediate reward than those from two-parent families. Father-deprived children may be at risk to have less mature impulse control because of a difficulty in trusting adults to follow through on commitments. Paternal deprivation in the first few years of life can also interfere with the development of the child's comfort in dealing with adults outside of the family. Even in infancy, children who have positively involved fathers as well as mothers tend to display less anxiety and impulsivity in unfamiliar social situations.

Internalizing Values

Parents should recognize the difference between being authoritative and being authoritarian. An authoritative parent is one who is able to provide guidance in what is right but who usually allows some leeway for the child's judgment. Authoritative parents may even modify their thinking concerning a particular issue after considering the child's point of view. The authoritarian parent, on the other hand, dictates morality to the child. This type of parent may force the child into submission through the use of intimidation or other physically threatening methods. Children with authoritarian parents generally have less mature moral development than those who have authoritative fathers and mothers.

Nurturant, supportive parents tend to have children who behave in a responsible and caring way toward others. With respect to Kohlberg's framework, children with nurturant and supportive parents are likely to get beyond stage-four morality. At least by adolescence most children who have warm authoritative parents are able to make moral decisions on the basis of internalized moral standards and their concern for the welfare of others. Clear, specific parental feedback stimulates children's moral as well as cognitive development. Parents should make it a practice to spell out to children the value ramifications of particular types of behavior. Parents should not hesitate to discuss the moral implications of their own as well as their children's actions.

With adequate family support and cognitive maturation, children gradually progress in developing more internalized standards rather than just conforming to externally presented controls. The morally mature individual understands not only the nature of rewards and punishments in society but also the meaning of personal conscience.

Conceptions of step-by-step progressions in moral development are at best oversimplifications. The parent's relationship with the child should not be predicated on stimulating some rigid notion of stage-based moral development. Children may actually benefit, after the fact, from being exposed to moral thinking far above their present level of functioning. Parents can share their ethical perspectives with the child. Throughout the child's development, parents need to make an effort not only to communicate expectations of appropriate moral behavior but also to act in a way that concretely emphasizes kindness, consideration and respect for others. In effect, the developing child can draw upon a backlog of incidents of admirable parental behavior. The child will have vivid memories to serve as beacons in later development.

Respecting Authority

Parents are the initial representatives of authority for the child. In a general sense, parents are the child's first police, first judges and first bosses. Within the context of fostering moral development, parents can provide a constructive foundation for helping the child to relate to other adults in positions of authority. Children also observe how parents themselves deal with authority figures, whether it be toward police or other institutional representatives like teachers or doctors. A big difference exists between considering the merits of what an authority figure requests and blindly following arbitrary demands.

Parental support of the child's relationships with other authority figures is also very important. Parents should not rigidly insist that children must, no matter what, unthinkingly conform to the demands of adults. Rather, they should convey the importance of mutuality and respect in any ongoing relationship. Statements such as the following may be helpful in communicating a more balanced approach to the child about a teacher's authority: "Carefully listen to the teacher and think about what is being requested." "The teacher has had more experience than you and deserves respect but don't do something if you believe it is wrong or unfair to you or someone else." "Be considerate of the teacher's feelings in voicing any disagreement or disapproval."

Both the parent and the child should have a general respect for those who have authority and responsibility. However, this does not mean that the behaviors or decisions of authority figures should be passively or uncritically accepted if they are questionable. When an authority figure has done something that is unfair, the parent must help the child to understand the specific issue and try to remedy it. Rarely does this call for the wholesale rejection of the individual as a competent authority figure. Individuals, parents as well as children, need to realize that no one always behaves admirably or always reaches the perfect decision. What is crucial is that those in authority strive to do the best they can to act responsibly even though they and the rest of society must be aware of their limitations. Intolerance of error by those subject to authority is one reason why widespread disrespect for the law is manifest in our society. The child who has grown up learning to accept authority appropriately would demand that bad laws be changed but would not reject all laws because of the ill-conceived ones.

Parents need to be aware of their true feelings concerning the child's moral behavior. Many parents give their children mixed messages about moral issues. They tell the child to behave in a certain manner but they themselves act in a quite different way. In effect, they communicate "Do as I say, not as I do."

Unfortunately, children are far more likely to model negative parental actions that can be explicitly observed than they are to follow well-intentioned verbal communications concerning what is appropriate behavior. Also, some parents are very critical of their child's poor conduct but at the same time provide much more attention for misdeeds than for appropriate behavior. Serious family problems can arise when parents get highly involved only when the child misbehaves but otherwise provide little attention. An especially ironic case of this type involved the family of a clergyman. His child had stolen money from a schoolmate, had broken windows, had defied a policeman and had sworn at the principal. The boy's behavior was the catalyst for the family to seek professional help. Although extremely distressed with the boy's behavior on the surface, the clergyman, supposedly a moral authority, smiled broadly as his son was recounting his misadventures. Further discussion revealed that he had, in effect, given his son far more attention for acting out than he had provided for socially appropriate behavior.

At our next session, I helped the clergyman discover that all the time that he was admonishing his son, he was also giving him a great deal of attention for his defiant actions. In later sessions, it became apparent that the clergyman was resentful at having been transferred to a less prestigious parish. His indirect encouragement of his son's delinquency was, in part, his vicarious way of expressing his own anger toward authority figures. Parents who are not able to deal directly with their own frustrations often, inadvertently, encourage inappropriate behavior in their children. The process of encouraging high moral standards in children provides parents with an especially important opportunity to examine their own behavior. To avoid the common pitfalls of mixed messages, parents should strive for consistency between their high expectations and how they behave with their children. This is the strongest foundation for supporting the positive development of morality.

Ethical Choices

Parents are often confronted with some moral issues about which their child needs guidance. The child who sees the parent systematically gathering information and then making a decision after very carefully weighing different factors has a good model for learning how to cope with complex choices. It is important for parents to try to make the steps involved in their deliberations as clear as possible so that the child can develop a frame of reference for making moral choices.

When my son Jonathan was a first-grader he was especially friendly with two boys at school. Jonathan was excited when he received an invitation to attend the birthday party of one of these friends. The next day at school, much to his dismay, Jonathan discovered that his other friend had not been sent an invitation to the party. He was very upset, finding it difficult to comprehend this turn of events. When I came home from work that evening Jonathan shared his concerns with me. Before jumping to conclusions, I suggested that we initially ask for more information about the party. I expressed appreciation about Jonathan receiving the invitation as the boy's father filled us in on the rather involved details. However, it soon became apparent that Jonathan's other friend was not invited because he was black. Jonathan and I had a long discussion about the specific situation as well as about the roots of racial prejudice. I made it clear that it was his choice whether to attend the party or not, but he decided to decline the invitation. After some further discussion, we invited his black friend to spend the day of the party with us. This moral problem-solving process was a significant learning experience for me and other family members as well as for Jonathan.

Gathering information relevant to many other types of choices, whether or not they have obvious moral implications, can have a very positive impact on the child who is an active participant in the decision-making process. Whether

Mary should be allowed to go on a camping trip or whether it would be wise for Jimmy to take an after-school job should not be an arbitrary parental decision but should include the child's input. A nurturant parenting approach sensitive to individual responsibility is most likely to be associated with the child's long-term positive adjustment. Parents should emphasize the gains their child has made rather than punish backsliding or inadequacies. What counts is that the child is making progress—making successive approximations toward more mature and responsible behavior. High-quality family relationships, with a healthy respect for individual differences, are the best assurance for the continued constructive development of both children and their parents.

SUMMARY

The nurturant father can contribute much to his child's development of self-control and moral standards. Paternal nurturance can be displayed in many ways and enhance the father's effectiveness as a role model, limit setter and communicator of positive family values. It is important for the father to take an active interest in his young child's daily endeavors. Fathers can increase their impact on the child's functioning when they demonstrate their emotional commitment and make themselves accessible to the child on a regular basis, providing a vivid example of paternal responsibility.

Discipline should be viewed as positive teaching rather than as punishment for misbehavior. Families function much better when both parents are clear about their expectations, behaving in the considerate manner that they wish their child to emulate. A democratic family environment facilitates the positive development of the father, mother and child. The committed father plays an especially important role in helping his child to develop a concern for the rights of others.

Children have a natural capacity for empathy and, with regular exposure to the nurturing behavior of both parents, they are likely to develop into adults with a strong internalized sense of morality. Parents can provide specific examples of their decision making involving value-based choices. As children mature, they become increasingly capable of morally responsible behavior, especially if they have experienced positive relationships with both of their parents.

FURTHER READING

Nurturing Behavior

Demonstrating Commitment

About research emphasizing the importance of paternal as well as maternal nurturance for both sons and daughters, see Biller (1971a, 1977c, 1981c) and Biller and Solomon (1986).

For study linking children's generosity with paternal nurturance, see Rutherford and Mussen (1968). For other research relating nurturant parenting with empathetic and altruistic behavior in children, see Clary and Miller (1986), Eisenberg (1987), Hoffman (1975, 1976) McClelland et al. (1978) and Zahn-Waxler, Radkle-Yarrow and King (1979).

Being Accessible

Concerning the importance of fathers as well as mothers being available on a daily basis for an hour or two of quality individualized interaction with the young child, see Biller (1971a, 1974c), Biller and Solomon (1986), Blanchard and Biller (1971) and Reuter and Biller (1973). Regarding research concerning the advantages of paternal presence for maternal success in limit-setting, see Biller and Solomon (1986) and Lytton (1979).

Active Interest

For basic guidelines for positive parental involvement, see Biller (1973a) and Biller and Meredith (1974). See Gordon (1970, 1989) for detailed suggestions regarding effective parent-child communication.

With respect to parents consistently modeling positive and responsible behavior in the context of nurturant family relationships, see Baumrind (1971), Biller and Meredith (1974), Clary and Miller (1986), Eisenberg (1987), Eisenberg, Lennon and Roth (1983), Hoffman (1975, 1976) and Zahn-Waxler, Radkle-Yarrow and King (1979).

On parents positively disclosing and conveying their feelings and values, see Biller and Meredith (1974), Eisenberg (1987), Hoffman (1975, 1976), Miller and Roll (1977), Sagi (1982), Schulman and Mekler (1985) and Zahn-Waxler, Radkle-Yarrow and King (1979). About children's natural tendencies to be empathetic toward others, see Eisenberg, Lennon and Roth (1983) and Schulman and Mekler (1985).

Parental Generosity

For parental perspectives on giving gifts to children, see Biller and Meredith (1974). For more detailed discussion of parents helping children to develop responsible attitudes toward money management, see Weinstein (1987).

Constructive Discipline

Maturational Considerations

Concerning basic perspectives on maturational readiness, see Gesell, Ilg and Ames (1977) and Kagan (1984). For individual differences in temperament, see Chess and Thomas (1986, 1987) and Kagan (1984, 1989).

For data relating to differential discipline practices with sons and daughters, see Biller (1971a), Sears, Maccoby and Levin (1957) and Sears, Rau and Alpert (1965).

Parental Teaching

On the importance of presenting positive parental values and expectations in a warm and supportive atmosphere with emphasis on specific behaviors and consequences to others, see Baumrind (1971, 1989), Biller and Meredith (1974), Brooks (1991), Gordon (1970, 1989), Lickona (1985) and Schulman and Mekler (1985).

About the strong impact that effective fathering can have in fostering an internal locus of control in children, see Biller (1971a, 1974c, 1982a), Biller and Salter (1989), Radin (1982) and Sagi (1982).

For examples of constructive socialization techniques and the need for parents to gear their expectations to the child's temperament and level of maturity, see Baumrind (1967, 1971), Biller and Meredith (1974), Chess and Thomas (1987), Gordon (1989), Maccoby and Martin (1983) and White (1988).

Resisting Maltreatment

On father-mother mutual support and sharing of parenting responsibilities as an important factor in preventing various forms of child maltreatment, see Biller and Solomon (1986). For detailed discussions of marital and family risk factors involved in different types of child maltreatment, see Egeland, Jacobvitz and Sroufe (1987), Garbarino (1981), Garbarino, Guttman and Seeley (1988), Gelles and Strauss (1988) and Van Hasselt et al. (1988).

Avoiding Punitiveness

With respect to alternatives to physical discipline and other forms of punishment, see Biller and Meredith (1974), Gordon (1989), Lickona (1985) and Schulman and Mekler (1985).

Moral Development

Different Levels

For his theory and data regarding moral development, see Kohlberg (1969, 1976, 1981). For criticisms and modifications of Kohlberg's theory, especially with regard to gender and cross-cultural issues, see Damon (1988), Gilligan (1982), Snarey (1985) and Schulman and Mekler (1985).

Family Influences

On parental factors in moral development, see Hoffman (1971a, 1971b, 1981), Hoffman and Saltzstein (1967), Holstein (1972) and Santrock (1975). For reviews of other parenting research relevant to moral development, see also Biller (1971a, 1974c), Biller and Solomon (1986) and Schulman and Mekler (1985). On research relating paternal factors and children's religiosity, see Clark, Worthington and Danser (1988) and Kiernan and Monro (1987).

For studies linking paternal deprivation with problems in self-control, see Fry and Scher (1984), Mischel (1961a, 1961b), Stern, Northman and Van Slyk (1984) and Wohlford and Liberman (1970). For reviews of research relating paternal deprivation to difficulties in self-control, see Biller (1971a, 1974c), Biller and Salter (1989) and Biller and Solomon (1986).

Internalizing Values

With respect to research contrasting authoritative and authoritarian parenting styles, see Baumrind (1967, 1971, 1989). On the capacity of some relatively young children to deal actively with complex moral and ethical issues, see Coles (1986) and Schulman and Mekler (1985). Regarding the importance of parents exhibiting explicit examples of morally sensitive behavior, see Biller and Meredith (1974), Clary and Miller (1986), Damon (1988), Gordon (1989) and Hoffman (1981).

Respecting Authority

For data emphasizing the development of children's ability to take the perspective of others as a factor in constructive self-assertion, as well as in fostering altruism, see Chapman et al. (1987), Damon (1988), Eisenberg (1987), Iannotti (1985), Schulman and Mekler (1985) and Zahn-Waxler, Radkle-Yarrow and King (1979). For very detailed and useful guidelines in helping children resist inappropriate demands by authority figures, see Schulman and Mekler (1985).

Concerning the importance of parents being consistent in their own behavior with respect to their expectations for their children, see Biller and Meredith (1974), Damon (1988), Driekurs, Gould and Corsini (1974), Ginott (1969), Gordon (1970, 1989), Lickona (1985) and Schulman and Mekler (1985).

Ethical Choices

For various types of ethical dilemmas, see Kohlberg (1969, 1976, 1981). For children's active striving to develop meaningful codes of social behavior, see Coles (1986), Damon (1988) and Schulman and Mekler (1985).

6

Intelligence and Creativity

The emphasis in this and the next chapter is on ways that a father can contribute to his child's intellectual competence. This chapter focuses on basic types of problem solving and creativity while chapter 7 discusses academic and educational issues. It is helpful to expose children to a variety of intellectually stimulating experiences while also allowing them to express individualized interests at their own pace. Fathers and mothers should expect increasing competence, but children should not be pressured toward particular intellectual accomplishments at the expense of their emotional and social needs.

INTELLECTUAL COMPETENCE

This section begins with a consideration of the complexity of intellectual functioning. Genetic predispositions and gender factors are discussed briefly before the focus shifts to family influences. Intellectual functioning involves many different processes and modes of behavior. Although there are numerous methods to assess various aspects of ability, as yet no single procedure exists that adequately captures the complexity of intellectual potential.

Multiple Abilities

It is erroneous to believe that intelligence is a simple process to define or measure. No test score provides a complete assessment of an individual's intellectual capacities. A child's performance on a standardized test may be a fairly accurate predictor of success in a traditional academic setting, but it is by no means a complete assessment of intellectual abilities. A so-called IQ score derived from most commonly used tests usually indicates how well an individual can communicate and understand language, but it does not necessarily measure problem-solving abilities in real-life situations. Any measure of intelligence must be interpreted with special caution. IQ scores can change and fluctuate considerably as the individual develops. Performance on an intelligence test does not indicate an individual's capacity to be creative or to deal with frustrating social encounters; nor will it reveal special talents in music, art or other areas.

Parents can definitely have some impact on the extent to which children optimize their abilities, including those that may be reflected in performance on an intelligence test. However, the child's intellectual (or emotional, physical or social) functioning is not just a reflection of parental influences. General intellectual ability can be viewed as being composed of several basic skills including those related to problem solving, verbal ability and creativity. This is only a partial list; visual, spatial and auditory memory skills, for example, are also involved in the production of so-called intelligent behavior. Intellectual development is affected by the individual's genetic potential and by many different types of stimulation both inside and outside of the family.

Exceptional intelligence may or may not be reflected in test performance. In reality there are many types or modes of cognitive competence. Psychologist Howard Gardner, for example, has cogently argued for the existence of several different domains of intelligence. Gardner brilliantly marshals evidence arguing for the existence of relatively separate linguistic, logical-mathematical, spatial, musical, bodily-kinesthetic and personal awareness-social intelligences.

Genetic Predispositions

Intellectual functioning is influenced by learning and experience in interaction with genetic predispositions. Each person is born with a unique patterning of potential intellectual abilities. The social environment, including experiences with parents and other family members, has much to do with the extent to which the individual's potential will be realized. The presence of a similar level of mathematical giftedness in a father and son, for example, often appears to be a function of both their common genetic heritage and positive paternal involvement in the child's activities.

Predicting a child's intellectual performance at some point in the future depends on many factors and is a chancy enterprise at best. Nevertheless, compelling evidence suggests some degree of correlation exists between the intellectual functioning of parents and children. In fact, taking a group of babies at random, level of eventual cognitive and academic performance can be predicted better from measures of the father's and mother's intelligence than from so-called infant tests. This is partly because infant tests are heavily weighted in terms of physical development, whereas those for older children and adults are primarily based on verbal functioning.

Because the educational level and socioeconomic status of parents, especially fathers, is highly correlated to differences among elementary schoolchildren's intelligence test scores, it has been argued that environmental factors play the most important role in cognitive development. However, studies of identical twins and adopted children indicate that various areas of intellectual potential (and social and emotional responsivity as well) also have a strong genetic basis. For example, identical twins separated at birth and reared in completely different family settings nevertheless as adults demonstrate an impressive amount of similarity in basic intellectual abilities and interests. Genetic factors and social learning opportunities interact with one another in influencing the individual's intellectual and personality development.

Growing up in primarily middle-class families, children adopted at birth, or shortly after, generally perform much better academically than their counterparts who remain in less economically advantaged social environments. But these children may not do as well in intellectual and academic endeavors as the biological offspring of their adoptive parents. Moreover, for children adopted even in early infancy, there tends to be a stronger correlation to the level of intellectual functioning of their biological parents than to that of their adoptive parents. From such research it is apparent that their adoptive parents' influence can make a big difference, but clearly genetic potential remains a very important factor in the child's development.

An individual's potential is influenced by different types of genetic endowment, some inherited through parents, some quite idiosyncratic. It is important to view genetic factors from a broad perspective. First of all, although some overall intercorrelation exists among parents and children and among siblings, family-related inheritance is only one type of genetic influence. An individual's genetic potential is unique, and in many ways it may be very different from other family members for a variety of reasons. Genetically influenced characteristics that are recessive show up in some family members but not in others. Furthermore, the individual's basic endowment may be greatly affected by other prebirth influences.

On a more practical level, individuals may be constitutionally predisposed toward different styles of learning and relating to their environment. Some individuals learn most from observing and imitating others, while some do best when allowed to master new materials by themselves. In order to develop their potential abilities children must have varied opportunities to learn in ways that most facilitate their processing and integration of new information.

Gender Influences

Some average gender differences are evident in certain areas of intellectual functioning, but they are much less significant than overall individual variations among children. Because many social institutions are controlled by men, the traditional tendency has been to believe that females have less ability to organize, understand and problem solve in complex situations than males. This chauvinistic stereotype is often reflected in a parental attitude focusing more on the education of male than female children. Probably innate tendencies contribute to some small, average sex differences in particular intellectual abilities. Studies indicate that females, on average, are better at perception of details, rote memory, language usage, verbal fluency, spelling and other skills requiring the quick shifting of perception, the use of fine muscle control and the interpretation of tactile stimulation. Males, on average, are more likely to excel at mathematical reasoning, spatial perception and mechanical aptitude.

Genetic and prenatal factors contribute to male-female differences in certain areas of intellectual functioning. For example, males as a group are more vulnerable to suffering from genetic-prenatal problems resulting in obvious retardation or in more subtle attention-deficit and learning disorders. On the other extreme, some data suggest that a greater proportion of unusually gifted individuals, especially in mathematical endeavors, are also males. However, the existence of some average sex differences, or those relating to atypical handicaps or talents, should not obscure the extremely wide range of abilities characteristic of both males and females. Parents should not let gender rigidly dictate the types of intellectual accomplishment that they encourage in their children. They should try to foster a broad range of intellectual competencies in children of both sexes.

Gender differences have little to do with the effective performance of most complex tasks. Among preschoolers, for instance, girls may draw and paint more accurately because of greater fine muscle control, but boys may be able to reproduce three-dimensionality better because of superior spatial perception. Looking at gender differences in a general way, it is not possible to determine whether boys or girls are naturally better artists. Most important, on an individual level, any particular girl or boy may possess especially great artistic, mechanical, mathematical, verbal or other talents. Children are in need of opportunity and parental support if their talents are to come to fruition.

Parental Stimulation

Although genetic predispositions are important, the development of various skills and other talents does not take place in a vacuum. For example, positive changes over time in the intelligence test scores of young boys and girls are influenced by increased motivation for independence and achievement. These characteristics are particularly stimulated by fathers and mothers who expect and encourage assertiveness and allow their children to take initiative. Psychologists Jerome Kagan and Howard Moss discovered that by late childhood, youngsters who displayed an active striving attitude in their early elementary school years were much more likely to achieve a significant gain in their intellectual performance when compared to those who were more passive in dealing with new situations.

Researchers have found that, on average, firstborns and only children are more intellectually and academically advanced than later-born children, especially those from very large families. Much evidence suggests that firstborns are more likely to be the recipients of a greater amount of individualized paternal and maternal attention, as well as higher parental expectations for achievement, than later-borns. Speculation has occurred that firstborns may experience a more biologically benign prenatal environment, particularly when compared to those later-born children who are very closely spaced in age and who may suffer from the effects of prolonged maternal stress. Many other family factors including gender and socioeconomic status can modulate the influence of birth order, but nonetheless, the relative intellectual and occupational accomplishments of only and firstborn children during adulthood are quite impressive.

As discussed in chapter 2, abundant evidence indicates that the father's positive attention can have an important role in fostering his young child's abilities. Even in the first year of life, infants with actively involved fathers are likely to have a relatively advanced level of functioning. Young children who experience a highly supportive relationship with their fathers have been found to be socially and intellectually advantaged compared to their less paternally stimulated peers.

Paternal nurturance can be a particularly significant factor stimulating intellectual development among children. In a pioneering study initiated by developmental psychology researcher Norma Radin, interviews and observations were conducted with fathers and their four-year-old sons. The sons were asked to remain in the room and play while their fathers were participating in the detailed interview process. The four-year-olds tended to become bored and fidgety during the lengthy interviews. The sessions were observed, tape-recorded and subsequently scored for how nurturant or restrictive each father was toward his son. Fathers who demonstrated positive attention toward the child such as asking their sons to show them what they were doing were considered to be nurturant. Fathers who tried to inhibit their children by telling them to sit down or be quiet were rated as restrictive.

Radin found that the boys' intelligence test scores were positively related to their father's nurturance. In contrast, paternal restrictiveness was negatively associated with the children's test scores. It was also observed that fathers who had children with high intelligence test scores tended to consult them more when filling out a questionnaire concerning home activities given after the interview. Fathers may, of course, be naturally more responsive and nurturant toward especially bright children as compared to those who are not as obviously intelligent. Nevertheless, some aspects of the child's intellectual functioning are clearly influenced by the degree to which parents encourage competence. Radin's follow-up study a year later revealed that the amount of father nurturance shown in the initial research was still related to the boys' intellectual functioning. The father's involvement in direct encouragement of such skills as counting or reading was significantly associated with his son's intelligence test performance at both four and five years of age.

Although much of my initial research focused on gender development in young boys, I also discovered that paternal nurturance was positively correlated with intellectual functioning, whereas father deprivation tended to lessen cognitive competence. In a study described in more detail in the next chapter, Robert Blanchard and I found that, even controlling for general intelligence level, degree of father involvement was strongly related to the academic performance of third-grade boys. Boys whose fathers were highly available to them earned much better achievement test scores and grades than those whose fathers were absent, especially if they had been absent during the child's infancy and early childhood.

In general, research indicates that fathers typically have a more direct impact on boys' than they do on girls' intellectual development. But in most families, fathers have tended to focus more of their attention on their sons than on their daughters. Studies of the family backgrounds of extremely successful women, in fact, indicate that they were much more likely than their female peers to have experienced a high level of paternal support and stimulation during early childhood.

Complex Factors

Children who are deprived of contact with their fathers often show less intellectual competence than those living in two-parent families. Psychologist John Santrock found that early father-absence tends to be associated with lowered intelligence test performance, especially for children growing up in relatively poor economic circumstances. Children who became father-absent before the age of five, and particularly before the age of two, generally scored significantly lower on measures of intelligence and achievement than those from two-parent homes. The strongest results were for father-absence due to divorce, desertion or separation rather than death.

Mavis Hetherington and her colleagues also reported data indicating that early father-absence can impede cognitive development. Young boys (five- and six-year-olds) who had lessened contact with their fathers for two years because of divorce scored lower on a standardized intelligence test than those from intact families. Data from this study clearly suggest that decreasing father availability during the two years following the divorce was a major factor in the boys' lower level of performance, although no clear-cut findings emerged for girls.

An impressive review of research concerning father-absence and intellectual performance was conducted by psychologist Maryann Shinn. She focused her discussion on twenty-eight studies that met some minimal methodological criteria: data were collected from nonclinical populations, some sort of father-present comparison group was used, and an effort was made to control for socioeconomic status. Father-absence due to divorce seemed particularly detrimental, and some evidence showed that early, long-term and complete father absence was especially likely to be related negatively to intellectual competence. More consistent results were reported from studies involving lower-class individuals and among males, and much evidence suggested that females' cognitive functioning was also negatively affected by paternal deprivation. The family instability and financial difficulty often associated with divorce and father-absence may be primary factors interfering with the child's cognitive functioning. However, the major disadvantage related to father-absence for children is lessened parental attention including fewer opportunities to model mature decision making and problem solving.

In our book, *Parental Death and Psychological Development*, Ellen Berlinsky and I emphasized individual differences among children in their capacity to cope with family-related changes. Children below the age of seven or eight typically have not reached a stage of cognitive functioning at which they can realistically understand and confront the loss or absence of a parent. On the other hand, older children or those who are intellectually precocious may have a great advantage compared to their less able counterparts in dealing with the loss of a parent or some other type of radical change in family living circumstances.

In homes in which the father is absent or relatively unavailable, the mother assumes an especially important position as a role model and source of nurturance and stimulation. Children who are strongly identified with an intellectually oriented mother are likely to do well in many facets of school adjustment, particularly in tasks involving verbal skills. Middle-class mothers are much more apt to encourage academic success than their less economically advantaged counterparts. Among lower socioeconomic status mothers, those without husbands are likely to be preoccupied with day-to-day activities and to think less frequently about future goals for themselves or for their children. Compared to middle-class mothers, those who are poor usually put considerably less emphasis on the long-term consequences of academic performance.

Success in early academic situations is based heavily on verbal abilities. However, there is far more to intellectual competence than language skills. Although they may stimulate the child's verbal and early school performance, some parents do not foster an active, problem-solving attitude. For example, they may be overprotective and dominating to the point that they interfere with their child's assertiveness and independence, characteristics that are so important in problem solving and creative endeavors.

PROBLEM SOLVING

Being able to analyze problems and to articulate solutions are great assets in the individual's successful adaptation to social as well as intellectual demands. The child's problem-solving skills can be greatly enhanced by experiences with each parent. Parents solve a wide range of problems in the course of their everyday family and work responsibilities.

Parent Differences

Traditionally, emphasis has been placed on males and females learning how to solve different types of problems. The feminine domain has been centered on resolving interpersonal and domestic conflicts, whereas males have been more focused on dealing with problems in the physical environment including those that require mechanical and mathematical solutions. Even when they were children, the focus of the father's and mother's problem-solving endeavors probably was quite different. For example, the father's childhood projects were more likely to have included building models, devising football strategies and computing batting averages.

As more and more women enter the business and professional worlds sharp distinctions are lessening between the problem-solving arenas of fathers and mothers. However, there are still going to be parental differences in the great majority of families whether or not they conform to traditional gender expectations. The employed parent experiences new challenges that accompany job changes or moves up the career ladder. The problem-solving endeavors of the mother who does not have a career usually occur in a domestic setting, at least while she is dealing with young children. Although the housewife-mother may face many difficult problems, they are likely to be very different from the day-to-day challenges that confront the parent who also has a career. In any case, it is advantageous for children to be exposed to two parents who, between them, deal with a varied array of activities. The child can learn much from observing how each parent deals with diverse problems on a day-to-day basis inside and outside of the home.

Both parents can encourage the child to learn about their respective responsibilities and interests. The father's activities may involve some features of household functioning that the child is less apt to encounter with the mother. For example, a father might be able to analyze why the heating system is not working or figure out how to set up a new television antenna. These examples should not be construed as suggesting that such activities are only part of the male parent's domain, but fathers and mothers are likely to be involved in dealing with different types of problem-solving activities. Understandably for many types of activities parents may not have the skill, patience or interest to encourage direct, joint involvement with their children. However, parents can still have a supportive role by exposing their children to the talents of others, whether they occur in the mundane workaday world or are very esoteric. In his autobiography, Benjamin Franklin described in detail how his father took him for walks to see various types of artisans in action and how he exposed him to his conversations with business, civic and religious leaders. Such diverse exposure to the skills of others as a young child, along with his great intellectual gifts, no doubt stimulated Franklin toward his vast number of diverse accomplishments.

Joint Ventures

Although the parent may feel that home chores are not that exciting or important, even mundane activities may appear very significant to the admiring young child. The toddler may be very interested in seeing someone change the oil in a car or fertilize a lawn. For the young child, chores that the parent takes for granted may represent important chances to learn. The attractive aura of many activities may be lost only in the eyes of the adult.

Either parent can involve the child in some basic problem solving that requires no technical training. Understanding how to operate a washing machine or vacuum cleaner can be quite stimulating for the preschooler, particularly with the patient teaching of the parent. More important than the specific types of activities the parent performs is the way that the child may be involved in problem solving. Parents can provide very natural learning opportunities for the child. The parent can explain the function of various household objects and the choice of a particular method to complete a task. The child can help by fetching materials or actually accomplishing part of the task.

Encouragement of the child's involvement in the decision-making processes concerned with various household problems can be especially important. The child's suggestions should be given careful consideration even if they are not immediately useful. Learning how to solve problems involves perseverance. Encouraging a child to take pride in getting things done may include specific activities that also might be new for the parent.

I remember a particularly challenging incident involving my son Kenneth when he was four years old. The issue itself was a small one—Kenneth had wanted to try a new brand of cereal that had been advertised on television. Kenneth and I went down to the neighborhood market to buy the cereal, only to find that they did not yet have it in stock. We went to another market and then another, still not finding the cereal. To both of us, the "Great Cereal Hunt" had become a special challenge. After several hours, we finally located a store that had just received a shipment of the new cereal. Kenneth had learned a valuable lesson—that you do not necessarily succeed at something the first time or even the eighth time, but that you can eventually succeed if you persevere. I also learned to scour the Yellow Pages when searching for a certain type of store and to call first before driving great distances to find a product that is not in stock.

Shared hobbies that both adult and child enjoy can also be a good way for a parent to encourage a son's or daughter's perseverance and problem-solving skills. However, too many parents supposedly working with their children on a project end up doing it all for them. One reason is that the parent may become impatient with the child's skill level. From the child's perspective, it may be more important to experience a sense of contribution to the finished product than to have no direct involvement in a more sophisticated project that turns out perfectly. Whether it be a garden, a tree house or a puzzle, a joint parent-child project can be a very satisfying experience for both participants.

Children can benefit from many types of leisure-time pursuits with their parents. Playing games with children can also aid in the development of their intellectual abilities. Parents need not wait until their children are old enough to master checkers or chess to use games as modes of encouraging strategy planning and problem solving. I have especially enjoyed playing various card games with my children. Card games were a major social activity in my family when I was a child. One of my greatest joys as a toddler and young child was climbing up and sitting on my father's lap during his weekly card games. The clatter of chips and conversation was very stimulating to me, as was the feeling of sharing a special activity with my father and his friends.

Analytical Approaches

Both parents can do much to help stimulate the child's problem-solving skills, but a focus on analytical issues may be an especially significant component of the actively involved father's behavior. Compared to those who are well fathered, paternally neglected children are more often at a disadvantage in terms of analytical ability. For instance, some research suggests that father-deprived children have more difficulty solving complex puzzle tasks and mathematical problems than adequately fathered children.

Lack of involved fathering seems to have more of an inhibiting impact on the mathematical skills of boys than it does for girls. However, this may be related to the fact that fathers usually make more of an effort to stimulate mathematical thinking in their sons than they do in their daughters. In order to overcome the negative influence of gender stereotypes, girls may need even more parental support and encouragement to develop their mathematical potential. As with other areas of competence, parents need to keep in mind that great individual differences in interest, motivation and basic talent occur among children regardless of their gender.

Being able to use mathematical concepts is very important, but it is only one dimension of analytical thinking. In addition to encouraging their children to learn how to weed out irrelevancies and solve particular problems, parents can support a discriminating approach to life in general. Throughout development individuals are bombarded with countless requests, temptations and other types of external pressures. Children must learn gradually to take more and more responsibility in making choices. A child may be in a situation where he or she is pressured from several directions to engage in various social activities. The parent by example and by discussion can help the child to learn how to sort out options and priorities. What is most crucial is that the child develops structures to make meaningful and responsible decisions, whether or not his or her choices agree with those of the parent.

Parents should not hesitate to talk out loud and share their decision-making process even with a young child. Mulling over the financial advantages and disadvantages about getting a new car versus taking an extended family vacation may help the parent clarify priorities. Furthermore, it can provide a child with insights into real-life problem-solving situations. Making parental reasoning explicit exposes the child to reflective thinking. And the child may ask a helpful question or add a provocative comment! Parents may be surprised, however, that the child's verbal response to their particular musings may not be initiated until the next day, week or even later. The explicit behavioral consequences of particular parent-child interactions may only be reflected when the child's developing maturational capacities later allow for the active use of earlier experienced situations.

Communication Skills

The speech of fathers and mothers differs in addition to their vocal quality. Although they certainly overlap, men and women tend to use different words as well as expressive styles. Such differences, in fact, can be quite stimulating for the child's vocabulary and social development.

Mothers tend to be more concerned about the impact that their words will have on other people's feelings whereas fathers may be more focused on conveying precise meanings in task-oriented situations. A business-oriented father might find such words as *produce*, *quota*, *organize*, *commitment* and *contract* to be quite representative of his normal day-to-day vocabulary. If both parents are employed, their occupations and technical vocabularies are still likely to be different, and the child can learn useful terminology from each of them. The words that parents use in leisure-time endeavors are also likely to vary. The father might have an excellent sports vocabulary, while the mother might have a good literary vocabulary, although the reverse is also true in some families. A wide-ranging vocabulary derived in part from experiences with both parents can be an important resource for the child.

In our complex society the ability to understand and produce language is especially important. Unfortunately, children and adults may be accepted or rejected by others simply on the basis of their ability to communicate. Even before they become capable of verbally expressing themselves, infants need the stimulation of hearing others speak to them. Young children who are exposed to very little verbal attention from other family members are more likely to develop language difficulties than those who are the recipients of at least a moderate amount of communication.

With respect to the development of communication skills, parental responsibility is mainly to encourage supportively the child's expressiveness. Parents should strive to provide clear models of effective verbal (and nonverbal) communication and be responsive in an unhurried fashion to the child's efforts at self-expression. But they should not pressure the child to speak or try to force clearer enunciation. Except in situations of gross deprivation, or where there is some sort of physically related disability, children begin to use words actively when they are developmentally ready. In most cases, the parent can do very little to speed up the timing of the child's initial sentence construction significantly. Given a relatively positive environment, the timing of verbal development in children is much influenced by maturational readiness.

The child should not be criticized for stammering, stuttering or other speech imperfections, or be made to feel self-conscious about verbal limitations. This may only make a child's speech difficulties more of a handicap. Parents who have questions about their child's speech development should not hesitate to seek professional help. A child who is not speaking in two-word sentences at sixteen months should not be a cause for excessive parental concern. But a child who cannot effectively combine simple words by the age of two should receive at least some initial professional evaluation.

Children growing up in quite similar circumstances can vary remarkably in the emergence of active verbal skills. Although parents can very much influence their children's eventual vocabulary and style of speech, the age at which the boy or girl is capable of constructing two- or three-word phrases is largely a function of child-specific maturational factors.

My oldest son Jonathan was quite verbal as an infant and toddler, putting together three- and four-word sentences by eighteen months. However, my experience with Jonathan did not prepare me for the verbal development of my next child, Kenneth. His cooing and babbling behavior was rather typical, but he appeared less vocal than Jonathan during his early infancy. Kenneth seemed quite serious in his facial expressions and often sucked his thumb intensely as he observed others. One day, at ten-and-a-half months of age, he removed his thumb from his mouth when his grandfather walked in the door and in a relatively mature-sounding voice said, "Take your coat off." At that point, Kenneth began to speak grammatically correct sentences superior to those of his older brother, who was then two-and-a-half.

Not surprisingly, Jonathan had considerable frustration coping with the attention that Kenneth received for his verbal precocity, but fortunately, he also had a positive sense of self-esteem and some well-developed cognitive and athletic competencies. Children are particularly sensitive to the fact that a younger same-sex sibling may be superior in general language or physical competence even if they themselves possess above-average abilities. It is easy for the sibling of an exceptionally gifted child to develop feelings of inferiority. Parents need to be supportive of the individuality and varied competencies of each of their children.

Productive Thinking

An often neglected facet of intellectual development is what may be termed the capacity for productive thinking. As important as it is for an individual to be able to analyze and communicate, it is also vital to be able to translate ideas and concepts into appropriate action. Most of us know at least one person with a hundred different plans who never seems to bring any project to fruition.

An all too common myth is that exceptionally intelligent children are apt to be unproductive, wasting their abilities because they are somehow socially immature. In fact, individuals who score at the very top levels on intelligence tests are as a group considerably more likely to be successful and productive in a variety of occupational and professional endeavors. Furthermore, in general they are at least as successful in their personal lives and social relationships as those whose intellectual abilities are more within the average range.

General and continuing advantages exist for individuals who test in the "gifted range" on intelligence tests during childhood. Even during middle and late adulthood, despite many exceptions, intellectually gifted individuals as a group are likely to continue to enjoy many more trappings of occupational and social success. However, because of still prevailing gender biases, exceptionally intelligent females may not attain the same level of occupational and creative success as their male counterparts.

Very high intelligence does not ensure superior social or emotional development, but well-developed cognitive skills may give individuals an advantage in understanding interpersonal situations. Nevertheless, exceptional cognitive skills are only one of many factors related to success in a variety of high-status occupations including those in the sciences, engineering, medicine and law.

Remember also that an individual may be exceptionally intelligent in one area of functioning such as verbal communication or mathematics, but not outstanding—or even handicapped—with respect to other abilities.

STIMULATING CREATIVITY

Scientists have had even more difficulty formulating an appropriate definition for creativity than for intelligence. Creativity can be viewed as the spice of the intellect. The creative process involves the imaginative joining or associating of ideas, materials or objects never before connected in a similar fashion. Creativity is expressed in many ways, especially in generating novel solutions to old problems.

Diverse Expressions

Creativity has been traditionally thought of as having to do with the arts and literature. However, creativity is now widely acknowledged as very important in science and technology too. Creativity can also be greatly in evidence in interpersonal and athletic endeavors, or for that matter in any aspect of life. Yet it is very difficult to pinpoint the essence of the creative process. Similar to other facets of intellect, creative potential is influenced by genetic predispositions that vary from individual to individual. But whatever their limitations, all individuals have some potential for creativity. Being creative is a basic dimension of human behavior, very much supported by our inherent curiosity and motivation to influence the environment.

Research by psychologists Michael Wallach and Nathan Kogan with elementary schoolchildren has supported the possibility of developing separate measures of creativity and intelligence. Measures of creativity focus on divergent thinking, the ability to give more than one possible answer to a question or to generate several alternative solutions to a problem. For instance, an individual may be asked how many uses there are for a coat hanger or how many objects might be represented by a particular abstract shape. Responses are scored in terms of both quality and originality.

Children who are both highly intelligent and highly creative can be viewed as cognitively competent in a more general sense. Although high verbal intelligence is generally related to doing well in school, level of creativity by itself does not seem to be linked strongly to success in most traditional educational settings. Children high in intelligence but low in creativity, and those high in both, generally perform similarly gradewise, but the latter more frequently confront and question teachers. Children high in intelligence and creativity also seem more likely to be socially assertive with peers and to assume more leadership positions than their highly intelligent but low creative counterparts.

On the other hand, children with relatively low scores on both intelligence and creativity measures, and those with relatively low scores in intelligence but high scores in creativity, fare much less well academically and socially than their highly intelligent counterparts. Children in the low intelligence, high creative group typically contribute the most members who have interpersonal conflicts with teachers. It should be emphasized that relatively low scores in intelligence or creativity are not meant to suggest that the children are retarded or disabled but just that they are below average with respect to their peers at school. Children in the Wallach and Kogan research labeled low in intelligence were actually as a group somewhat above average for the general population, although within their highly competitive school situation they were at a clear disadvantage when compared to most of the other students.

Basic Suggestions

Creativity is fostered when the child is allowed considerable independence, both of thought and of action. The child can be encouraged to take a constructive approach in questioning authority and the traditional ways of doing things. The child will thus feel freer to discover new perspectives, knowing that there is not only one way to understand a situation or to solve a problem.

Strategies to improve creative thinking may be easier to describe in the abstract than actually to put into reality. Indeed, parents have a basic responsibility for ensuring the safety of their child and for setting reasonable limits. But within this context, great respect for the child's comments, ideas, questions and preferences can be given, and the parent can strive to avoid unnecessary assertions of authority. A flexible give-and-take relationship can facilitate creativity for the parent as well as for the child.

Certain children are particularly sensitive to their physical environment, some to their social surroundings, while still others are more involved with their own thoughts. Every child is greatly influenced by constitutional predispositions as well as by family and school experiences. Some children are much more comfortable dealing with ambiguous situations whereas others need a predictable structure. Some children enjoy dealing with alternative suggestions whereas others are apt to take any divergent comment as criticism. Parents can certainly encourage flexible thinking, but they must keep in mind that the child's temperament may have much to do with the impact of their efforts. Parental stimulation of intelligent and creative behavior does not require highly pressured or formal teaching situations. Learning new information and modes of discovery can be fun and take advantage of the child's natural curiosity. The following suggestions may be especially relevant for parents with young children.

The child needs a place for the unfettered use of imagination. The child should know that this is an area where there is no concern about neatness, where there is freedom to use messy paints or to play loudly. The child can be given a large space on which to draw, perhaps a wall covered with plastic or other washable material. Shelves, a workbench, tables and chairs can be added to facilitate the child's efforts. Even if a large closet or a divided-off portion of a room is used, it is the child's own free space. The child may also be provided with a small portion of the yard to store possessions, dig holes and construct whatever can be imagined, whether it be a tunnel to China or a rocket ship to another galaxy.

Watching adults enjoying interesting endeavors helps to encourage the child's curiosity. What is fun for the parent may also be stimulating for the child. Children can become interested and involved in so-called adult endeavors but enjoy them at their own level. Parents should not hesitate to read out loud, even if they think the child cannot understand everything. The parent can paraphrase certain sentences or stop and have a discussion with the child. Active interactions during reading can greatly enhance the child's interest. The child can benefit from time spent being read to by each parent because it shows that an adult interest in books is in no way restricted to a particular gender.

Encouraging Flexibility

Rigid gender stereotypes can interfere with creative thinking. Because creativity contains a feature traditionally considered masculine—independence—and another rigidly labeled feminine—sensitivity—both boys and girls can become inhibited when subjected to a parent's stereotyped views of gender roles. For example, the father who comments to his son that sensitive males are somehow unmasculine or to his daughter that independent females are unfeminine is not doing something constructive to foster his child's social and intellectual development.

Some theorists have taken a somewhat different but still rather stereotyped view in conceptualizing the creative process. They have equated creativity in men with femininity and in women with masculinity. In fact, highly creative men and women typically are not afraid to break away from traditional gender stereotypes, revealing themselves as relatively well-rounded individuals who possess a productive mix of competencies.

Because of peer and other social pressures, certain periods of development seem to occur when children need special parental support for attempts at creativity. Parental encouragement of the child's creativity and independence during these times may be particularly important. The child will be much better able to withstand teasing by peers if clear evidence of family acceptance is given. The third and fourth and the seventh and eighth grades in school tend to be two time periods during which creativity and nonconformity may be especially inhibited by peer-group pressure. During the third and fourth grades, cliques—usually all-boy or all-girl—are formed as youngsters explore farther afield in their social world. During this period children may be extremely sensitive about participating in any activity that may provoke ridicule and damage their standing within the peer group. During the seventh and eighth grades, many children are experiencing puberty and a growing interest in the other sex. Bodily changes may contribute to children being particularly uncomfortable about being different in any way from friends.

Children who are confident of parental approval in their search for new ways of doing things are likely to have greater resilience in the face of intolerance by

peers or adults. A good general rule for fostering creativity is to provide encouragement and the opportunity to view things from many different perspectives. Creativity can be involved in resolving interpersonal issues as well as in
dealing with more task-related or artistic situations. Role playing may help the
child resolve a problem with a bully, a teacher or a friend. A parent can role
play the specific problem with the child, acting out a part of the relationship.
The parent and child can then work out different ways to deal with a particular
problem.

When confronted with household problems, the parent can initially ask the
child how many ways the job can be done. How many ways, for instance, can
furniture be rearranged or water be removed from a flooded basement? The child
can be encouraged to visualize different solutions and to speculate on outcomes
in terms of convenience and practicality.

Family Support

Insufficient recognition has been given to the family backgrounds of unusually
creative individuals who had highly involved fathers or, more likely, had two
parents who were very supportive. Indeed, if the child has the genetic potential,
outstanding creative accomplishment is most likely to be fostered when both
parents are positively involved in the family.

Albert Einstein's development is a good example for illustrating the importance
of both parents. Einstein's father was a warm, encouraging, optimistic man who
took a great deal of interest in his son. He enjoyed taking his family on outings
and was a nurturing and accepting parent. Einstein's mother possessed a broad
range of knowledge and talent in both literature and music. During his childhood,
Einstein seemed to develop slowly in some areas, and one of his teachers even
perceived him as intellectually limited. However, his parents were not swayed
by the negative evaluations of others concerning their son's potential. Although
quite different from each other in temperament and interests, they were discriminating people who accepted little without analysis. They were not afraid to
question authority or to establish their own independent family life-style.

From both of his parents Einstein derived that special form of nurturance and
encouragement that allowed him to explore the world in his own way. His mother
supported his musical interests, from which he gained an appreciation of underlying mathematical structures as well as another creative outlet. His father,
an engineer, gave him access to scientific paraphernalia and to other adults from
whom he could learn. When Einstein was five years old and sick in bed, his
father brought a pocket compass to show him. Seeing the iron needle always
pointing in the same direction, Einstein for the first time became impressed that
the space he had always considered empty was actually filled with invisible
forces. Of course, Einstein was not just a product of his parents' nurturance.
Genius like his is an extremely rare commodity, but every child has some degree
of creative potential that can be fostered by positive parental interest.

Research with children who show early signs of unusual creativity has yielded interesting findings concerning parental behavior. Some data suggest that fathers play a particularly supportive role with daughters, and mothers with sons. A constructive relationship with the parent of the other sex may be especially helpful in giving the individual with high creative potential encouragement to overcome inhibiting gender stereotypes. Most important, the positive interest of both parents is likely to give the child a greater awareness of varied possibilities.

Perhaps most significant is the example that the parents set for their child. Parents of creative children tend to be highly educated, often having advanced professional training. But in addition, they are also much more likely than those parents with similar educational backgrounds to strive for an independent outlet for their abilities. In the families of creative children, fathers with scientific or other advanced degrees more often worked in a relatively autonomous situation as compared to those from similar educational and socioeconomic backgrounds. The fathers of creative children were more likely to have personal control over their work schedule rather than being under the direction of superiors within a highly structured organization. Parents with such creative life-styles also have more opportunity to spend flexible time periods with their children.

SUMMARY

The father plays an important role in stimulating and encouraging various types of intellectual competance. However, consideration must also be given to the influence of biological predispositions and other family and social factors that impact on the child's cognitive functioning. Individual differences involving particular abilities must be taken into account in understanding the complex nature of intellectual development.

Involved fathers, who actively play and communicate, contribute to their child's development even during infancy. By including the child in some of his daily activities, the attentive father provides stimulating developmental experiences. In the context of their day-to-day play and other joint endeavors, the father is likely to expose the child to a different style of verbal and problem-solving behavior than the mother or other females. The father's nurturant involvement can be especially important in expanding the child's curiosity and problem-solving skills.

The child who has a positive relationship with both parents is more likely to develop broader perspectives in analyzing problems and constructing alternative solutions. Analytical and creative behavior can be expressed in many arenas, ranging through the arts, literature, science and technology and even including various social and athletic endeavors. Parents should encourage basic intellectual accomplishments but also realize that children vary in their interests, talents and maturational readiness. The child with a nurturant, accepting and accessible father and mother is likely to develop a strong sense of self-worth in conjunction with solid intellectual and social skills.

FURTHER READING

Intellectual Competence

Multiple Abilities

On the complexities of "intelligence" and the existence of various domains of cognitive competence, see Flavell (1985), Gardner (1983), Guilford (1967) and Sternberg (1985).

Genetic Predispositions

For discussions of data relating to genetic/environmental interactions in intellectual development, see Holden (1980), Horn (1983), Loehlin and Nichols (1976), Plomin (1987, 1989), Scarr and Kidd (1983) and Scarr and Weinberg (1976, 1980).

Gender Influences

Concerning gender differences in cognitive abilities, see Feingold (1988), Halpern (1986, 1989), Lips (1988), Maccoby and Jacklin (1974) and Nash (1978). For "average" advantages that girls have even in infancy with regard to language-related skills, see Friedman and Jacobs (1981), Gunnar and Donahue (1980), Halpern (1986) and Maccoby and Jacklin (1974). For "average" advantages that males have in developing certain mathematical and spatial skills, see Benbow and Stanley (1983), Halpern (1986), Lips (1988) and Maccoby and Jacklin (1974).

Parental Stimulation

With regard to findings indicating a relationship between children's personality styles and developmental changes in intelligence test performance, see Kagan and Moss (1962). About the advantages of firstborns and only children, see Cicirelli (1982), Falbo (1982), Glenn and Hoppe (1984), Lamb and Sutton-Smith (1982) and Zajonc (1983). For the constructive impact of positive paternal influence on the intellectual development of children, see Blanchard and Biller (1971) and Radin (1972, 1973, 1976, 1981). For research on the father's influence during infancy and the preschool years, see Belsky (1980b), Easterbrooks and Goldberg (1984, 1985), Pedersen, Anderson and Cain (1980), Pruett (1987) and Yogman (1981, 1982).

About data relating to divorce, family atmosphere and cognitive functioning in children, see Hetherington, Cox and Cox (1978b, 1982), Radin (1981), Santrock (1972) and Shinn (1978). For reviews of research linking father and mother influences to various aspects of children's cognitive development, see also Biller (1974a, 1974b), Biller and Salter (1989), Biller and Solomon (1986), Gottfried, Gottfried and Bathurst (1988) and Radin (1981).

Complex Factors

Concerning different types of parent loss with respect to their impact on cognitive development, see Berlinsky and Biller (1982). For varied factors that interact with the parenting environment to influence intellectual performance, see Biller (1974a, 1974b) and Radin (1976, 1981).

Problem Solving

Parent Differences

For extended analyses of the impact of sex differences and gender stereotypes in various occupational domains, see Basow (1986) and Lips (1988). On the special types of stimulation each parent offers to the child, see Biller (1971a, 1974c, 1976b, 1982a), Biller and Meredith (1974), Lamb (1981b, 1987), Parke (1981, 1985), Pedersen (1981), Pruett (1987) and Yogman (1981, 1982).

Joint Ventures

For helpful suggestions for playing with infants and children and involving them in appropriate ways in various home-based activities, see Singer and Singer (1977), Sutton-Smith (1979, 1985) and White (1986, 1988).

About involving young children in everyday adult-oriented activities, see Biller (1973a), Biller and Meredith (1974) and Biller and Salter (1985).

Analytical Approaches

For research relating paternal deprivation to lessened ability in analytical and mathematical endeavors, see Barclay and Cusumano (1967), Berlinsky and Biller (1982), Biller (1974a, 1974b), Biller and Salter (1989), Carlsmith (1964), Dyk and Witkin (1965), Lessing, Zagorin and Nelson (1970), Lifshitz (1976), Parish and Copeland (1988), Reis and Gold (1977), Shinn (1978) and Wohlford and Liberman (1970).

Communication Skills

Concerning the development of communication skills in infancy and early childhood, see Brown (1973), Bruner (1983), Chess and Thomas (1987), Gleason (1988), Rice (1989), Slobin (1972), Tannen (1990), and White (1986, 1988).

Productive Thinking

For perspectives on productive thinking, see Greeno (1989) and Sternberg (1986a). For longitudinal research on gifted individuals, see Sears (1977), Shneidman (1989) and Terman and Oden (1959).

Stimulating Creativity

Diverse Expressions

With respect to various forms of creative and intelligent behavior, see Gardner (1983), Guilford (1967) and Sternberg (1985). For research relating to the differentiation of creativity and intelligence, see Hattie and Rogers (1986), Kerschner and Ledger (1985), Simonton (1984) and Wallach and Kogan (1965).

On ways to support creative endeavors in children and adults, see Biller and Meredith (1974), John-Steiner (1986), Monroe (1988) and Simonton (1984).

Basic Suggestions

For suggestions about specific types of toys, games and play activities that stimulate intellectual and creative growth in young children, see Segal and Adcock (1981), Singer and Singer (1977), Sutton-Smith (1979) and White (1986, 1988).

Encouraging Flexibility

Regarding personality characteristics involved in the creative process, see Barron (1969), Biller (1974b), Biller, Singer and Fullerton (1969), John-Steiner (1986), Monroe (1988), Simonton (1984) and Tyler (1983).

Family Support

For descriptions of Einstein's early development and family background, see Clark (1971). On research relating to paternal and maternal influence in the backgrounds of creative and gifted individuals, see Biller (1974c), Dauw (1966), Eisenstadt (1978), Goertzel and Goertzel (1978), Helson (1971), Weisberg and Springer (1961) and Werts and Watley (1972).

7

Family, School and Education

The first half of this chapter focuses on how the child's elementary school experiences may be influenced by paternal involvement. The second half is devoted to educational opportunities outside of school, especially informal learning that can be stimulated by everyday family contact with the father. As in chapter 6, the emphasis is on providing parenting guidelines for fostering problem solving and creative abilities.

BUILDING PARTNERSHIPS

The father and mother should share in the responsibility for the child's education. Children benefit greatly when respect and positive communication occur among themselves, parents and teachers. Neither parents nor teachers can be expected to assume total responsibility for the education of children. A major goal of this chapter is to encourage a more active family-school partnership, especially in recognizing the important role that men can have in enhancing the intellectual development of children.

Parent Involvement

Children who have two positively involved parents are likely to fare better in academic situations than those who suffer from some form of paternal deprivation. Just because a father lives in the home does not mean that he will be effective in helping his child do well in school. Research with children from two-parent families who are relatively intelligent but do poorly in school has suggested that most of them have inadequate relationships with their fathers. Conversely, children who do well in school are much more likely to have constructive relationships with both of their parents.

Robert Blanchard and I did a study that indicated a strong connection between paternal influence and children's grades and achievement-test scores. We collected extensive data relating to the family backgrounds and academic performance of third-grade boys. In our study, children were initially grouped according to their level of father availability: early father-absent (before age three), late father-absent (beginning after age five), low father-present (less than six hours of contact per week) or high father-present (more than two hours of contact per day). We attempted to control for factors such as the child's basic intelligence, birth order, socioeconomic status and maternal employment. Each early father-absent subject was individually matched with a member of the other three groups so that the only apparent difference in their family backgrounds involved level of paternal influence. The groups differed with respect to father availability but not in terms of many other family and social factors. In addition, teachers did not have access to the children's achievement-test scores until after they had assigned grades.

High father-present boys generally received superior grades and performed about a year above their expected age level on achievement tests. The late father-absent and low father-present boys scored a little below grade level on achievement tests, with teacher evaluations of their classroom performance being generally average or below. The lowest test scores and grades were most often obtained by boys in the early father-absent group. Our findings suggested that involved and available fathers can help their children's academic performance. We did not focus on the specific activities of fathers but on the degree of their availability to their children. The father's general support and interest seems to be more crucial in the development of the child's confidence and motivation than his direct participation in school-related activities. In fact, many children clearly react negatively to parents who pressure them academically but provide little interest and involvement in other aspects of their emotional and social development.

Father deprivation can also be a major factor contributing to an already economically disadvantaged home situation. The association between low socioeconomic status and frequent difficulties in children's cognitive, academic and social development is amply documented. Some researchers have even argued that the impact of father-absence and divorce on children's development is, for the most part, an artifact of lowered socioeconomic status. However, some data suggests that single-parent family status may actually be a more powerful predictor of the academic and social functioning of young children than their socioeconomic background. Educational psychologist John Guidubaldi and his colleagues have reported striking evidence that family structure is highly predictive of performance and social competence in academic situations. Children from single-parent homes have been found to be much more at risk for poor academic performance and behavior problems in first grade than children from two-parent families.

Nevertheless, father deprivation tends to be associated with much more serious academic consequences for lower-class children than for middle-class children. Middle-class father-absent children often do well in situations requiring verbal skills. For instance, Alan Dyl and I found that, although lower-class father-absent boys tended to perform poorly in reading, most middle-class father-absent boys functioned quite adequately. Because initial academic achievement is so heavily dependent on verbal and reading ability, father-absent middle-class children do not seem to be generally disadvantaged in classroom performance. Among single mothers, those from middle-class backgrounds in comparison to those from poor families are more likely to stimulate academically relevant verbal skills in their children.

Correcting Imbalances

Extremely few males teach in our elementary schools, particularly in kindergarten and the lower grades. The ratio of female to male teachers in elementary schools is about six to one—and more than fifty to one in the first few grades. Considering the extent of paternal neglect outside of school, children could derive something very special from regular contact with an interested and effective male teacher during their preschool and early school experiences. For a very large proportion of young children in our society, lack of contact with male adults at school is piled upon existing father deprivation at home.

I am not suggesting that having more male teachers would solve the problem of paternal deprivation in our society or necessarily improve the early school performance of most children. Some studies suggest that boys generally do better academically in societies where there are more male teachers. Research in the United States is inconsistent in this regard. However, a few studies support the notion that many young children, especially those who have been paternally deprived, improve their attitude, if not their immediate academic performance, when taught by supportive male teachers.

The shortage of male teachers certainly should not be viewed as a blanket indictment of the American educational system. Most teachers in both public and private schools try their best to meet the needs of children. Unfortunately, teachers often become discouraged and burnt-out after a few years of trying to help students. Lack of appreciation for their efforts from parents and school administrators as well as resistance from children can rapidly deplete their initial enthusiasm.

The positive socialization of young children into the classroom is an extremely important and challenging endeavor. Complicating the teacher's role is the frequent presence of children who are not developmentally receptive to basic classroom structures and who have not received adequate family support prior to school entrance. For many teachers and students the elementary school experience can be extremely disconcerting and stressful.

The typical elementary school classroom is likely to involve more obvious problems for boys than girls. A boy, especially one who is father-neglected, may perceive the teacher as just another controlling female authority figure. He may rebel against her in his general attempt to assert himself in the presence of females. The teacher, feeling threatened, may increase her efforts to control him rather than attempting also to sensitize herself to his basic insecurities. Many boys begin to view school and intellectual pursuits as female-oriented because they never get a chance to see a male adult who values academic pursuits.

Desperately trying to bolster their insecure identities, such boys may reject the educational efforts of their female teachers. At the elementary school level, the stressful relationships that teachers have with a relatively small proportion of male students may contribute to an already existing bias against boys and their activities.

In part because they tend to be more disruptive, boys typically elicit greater negative attention from teachers than girls do. Boys receive many more warnings and scoldings, and teachers are more likely to use harsh words with them than when reacting to girls who display similar behavior. Indications are that many female teachers also tend to give girls better grades even when boys have objectively achieved a higher level of performance.

Learning Problems

Far more young boys than girls have handicaps that interfere with their ability to learn to read and with other academic activities. More boys than girls have learning disabilities, and four or five times as many are referred to reading clinics. The higher incidence of reading problems among boys may also in part be a reflection of differential teacher treatment. Females are, on average, somewhat more developmentally advanced upon entering school and are much less likely to suffer from basic learning disabilities, but this does not explain why so many more boys who seemingly have no basic handicaps still have difficulties with reading.

In general, teachers react less favorably toward boys than girls during reading lessons and also tend to allow them less oral-reading time. In many cases teachers may just be encouraging the general initial superiority that girls may enjoy compared to boys. Throughout elementary school, girls tend to be consistently more interested and competent in reading. Compared to boys, girls are found to attach more prestige to reading. At least during the elementary school years, boys generally do not regard reading as a masculine virtue. Girls also have a definite advantage in the elementary school classroom because of the presence of a same-sex adult model who is a highly competent reader.

From an educational perspective, it is hard not to overemphasize the significance of reading. Children's feelings about academics as well as their general learning and achievement are highly related to their level of reading competence. When the proportion of boys who have relatively slow maturation or specific learning handicaps is coupled with the biases of the feminized classroom, it is no wonder that girls generally perform at a superior level in reading and other academic endeavors in the early elementary school years. Yet, despite such disadvantages, under different circumstances most boys can learn to read as well as girls. In one study, when children were given programmed, independent reading instruction, boys and girls functioned at about the same level. But when children were taught in small reading groups that featured close contact with a female teacher, girls demonstrated superior performance.

Reading skills can be influenced by cultural factors. Boys who go to school in societies where male teachers are plentiful at the early elementary school level may experience fewer reading-related difficulties. Among Japanese children who are taught in communities in which about 60 percent of the teachers are males, no difference seems evident between boys and girls with respect to the frequency of reading difficulties. German boys have been reported to have significantly better reading scores than girls and to be less likely to suffer from severe reading retardation. In Germany, elementary school teachers are usually males, and reading is considered a masculine talent. In contrast to the general situation in the United States, the German elementary school system may actually be biased against the development of girls' reading competence.

Needed Changes

Although the form of discrimination may be different, girls as well as boys can also be victims of the biases of the elementary school classroom. Girls tend to be more sensitive to the attitudes of others and especially to the prejudices of authority figures. The girl's independence, achievement motivation and assertiveness may be hindered by traditional female teachers. While female teachers usually react more negatively to boys, the overall elementary school atmosphere may subtly downgrade the importance of long-term achievement for girls.

Despite the preponderance of female teachers, they tend not to be well represented in the administrative hierarchy. A girl's impression of the school bureaucracy may also bruise her pride because the typical female teacher is usually working under the supervision of a male principal. The outmoded paradigm of adult females being subservient to male authority figures is a routine part of the educational system.

But females are often confronted with the most severe inhibitions to their educational development in high school and college. In elementary school, education is typically feminine-focused while in high school and college it is likely to become much more masculine-oriented. Male teachers and male students may put subtle pressure on an adolescent girl to be "feminine" in the sense of subduing her competitiveness in order to conform with their stereotype of the passive female. Many females become intimidated by the social implications of achieving in competitive situations with males.

Having a supportive, encouraging male teacher early in the educational process can be important for the girl as well as the boy. If a girl has been exposed only to female teachers in elementary school and has never had an adult male show her that he values learning and achievement as a natural feminine characteristic, she may find it more difficult to assert herself intellectually as she matures into adolescence and adulthood. Without such early self-confidence, she is likely to take the path of least resistance and conform to more restrictive gender stereotypes. A major remedy to the feminized classroom would be the presence of more male teachers in the early elementary school grades. However, this is not an easy task to accomplish. A great change away from the attitude portraying early childhood education as only women's work has to take place.

A broad-scaled attack on paternal deprivation in our society needs to take place. More support should be given to the general importance of the adult male role with young children in educational contexts as well as to the father's significance within the family. Regardless of their gender, more flexible teachers could concentrate less on demanding obedience and conformity and more on encouraging both boys and girls to be assertive and creative. Male and female teachers could support one another in allowing freer, more open classrooms. Children should see men and women working together cooperatively inside and outside of the classroom.

More focus on the needs of the individual child is required. Especially in the early grades, the child should have more time to relate to the teacher in a one-to-one fashion. The emphasis should be on fostering a more positive attitude toward school rather than just concentrating on the child's conformity or level of performance. Many relatively immature children, especially boys, are pushed into structured academic situations for which they are not at all ready. Exposing young children to stimulating intellectual activities is one thing; endlessly requiring them to fill in the blanks on dittos is another. Related issues that should be addressed include the frequent emphasis on overly repetitive homework and the great need for more opportunities for active play during the school day.

Any discussion of education should not, of course, ignore the disadvantaged circumstances of children living in poverty. In far too many communities a double-standard exists in educational opportunities; poor children are provided with all too little support for educational achievement at home or at school. Head Start-type programs have helped to prepare many economically disadvantaged children better for the challenges of elementary school, but much more needs to be done on a continued basis to ensure high-quality educational opportunities for all children, not just those from affluent families.

Expanding Participation

For the most part, mothers are the parents who deal directly with the school. Mothers typically communicate concerns that they may have about their child, or they are the ones who are usually contacted by the teacher if there is a problem. Similar to other institutions serving children, the school is oriented toward dealing with mothers. School administrators vary greatly with respect to their encouragement of parent-related involvement, but typically relatively little support is extended for the input of interested fathers.

More fathers as well as mothers should become knowledgeable about the early elementary school experiences of their children. In fact, fathers may be in a better position than mothers to be sensitive about problems with the feminized classroom and the need for more male input. Parents should advocate that every child has some regular contact with a male teacher during the early elementary school years. Some immediate changes might be made by giving male teachers already in the system incentives to spend some of their classroom time with students in the lower grades.

Changing the proportion of male teachers in elementary schools is a very complex issue with no easy resolution. It has traditionally been very difficult to recruit qualified male teachers, especially for the early primary grades. A tremendous need exists for greater financial and professional incentives to attract highly qualified men and women into teaching young children. A corresponding need is identified for more female administrators, especially at higher levels. Probably the biggest source of resistance to interesting more men in teaching young children is the prevalent social attitude that early childhood education is a feminine endeavor. Although our gender stereotypes appear to be lessening, some male elementary school teachers, especially those who teach at the kindergarten level or in the lower grades, still feel that they are not regarded by others as adequately masculine. However, many males choose to be elementary school teachers because they have integrated a sensitivity to the needs of young children into their very positive masculine self-concepts.

Fathers as well as mothers should be involved in the family-school partnership. More support is needed for both parents to visit their child's school and meet with teachers. The father, perhaps having unpleasant memories about his own early educational experiences or being hesitant to enter a world that sometimes seems excessively feminine, may require special support in order to feel comfortable communicating with school personnel. It is advisable for parents to try to establish a positive rapport with the principal and teacher before either perceives a problem or difference of opinion. Such an approach improves the chance of later cooperation between the family and school if the child does experience classroom difficulties.

Every school can also benefit from a program bringing parents into the classroom. An accountant could give a lesson in basic budgeting procedures, a pilot could lecture on the fundamentals of flying airplanes, and an insurance agent could explain the nature of actuarial practices. It is important to have women as well as men describe their occupational activities to children and, it is to be hoped, lessen gender stereotypes relating to educational and career opportunities.

LEARNING OPPORTUNITIES

Being a competent parent does not necessarily mean being directly involved in the child's formal schooling. Some children whose parents never talk to a teacher or visit the school are very happy and competent students. However, parents can add a significant dimension to their influence by encouraging their child's school-related activities.

Constructive Homework

After-school assignments may provide an important avenue for helping the parent and child learn together. Homework can give the child a positive opportunity to involve the parent in school-related endeavors. A proliferation of cartoons picture a baffled parent hunched over the child's homework. Although parents may constructively demonstrate solutions to parts of an assignment, they should not do all of their child's homework. Even if help is required at many points during a difficult assignment, the child should go through the process to the final answer as much as possible. If necessary, the parent can encourage the child by asking focused, step-by-step questions. A good example of constructive parental help was provided by a father whose child had decided, as part of a science assignment, to prepare a report on new techniques in radiology. The father was a physician and could have done much of the work for his daughter. Instead he discussed some of what he knew about X-rays but encouraged her to visit the local hospital and interview a radiologist.

Many family conflicts revolve around children's school performance and their reluctance to complete homework. Parents should not threaten or punish their children but express their concern in a supportive manner. They can communicate their positive expectation that the child will demonstrate more commitment and follow through on future assignments. Parents should avoid making education such a transcendant issue that academic success is the child's only basis for feeling self-worth. Some children are just not that interested in academic competition or are simply not able to keep up with classmates. Special educational arrangements may be necessary but the child's basic self-acceptance is far more important than his or her relative success in school. Parents need to be supportive whether or not their children are academically successful.

A young child's life should not just revolve around academic activities. Parents should not hesitate to speak up when they think their child is being overloaded with homework. They should ask whether it really contributes to the child's understanding or is simply busywork. They should communicate with the teacher if they think the child may be getting too much pressure at school. Consideration of the child's other commitments is also needed. Many children are overscheduled. They have religious training, sports activities, music lessons and other out-of-school commitments. They hardly have a free moment for spontaneous play. Consider also that children usually need more sleep than adults. Excessive homework is often the final insult to a child's free time.

Helping children to schedule their time can be a very important role for parents. In fact, in trying to help their child, parents may well find that they, too, have overscheduled themselves. Individuals vary in terms of their ability to deal with schedules. Just because a parent may feel good about cramming many activities into a short time span does not mean that this is comfortable for the child. Parents should avoid a frantic and hurried life-style for themselves and their children.

Sharing Activities

Parent-child communication works best as a reciprocal process. This means establishing a history of rapport in which parents are willing to talk about their activities and responsibilities with their children. For example, parents who have consistently volunteered information about what they are doing at work are more likely to have children who are responsive in talking about school activities.

As discussed in chapter 6, the parent can do a lot to encourage the child's learning experiences outside of school. Family interactions may indeed provide the most meaningful learning experiences for the parent as well as the child. Moreover, the degree of family support for learning is generally at least as significant a factor in children's intellectual and educational attainments as the specific quality of classroom teaching that is provided for them. In many ways the most important aspects of the child's education take place outside of school. Although a large proportion of time is spent in school, it by no means fulfills all the child's learning needs. Parents can provide special opportunities not readily available within the typical school.

Unfortunately, classroom experiences all too often encourage passivity by requiring children to learn but not necessarily to develop their own ideas. The emphasis in most school situations is normally on convergent thinking focusing on issues such as mathematical solutions or historical facts where only one correct answer to a question is usually presented. Divergent problem solving emphasizing alternatives to different situations, so important for competence and creativity, is rarely encouraged in the classroom. The concept of the open classroom, allowing students to work at their own pace on their own projects, can be a step in the right direction. However, in most schools a child is still expected to complete a very prestructured, standardized course of study. The child's elementary school curriculum will probably not provide the opportunity to visit a bustling construction site or do myriad other things involving exciting learning experiences.

Family trips can provide excellent opportunities for joint parent-child learning experiences. When traveling by automobile, parents can play various word games with children, stop and show them sights or share information about the localities they are passing through. But parents should not feel that they have to keep busy every minute of a vacation. Parents may be so intent on cramming every possible activity into a limited time period that they return from a vacation feeling much more stressed than when they left. Tourist attractions such as Disneyland can be great fun for the whole family, but parents should also try to balance such excursions with those having a less frenetic pace. Canoe trips, visits to museums and historical sites or other less structured activities offer excellent opportunities for parent-child interaction. If the parent spends individualized time with the child, even a trip to the local dump can be a very positive learning experience. With a large family, it may be difficult for parents to have individualized interactions with each child on a regular basis. Parents with more than one child should try to take a short mini-vacation with each of them. It need only be a visit to the zoo or an overnight camping trip to make the child feel special.

Perhaps the most important parental role from an educational standpoint is to encourage the child's receptivity to new learning opportunities. Children benefit from feeling that mutual respect and cooperation exist between their parents and their teachers. Having a positive attitude linking family and school also helps to provide the child with more of a sense of the tangible benefits of the educational process. Working parents are in an excellent position to provide the link between schooling and practical benefits. Either the father or the mother may be the individual in the family who has received the most obvious benefits from education. Parents can discuss the connection between the family's economic well-being and their education with the child.

Occupational Influences

Most children can be positively influenced by some exposure to their parents' occupational activities. What the father and mother do at work may not be very visible to the child, but the nature of their employment still greatly influences the quality of family functioning. In two-parent households, the father's occupation is typically the single most important determinant of the family's social and economic status. However, the interrelationship between the father's work and his parenting style is much more than just a reflection of his annual income. The type of work the father does, and how he feels about it, can influence his parenting style. For example, the father whose success depends upon assertiveness and independence is likely to encourage these characteristics in his child, whereas the parent whose job security is based on pleasing authority figures is more likely to value submissiveness and conformity. But the major issue transcending the father's occupation is his willingness to make a positive commitment to parenthood, sharing his interests and activities constructively with his child. Either chronic work dissatisfaction or career preoccupation can interfere with the father's ability to develop a close relationship with his child.

When the father's work schedule severely limits interaction with his child, the mother may also be restricted in her parenting effectiveness. By assuming all the family's domestic responsibilities, she may have little energy left for playful and stimulating activities with her child. Because of the father's unavailability, she may have fewer opportunities to participate in social endeavors with other adults, further limiting her effectiveness as a role model for her child. Even though the majority of mothers with young children are now employed, their jobs and career patterns are likely to be quite different from those of fathers. Compared to men, because of gender stereotypes women have not been as prepared for professional and technical jobs. They have tended to be channeled into certain occupations, such as secretary or clerk, or else trained for traditionally female careers, such as nursing and teaching.

Compared to the mother, it is still the father who is far more likely to have the opportunity to introduce the child to the world of the advanced professional or skilled technician. Daughters as well as sons need to learn about various career options. Both parents, if they are employed, should expose the child to some of the details of their work. When both parents are employed, the child is likely to know more about the mother's than the father's work. Even when they are employed, mothers tend to maintain primary parental responsibility for their children's activities. The work that the mother does outside of the home may also be much clearer to the child than are the occupational endeavors of the father. A lack of awareness about their father's work activities contributes to the paternal deprivation of many children.

Most fathers go off in the morning to do something that, at best, is usually very amorphous to their young children. When friends or even teachers ask children what kind of work their father does, the response they get all too often involves a comment that he gets in his car and drives away someplace every day. Not only the children of salesmen or bus drivers but many other preschoolers perceive that their fathers simply get paid for driving a vehicle, having no awareness of any of the actual details of their parent's career.

Although preschoolers may not be able to grasp the significance of their parents' jobs, they certainly are capable of articulating a more differentiated view than one simply involving the father or mother driving off in the morning and coming home at night. Parents may indeed find it difficult to expose their young children to their work. Nevertheless, even in those cases where children cannot directly observe their parents at work, they can still learn much about their specific job-related responsibilities. Parents can show the child pictures of where they work, verbally describe and role play details of their activities and in other ways share information about their occupations.

Children should at least have an occasional opportunity to spend some time with their parents at work. In the past there was good reason for excluding children from some work settings such as factories because they were quite dangerous places. Today, however, safety regulations are generally well enforced, and many parents work in offices where the most dangerous injury a child might sustain would be a paper cut. Most of the reasons that children are not encouraged to visit with their parents at work have nothing to do with health and safety issues.

Child Awareness

Parents may be surprised at the lack of information their children have about their careers. Whether three or thirteen years old, the child should be able to understand something about a parent's work. The older child would be expected to have a much more detailed grasp of parental job responsibilities, but even the younger one should be able to describe some of the kinds of activities a father or mother does at work.

Because of the nature of my career, I have always felt relatively comfortable taking my children to work with me. For example, my youngest son Benjamin, even when he was less than a year old, usually spent much time with me during weekdays while I was in my office and teaching classes at the University of Rhode Island. To some extent, it could be argued that I had a built-in rationale for bringing Benjamin to class since much of my teaching involves issues in child and family development. But my disposition to include my children is also very much related to my own very early and treasured memories of times that I was with my father or grandfather when they went to work. In fact, Benjamin was with me in Washington when I was invited to testify before the House of Representatives Select Committee on Children, Youth and Families in November 1983. He was five months old at the time, and I held him in my arms while discussing relevant research on the father's role in the family. Benjamin actually had his name entered into the proceedings twice by Representative Patricia Schroeder, cochair of the committee, thanking him for his very visible participation.

Even in a university setting, however, some people are uncomfortable when parents bring their children to work or to class with them. Negative as well as supportive comments were made by my colleagues regarding Benjamin's presence as an infant and toddler. Some graduate students and an occasional female faculty member have also brought infants to the university, but typically not on such a consistent basis. Great variability in employment settings exists, but parents should try to take their child to work with them at least a few times a year. As new phases of development are reached, the child will become more aware of different facets of a parent's work responsibilities.

Consider, for example, the situation of a parent who is involved in complex data analysis and economic projections at a large company. The toddler may be most interested in the office bubbler, candy or soda dispenser, but by age four the child will become more aware that the parent sometimes works with machinery with lots of lights and numbers. Within the next few years, the child will realize that the parent is working with computers and will gain some understanding of their operation. By the age of eleven or twelve, the child will probably be able to grasp that the parent does economic systems modeling and what that entails.

Many parents also have paperwork that they have to complete at home. I do a lot of writing, often at the dining room or kitchen table. As each of my children has matured, they have tended to adopt a particular mode of interacting with me while I am working. As toddlers, they typically climbed up on my lap to watch me for a few minutes or to scribble with pencil and paper "just like Daddy." When the children began getting homework in elementary school, they frequently did it sitting near me while I was working. As an infant, my son Benjamin would often see his older brothers Cameron and Michael doing school assignments as well as me working on a book. When he was about eighteen months old he sat next to me with a pencil and some paper, exclaiming that he, too, had "homework." To varying degrees my older children have helped me with my work, doing some proofreading or discussing an issue in family development.

Many parents are frustrated because their jobs demand a significant amount of overnight travel and separation from their children. However, work-related trips can provide excellent opportunities for parent-child involvement. If parents go on business trips, they should consider taking their child with them at least occasionally. In most cases, the child gets reduced airfare and typically little or no extra cost for the hotel room is involved. Even a relatively young child can greatly enjoy accompanying a parent on a business trip. Although the child may not understand the significance of meetings or conferences, there are usually intervals of time that allow for enjoyable interactions with the parent. During the parent's time off the child will certainly be stimulated by the sights of a new city. If the child is old enough, he or she may even choose to stay in the hotel room during some of the time the parent is at meetings in another part of the building. All the child has to do is dial the front desk in order to locate the parent if the switchboard has been notified beforehand. And, of course, many hotels provide child-care services if necessary.

Business trips can give parents the opportunity to get to know their child better and to share special and particularly memorable experiences. My older sons and I still fondly talk about professionally related trips that I took them on fifteen or even twenty years ago. Having one of my children along even made time spent in airports or train stations much more interesting than if I had been alone.

Differing Interests

Parents can also emphasize the relatively intangible benefits of education such as the increased ability to appreciate art, literature and music and the development of a broader social perspective. But the best way to encourage the child's interest in these aspects of life is by parental actions rather than by uttering platitudes about the importance of education. Exposing the child to parental activities can set a very vital example of the benefits of education. Having frequent opportunities to observe the self-educative behavior of parents provides the child with a particularly significant lesson. If the more formal educational process is to have ultimate meaning, it should serve as a catalyst to strengthen natural curiosity. The criterion of an excellent education is actually the degree to which it stimulates the individual's motivation to gain further understanding and knowledge outside of the classroom.

The child may seek new knowledge in areas different from the parent's interests. This can be an opportunity for the parent to learn along with the child. But whether or not the parent feels directly involved in the specific subject matter, it is important that the child perceives that self-directed learning is a valued process. Some parents get more enthusiastic about a son's or daughter's interest in science than they would if the same child became very involved with art or literature. Other parents have just the opposite reaction. Even if parents cannot enthusiastically relate to a particular educational activity, they should not devalue it.

Whatever their particular interests, enjoyment of reading is a great asset for parents and children. The child's reading skills are much influenced by parental example. Parents generally have more impact on their children's overall enjoyment of reading than do teachers. In a very extensive study of seventy thousand high school students in nine countries, educational researcher Alan Purves and his colleagues found that the home environment was the most critical factor related to student involvement in reading. Teachers typically did little to develop the aptitudes of their students to enjoy or analyze literature although they did play an important role in the acquisition of basic reading skills. The number of books and magazines in a student's home bore an even greater relationship to academic achievement than did family income or educational level. A student's motivation to read is likely to be much more affected by family experiences than it is by the particular type of teaching procedure used at school.

Parents should make sure that their child has ready access to books and magazines. I have always enjoyed taking my children to the library, partly because of my own interest in finding books we have not read before. In addition, many libraries have various exhibits and activities geared especially for children. Encouraging curiosity and the fun of learning is more important than the specific details that the parent may directly teach the child.

Parents should take a positive approach, sensitive to the child's individuality. They can purchase books tailored to the child's interests and, moreover, indicate by their own behavior that reading is a great leisure-time activity. Some young children, in fact, seem to increase their interest in books when they discover that their parents are more tolerant of letting them stay up late to read than to watch television. However, to try to force an activity that is not compatible with the child's interests may backfire despite the best of intentions. Being a good reader or conversationalist is not the measure of an individual's worth any more than being a good tennis player, dancer or flutist. People vary in what they value in others and in themselves. Intellectual pursuits should be encouraged, but the fundamental responsibility of a parent is to help the child develop a sense of self-worth.

Television Watching

Many social critics claim that television has had a very negative impact on the development of children. Certainly a fixation on television watching to the exclusion of other kinds of experiences can impede the child's development. However, television should not be used as a scapegoat to camouflage deficits in parental involvement. Unfortunately, in many families other types of nonpressured recreational opportunities for children are missing.

The relative seductiveness of television for young children, and individuals of all ages, is a function of what other alternative activities are available. For example, an enthusiastic offer by the father to play a game, to read a book or to go for a walk is a much better approach for redirecting the young child than simply unplugging the television set. If both the father and the mother are positively involved with the child, excessive television watching is unlikely. However, a problem definitely exists when television does become the primary socializer and the child is not actively involved with other family members and peers. Similarly, there can be a problem if parents sit in front of the television during and after meals, not communicating with one another or with their children. But so, too, is it detrimental if parents are always too busy working or engaged in other pursuits to spend relaxed times with their children. For some individuals, watching television is a way of relaxing; for others it becomes a mode of chronically avoiding interaction with others.

Children are more influenced by what their parents do than by what they say. Parents can set specific limits on television watching, both for themselves and for their children. These limits can be flexible to accommodate an unusual number of good programs in a given week. An effective way to teach children to plan ahead is to use a weekly television schedule, marking off selected programs. Both the parents and the child should be able to articulate their reasons for choosing a particular program. The parents can make it clear to the child that television is allowed only if chores, homework and other tasks have been completed in a responsible manner. This approach may be helpful for some but not all families. A more structured life-style fits better with the values and dispositions of some parents and children than it does for others. The important issue is to prevent television from becoming the dominating force in the family. Television can play a constructive role if it is kept in perspective.

Parental reactions to television programs can stimulate the child's learning. Though fathers and mothers who talk back to television commentators may seem to be easy targets for humorists and cartoonists, such parents may be demonstrating the value of critical thinking. Children should be brought up to realize that what they see on television is not necessarily the correct or whole story. Parents should not hesitate to be critical when they watch documentaries or other special programs. They can talk about the contents and discuss how the program relates to their own life and family. They can analyze the ploys behind commercials and particularly the flaws in logic contained in many advertisements to buy a product. Television has received especially strong criticism because it typically provides information without requiring very much thinking or initiative on the part of the viewer. However, many ways can be demonstrated to encourage children to take a more active approach while watching television.

Some issues similar to those relating to television are also involved with the explosion of computer technology directed at children and families. Most parents, especially if they can afford them, view home computers as providing very positive benefits to their children. Advertisers are even capitalizing on parents' fears that their children will not be able to keep up with peers in school unless they have access to a home computer. Potential disadvantages of computers are often overlooked in the zeal for state-of-the-art educational opportunities. As with television, the home computer can be an object that helps to isolate the child or parent from other family members and peers. Although it certainly does not have to be the case, a computer can also provide overly passive access to new information.

The danger is that the child will not be as stimulated to develop critical thinking processes if the answers to basic mathematical, scientific or other problems just require the pushing of a button. Similarly, with user-friendly word processors, the child may not need to have much of a concern for developing basic spelling and language-usage skills. Children should be encouraged to develop their intellectual skills in an active manner and not just to be mere button pushers. Boys and girls can learn to initiate and create computer programs, especially with the support and encouragement of parents and teachers. However, adults should also be wary of pressuring children into computer-related activities before they have developed more basic intellectual skills.

It is especially important to remember that children are likely to learn as much in informal interactions with nurturant adults as they are in highly structured information-oriented situations. In many families other adults in addition to parents may serve as significant resources.

Generational Links

Grandparents can provide many different types of positive experiences for their grandchildren. Sociologists Andrew Cherlin and Frank Furstenberg interviewed grandparents concerning their activities with their grandchildren during the previous twelve-month period. More than a third (38 percent) of grandparents reported taking a grandchild for day trips. Although most of them did not spend this kind of intense one-to-one activity with their grandchildren, emotionally nurturant interactions including talking about their own childhoods (77 percent) and giving advice (68 percent) were mentioned by the majority. Many grandparents alluded to other examples of their involvement, including discussion of the grandchild's problems (48 percent), teaching the child how to do something (24 percent) or helping to settle a parent-child disagreement (14 percent). Less socially active contacts, including providing money (82 percent) and watching television together (79 percent), were also mentioned by most grandparents.

Sadly, most grandparents and grandchildren do not seem to have particularly close relationships. Psychiatrist Arnold Kornhaber, interviewing more than three hundred school-age and adolescent children, discovered that only about 5 percent perceived a very close and positive relationship with their grandparents. However, much more self-acceptance and feelings of specialness occurred among children who were highly attached to their grandparents as compared to those who reported distant relationships. Strong grandparent-grandchild relationships were characterized by a mutuality and spontaneity in expressing love and unconditional acceptance. Children who were highly attached to their grandparents found it easy to relate to people of various ages. They had a generalized comfort toward elderly people and were less anxious about illness, aging and death-related issues. Having positive attachments with grandparents as well as parents broadened the child's ability to express sensitivity, empathy, compassion and humor.

In contrast, those children who were not close to their grandparents had greater discomfort with older people and more anxiety about illness and the aging process. They, perhaps realistically, perceived their grandparents in a negative way, often describing them in terms of their irascibility, insensitivity or intrusiveness. No special bond formed with grandparents when grandchildren had little contact with them, even in cases where evidence existed of much financial generosity. Paralleling some of my research findings concerning fathers and children, those grandchildren who had grandparents who were highly available in the sense of physical proximity but emotionally distant seemed to be at risk for difficulties in their personal adjustment.

Grandfathers are more likely to have distant relationships with their grandchildren than grandmothers are. Adult-child attachments need a foundation of caring and commitment. Adult males, whether fathers or grandfathers, have to be available and nurturant toward children for positively meaningful relationships to develop. Paternally deprived children are in special need of a supportive relationship with a grandfather. Either grandparent can play a highly significant role in helping the single-parent family expand its adult resources. However, given the general paternal deprivation in our society, even in two-parent families the presence of a positively involved grandfather may be particularly beneficial for children.

The mutual attachments between grandparents and grandchildren can be just as significant as those between parents and children. In fact, if it is strong, the grandparent-grandchild connection may have advantages because it is less likely to be fraught with underlying competitiveness and rivalry and more apt to be marked by mutual sharing and empathy. Becoming a first-time grandfather unleashed a complicated set of emotions for me. My basic reaction to my grandson Conor's birth was one of intense engrossment and pride. In addition to an even more strengthened connection with my son Jonathan, Conor's birth triggered especially intense feelings of identification with my beloved grandfather who was a major source of nurturance in my preschool years. But I also mourned the fact that my father had never had the chance to be a grandfather as I now was. Fortunately, most adults have continuing opportunities to further develop their self-understanding and nurturing capacities in the context of relationships with grandchildren.

SUMMARY

Fathers as well as mothers should strive to collaborate with teachers in supporting an active school-family partnership. The absence of adult male involvement in preschool and elementary school settings is a particular problem for many children. Paternal deprivation in the family is compounded by the lack of nurturing adult males during their early educational experiences. More participation by men, both formally and informally, is needed in programs serving young children.

Children with involved fathers generally experience much more success in school than those who come from paternally deprived families. It is important for the father to demonstrate consistent support, interest and encouragement for his young child's day-to-day school-related activities. However, the father can also contribute much to his child's education outside of school.

The father can include the young child in many types of activities that can greatly enhance and expand learning opportunities. He can involve the child in positive individualized endeavors that are unlikely to be encountered in the elementary school setting (or in the context of interacting with the mother or other female adults). He can also talk about his career-related activities, at least occasionally taking his child to work with him. Regardless of his occupation, he can model a curiosity about learning new things about people, places and events. On a more day-to-day basis, he can demonstrate his constructive approach to dealing with new situations whether commenting about something controversial on a television program or dealing with family issues. The grandfather, too, can do much to enrich the child's development, and strengthen intergenerational family connections.

FURTHER READING

Building Partnerships

Parent Involvement

On father availability and academic performance, see Blanchard and Biller (1971). For reviews of research linking paternal influence, cognitive functioning and academic achievement, see Biller (1974a, 1974b), Biller and Salter (1989), Biller and Solomon (1986), Radin (1976, 1981) and Shinn (1978).

For data relating to divorce, school behavior and academic performance, see Guidubaldi (1983), Guidubaldi and Perry (1984) and Hetherington, Cox and Cox (1978, 1982). Concerning father-absence, social class and reading achievement, see Dyl and Biller (1973). For academic problems often encountered by lower-class paternally deprived boys, see Biller (1974a, 1974b).

Correcting Imbalances

With regard to the so-called feminized classroom, see Biller (1974a, 1974b), Biller and Meredith (1974), Fagot and Patterson (1969) and Sexton (1969). On the lack of male teachers in early childhood education, see Biller and Meredith (1974), Gold and Reis (1982), Klinman (1986), Lee (1973) and Lee and Wolinsky (1973).

Learning Problems

About learning disabilities including those involved in reading handicaps, see Dusek (1985), Eccles (1987), Levinson (1980, 1984) and Silver (1984).

Concerning more extended analyses relating to gender stereotypes and academic interests, see Basow (1986), Biller (1974c), Lips (1988), Stein (1971) and Stein and Bailey (1973).

For data suggesting that boys respond well to programmed reading instruction, see McNeil (1964). For research suggesting that boys have fewer academic problems in societies in which there is a relatively high ratio of male teachers, see Biller (1974a, 1974b), Kagan (1969) and Preston (1962).

Needed Changes

On ways that girls as well as boys may be handicapped because of gender stereotypes in the classroom, especially as they advance beyond primary education, see Biller (1974a, 1974b), Busch-Rossnagel and Vance (1982), Klinman (1986), Sexton (1969), Stein (1971) and Stein and Bailey (1973). For reviews of research relating to gender stereotypes and educational issues, see Basow (1986), Eccles (1987) and Lips (1988).

For research indicating that competitive and achievement-oriented students perform well in flexible classrooms but that more dependent students need greater structure, see Peterson (1977). Regarding the educational disadvantagedness of the poor and many minority groups, see Bronfenbrenner (1967), Dusek (1985), Tharp (1989) and Zigler (1985).

Expanding Participation

About increasing the involvement of fathers and other men in early childhood education, see Biller and Meredith (1972, 1974), Klinman (1986), Klinman and Kohl (1984) and Sexton (1969).

Learning Opportunities

Constructive Homework

Concerning the negative side effects of overscheduling young children with unrealistic academic demands, see Elkind (1981, 1984, 1987), Kagan (1984) and Zigler (1987).

Sharing Activities

For relaxed parent-child play activities that may encourage intellectual development, see Biller and Meredith (1974), Segal and Adcock (1981), Singer and Singer (1977) and Sutton-Smith (1979). On the relevance of cooperative learning in the classroom and children's achievement, see Slavin (1987).

Occupational Influences

For detailed discussion of gender stereotypes and different employment patterns among men and women, see Basow (1986), Eccles and Hoffman (1984) and Lips (1988). On how parental occupation may influence the child's socialization, see Barclay, Stillwell and Barclay (1972), Benson (1968), Biller (1971a, 1975a, 1978, 1982a), Kohn (1979), Kohn and Schooler (1978), Lynn (1974, 1979), Piotrowski (1979), Pleck (1984, 1986) and Pleck and Staines (1985). For how four-day work schedules may contribute to fathers also spending more time with children throughout the week, see Maklan (1977) and Pleck (1986). For the negative effects of paternal job loss on children and families, see McLoyd (1989) and Ray and McLoyd (1986).

Child Awareness

With respect to issues relating to children visiting the parent's workplace, see Biller (1973a), Biller and Meredith (1974), Hughes and Galinsky (1988) and Pleck and Staines (1985). Regarding suggestions for balancing career and child-rearing responsibilities, see Biller and Meredith (1974), Brooks (1991), Grollman and Sweder (1986) and Loman (1984).

Differing Interests

For family influences that may stimulate children's interest and competence in reading, see Boegold (1984) and Purves (1973).

Regarding research indicating that family background generally has great impact on children's educational attainment, see Biller (1974a, 1974b), Biller and Salter (1989), Forehand et al. (1986), Lynn (1974, 1979) and Purves (1973). For the importance of the quality of schools and teachers, see Busch-Rossnagel and Vance (1982), Rutter (1983), Rutter et al. (1979) and Tharp (1989).

Television Watching

About the impact of television, as well as practical suggestions for parents in encouraging constructive viewing habits for their children, see Liebert and Spratkin (1988) and Singer and Singer (1987).

Concerning some developmental implications of computer usage, see Galinsky and David (1988), Lepper and Gurtner (1989), Lockheed (1985) and Marone (1988).

Generational Links

For data detailing the variations in quality of grandparent-grandchild relationships and their significance for both the child and the adult, see especially Cherlin and Furstenberg (1988), Kornhaber (1987) and Radin, Oyserman and Benn (1991).

Regarding specific dimensions of the male's parenting behavior that seem to facilitate positive development, see Biller (1971a, 1974c, 1982a) and Reuter and Biller (1973). For gender factors relating to grandparent-grandchild relationships, see Bengston (1985), Cherlin and Furstenberg (1988), Haggerson (1981) and Thomas (1986).

8

Assertiveness and Independence

Gender stereotypes have generally supported males in being assertive and independent while inhibiting females from expressing themselves in ways that could be construed as aggressive or competitive. Fathers have especially important roles in supporting both their sons and their daughters to develop a constructive sense of assertiveness and independence, to be achievement-oriented without succumbing to the traditional masculine stereotype of disregard for the feelings and welfare of others. In fact, assertiveness and interpersonal sensitivity complement one another in contributing to healthy personality functioning.

ENCOURAGING ASSERTIVENESS

Important distinctions are to be made between different types of aggressive and assertive behavior. Assertiveness refers to the ability selectively and advantageously to demand one's rights. Physical aggressiveness is one way of expressing assertiveness, but it may become seriously maladaptive if it is directed at hurting others.

Gender Variations

Cross-cultural research has consistently revealed gender differences in physically aggressive behavior. From birth onward males are the more physically aggressive of the two sexes. Boys play rougher, get into trouble and court danger more than girls do. Although girls are capable of rough-and-tumble play and many are highly competent in athletically demanding activities, a far greater proportion of boys seem motivated to engage in intense and strenuous physical endeavors. In most subcultures, boys also receive much more encouragement for physical aggression from parents, other adults and peers than do girls. But certainly some girls become physically aggressive while many boys remain quite inhibited even when their level of frustration is very high. Temperamental variations among individuals are ultimately more significant than gender differences. Average group differences between boys and girls in aggressive behavior represent just another example of the intermix of biological predispositions and social expectations.

Regardless of the individual's gender, it is important to distinguish between physically assertive behavior and maladaptive aggression. Both an assertive and a negatively aggressive child may punch someone in the nose. However, the assertive child does it only when necessary—in self-defense or when defending others. In contrast, overly aggressive children may feel an inner need to react to frustration by hurting others. Assertiveness has a definite and important place in an individual's life and is not a trait to be smothered in either boys or girls. Achievement, confidence, independence and even nurturance all have elements of assertiveness in them because they all require extension of the self outward to others and to the physical environment.

Constructive Responses

There are many dimensions of assertive behavior. Being assertive does not only relate to responding to certain situations in a physically aggressive manner. It also means making oneself heard, standing up for one's rights and having the confidence to do something one thinks is right even when it is an unpopular choice or others say it is futile. Learning to be assertive in a constructive manner is a crucial factor in developing a healthy sense of control in one's life. Children need to learn how to be effective in communicating their choices and preferences. They need the confidence to resist arbitrary power assertion from others, including parents and teachers as well as peers.

Although individuals may differ in their temperamental dispositions toward various expressions of assertive behavior, it is important to support each child's feeling of having an influence in day-to-day endeavors. Becoming adequately self-assertive is also a major way for a child to avoid being maltreated by adults or peers. Learning how to protect oneself from being manipulated, sometimes simply by saying no, is just as important for the young child as it is for the adolescent or adult.

In two-parent households, the adult who is most influential either in a positive or negative way with respect to children's assertiveness is often the father. He is usually bigger and stronger than other family members and he typically represents more of a potential physical threat than the mother. The father may offer an especially potent model for assertiveness. Compared to the mother, he is likely to be naturally more aggressive and also to be more often in situations where self-assertion is expected.

On the other hand, the poor conduct of the inappropriately aggressive child is frequently very much related to the father's negative parenting behavior. Ironically, parents who use physical punishment in response to aggressive behavior may stimulate their children to act out even more. Many overly aggressive children have parents who punish them physically, restrict their activities and refuse to allow them to express any anger constructively in their presence. Children often display hostile behavior toward peers because they are frustrated by parental punitiveness but cannot retaliate in any direct manner. Furthermore, they tend to imitate what they observe in the behavior of their parents. If a parent resorts to frequent physical violence toward family members, the child may come to see force as a preferred form of action to use in dealing with peers.

However, the parent's and child's behavior do not always match directly. Highly punitive parents may in fact stimulate very different behavior patterns depending on how much they are generally nurturant to their children. If a parent is cold and punitive, the child may become overly aggressive. On the other hand, having parents who are relatively nurturant but also highly punitive may contribute to the development of a submissive, excessively conforming son or daughter. Children need to learn to discriminate between when aggression is appropriate and when it is destructive. As long as the child's expression of frustration or anger does not extend to abusive behavior toward others, it can be a healthy outlet for intense feelings.

If the child's behavior begins to get out of hand, parents can provide a cooling-off period. They can help to provide a calm atmosphere for the child to voice complaints and frustrations. Tensions can be lowered even if no immediate solution to the problem is available. Many parents feel that a child's anger represents either a threat to them or a sign of ungratefulness. Parents should, rather, see their child's anger as a natural reaction to an affront or frustration. As the child matures, anger becomes more differentiated, more directed at both self-failure and disappointment at the unreasonable behavior of others. A forth-right sense of indignation, based on a sound set of values, is a trait to be treasured in a child as well as an adult. Parents who can express their frustration in a specific but nonhostile manner provide a good example for their children. Making a comment about what is wrong with someone else's behavior without attacking their character is an important talent to be nourished in both adults and children.

Expressing Frustrations

It can be difficult to learn to be assertive in the context of the traditional adult definition of being a "good" child. Extreme deference and restraint toward authority figures and other adults is all too often considered the hallmark of the well-behaved child. Such expectations can encourage a child to become inhibited and passive instead of being constructively assertive. Most children can be encouraged to use assertiveness intelligently and selectively. They can learn to challenge effectively the opinions of authority figures including parents with a diplomatic style of disagreement.

Parents sometimes make the mistake of encouraging their children to be assertive without also focusing on appropriate self-control. Charlie, an energetic six-year-old, was sent to the school counselor because he was continually getting into fights with peers. If a child bumped into him in the lunch line or Charlie thought someone made a face at him, he would immediately lash out at the child. School personnel became increasingly concerned about Charlie's indiscriminate aggressiveness, and his parents were asked to meet with his teacher and the school counselor. When Charlie's behavior was described by the teacher, his father responded with pride rather than dismay. He insisted that Charlie was just acting assertively whenever he felt there was an infringement of his rights. Charlie's father was pleased that his son would tell him every time he had been in a fight at school. The father's reaction would be to laugh and then congratulate him for his aggressiveness. Charlie's mother voiced agreement and smiled as her husband described their child-rearing philosophy.

Rather than simply discussing the child's behavior in the abstract, the principal gave Charlie's parents the opportunity to observe their son during recess at the school playground. Though Charlie had never been a discipline problem at home, his father watched him punch a boy for not throwing a ball to him, take a jump rope away from a girl and kick another child who was in his way. Charlie's parents finally began to realize that merely encouraging aggressiveness without any consideration for the rights of others was not a sound parenting approach.

Some children need special attention in learning an appropriate degree of self-control to modulate their natural aggressiveness. Others are more likely to struggle with pressures that overly inhibit their aggressive tendencies. Compared to boys, girls receive much less support from adults and peers for being assertive. The emphasis in the socialization of girls focuses more on physical restraint. Many young females are instructed that it is never proper to fight or argue, regardless of the circumstances. Parents must recognize that daughters as well as sons need support in developing the ability to be assertive in a confident and constructive manner.

Innate differences occur among children in their proclivity to be assertive, but parents should try to avoid gender stereotypes. While females are told that nobody likes pushy or bossy women, their male counterparts are admired if they are dynamic, assertive or natural leaders. Parents should give both sons and daughters the confidence to see through this restrictive double standard. The individuality of each child deserves support and encouragement.

Permitting Disagreement

Much of the child's attitude toward authority figures is related to interactions with parents. Fathers and mothers should strive to consider calmly their child's opinions and preferences, even when they run counter to their own viewpoint.

Parent-child discussion is crucial in establishing a constructive family learning process. The opportunity to express and discuss opinions freely with parents provides a basis for the child's growing ability to interact both sensitively and assertively with other adults. Rather than evolving into power struggles, meaningful parent-child discussions can become more the rule than the exception. Incidentally, but very importantly, such family interactions can do much to stimulate the child's verbal communication skills.

How parents argue with their children can have a great deal to do with fostering constructive assertiveness. Many parents find it difficult to use positive techniques in resolving conflicts with their children. If they come home tired from a day of controversy with their colleagues at work, they may be very reluctant to discuss anything with their child. Or they may make any conversation a contest of wills, refusing to acknowledge the child's viewpoint. Given their greater experience, it is also true that parents are usually more realistic in their arguments, especially compared to young children. However, even the young child's viewpoint should be respected and taken into consideration. Merely to dismiss a child's ideas because they are based on less life experience is not a constructive parenting approach. Intelligent, patient argument helps to teach the child that the governing force behind parental decisions is reason rather than arbitrary power. It reinforces the value of using a rational approach in dealing with others. The father or mother who refuses to discuss issues may find that their child has decided that tantrums and threats are an effective tool in influencing others. When parents allow discussion, they also teach their child to use verbal assertiveness rather than physical intimidation.

Discussion with a two-year-old and a twelve-year-old differs greatly. However, when parents exhibit patience, even two-year-olds may be surprisingly cooperative. On the other hand, twelve-year-olds may still be throwing tantrums if parents have not exhibited a respectful attitude toward their feelings during earlier childhood. Fathers and mothers who do not listen to their children are likely to have sons and daughters who seem totally uninterested in parental opinions. One ironic but all too typical example involved a family with a fifth-grader referred for help with a severe discipline problem. During the first family session, the father reported that the child never listened to him. He obsessively recounted how pleas to stop unwarranted behavior were constantly ignored by the child. After being subjected to several minutes of parental criticism, the son started to say something but was promptly interrupted by his father who told him to be quiet while he was talking.

Building Confidence

Even if they disagree, the parent and child should pay attention to each other's point of view. Rather mundane situations can serve as learning experiences for both child and parent. For example, take the case of a parent and child argument regarding the trade name of a particular brand of cookies. The father insisted the cookies were called Nabiscoes, but the young son corrected him by saying that they were Biscoes. The son abruptly got up from the table, stood on a chair and pulled out the box of cookies from the kitchen cupboard. He proudly showed his father that he was right by pointing to the label on the cereal box. The father admitted his mistake and congratulated his son for being so perceptive. Had this father been like some parents, he would have thoughtlessly demeaned the child's comment, criticizing him for being disrespectful. Instead, he allowed his son to assert himself and gather evidence for his case, giving the boy his due when it turned out that he was right.

Family discussions can provide parents with opportunities to examine their own underlying biases. They may react very illogically and inappropriately when their point of view is questioned by their child. Give-and-take family discussions can do much to stimulate the parent's insight as well as to foster a child's intellectual growth, independence and assertiveness. Constructive parenting does not mean always letting the child's opinion prevail any more than it calls for the adult being tyrannical. Rather, as much as possible, a meaningful resolution to disagreements should occur, where neither the adult nor the child feels like a loser. On a more general level, the child can learn that it is all right for two people who love and respect one another to have differences of opinion.

There is no single ideal family atmosphere. When either parent or child is very emotionally reactive, more conflict in the family is apt to occur. More stress is also likely when several children close in age are in the household. Nevertheless, it is important for the parent, within his or her own limitations, to try to give each child an opportunity to express opinions and preferences while also providing a clear frame of reference.

Every parent, at some time or other, exclaims (or shouts) "Do it because I told you so!" or "You don't have a choice, I'm the boss." But it must be realized that fathers and mothers who consistently take such an authoritarian approach are not encouraging the child's assertiveness and self-confidence. What an appropriate level of discussion is varies from child to child. A very sensitive child may be intimidated at a slight increase in the parent's tone of voice whereas a more resilient one may be impervious to seemingly intimidating words.

A major parenting goal should be to help children feel confidence in expressing their needs and opinions. This is not the same as fostering a belief in children that they can control the lives of parents, other family members or friends. Children should feel that they are effective individuals while at the same time respecting the needs and rights of others. Parents can encourage their children's self-confidence by being attentive to their strengths. If done thoughtfully, parents can also strengthen their child's confidence by being realistic about their own weaknesses. Effective parenthood involves honest self-reflection.

The parent may be a great golfer but a poor swimmer, excellent at thinking up new ideas but abysmal at following through on details; may feel right at home with machines or mathematical concepts but very uncomfortable in large social gatherings. Whatever their limitations, parents can try to disclose them constructively to their child. A major mistake that many parents make is to try and appear to be moral and physical superpersons to their children. The child should become aware of the fact that every individual has limitations but that these do not have to affect his or her overall happiness or competence as a human being. Men typically have a much more difficult time than women in talking about their weaknesses, for they have been socialized to emphasize achievement and to fear failure of any kind.

Parental Disclosure

Sometimes a child finds great comfort in knowing that a parent has encountered a similar problem. A young man was embarrassed to tell his peers that he invariably got seasick in even slightly choppy water. He was always quite self-conscious whenever he was on a boat, thinking it was unmasculine to admit such feelings. After one particularly horrid bout of seasickness, he reluctantly confided this problem to his father. Despite having never mentioned it for the first twenty-five years of his son's life, the father finally admitted that he too got severely ill in boats. The father further confided to the son that this was the reason why he had never taken him deep-sea fishing even though they lived only ten miles from the ocean. Needless to say, the son felt a great measure of relief, knowing that not only he but also his revered father was prone to seasickness.

Parents who frankly discuss their shortcomings can have a much broader effect than just aiding the child's personal sense of confidence. A realistic view of parents, including their faults, can be related to a relatively objective evaluation of the outside world. When children are not allowed to see that their parents have shortcomings, they may deify them in a very simplistic manner. Children cannot hope to match the illusions of perfection that parents may encourage about themselves. Children brought up in an authoritarian and perfectionistic family atmosphere are likely to have feelings of hostility toward individuals and groups who do not fit into the neat but rigidly defined picture their parents have given of the world.

Admitting current weaknesses can be very uncomfortable for some parents. Perhaps not so difficult to share are the trials and troubles experienced when they were children. For instance, if a child is frustrated in a particular course, parents can reveal the subjects that they had trouble with in school. A child may be amazed and relieved to hear that a seemingly accomplished parent was not always a whiz in math or spelling. Parental self-revelation also can convey the confidence that it is possible to overcome childhood limitations and grow up to be a competent adult. Admitting that I was not a very successful student until I was in college actually seemed to make my children less anxious about their performance in school.

Each parent has his or her unique blend of strengths and weaknesses. What is important is that children realize that their parents are real people. Some disclosure about parental frustrations and failures as well as successes during childhood can help the child have a more realistic view of life. The child can profit from the perspective that difficulties at one phase in development do not necessarily translate into lifetime limitations. The parents' ability to view themselves in a realistic manner makes it much easier for their child to develop a more objective self-concept. Realizing that a parent, although admirable, is not perfect helps the child to achieve a more balanced self-acceptance and to be responsive to well-placed criticism.

If parents disclose the long, difficult road they traversed in gaining some skill, be it bowling or calculus, the child may gain confidence that he or she can do it too. Parents should support the child's areas of interest and competence, not focus on shortcomings. Similar to adults, children, at least by the time they reach school age, can become all too obsessed with their deficiencies rather than feeling satisfaction with their positive qualities.

SUPPORTING INDEPENDENCE

The developing child expresses some individualized blend of relatively independent exploration and need for parental reassurance. Keep in mind that there
are varying subtypes of independence and dependence. Because individuals demonstrate a relatively mature sense of independence does not mean that they are
without any need for being dependent on others. For example, well-adjusted
individuals have the competency to carry out many tasks by themselves but at
the same time have the motivation to form intimate relationships to meet their
needs for emotional support.

Child Needs

To push a young child to focus overly on a particular activity whether it is
reading, tennis, swimming or playing the violin may interfere with well-rounded
functioning and, just as significantly, inhibit a sense of control and self-
determination. It is the parent's responsibility to provide a supportive environment, but this does not mean that the very young child needs to be pressured
with special lessons and highly structured learning opportunities.

Unless severely impaired, individuals regardless of age or maturational level
naturally strive, within their limitations, for a sense of mastery and self-
fulfillment. A propensity toward influencing one's environment is inherently
human whether it emanates from the infant or the elderly adult. The drive for
mastery and control is a continuing motivation throughout life, though it is greatly
affected by individual differences and social opportunities. Children have a
remarkable innate capacity to relate to their environment in a way that is interesting to them and is commensurate with their own maturational level. What
children need most is emotional support and realistic concern for their safety
but not excessive channeling or coaching. Given loving interest by parents, they
will typically communicate their need for help or their desire to do things by
themselves.

Just because a certain birthday has been attained, or because parents or other
siblings at a similar age were functioning in a particular way, does not mean
that a son or daughter will necessarily manifest the same capabilities or interests.
Allowing some latitude in achieving specific milestones and competencies is
crucial in the child's development of self-acceptance and a sense of well-being.
The importance of parental sensitivity to developmental readiness does not just
apply to early childhood. At later phases of the child's development, premature
parental pressure can lead to family conflicts. An undue focus on academic,
athletic or social accomplishments can lead to problems for the parents as well
as the child.

A theme throughout this book is on simultaneous parent and child growth.
The parent's continuing sensitivity to the child's uniqueness is essential throughout development. Family functioning is enhanced when parents can differentiate

between their own needs and interests and those of the child, often a very difficult accomplishment.

Parental beliefs concerning appropriate child-rearing techniques are very much influenced by values relating to the alleged essence of human nature. Many parents view the child's basic nature as one that must be inhibited or rechanneled. According to such a value system, the child is destined to be wild, uncontrollable, selfish and aggressive unless rigidly socialized. From this perspective, parents and the family are viewed as forces to reshape the supposedly resistant, narcissistic and self-indulgent nature of the child. This is a far too gloomy view of the basic nature of children. Given adequate parental attention, children are innately predisposed toward identifying and empathizing with others. Even infants have an inherent proclivity to respond to nurturant care and actively relate to others.

The parenting process also provides fathers and mothers with the opportunity to improve their nurturing skills and, in a sense, to continue to be positively socialized while being responsible for the welfare of children. Optimally, both parents and children become better people because of family connections. Human beings have at least as much potential for kindness and generosity as they do for self-centered destructiveness. Much of how well the child develops a balanced concern for others is a function of the quality of treatment received from parents. Children who are consistently derogated, criticized, neglected or otherwise mistreated are not likely to develop into caring, sensitive and kind individuals.

Providing Choice

As much as possible the child should be allowed to make choices, as long as these decisions are not destructive and do not grossly impinge on the freedom and rights of others. A young child wanting a sandwich for breakfast, wearing one green and one red sock, demanding to stay up another half-hour or insisting on going outside in rather cool weather without a sweater may offend the parent's sense of order. However, such seemingly immature choices need not be harmful to either child or parent. For example, it is far better for the resistant child to choose voluntarily to put on a readily available sweater, once outside and after realizing it is cold, than to succumb angrily to parental pressure to wear extra clothing before leaving the house. The more children feel in control concerning areas that are important to them, as long as the parents' and others' rights are not infringed upon, the more they may attain a healthy sense of self-confidence.

Parents vary greatly in their ability to comfortably allow children to make choices. Some parents are very concerned about predetermined structures or have particular areas where deviance from expectation is especially troublesome for them. On the other hand, children have a basic desire to structure their environment in a personalized way if given a chance to do so. A frequent cry of dismay by parents is that their young child (or adolescent) wants complete self-determination. Parents often express their frustration as if childrens' desires to make all their own decisions are unnatural. It is basic to human nature to want to control one's environment. Certainly at times an individual feels anxious, uncomfortable, fears the unknown or wants to defer a decision to someone else, but in general, the desire for self-determination is a basic human disposition.

This is not to deny that there are constitutionally based individual differences, as well as subcultural variations, that influence motivation for self-determination. Some children have special problems dealing with externally imposed structure while others appear helpless when not being given adult directives. Some children will, within their physical capabilities, rather passively conform to almost any parental demand. Positive adjustment involves a balance between self-interest and concern for others. Being considerate is not the same as always conforming to the expectations of others. The child must acquire a respect for the rights of others and the ability to empathize with their particular situations.

A child does not have the right to go around hurting other individuals, whether they be peers or adults. A child does not have the right to abuse others or their property. Limits need to be set more firmly for some children than for others, but boys and girls have an increasing capacity to make positive decisions about how they choose to treat other people. Many adults who decry the child's striving for control are frustrated themselves because they are relatively passive pawns with respect to the expectations of others. Such parents can resent the child's potential freedom, and they demonstrate a displaced need to program greater conformity.

Although young children are often depicted as thoroughly egocentric, their capacity for caring and nurturance for others is also quite evident. Empathy is an inherent human tendency. As children mature, their consideration of the needs of others expands, at least when they have had an opportunity to grow up in a loving, supportive family. As they advance through development, children develop a respect for the time and space of others if they have been treated with kindness and consideration. Allowing children to make concrete choices in turn provides them with a basis for respecting their parents' preferences for particular activities. More specifically, children who are nuturantly allowed to choose how they spend their time are more likely to understand a parent's decision to read a book, talk to another family member or do something else rather than immediately engaging in an activity with them. Receiving consistent parental support for personal choice, the growing child begins to realize the importance of mutual respect among family members for their separate and individual preferences. All individuals need to develop some sense of control over their time and activities, whether they be children or adults.

Stimulating Initiative

Children need to develop a positive sense of autonomy at their own pace. As much as possible, parents should take their cues from the child. Parents should consider their child's individuality and remember that maturation is an ongoing process. What counts is that the child is making some gradual improvement in developing more independent patterns of behavior. In learning to tie shoelaces, young children may at first only succeed in constructing some incredible knots, but they will eventually master this surprisingly complex process. Children profit from parental patience and encouragement whether it is learning how to tie shoelaces, ride a bike, add numbers or hit a baseball.

Fostering independence provides a good example of the advantage for the child of having two actively involved parents. A father's encouragement of a child's independence often offsets a mother's overprotective tendencies. Excessively mothered children without men in their lives are much less likely to be allowed exploratory freedom or to be encouraged to develop an assertive and independent attitude. Mothers may tend to be overprotective, especially with their firstborn, while fathers may prematurely expect an unrealistic degree of autonomy and independence, particularly from a male child. When both parents are involved in child rearing, their combined expectations usually result in a more realistic and less extreme approach. The sharing of parenting responsibilities by the father and mother can have a healthy modulating effect as they learn from each other's behavior.

Compared to men, women are more likely to have been reared as if they were fragile and delicate creatures. Women treated in this manner tend to be overly fearful of injury and are likely to stifle their children's attempts for active play and exploration. On the other hand, mothers can offset the common tendency of fathers to pressure children unrealistically toward excessive self-reliance or independence. However, in some households the father may be the most over-protective parent, especially if he has a daughter.

In most families, clear differences tend to occur in the types of relationships that boys and girls have with their parents. Girls typically feel closer to their parents and less pressured to become independent. Boys usually receive greater encouragement to spend time outside the family with peers and in contact with the broader society. Boys do look to their parents for support, but the attention they receive becomes increasingly connected to accomplishments away from their household. The greater support that boys receive to strike out on their own is related to a complex intermix of biological and social factors. Young girls tend to be less aggressive but more advanced in self-control than boys at a similar age. In general, prior to adolescence girls are typically easier for parents to control than more intensely active boys.

Parents may also not encourage independence in their daughters because they see them as more vulnerable to physical harm as compared to their sons. Fathers, in particular, tend to be much more protective of daughters than sons. Much of the family's and society's protective attitude toward females relates to concern that they will be sexually abused or otherwise physically intimidated by stronger males. In actuality, many females can more than hold their own in confrontations with men. Nevertheless, parents have a responsibility for the safety and well-being of their children. Parents can help their daughters as well as their sons by providing instruction in self-defense and ways to respond to emergencies. Most of all they can encourage an assertive, independent attitude for making decisions so that the child is less likely to be taken advantage of by others.

Our social structure does not provide enough support for females to develop a sense of control over their lives. But unrealistic fears should not prevent parents from nurturing competency in their daughters. Although parents may still feel more protective toward a daughter than a son, they should not let their attitude interfere with her becoming assertive and independent. Parents should carefully consider whether they are unnecessarily restricting their daughter's independence. For example, her request to take a bus into the city by herself or to go on a hike without adult supervision should be treated with respect. They should take into account how mature she is, if the activity is really dangerous or whether they are being overly protective just because she is a female.

Relationships with both parents often generalize to the child's broader social functioning. In particular, a girl who has been encouraged by her father to be independent in making decisions, while at the same time knowing that she can count on him for love and support, will probably develop very positive relationships with other males later in her life.

Achievement Motivation

Having a strong sense of self-esteem and independence gives the child a solid basis for developing a high degree of positive achievement motivation. Such motivation can also contribute to the growth of the child's intellectual, athletic and other talents. No matter how gifted, individuals will never fully develop their potential without some motivation for achievement. Assuming a nurturant family relationship, parents who expect to succeed in their own endeavors are very likely to pass this attitude on to their offspring. Parents who encourage initiative, autonomy and independence foster achievement motivation in their children. At the same time, parents should not be so obsessed with particular types of achievement that they are overly critical of their children, or so impatient as to not allow them the luxury of learning from mistakes.

The behavior of both parents can do much to influence the achievement motivation of children. Traditionally, fathers have been the parents who most clearly have presented models of achievement in outside-of-the-home endeavors. Fathers of low-achieving children have often been found to be relatively neglectful and uninvolved in their children's lives. Children who have obvious potential to succeed but nevertheless do poorly often have parents who relate to them in a very limited way, tending to respond only to what they perceive as problem behavior.

For example, many academically low-achieving children have what might be termed a "report-card father." Such a parent does not really have much to do with his children, except when it comes time to sign their report cards. The report-card father enters into a cycle of bribing, cajoling and demanding that the child get better grades. He may even help his child with homework for a few nights. He may do the whole assignment because he is unwilling or does not know how to encourage the child more positively. Within a week or so, however, this kind of father is again preoccupied with his own endeavors until it is report-card time again.

Although it is probably not the father's conscious intention, he is actually giving the child much more attention for poor performance than he provides on a day-to-day basis for competent behavior. It is not surprising that some children repeatedly perform poorly given that their negative behavior elicits such a strong response from their otherwise aloof parent. Parents need to convey an appreciation of their children's particular abilities whether or not they extend to academic endeavors.

Parents may stimulate a very narrow view of success and achievement. Lionel, a self-made millionaire, was quite influenced by his workaholic father. The only real contact Lionel had with his father was in the context of observing his day-to-day business dealings. His father constantly reminded his son that a preoccupation with making the right deal was the key to success but otherwise had little to communicate about life. Though Lionel became a very wealthy real-estate promoter, he had serious problems with his marriage and his children. He knew little about how to function as a man outside of his business. He had learned from his father only to value financial success.

Some father-neglected individuals become obsessed with achieving, continually seeking approval for their actions in the form of money, fame or power. Yet underneath their material success, they are usually not happy with their lives. The father should be involved enough in family life so that his children have a whole man for a parent. It is important for parents to encourage a perspective that involves leading a successful life rather than just providing a narrow focus on academic, athletic or financial achievement. Parents who communicate pride in both their career achievement and their committed involvement with their children are the best role models. The child with a father and mother who gain satisfaction from both a career and parenting is at a definite advantage.

Having parents who are achievement-oriented can be very positive for children if it is in the context of warm, supportive family relationships. But children's avoidance of achievement-related activities often represents a reaction against parents, especially fathers, who have overemphasized their work activities at the expense of family involvement. Financial security without positive family relationships is likely to end up being very unsatisfying for both children and parents. Fathers and mothers should be careful to emphasize other values in addition to educational and economic success. A person can be just as unhappy from a lack of personal commitment as from a low salary. A child should be encouraged to strive for self-esteem and a sense of self-determination in addition to getting a good education and a well-paid job.

Encouraging Females

Until relatively recently, females have not been given much support to achieve in the world outside of the home. While men traditionally have been socialized to be concerned with achievement in business, industry or science, women have been encouraged to view home and family as their chief or exclusive spheres of accomplishment. A focus on domestic endeavors can be a challenging arena, but many females have been channeled into circumscribed roles that do not fit with their own individualized blend of aspirations and competencies. Compared to males, females tend to define their achievement and self-worth more according to relationships with others. Males, on the other hand, tend to take more pride in task-oriented achievements. A daughter needs to realize that a sense of achievement and independence can be a meaningful characteristic of her feminine identity just as a son should enlarge his concept of masculinity to include the importance of caring and sensitive relationships.

Parents should value a sense of achievement within their conceptions of femininity. They should make it clear to their daughter that they perceive her as positively feminine, whether she wants to be an engineer or a housewife. They should be at least as appreciative of her when she earns a top grade on a math test as when she prepares a delicious family meal. By helping their daughter to have solid confidence in her femininity, regardless of her activities, they are supporting her to develop a broader range of competencies. The father's encouragement of achievement is particularly significant because the support of men is vitally needed to help overcome lingering. social resistance to women actualizing their potential in traditionally masculine endeavors.

Researchers have found that many women actually seem to fear certain types of success. They are afraid that if they achieve in traditionally masculine arenas, they will be considered aggressive and unfeminine. They fear that the potential consequences of success may involve being rejected by friends, lovers and family. Psychologist Matina Horner, in the 1970s, found this type of fear vividly illustrated in research she did with college students. She provided female students with the following sentence: ''After first-term finals, Anne finds herself at the top of her medical school class.'' She then requested that they use the sentence to write a story. She gave the male students a similar task, except that the sentence contained the name of John instead of Anne. Stories written by males tended to emphasize John's dedication, striving, achievement-orientation and self-confidence. Females, in marked contrast to males, wrote stories emphasizing Anne's conflict between doing well in medical school and her anxiety concerning romantic relationships. Common story endings by females involved Anne deliberately reducing her level of performance, getting married and dropping out of medical school.

More recent research has revealed other factors besides achievement motivation that influence gender differences in response to such story completion tasks. For instance, females writing nonachievement story endings may not be reflecting their own personal attitudes but rather responding to task instructions that elicit traditional views about women. In any case, Horner's research was very important in dramatically highlighting clear-cut gender stereotypes that discourage many females from pursuing certain types of career achievements.

Lessening Inhibitions

Parents should reassure their children that they need not fear success. The father's support can be especially important for his daughter since he can serve as a clear counterforce to prevalent male biases. If the daughter is ridiculed by her classmates for being too smart or too aggressive, he can help her to maintain her sense of self-worth. He can assure her that although some males are indeed threatened by competent women, he and many others find them to be very admirable and attractive. In the course of giving support to his daughter's particular brand of achievement motivation, the father is acting as a forerunner of men to whom she may be attracted later in her life. He is giving her the confidence that she will encounter men who will accept her achievement orientation and that she will be able to have a healthy, sharing relationship with them. The father should make her aware that she will also come into contact with many men and women who equate femininity with incompetence, but he should encourage her to be confident enough not to be inhibited by such attitudes.

Along with supporting his daughter's motivation for achievement, it is important that the father shows his respect for her mother as a competent individual. Children greatly benefit from observing two involved, mutually supportive parents. It is in the child's best interests to have a father and mother who accept and support each other's respective competencies.

Parents should also remember that more than one path leads to self-fulfillment. The daughter, despite the father's and mother's active encouragement, may simply not be interested in achievement with respect to a career. Both parents should value their daughter's individuality and her right to choose actively the type of life-style that fits her needs and goals. Many women today, including some who blossom into achievers in nondomestic endeavors only after several years of being wives and mothers, may have to establish their femininity with a husband and children before they can become motivated enough to pursue a long-term career. Different sequences of achievement fit some individuals better than others.

If a daughter does not feel any incompatibility between being feminine and career-oriented, she will be less likely to use a husband and children as the total basis for her identity. Those women who first complete their education and have a successful career may enjoy more egalitarian family relationships when they later marry and become mothers. Indeed, they may present their own daughters with especially effective examples of feminine competence.

The mother is a very significant role model for her daughter. If she is happy with being a parent and with working, her daughter more likely will view both roles in a positive way. However, if she resents working or sees parenting responsibilities as a detriment to her career, her daughter is less likely to be positively motivated to be both a mother and a career woman. The daughter's long-term aspirations can be very much influenced by the degree of warmth in her relationship with her mother. If the daughter feels that she always plays second fiddle to her mother's work, she may be very ambivalent about pursuing a career for herself. The father's support of the child and the mother is very important. The daughter who feels close to an attentive father is less likely to resent a working mother, especially if he is also supportive of his wife's career.

Increasing Options

Parents should try to be supportive of their child's interests, even if they do not fit neatly into traditional stereotypes. For instance, a daughter may have aspirations to become a civil engineer or a neurosurgeon rather than to plan for some more traditionally feminine career.

Cindy at fourteen was a positive example of a girl already well on her way to exceptional intellectual accomplishment in a nontraditional career. She was a brilliant student, especially gifted in math, and had already been accepted into a calculus course usually open only to juniors and seniors. Her father, an accountant, was proud of her achievements. One day, however, Cindy came home from school in a very somber mood after she had deliberately done poorly on a calculus test. Her father tried to find out what had happened, but initially could not get an answer from Cindy. Finally, in tears, she told her father that the othe: girls in the class were very critical of her because she was doing so much better than everyone else. The next day she admitted that she became particularly self-conscious when she discovered that she had scored higher on the previous exam than Jimmy, a very bright eleventh-grader. She had hoped that Jimmy would invite her to his junior prom, but her female peers had told her that no boy could be interested in such a "brainy" girl.

Her father tried to explain to her that doing well on tests was not incompatible with being feminine and attractive. Most important, he introduced her to one of his clients, a woman who was a professor of mathematics at a local university. After meeting this woman and learning about her experiences, Cindy refused to allow the taunts of her peers to influence her performance. She knew that her father valued her competence and she had met an attractive woman who was also a successful mathematician.

Cindy developed clear talents and career goals even in early adolescence, but most teenagers have much less articulated aspirations. Many high schools and most colleges offer vocational counseling services. The opportunity for a thorough assessment by a trained professional may reveal that an adolescent's interests, preferences and abilities are similar to those of persons who have been successful in particular occupations. A special advantage of such assessments is that individuals may discover that their interests fit rather well with careers about which they had very little information beforehand.

Post–high school educational and career choices are not quite as gender stereotyped as they were in past decades. However, in most families some different feelings are usually involved in a daughter's as compared to a son's career-related decisions. A daughter may desire a full-time career or may want something she can enter and leave as her life-style changes. Or she may want a job only to earn money until she marries. More young women than ever before are pursuing careers, but many adolescent females still focus their perceptions of the future on the traditional domestic role of wife and mother. In reality, more than nine out of ten women work outside of the home at some time during their lives. Parents should be supportive of career aspirations of daughters as well as sons. The daughter's choice should be influenced by her own personal standards, interests and abilities and not by rigid gender stereotypes.

Career Issues

Fathers, in particular, need to be wary of rigid gender stereotypes concerning career issues. Two especially unfortunate patterns relate to closed-minded parental views of a daughter's career. Some parents blatantly aim their daughters toward very limited education and careers. When their daughters are fifteen or sixteen, or younger, they focus them on preparation for a so-called feminine career. The daughter is channeled by her parents into home economics or typing courses. A second limiting perspective involves parents who are quite supportive of their daughter's desire for some higher education but have very circumscribed perceptions of her long-range career potential. The daughter is expected to complete college but is not given an orientation toward individualized career accomplishment. She is encouraged to major in art, literature or philosophy but she is not expected to contribute in a creative way to these fields or to use her education in a practical, job-oriented fashion.

Even if she does receive a degree in an area with quite varied career opportunities, such as chemistry, she is likely to be encouraged toward high school teaching rather than research or a career in medicine. This is not meant to demean a high school teaching career but to point out that many young females who have the talent do not get parental support for careers that may be relatively nontraditional for women. What is most important is that females as well as males have the freedom to consider various career options without being weighed down by outmoded stereotypes.

If it is a well-thought-out personal choice, deciding not to pursue a full-time career outside of the home can have special advantages. No one should disparage the housewife-mother role, which can, in fact, be an especially challenging career. The middle-class housewife often has the potential to schedule her time much more flexibly and creatively than the typical male or female wage earner. She may choose to fulfill herself with a wide variety of activities including charitable work, a home business, professional consultation or the fine arts.

In terms of male liberation, it is unfortunate that more social support is not given to men to develop their competencies as "househusbands" or in various work roles that they can pursue while maintaining a primary parenting role for young children. Some fathers as well as mothers derive their income from freelance work, writing or other types of endeavors that can be carried out at home. Technological advances, especially those relating to computers, will allow more fathers to work at home with a flexible schedule. It is to be hoped that a larger proportion of fathers and mothers will be able to balance child-rearing and career responsibilities in a personally fulfilling manner.

SUMMARY

Fathers have especially important roles to play in supporting the development of a constructive sense of assertiveness and independence in their sons and daughters. A major goal of parental involvement should be to encourage an active sense of self-determination in all family members. The father who demonstrates a sense of personal efficacy while maintaining positive family relationships facilitates his own and his child's development. The father's sensitivity to the individuality and needs of other family members greatly contributes to his impact in fostering a sense of inner-directedness and purposefulness in his child.

Social expectations have generally helped males to be assertive and independent while inhibiting females from expressing themselves in ways that could be construed as selfish, aggressive or competitive. Positive paternal involvement can stimulate sons and daughters to be assertive, independent and achievement-oriented without succumbing to the traditional masculine stereotype of disregard for the feelings and welfare of others. In fact, self-confidence, assertiveness and interpersonal sensitivity complement one another in contributing to healthy personality functioning in children and adults.

An important dimension of paternal involvement concerns the father's support of the child's individuality and ability to make personally relevant choices. Nurturant fathers who encourage free expression of opinions, initiative and perseverance are helping to develop a solid foundation for their children's independence and later life achievements. Positive paternal relationships can be especially crucial for daughters in their efforts to become competent, achievement-oriented and successful in nontraditional educational and career areas.

FURTHER READING

Encouraging Assertiveness

Gender Variations

For data indicating that males are generally more physically aggressive but typically less verbally oriented in expressing their feelings than females, see Basow (1986), Lips (1988) and Maccoby and Jacklin (1974). For temperamentally based individual differences relating to sociability, assertiveness and aggressiveness, see Chess and Thomas (1986, 1987) and Kagan (1984, 1989).

Constructive Responses

Regarding family factors and the development of children's social competence, see Baumrind (1967, 1971, 1989), Biller (1971a, 1974c), Biller and Meredith (1974), Pettit, Dodge and Brown (1988) and Schulman and Mekler (1985). For perspectives relevant to coparenting and child's appropriate control of aggressive impulses, see Biller (1971a, 1974c), Biller and Solomon (1986), Gordon (1989) and Lytton (1979). Concerning sociobiological formulations relating variations in paternal availability to sex differences, see Draper and Harpending (1989) and Smith (1989).

On the negative effects of physical punishment and family violence in stimulating hostile and destructive behavior among children, see Biller (1989b), Biller and Solomon (1986), Gelles and Strauss (1988), Patterson, DeBarshye and Ramsey (1989) and Van Hasselt et al. (1988). For situational determinants of physical aggression among females, see Shortell and Biller (1970) and Steinmetz (1988).

Expressing Frustrations

For research on temperament and individual differences in children's reactions to frustration, see Chess and Thomas (1986, 1987) and Kagan (1984, 1989).

Permitting Disagreement

Concerning the importance of parents allowing children leeway to express their own opinions and values, see Baumrind (1967, 1971, 1989), Biller and Meredith (1974), Coopersmith (1967), Gordon (1989), Herzog (1982) and Pettit, Dodge and Brown (1988).

Building Confidence

For suggestions for constructively dealing with parent-child disagreements, see Biller and Meredith (1974), Driekers, Gould and Corsini (1974), Faber and Mazlish (1987, 1988), Ginott (1969), Gordon (1970, 1989) and Patterson (1975).

About the significance of both parents in the development of children's confidence and self-esteem, see Biller (1971a, 1974c, 1982a), Biller and Solomon (1986), Block (1971), Coopersmith (1967), Lozoff (1974), McClelland et al. (1978) and Pettit, Dodge and Brown (1988).

Parental Disclosure

For perspectives stressing the importance of fathers and mothers respecting their children and sharing accurate information about themselves with them, see Baumrind (1967, 1971), Biller and Meredith (1974), Coopersmith (1967), Gordon (1989) and Schulman and Mekler (1985).

Supporting Independence

Child Needs

On children's intrinsic motivation to master their environment and to be assertive, see Biller and Meredith (1974), Chess and Thomas (1986, 1987), Kagan (1984, 1989), Piaget (1967) and White (1960). For consideration of potential conflicts between parent and child needs at different phases in development, see Galinsky (1981), Gordon (1989) and Rapoport et al. (1977).

Providing Choice

For perspectives on the basic human need for freedom to make choices and assume a sense of personal responsibility, see Biller (1971a), Biller and Solomon (1986), Gordon (1989), Haslow (1971), Rogers (1980) and Schulman and Mekler (1985). On cognitive-behavioral approaches to self-determination, see Bandura (1986) and Meichenbaum (1977).

Regarding research relating to parenting, empathy and altruism and the encouragement of children to be kind, just and responsible, see Gordon (1989), Hoffman (1976) and Schulman and Mekler (1985). See also Biller and Meredith (1974) concerning parental responsibility for taking the feelings and opinions of children seriously by exhibiting caring and compassionate behavior.

Stimulating Initiative

On the father's role in encouraging autonomy, self-esteem and initiative, see Baruch and Barnett (1981), Biller (1971a, 1974c, 1982a), Biller and Meredith (1974), Biller and Solomon (1986), Block

(1971), Coopersmith (1967), Dyk and Witkin (1965), Lozoff (1974) and Witkin and Goodenough (1981).

For research indicating that fathers can have a strong role in encouraging an internal locus of control in sons and daughters, see Biller (1971a, 1974c, 1982a), Biller and Salter (1989), Fry and Scher (1984), Radin (1982) and Sagi (1982). For data indicating the typically greater family dependence of daughters relative to sons, see Basow (1986), DuHamel and Biller (1969), Lips (1988) and McGoldrick (1988b).

With regard to the importance of both parents in positive social and personality development for sons and daughters, see Biller (1971a, 1974c), Biller and Solomon (1986), Block (1971), Block, von der Lippe and Block (1973) and Lozoff (1974).

Achievement Motivation

For discussions of parenting and gender-related issues in intellectual and academic achievement, see Biller (1974a, 1974b), Biller and Salter (1989), Eccles (1987), Heckhausen (1986), Radin (1981, 1982) and Schulman and Mekler (1985). For reviews of research on the development of achievement motivation in children, see Nicholls (1983) and Nicholls and Miller (1983).

About the importance of parents being available and nurturant models for their children, see Baumrind (1967, 1971), Biller and Meredith (1974), Blanchard and Biller (1971), Block (1971), Coopersmith (1967), Lozoff (1974), Pettit, Dodge and Brown (1988) and Reuter and Biller (1973). For research linking paternal warmth and positive fathering with generalized achievement motivation in sons, see Biller (1971a, 1974c, 1982a), Biller and Salter (1989) and Radin (1981, 1982).

Encouraging Females

For research relating to fear of success in women, see Horner (1972, 1978). For other research relating to the complexity of achievement motivations among women, see Basow (1986), Eccles (1987) and Lips (1988).

Lessening Inhibitions

Regarding the father's role in fostering competence and achievement in daughters, see Biller (1971a, 1974c, 1982a), Biller and Solomon (1986), Biller and Weiss (1970), Block (1971), Block, von der Lippe and Block (1970), Eccles (1987), Lasser and Snarey (1989), Lozoff (1974) and Marone (1988).

Increasing Options

For data underscoring the lack of information most adolescents have concerning meaningful job and career options, see DeFleur and Menke (1975), Eccles and Hoffman (1984), Greenberger and Steinberg (1986) and Vondracek and Lerner (1982).

Regarding family influences on children's vocational development, see Bell (1969), Eccles and Hoffman (1984), Grotevant and Cooper (1985), Havinghurst (1982), Landy (1989), Lynn (1974, 1979), Schulenberg, Vondracek and Crouter (1984) and Vondracek and Lerner (1982). For data indicating that the extent to which the father's work values influence the child is related to the relative closeness of their relationship, see Biller (1971a, 1974c) and Lynn (1974, 1979).

Career Issues

Concerning the influence of sex differences and gender stereotypes on adolescents' educational and work choices, see Eccles and Hoffman (1984), Greenberger and Steinberg (1986) and Lips (1988). For the importance of parental support in children's choice of creative and nontraditional careers, see Biller and Meredith (1974), Dauw (1966), Goertzel and Goertzel (1978), Helson (1971), Lynn (1974, 1977), Weisberg and Springer (1961) and Werts and Watley (1972).

Regarding the need to encourage broader and less stereotyped perspectives relating to post–high school education and career choice, see especially Eccles (1987), Eccles and Hoffman (1984), Greenberger and Steinberg (1986), Lips (1988) and Lock (1988).

9

Body Image, Athletics and Fitness

Parents can have much impact on their child's physical fitness. Fathers and mothers can be very influential in encouraging their sons and daughters to develop feelings of self-acceptance and pride in their bodies. Health, fitness and a positive body concept are important for every family member, and the responsibility of being parents can also be a constructive impetus for fathers and mothers to take better care of themselves. Parents can improve their own physical fitness in the process of serving as effective models for their children.

BODY CONCEPT

The involved father is likely to have a particularly significant influence on his child's body image, fitness and interest in athletics. Compared to mothers, fathers are more apt to spend a greater proportion of their time in physically oriented play and sports, especially with their sons. There is even a tendency in households where the father assumes a significant amount of child-care responsibility for him to be more focused than the mother toward engaging the infant in high-intensity physical play activities. A strong interrelationship exists among the developing child's feelings of physical competence, body image and self-concept.

Realistic Expectations

Fathers play a very important role in nurturing their children's sense of bodily adequacy and self-esteem. But they have to guard against unrealistic expectations concerning the physical capacities of children. For example, they should not expect a three-year-old to be able to catch a small ball or a four-year-old to tie shoelaces or ride a bicycle without training wheels. Most children are not maturationally ready for such accomplishments until they are at least five or older.

Parents also need to realize that it takes some children much longer to reach a particular level of physical competence than it does for others. But the ability to perform more complex achievements in coordination continues to increase throughout childhood and into adolescence. An individual's strength, speed and precision of movement can all show improvement well into adulthood. Throughout childhood and adolescence, boys usually continue to gain in strength and speed while girls typically taper off earlier, especially if they are not involved in athletic endeavors. Children typically improve their coordination during their adolescent years. Teenage awkwardness is usually due more to social ineptness and self-consciousness than actual physical clumsiness.

As with earlier physical achievements, children vary greatly in the rate and timing of their development. The child who remains physically immature in his mid-teens may need the special confidence afforded by an understanding father to counteract the stigma of being "different." If a child's physical development is extremely delayed, parents should consult a physician who specializes in growth problems. Adolescents are especially sensitive to how their physical development compares to that of their peers. Girls may be distressed by what they feel is too little or too much development of their breasts, hips or various other aspects of their appearance. Boys may be particularly embarrassed by delayed growth or lack of muscular development.

Parents may be able to give a boost to their child's sense of confidence by talking about some of the bodily concerns that they themselves had when they were younger and how they learned to cope with them. A father, for example, may have worried about his big feet, short legs or long neck but discovered that these "defects" turned out not to be as serious as they seemed at the time. Parents need to be sympathetic and not act as if the child's bodily concerns are frivolous and unworthy of attention.

Physique Differences

Parents should be careful not to stereotype their children, but they should be aware of the potential impact of body type on self-perceptions, physical and social development. Extensive research concerning physique-related behavioral differences was conducted by psychologist William Sheldon during the 1930s and 1940s. According to Sheldon, there are three basic body types: the mesomorphic (muscular build), the endomorphic (plump build) and the ectomorphic (slender build). Rather than being pure examples, most people are to some extent combinations of these basic body types. The mesomorphic endomorph or the ectomorphic mesomorph are examples of such variations. The mesomorphic endomorph tends to be large but less muscular and more obese than the classic mesomorph. The ectomorphic mesomorph tends to be lean but muscular.

The most controversial aspect of Sheldon's work was his insistence on body type and temperament connections. Even among those who represent quite pure examples of basic body types, variations in temperament occur. But despite individual variations among those with particular kinds of physiques, some behavior tendencies do seem generally to be associated with relatively distinct body types. Although the relationship between physique and temperament is not as strong as Sheldon argued, when large groups of individuals with particular body types are compared to one another, some differences do emerge. Mesomorphs tend to have high energy levels and to be assertive, extroverted, dominating and relatively fearless and impulsive. Endomorphs tend to be less vigorous and aggressive and to be more cooperative and comfort loving than mesomorphs. Endomorphs are apt to be more easygoing and react less intensely to their environment.

In contrast, ectomorphs tend to be very sensitive to environmental fluctuations. Their reactions to the outside world tend to be more influenced by reflective thought than by vigorous activity as with mesomorphs. Nevertheless, such associations of physique and behavior are applicable at only a very general group level; for some individuals relatively little fit seems to occur between body type and temperament.

Everyday experiences can have a differential impact depending upon the individual's body type and temperament. For instance, compared to the typical ectomorphic or endomorphic child, the mesomorphic boy or girl may have more energy and a greater motivation for vigorous play with peers. Such a behavioral style is likely to result in an early and strong social confidence. In contrast, the endomorphic child is apt to be less physically energetic and may spend more time in sedentary activities.

Even among young children, some general connection exists between body type and behavior. In an extensive series of studies with nursery-school-age children, psychologist Richard Walker clearly demonstrated that among both boys and girls, those with a mesomorphic body type were likely to be particularly assertive, socially active and dominant in peer group activities. Endomorphic and ectomorphic children were usually at a competitive disadvantage in physical activities when compared to mesomorphic children. Adults, including parents and teachers, consistently rated the behavior of mesomorphic boys and girls as more socially positive than that of children with a nonmesomorphic body type.

My research with kindergarten-age children also suggested that being relatively tall as well as mesomorphic was associated with positive social behavior. Tall boys typically were rated as more socially influential, assertive and dominant than short boys. However, the most clear-cut advantages occurred when tall mesomorphic boys were compared to those who were short and had a nonmesomorphic body type.

Depending on their body type and temperament, children are likely to be treated differently by parents and teachers. The mesomorphic child may be punished more for being vigorous, and the ectomorphic child may receive more teacher approval for being quieter and more studious. Peers and adults respond to various aspects of the child's bodily appearance and temperament.

Gender differences in behavior are also influenced by body type factors, being partially determined by average physique and temperament variations between the sexes. For example, although various body types are represented among both males and females, even among young children, a greater proportion of boys are relatively mesomorphic while significantly more girls are relatively endomorphic. Some underlying body-type continuity tends to persist throughout the life span, but children's physiques are by no means static entities. On the other hand, bodily appearance is not as easy to modify as many individuals might desire. It is much more difficult for some children to develop a lean or muscular physique than it is for others. Bodily appearance can definitely be affected by exercise and diet, but it is also very much a function of genetic predispositions.

Parenting Implications

Parents have important roles to play in facilitating children's positive adaptation to their particular physique and temperament. They should provide support and encouragement so that the child can gain self-acceptance and a sense of confidence as an effective person. For instance, parents may caution their mesomorphic son about becoming a bully, but also remind his teacher that the boy should not be punished merely for being assertive and vigorous.

In setting realistic expectations, fathers and mothers need to give some consideration to the child's physique and temperament. The endomorphic child may shrug off or passively accept parental criticism. An ectomorphic child may brood about the scolding and take it more to heart. In contrast, a mesomorphic child is more likely to react in an aggressive manner. A reflectively oriented ectomorphic child may be especially receptive to calm, rational discussions. A vigorous mesomorphic child, on the other hand, may require more definite limits to aid in impulse control. These are just some possibly relevant examples. For many children, little correlation exists between body type and temperament, or developmentally related changes occur. Parents have to discover a successful approach for dealing with each individual child.

The vigorous, muscular father with a robust son or daughter may never even have to give physique-temperament differences a thought, for both parent and child may be relatively assertive, outgoing and athletic. In contrast, the slim, delicate parent with a mesomorphic son or daughter may be in an altogether different position. Care must be taken by the parent not to stifle the child's vigor, either by devaluing exercise or by scolding naturally boisterous behavior. In this context, a father comes to mind who was very effective in encouraging his athletically inclined son even though he himself was very frail, physically awkward and uninterested in sports. This father did not get out and play with his son but he encouraged him in other ways. He helped his child develop a positive feeling in his chosen interests even though he was not able to model athletically skillful behavior. He attended his son's baseball and football games and also set up a backyard basketball court and basement exercise room for him.

Keep in mind the danger of stereotyping according to body type and stature. People in our culture tend to prejudge very skinny or heavyset individuals in a negative manner while viewing those who possess more muscular builds, especially males, in a much more positive fashion. Individuals of both sexes tend to portray mesomorphs as having leadership ability and being friendly, strong and capable, but typically describe ectomorphs and endomorphs as being weak and incompetent. Short children, especially boys, are also likely to be viewed as less generally competent than their taller counterparts by peers, teachers and parents. Physique-related stereotypes develop even among preschool-age children. The negative bias toward very thin individuals seems somewhat ironic given that slim female models are portrayed as ideal for wearing fashionable clothes. However, consistent with the prevalent contemporary prejudice against obese individuals, the endomorphic physique tends to be described in especially negative terms.

Parental acceptance of the child's body is very important in fostering self-confidence. Unfortunately, children with short, thin or heavyset physiques may automatically be viewed by some peers and adults in a negative light irrespective of any fit between their personalities and social stereotypes. Parental attitudes can have much impact on whether or not a child with a negatively stereotyped physique can develop an adequate body image and sense of self-esteem.

Puberty Variations

Whatever the specific age of the child, the onset of puberty and adolescence may put considerable stress on family interactions. At the least, parents have to face a significant reorganization of their perceptions of their child's body and how this fits with their parental identities. If parents have not negotiated earlier transitions in family development with respect to dealing with differences between themselves and their children, adolescence can be particularly tumultuous. In a sense, preparation for dealing with an adolescent begins early in the toddler period when the opportunity is afforded to begin giving the young child more and more autonomy and independence, safely and gradually.

Early adolescence is perhaps the most dramatic period of development, especially for those individuals whose onset of puberty is marked by very visible physical changes taking place in a relatively short time frame. Tremendous individual differences are associated with the onset of puberty. For girls, the range for initial menstruation is roughly between age nine and thirteen. Boys tend to be a year or two behind girls, with their most intense puberty-related changes and growth spurts typically occurring somewhere between the ages of eleven and fourteen. The age at which biological changes associated with puberty are evident can have tremendous significance for the individual's development. Early maturing boys are usually at a great advantage compared to their peers with respect to social influence and athletic activities. They tend to behave in a much more mature manner and are usually viewed by others as more capable and competent, particularly in comparison to their late maturing male counterparts.

Females as a group are relatively more mature both physically and socially than males at similar ages, but advantages for early maturing girls are not usually as clear-cut as for early maturing boys. Nevertheless, early maturing girls generally are more socially advanced than their later maturing female peers. The early maturing girl may appear especially out-of-phase compared to her class-mates, and this may be associated with some disadvantages as well as advantages.

The timing of puberty-related changes varies greatly from child to child. For many children puberty may begin at age nine or ten, though for most it is not apparent until after the age of eleven or twelve. Some children seem to go almost directly from a rather stable middle childhood to a rather full-blown early ad-olescence, while for others the process is much more gradual and less discordant. The eleven- or twelve-year-old is usually beginning to have to adjust to a speeding up of biologically based changes much greater than those that had been occurring in more subtle ways during the previous several years. A quite noticeable growth spurt may be associated with restlessness, moodiness, distractibility and alter-nating periods of great energy and intense tiredness. A calm and predictable ten- or eleven-year-old may temporarily turn into a negativistic and stubborn eleven- or twelve-year-old.

The onset of puberty often corresponds roughly with the child's graduation from elementary school and entry into the next phase of education. Such tran-sitions, even if looked forward to, are bound to be somewhat stressful for the child and parents. It is quite disconcerting for children to go from a school situation in which they felt well established to one in which they are now starting over at the lowest level. When the child's entry into a new school also coincides with the beginning of puberty, the family may be in for an especially difficult and unsettling period. Whether the change emanates primarily from the child or is more related to external pressures, developmental transitions are likely to go much more smoothly when the father and mother have a mutually supportive parenting partnership. Some increase in family stress is a natural outgrowth of the changing social expectations associated with puberty, but parent-child con-flicts are much less likely to be severe in families with a history of positive paternal involvement. When the father is an attentive parent, serious mother-adolescent conflict is less likely. The father's respect for both the mother and the child and his willingness to engage them in individualized discussions helps to alleviate tension in the mother-child relationship.

Perhaps at no time in development is the variation of individuals of the same age more apparent than in early adolescence. Among twelve-year-old males, for example, some may appear more like the average third-grader while others could easily be mistaken for college students. Maturational factors dramatically influ-ence social relationships both within and outside of the family. However, stature and other aspects of appearance have influenced the child's self-concept and social development well before the onset of puberty. Adolescents do generally become more preoccupied with their appearance and how they compare to others, but for most children these are certainly not new concerns. The self-concepts of children are greatly affected by their relative physical maturity, stature and body type. Those children who are early maturers, attractive and well built are likely to be socially active, self-assured and successful in peer group and leadership activities during early adolescence.

The adolescent's physical development can be a very strong catalyst for parental reactions. Parents who have much anxiety about their own physical appearance may find it quite difficult to be supportive of their child's burgeoning maturity. Feelings of inadequacy and jealousy are quite common, particularly if the parent is on the clear downside in self-perceived physical attractiveness. On the other hand, the child's entry into adolescence can be an impetus for parents constructively to improve their own physical appearance and fitness.

Countering Prejudice

Enlightened segments of our society frown on racism, sexism and religious persecution, but not enough attention is given to prejudice relating to body type and stature. In *Stature and Stigma*, Leslie Martel and I reviewed a great deal of research relating to the significance of height and body type as factors in personality development and social relations. The short endomorphic or short ectomorphic child is especially likely to have problems in self-acceptance and in succeeding in social situations, whereas the tall and mesomorphic male is much more apt to attain a high peer status and a position of leadership.

Relatively short stature, in itself, can be a continuing social handicap. Our research with successful middle-class college students clearly revealed that young men who were short (defined as 5 ft. 2 in. to 5 ft. 5½ in.) were more likely to have anxiety in social, dating and job-related situations and were less confident in their ability to influence others than were their average-height (5 ft. 8 in. to 5 ft. 10½ in.) and especially their tall (6 ft. to 6 ft. 4 in.) counterparts. Regardless of their own height, college students generally perceived short males as much less competent than tall males. Compared to other males, those that were tall tended especially to value stature and have the most negative attitudes toward their smaller peers.

Short females as well as short males report that others tend to treat them as if they were younger and less experienced and knowledgeable than their peers. Furthermore, short individuals are more often the targets of condescending, manipulative and physically abusive behavior than their taller peers. On the other hand, taller individuals are routinely at an advantage in social endeavors, although little public acknowledgment is made of this fact. Being tall is positively related to greater social power and economic status.

Quite formalized types of job discrimination relate to stature. This is the case when an explicit criterion for minimal stature is set with the assumption that those below a certain height do not have the physical competence or social influence necessary to do the job. Traditionally, for example, entry into positions in police and fire departments has been closed to individuals with short stature (typically defined as less than 5 ft. 7 in. or 5 ft. 8 in.). Fortunately, legal pressure has been exerted to develop more competency-based standards that will not automatically exclude those with short stature; height requirements have been particularly discriminatory toward individuals who tend to be shorter than average, such as minority group men and women from lower socioeconomic backgrounds.

Our society needs to confront stereotypes relating to stature and other dimensions of physical appearance. To deny that such stereotypes exist or to pretend that they do not have a powerful psychological and social impact is counterproductive. Part of parent and teacher training, for example, should include an examination of stereotypes about stature and body type in a way that highlights their existence but also cautions against generalizing their meaningfulness to specific individuals. Adults should become more aware of their own potentially discriminatory attitudes toward individuals who significantly deviate from culturally idealized body types. They should be careful to make sure that their judgments are based on behavioral information rather than on stereotypes. Children should not be discouraged from performing a particular activity simply because of their stature or body type, but they should also be prepared for the possibility that others may prejudge their competence.

With parental support, children can develop the confidence and competence to surmount discriminatory attitudes. Whether children are striving for respect for their opinions, social acceptance, a leadership role or a position on an athletic team, assertiveness in countering stereotypes is extremely important. In some ways, the issues are quite similar to those confronting individuals who face discrimination because of their racial or cultural identification.

Coping Patterns

Differences among individuals relating to stature and body type have a definite impact on social relations. There are, for example, some likely disadvantages in being much smaller and shorter than one's peers. Disadvantages may range from lesser strength and leverage to more subtle social handicaps relating to having constantly to look up at peers and having a more restricted sense of personal space. Difficulties in peer relations in childhood may appear far removed from adulthood concerns, but such experiences are important in molding long-lasting attitudes and self-perceptions. How much of a handicap shortness, or any other perceived body-type or appearance deficit, remains during later development depends on myriad factors including family and cultural influences. The interactions among such factors as temperament, intellectual resources, parental influence, peer values and socioeconomic status must all be taken into account in order to understand the way in which an individual may deal with a potential handicap.

As Alfred Adler emphasized, those who feel that they are not quite adequate on a physical level may develop an inferiority complex. Attitudes about the adequacy of bodily characteristics play a crucial role in personal and social adjustment. The individual who feels physically inadequate may be at a great disadvantage in dealing with others, particularly because of fears of vulnerability and rejection.

It is possible to make a very general analogy between appearance deficits and other types of handicaps such as learning disorders in the sense that individuals differ greatly in their capacities to cope successfully with such problems. Given appropriate resources, individuals can usually manage with either a learning handicap or physical disadvantage, but if other personal or family limitations are present, their feelings of self-worth may suffer long-term damage. Family environment forms the basis for the successful development of self-esteem and interpersonal competence. Emotional security within the family may serve to inoculate the short or otherwise appearance-handicapped child from difficulties in the larger social arena. If a solid sense of self-worth has been fostered within the family, body type or stature stereotypes may have a very minimal impact on the individual.

In contrast, an unsupportive family places individuals with appearance deficits at great risk for the development of psychological problems. The child with a stature or body-type disadvantage seems especially vulnerable to emotional difficulties when also suffering from some form of parenting inadequacy. Children who feel a lack of peer acceptance are in particular need of the support of both parents if they are to develop a healthy sense of self-worth.

Important benefits can accrue from the successful negotiation of an initial physical disadvantage, whether it be related to a deficit in stature, body type or other aspects of appearance. Surmounting difficult issues during early development may serve to enhance character strengths. Coping well with adversity can increase self-confidence and feelings of personal empowerment. Parents can do much to help their children overcome initial disadvantages and develop a solid sense of self-acceptance. As they grow, children need support in updating their body images. Unfortunately, many quite attractive adults, who were awkward or ungainly children, still are fixated on their previous experiences of not physically measuring up to others. Parental support is very crucial in allowing a child realistically to overcome feelings of inferiority originally initiated by clear physical disadvantages vis-à-vis siblings or peers.

Parental love and acceptance of the child as an individual, as a special person, is crucial in encouraging a healthy body image and self-concept. A child who is fortunate to have two accepting and supportive parents is very likely to have a positive body image. A child is more vulnerable to self-doubt when only one parent is actively involved and nurturant. When love and respect is communicated by two quite different people, it provides a kind of consensual validation of the child's feelings of self-worth.

Gender Issues

Regardless of their child's particular stature or physique, both parents should be supportive of the development of competence. The same-sex parent may play a particularly significant role in the development of the child's body concept. For example, the young boy will inevitably compare his physical assets to those of his father. The boy's body concept can be positively supported by paternal assurance that he is developing well and will with time possess a mature male physique. When the parent and child of the same sex are very dissimilar in physical appearance, special difficulties may arise. The slim mother may subtly or unsubtly devalue her heavyset daughter, or the muscular father his skinny son. Either parent's comments may bolster or deflate the child's sense of bodily adequacy.

Feelings of inadequacy about the sexual aspects of one's body have particularly negative implications for the development of self-esteem. Unfortunately, some parents teach their young children that any personal contact with the genital area is dirty and repellent. A positive body concept is an important ingredient contributing to sexual adjustment during adulthood. Parents should avoid derogatory statements concerning their child's body-type and stature. As with other areas of child rearing, parents need to examine their own self-perceptions and attitudes. Insightful parents have the opportunity to reassure a child constructively by sharing their own early experiences.

Sometimes parents who themselves have had body-image problems inadvertently contribute to the development of similar difficulties for their children. Ray perceived that his son Jack was handicapped by his pudgy appearance and rather slow running speed. However, in responding to a therapist's comments, Ray finally realized that he himself was adding to his son's anxiety by his negative attitude about the child's athletic ability. Ray was then able to share with his son some of the similar problems he had encountered as a child and how he had learned to cope with teasing by peers. He could acknowledge that he himself no longer felt as handicapped as he did when he was a child. Realistic parental support can help children avoid severe body-image problems and give them the hope that their physique will improve with maturation, or at least that it does not have to be a disability when they reach adulthood.

Compared to boys, girls usually receive much less parental interest in their relative fitness, strength and athletic abilities. A major mistake many fathers and mothers make is in not encouraging their daughter's physical competence. Both girls and boys can greatly benefit from developing a sense of pride about their fitness. Leah was stifled by overprotective parents who believed that females were naturally fragile. She often became tense, nervous and distracted when involved in play activities with other children, overreacting any time she had even the slightest sniffle or bruise. With family counseling, Leah and her parents were able gradually to sort out realistic concerns from rather sexist thinking about beliefs in innate female fragility. Leah later enjoyed playing on the girls' basketball and volleyball teams at her high school. When the father supports his daughter's physical competence, it enhances her self-confidence and assertiveness as well as her potential for success in athletics. A father's positive involvement in encouraging his son's or daughter's interest in athletic activities, regardless of the sport, can contribute in significant ways to the child's personal and social adjustment.

PROMOTING FITNESS

Perhaps the most important teaching fathers and mothers can do in helping children develop a healthy body concept is to set a positive example. Parents who value their own bodies and take care of their health and physical fitness are providing very cogent models to their children. Even very young children can become playfully involved in athletic and fitness activities with their parents. For example, Benjamin began an after-supper ritual of exercising with me when he was still a toddler.

Organized Sports

In addition to helping the child to develop a positive body image, parents can also foster pride in athletic competence. Parental attitudes concerning competition can have much impact on the child's interest in participating in organized as well as informal sports. However, parents should be careful not to put undue pressure on children, because it may interfere with their ability to enjoy athletic competition. Many parents, because of their unfulfilled fantasies, pressure and hurry their children into arduous practice and competition. Young children are not emotionally mature enough to cope constructively with unrealistic parental expectations. When a child enjoys a particular athletic endeavor or sport, it can be a very positive developmental impetus. But when the child is practicing and performing primarily to meet the father's or mother's needs, the result is much less apt to be beneficial.

Added pressure on the child whose parent is the coach is likely. Other parents may rightly or wrongly feel that the son or daughter of the coach is receiving preferential treatment. A potential problem with adult-organized teams in various sports is that they may hurry children into overly structured, competitive activities. Parents, especially those in coaching roles, have a tendency to get over-involved, expecting an unrealistically high level of performance from their children.

A child should not be arbitrarily forced to participate in organized sports activities. Choices should be made on the basis of the child's interest and readiness. It may be better for the child to play a sport informally with one or two friends, gradually improving skills, rather than being exposed to intense competition before the development of sufficient self-confidence. Even those children who love sports may find organized activities too structured and rather boring. Although some teams have lengthy scheduled practices, the younger child may spend only a very small proportion of this time actually involved in active play. For many children, informal half-hour sessions a few times a week practicing a sport with their father or mother are far more enjoyable and productive, whether it be hitting tennis balls, shooting baskets or taking batting practice. On the other hand, a child who is eager to join an organized league should be given the opportunity.

Pressure from parents and coaches may be even greater when young children are participating in more individualized sports such as tennis, swimming and gymnastics. Tremendous amounts of adult time, money and effort may be spent in grooming preschoolers as well as elementary school-age children for athletic accomplishment. Whether they be directed toward excellence in athletics or other areas such as music or dancing, hours of highly structured and pressured daily practice are not likely to be compatible with the emotional and social needs of young children.

Many coaches do contribute in very constructive ways to the development of children. Having a positively involved and caring coach who views each participant as an individual can be a great experience for children, particularly if they have not been treated this way at home. Similarly, in the context of organized sports activities, some parents may be able to exhibit a very admirable dimension of caring and support to other members of the team as well as to their own child.

Positive Support

In a general sense, guidelines for fostering athletic competence are similar to those that are relevant to other areas of accomplishment. Just as the child should be encouraged to strive for improvement in academic areas, a similar attitude should be encouraged in athletic endeavors. But equally as important, children should have some freedom of choice and not simply engage in activities selected by their parents. Positive support should be provided for the child to compete at an appropriate level. The child can be encouraged to appreciate self-improvement as well as competition with others, to experience the joy of achievement relative to personal standards.

Involvement in certain types of athletic activities can be an excellent way to bolster the confidence of a child who has experienced a deficit in body image. Many adolescents take up weight lifting because they feel insecure about their bodies. Parents should take a keen interest in their child's progress in fitness and strength-inducing endeavors. The child may even welcome parental participation in a cooperative training program.

An individual's functioning is not neatly divided into areas of physical and nonphysical development. The child's temperament, maturity and time perspective should be taken into account with regard to encouraging participation in sports. When I first went bowling with my son Cameron, then four years old, he tended to lose interest rather quickly, fidgeting and wandering around. It finally occurred to me that the time between turns was too long to sustain his interest, but when I allowed him to bowl as long as he wanted to, his enjoyment and proficiency increased enormously. Another perspective that has helped me when dealing with children of diverse ages and abilities is to strive to find ways for each to experience some success. For example, when playing baseball with a preschool-age child, I use a much easier-to-hit, large ball. When it comes time for an older child to bat, I simply revert to the use of a standard baseball. Similarly, in playing basketball, the younger children get to stand closer to the hoop, the older children and I shoot from progressively greater distances.

A common family problem involves a parent who may overemphasize athletics even though the child may not enjoy competitive sports. Insensitive parental pressure can have a very negative influence on the young child's self-image. It is important that children receive parental support to discover what types of activities are interesting for them rather than being pushed into endeavors that they do not enjoy. I experienced much initial frustration when my son Michael displayed little interest in team sports despite much family encouragement. Even though he was bigger as a young child than any of his older brothers at a similar age, he showed none of their desire to play football, basketball or baseball. Relating to my children through sports participation has been very important for me but, fortunately, was not my only way of connecting to them. I gradually began to realize that Michael was not motivated to engage in group sports with peers. Despite his relative aversion to traditional team sports, Michael has become an excellent swimmer, by far the best in the family. Even though not a highly competitive individual, he nonetheless won many YMCA-sponsored freestyle swimming races as a teenager.

Family Opportunities

Compared to boys, girls do not receive as much support to develop their athletic competence and fitness. Parents can be very influential in encouraging their daughters to participate in various types of athletic activities. Being a competent athlete can be just as beneficial for females as it is for males with respect to developing physical fitness and feelings of self-confidence. And there is no reason why girls cannot be athletically competitive and still retain a basic sense of acceptance of themselves as positively feminine.

If their daughters are motivated, parents can help lessen still-prevalent gender stereotypes by encouraging them to engage in athletic competition. They can help their daughters to develop a strong enough feminine self-image to overcome any social or peer group stigma attached to their involvement in physically competitive endeavors. A daughter can especially profit by the encouragement from a father who sees no incompatibility between her being both positively feminine and athletically competitive. As the primary male in her life, the father can provide a strong sense of acceptance for her athletic interests.

The great tennis star Chris Evert owes much to the careful, involved coaching of her father. She has fond memories of her father throwing tennis balls to her when she was six years old. He patiently, and with humor, encouraged her initial awkward attempts to hit the ball back over the net, devoting a significant period of one-to-one time to her on a daily basis. He was an important influence in helping her to achieve a strong sense of physical competence as well as a very positive self-image.

Athletics can be a particularly significant vehicle for parent-child communication. The specific athletic endeavor is not the issue; rather it is the fact that the child can observe the parent engaging in an enjoyable physical activity that involves some form of coordination and muscular exertion. It is also important for the child to be aware that the parent does not view success in athletics and intellectual endeavors as mutually exclusive. A well-rounded individual—male or female—can feel just as comfortable on the playing field as in the library. Furthermore, a high level of competence in many sports requires a conceptual understanding of complex strategies and alternatives.

I will always remember some conversations I had with my son Cameron when he was five years old. He seemed to be having a difficult time imagining that the same individual could be interested in both intellectual matters and sports. Like many young boys, he was impressed with his father's athletic competence but it took him much longer to realize that someone like myself, who enjoyed sports and physical challenges so much, could also be successful in more intellectual pursuits. Unfortunately, at least through adolescence, many of us have to struggle with certain social stereotypes that suggest some impermeable barrier separates so-called intellectual and athletic skills.

Self-Defense

Physical competence developed in the context of athletic and fitness activities can increase confidence in being able to defend oneself. The traditional picture of the father instructing his son how to box gives an incomplete picture of the learning experiences involved in self-defense. A daughter needs to be taught something about assertive self-defense as well, and both boys and girls should be aware of physical and nonphysical techniques that may be useful in protecting themselves and others. A father may be in a better position to encourage the child's competence in self-defense, but there is no reason why a mother cannot also be an active participant.

The child should learn a variety of verbal strategies to deal with the threat of attack or intimidation, but a physically assertive defense is definitely an appropriate reaction in some circumstances. On occasion physical force, or its potential use, is the only viable alternative. Individuals need to have the confidence of knowing how to defend themselves. Parents should instruct the child in different alternative modes of responding to the possibility of being assaulted by others. They should emphasize ways to use words to calm a situation as well as to make sure that the child knows how to ask for the help of others. Nevertheless, parents must realize that their son or daughter may encounter situations where some display of at least potential physical prowess is necessary for self-protection.

The child may have to learn to live in an environment that contains a certain amount of risk of being assaulted by others. A son or daughter may encounter intrusive bullies, people to be protected and instances requiring the physical ability to control someone who is being abusive or violent. Training in self-defense by a parent or other adult can aid a child's confidence to act appropriately and in a manner that minimizes anyone being hurt. However strongly they may adhere to a philosophy of nonviolence, few parents would wish their child or themselves to be a passive target for physical abuse or injury.

Parents and children need to have some means of active physical defense at their disposal. Being confident and athletically fit is certainly helpful, but having been trained in a more formal self-defense program can be especially relevant. Instruction in martial arts such as karate can benefit children not only in learning how to defend themselves but also in providing a more general sense of self-discipline, confidence and fitness. As always, however, parents should not overly pressure children into time-consuming or competitive activities. In fact, parents who feel a lack of confidence in physically threatening situations can profit from learning self-defense techniques themselves that they can then teach in a more relaxed manner to their children. Even very young children can learn basic techniques of assertiveness and self-defense, which can greatly minimize the danger of being physically abused or molested by others.

Parental Benefits

Participation in sports and regular exercise can benefit parents as well as children. The importance of spending active time with a child constitutes a very cogent reason for parents to engage regularly in fitness endeavors. For many parents, feelings of embarrassment about running or playing ball evaporate with the addition of a child's excitement and interest. Furthermore, an adoring young child can help the parent stick with an exercise program. Regular athletic endeavors with the child have definite advantages for a parent. The companionship can be relaxing, and the exercise itself may help to reduce the likelihood of the parent suffering health-related problems. Being able to enjoy vigorous sports activities with a child definitely has benefits for the well-being and fitness of parents.

This is not to say that to be a good parent one has to participate actively in particular types of child-oriented sports. For some parents, certain kinds of activities may be uncomfortable or stressful. Nevertheless, various forms of regular athletic participation can help maintain the health and fitness of all family members.

Parental health-related problems can have quite dramatic effects on a child's life. A physically imposing parent can rather suddenly be transformed into a very passive and helpless individual. When parents responsibly take care of their health and fitness it can also be a reflection of their concern for the well-being of their children. Ramifications of parents neglecting or abusing their own health are often reflected in their child's behavior. Francine and Ralph came for family counseling because their twelve-year-old daughter Stephanie had been taking stimulant drugs in the company of older children. Discussions with the parents revealed that they were both quite dependent on alcohol and sleeping pills. They had also always been very quick to dispense medication to their daughter at the slightest sign of illness.

Family treatment involved structured programming for both the parents' and the daughter's addictions, along with a focus on the father providing his wife and daughter with more appropriate support and attention. Part of the success of treatment was related to the parents setting an example for their daughter in abstaining from unnecessary medication. Ralph, in his role as father and husband, had to recommit himself to consistent day-to-day attention to his family, prioritizing his time so that he was not constantly preoccupied with his business. Ralph began to participate in more sports-related activities with his wife and daughter, including tennis and skiing, which also helped to improve his health and fitness levels.

Parents who do not take care of their bodies set a poor example. Especially detrimental to their children are those parents involved in a self-destructive pattern of drug addiction. The alcohol-troubled or otherwise drug-addicted parent is typically inconsistent, abusive or neglectful toward children and other family members. Parents need to take a hard look at their life-styles for the sake of their well-being and that of their children. Smoking, drinking and the use of other drugs, negligent personal hygiene and lack of regular exercise can all negatively impact on the child as well as the parent. Individuals who become excessive drinkers and smokers, for example, are more likely to have had parents who suffered from similar addictions than those without such habits. Hereditary factors may be involved in the child's susceptibility to addictions, but what parents convey by their behavior is extremely important. Respect for the body and health provides a highly significant example for a child. A key ingredient in being an effective parent is taking good care of oneself as well as one's child.

SUMMARY

When fathers are regularly involved in family activities, they are more likely than mothers to engage their children, especially their sons, in high-intensity, physically oriented play activities. They are more apt to encourage physical challenge and an interest in competitive sports. Quality paternal involvement can be an important factor in fostering a healthy body image and feelings of physical competence in both boys and girls.

The father's positive acceptance of the child's gender and bodily appearance has a great impact on his son's and daughter's self-concept. Body type and stature variations can have considerable influence on the child's social relationships and sense of personal adequacy. The child whose physique does not conform to culturally valued stereotypes may be in special need of a nurturant, involved father. Girls and boys deserve paternal support to find physically stimulating activities that are enjoyable to them, whether or not they are interested in organized sports.

Regardless of body type, all individuals should have the opportunity to develop a positive self-image and concern for physical fitness. Parents who value their own bodies and take care of their health are providing cogent examples for their children. Even very young children can become playfully involved in athletic and fitness activities with their parents. The father can improve his own physical fitness in the process of serving as an effective role model for his son and daughter. Abstaining from the inappropriate use of alcohol and other drugs is another important way that he can help himself and his child.

FURTHER READING

Body Concept

Realistic Expectations

About the general importance of considering the child's maturational readiness for particular activities, see Elkind (1981, 1984, 1987), Kagan (1984) and Zigler (1987). On individual differences in so-called bodily kinesthetic intelligence, so important in competitive athletics as well as in other areas such as dance performance, see Gardner (1983).

Physique Differences

For basic research on body types, see Sheldon (1940) and Sheldon and Stevens (1970). For discussion and criticism of body-type research, see Hartl, Monnelly and Elderkin (1982) and Martel and Biller (1987).

Concerning research relating body type and temperament in young children, see Walker (1962, 1963). For data relating to height, body type and social functioning among kindergarten-age boys, see Biller (1968a).

For differences between early and late physical maturers, see Brooks-Gunn (1988), Chumela (1982), Jones (1957), and Nash (1978).

Parenting Implications

On ways that the child's physique can influence parental perceptions and expectations, see Brackbill and Nevill (1981), Martel and Biller (1987), Walker (1963) and Washburn (1962). Concerning the role of paternal and maternal factors in the development of body image problems and eating disorders, see Humphrey (1986) and Klesges et al. (1990).

Puberty Variations

With respect to the timing and impact of puberty on family relationships, see Ames, Ilg and Baker (1988), Brooks-Gunn (1988), Chumela (1982), Daniels et al. (1985) and Steinberg (1988).

For transition from middle childhood to early adolescence, see Lerner (1987, 1988). For physical appearance, sex-role and sexuality issues during adolescence, see Biller and Liebman (1971), Chumela (1982), Dreyer (1982) and Martel and Biller (1987).

Countering Prejudice

Concerning the difficulties encountered by relatively short individuals, especially males, see Martel and Biller (1987). For examples of job discrimination related to short stature, see Hogan and Quigley (1986) and Keyes (1980).

Regarding the impact of physical appearance on social acceptance and self-concept, see Biller and Liebman (1971), Hatfield and Sprecher (1986) and Lerner, Karagenick and Stuart (1973).

Coping Patterns

For a provocative discussion of bodily limitations and inferiority complexes, see Adler (1956). For research on body image and personality adaptations, see Fisher (1986), Hatfield and Sprecher (1986), Keyes (1980) and Martel and Biller (1987).

Gender Issues

About gender stereotypes, physical attractiveness and body image, see Dion and Berscheid (1974), Eitzen (1975), Chernin (1981), Fisher (1986), Lerner, Orlos and Knapp (1976), Martel and Biller (1987) and Staffieri (1967). Regarding gender similarities and differences in the development of athletic skills and physical fitness, see Bunker (1987), Smith, Smith and Smoll (1983), Thomas (1984) and Thomas and French (1985). On the positive benefits of fathers supporting daughters in their athletic endeavors, see Biller and Meredith (1974) and Snarey (1992).

Promoting Fitness

Organized Sports

For parent roles in supporting physical and athletic competence and achievement in children, see Biller and Meredith (1974), Glover and Shepherd (1989), Seefeldt (1987), Smith, Smith and Smoll (1983) and Snarey (1992). See also Roberts (1983) for children's achievement and social motivations for participating in sports.

Regarding the importance of the coach's sensitivity toward the needs and individuality of children, see Seefeldt (1987), Seefeldt et al. (1981), Smith, Smith and Smoll (1983) and Smoll and Smith (1979, 1984).

Positive Support

For the relationship between strength, fitness and self-esteem, see Chernin (1981), deVries and Hales (1982), Eitzen (1975), Glover and Shepherd (1989), Gould (1984), Lerner, Orlos and Knapp (1976) and Martel and Biller (1987). Concerning the importance of fathers actively encouraging both sons and daughters in athletic and fitness activities, see Biller and Meredith (1974) and Snarey (1992).

Family Opportunities

For detailed suggestions for family fitness and sports activities, see Glover and Shepherd (1989).

Self-Defense

With respect to principles of self-defense applicable for both children and adults, see Peterson (1979, 1984) and Tegner (1975).

On the importance of assertiveness in resisting various types of maltreatment by others, see Biller and Meredith (1974), Biller and Solomon (1986) and Schulman and Meckler (1985).

Parental Benefits

For continuing advantages of exercise in maintaining health and fitness throughout the life span, see deVries (1970, 1974), deVries and Hales (1982), Glover and Shepherd (1989), Keller and Seraganian (1984), Kobasa, Maddi and Kahn (1982), Kobasa et al. (1985), Taylor (1986) and Wiswell (1980). Concerning family system influences involved in alcohol abuse and other drug problems, see Barnes (1984), Elkin (1984), Krestan and Bepko (1988) and Stern, Northman and Van Slyk (1984).

With respect to the linkage between various types of parental involvement-noninvolvement and the child's health and physical well-being, see Guidubaldi and Cleminshaw (1985), Guidubaldi et al. (1986), Houston and Vevak (1991), Humphrey (1986), Klesges et al. (1990), Peterson, Farmer and Kashani (1990) and Pratt (1973). Regarding evidence that the quality of the relationships that men have with their children can influence their physical and mental health, see Barnett, Davidson and Marshall (1991), Barnett, Marshall and Pleck (1991) and Julian, McKenry and Arnold (1990).

10

Intimacy, Sexuality and Social Adjustment

As emphasized in previous chapters, the nurturant father's encouragement of assertiveness, body pride and basic self-esteem increases the likelihood of the child having successful social experiences with both age-mates and adults. This chapter elaborates on how the child's social and sexual development can be greatly facilitated by a caring, accessible and dependable father who fosters a sense of closeness, sharing and trust. The focus in the first half of the chapter is on the importance of the father conveying constructive values about intimacy, sexuality and male-female relationships. The second half of the chapter is directed more at examining how the quality of fathering during childhood may be linked to the son's or daughter's sexual and social adjustment during adulthood.

INTIMATE RELATIONSHIPS

Children are exposed to a gradually widening network of adults and peers, but their experiences with their parents remain a central core in the development of their social competence. Being able to form close relationships with others is an important ingredient in overall social adjustment. The ability to communicate and empathize with both males and females becomes an increasingly salient issue as the child progresses through different phases of development. The nurturant father can have an especially crucial role in supporting his son's and daughter's capacity for positive intimacy.

Family Dynamics

For the child, the father-mother relationship is generally the most significant model of male-female interactions. How the parents exhibit their affection for one another, whether they are aloof or loving, formal or relaxed, is closely watched and imitated by the child in his or her own relationships. When parents are considerate of each other's feelings and needs, very likely their children will develop positive attitudes toward both males and females. The child can gain a sense of security from living in a family where the parents have a warm, loving relationship. Most young children have very romanticized views of their parents. The four-year-old daughter's emotional declaration of everlasting romantic devotion to her father or the five-year-old son's marriage proposal to his mother are perfectly natural. Young children are learning about adult roles and are particularly fond of imitating their same-sex parent.

Indications of so-called Oedipal rivalries do occur in many families. However, strong, enduring rivalries between a son and a father for the mother's love or between a daughter and a mother for the father's love are by no means a necessary part of family development. For example, boys usually have chronically rivalrous feelings toward their fathers only when a strong father-son attachment has not developed in the first few years of the child's life. A son who has suffered from paternal neglect is at risk to feel intense anger toward his father in the context of competing for the mother's attention.

Parent-child rivalries may be somewhat defused during the elementary school years only to reemerge in an even more dramatic fashion when the child reaches adolescence. The physical maturity of the child brings with it some natural implications for rivalry with the same-sex parent. In families where the child has not developed a solid attachment with the father, rivalry and other forms of conflict may become especially intense. On the other hand, a strong father-child bond decreases the likelihood of family problems.

Some fathers have difficulties in being nurturant because of an underlying fear of losing control of their sexual impulses. Psychologist Robert Sears and his colleagues discovered that anxiety concerning sexual matters was associated with parents having conflicts dealing with the bodily functions of their children. High parental sexual anxiety, for example, was correlated with a tendency toward discomfort when bathing and dressing babies. Some fathers may feel inhibited in expressing nurturant behavior because they cannot distinguish between sensuality and sexuality.

Sensuality in the context of positive parenting includes the enjoyment of being physically close and of appropriately touching and hugging the child. Sensuality is not equivalent to sexuality. In fact, the most effective antidotes to a variety of problems between parent and child often include a hug and a feeling of physical closeness and acceptance. Fathers and mothers should make appropriate use of their capacity for a nurturant sensuality in the parenting process. Sensuality and sexuality can be conceived of as two interrelated ways of expressing feelings, but being physically close to a child should not get confused with the satisfaction of adult sexual needs. A father, for example, may feel uncomfortable about hugging his child, believing that such enjoyment is somehow unmanly or even symptomatic of a sexual perversion. However, enjoying feelings of physical closeness with the child is a natural part of fathering as well as mothering.

Because of traditional definitions of femininity and mothering, it seems perfectly natural for the female to come into close physical contact with infants and young children. Mothers tend to be more flexible in expressing their affectionate feelings than fathers. Parents need to be concerned about the appropriateness of their physical intimacy with children, but this should not rule out playful, reciprocal physical contact. Serious problems emerge when parents and other adults cannot differentiate between normal feelings and potentially destructive impulses. However, parents can become so upset with what are basically normal feelings that they overly distance themselves from the child. For example, the father who becomes mildly aroused when taking a bath with his infant may reject any further physical closeness with the child. Similarly, a highly anxious father may avoid any individualized contact with his daughter because he feels an erotic attraction to her.

Parents who feel sexually stimulated by their children should certainly exercise caution in the particular ways that they express physical affection toward them. It is crucial for the parent to avoid sexually directed contact with the child while at the same time allowing for the healthy expression of physical closeness. Parents must distinguish between sensuality and sexuality, taking the responsibility to recognize and control inappropriate and destructive impulses.

Sharing Values

Sexuality involves far more than physical interaction between two people. Parents can communicate a moral basis for appropriate sexual behavior to their children. Morality relates to the sensitivity and consideration given to others whether or not it is in the context of a sexual relationship. Parents can explain how love can be expressed through sexuality, but also how being considerate of another person's feelings is important. Children may be just as interested to know the why of sexual behavior as the how.

Books can also be useful in the sex education process in several ways, not the least of which is to help parents educate themselves so that they can better respond to their child's questions. Many parents are uncomfortable about sex education because they are reluctant to admit that they do not know everything about the subject. Even if they had discussions earlier about explicit sexual issues and have continued to have open communication about many varied topics, most parents find that their adolescents are unwilling to disclose intimate details of their relationships with others. Older children and adolescents need to feel an independence from their parents, especially concerning issues of intimacy and sexuality. Parents should rely more on being positive examples of responsible behavior than on expecting to have detailed discussions about sexuality with their children.

Long before children reach adolescence or even school age, parents have the opportunity to communicate positive sexual values to them. For instance, when the son asks about genital sex differences, the father can explain that females have their sexual organs inside, not that they "don't have a penis." If the father does not belittle females as if they were physically inferior, the son is less likely to have a sexist attitude. There are, however, limitations in the young child's ability to understand abstract principles. No matter how bright, the preschooler is usually not capable of taking the same perspective as an adult. No matter how egalitarian are parental attitudes, children may still insist very strongly that it is much better to be a member of their sex or that the other gender is clearly inferior.

Parents should consistently express views that indicate a respect for the other sex. Parental example is the best way to increase the likelihood that the child will eventually internalize similar values. Verbal power struggles are not likely to convince the child of the validity of parental beliefs.

If the issue comes up, the parent can let the child know that masturbation is a natural behavior and is usually perfectly harmless. According to survey data, more than 90 percent of males and 60 percent of females masturbate at some time in their lives, although, on average, females do it about half as often as males. About twice as many boys as girls have masturbated by the age of thirteen. Some parents view masturbation as inappropriate and even respond in punitive ways toward the child for engaging in such behavior. Parents vary widely in their attitudes toward masturbation and other sexual activities as a function of their own family and religious training. However, parental sexual conflicts can be quite disruptive for both the marital relationship and the child's development.

It is important for both parents to communicate constructive attitudes toward sexuality to their daughters as well as their sons. The mother's positive acceptance of her own biology can make it much easier for her daughter to feel comfortable as she physically matures. The daughter's discovery that she is different from males and that she will one day be capable of becoming a mother herself should be treated in a highly supportive manner by both of her parents. Some parents have particular discomfort when dealing with their daughter's sex education. From a traditional perspective, the emphasis is on defining the daughter's morality in terms of her exerting self-control and inhibition in sexual situations. Parents may fear that talking about sex will somehow make their daughter vulnerable to promiscuity.

Just as the mother can talk with a special kind of expertise about women with her son, so the father can discuss men with his daughter. The father, for example, can emphasize to his daughter that sexual intimacy, though extremely significant, is only one part of committed adult male-female relationships. The father can provide an example of a man who values sexuality but does not allow it to obscure other dimensions of his personality. He can communicate his views concerning the importance of sexual relationships in the context of intimacy between two consenting adults.

The father can be a particularly good coach for his daughter on how to relate constructively to males. For instance, he can talk to her about what makes a girl attractive to boys in more than a physical sense. He can encourage her to be assertive about her interests and can emphasize that females are not passive creatures to be manipulated by males. In a practical vein, a father's coaching in self-defense has helped many females save themselves from rape and other forms of physical manipulation.

Fostering Trust

The father's role is very influential in his daughter's sexual development. Constructive heterosexual relations involve learning how to interact with the other sex in ways that establish a sense of trust between males and females. Daughters may have even greater difficulty than sons do in forming positive heterosexual relationships if they are victims of inadequate fathering. Young boys who suffer from paternal deprivation usually have ample opportunity to form relationships with females. Even if their mothers are relatively neglectful, they are still likely as young children to encounter other women who will be reasonably nurturant toward them. The situation tends to be quite different for paternally deprived girls. They are much less apt to encounter a male who will express consistent kindness and sensitivity toward them.

The father is the first man in his daughter's life, and she will see him as the major representative of the other sex. During her early development, she will begin gradually to realize some sex-related differences between her and her father. As a young child, she will look to him for positive support of her femininity. As she enters adolescence, the father's role both as a male prototype and as a judge of her feminine adequacy will intensify. A solid relationship with her father during adolescence will help her weather insecurities in her interactions with male peers. With the background of a supportive paternal attachment, the daughter can more confidently enter into meaningful peer interactions with males and later develop a constructive heterosexual relationship.

Appropriate paternal involvement has very positive effects on a daughter's sexual development. College women who have successful long-term romantic relationships, for instance, report being relatively close to their fathers during childhood. On the other hand, women who have unstable sexual associations and broken marriages are much more likely to recall highly conflictual relationships with their fathers and paternal absence or inadequacy during childhood.

According to the results of psychologist Seymour Fisher's research, a woman's childhood relationship with her father may still play an important role in her relative sexual satisfaction as an adult, even in her ability to experience orgasm. Fisher analyzed the personality and marital adjustments of over three hundred middle-class housewives. His research project involved in-depth interviews and the administration of a comprehensive battery of psychological tests. Fisher found that a woman's confidence in herself and others relates very strongly to her ability to have an orgasm. Highly orgasmic women generally recalled their fathers as having a definite set of values and having high expectations for them. The responses of highly orgasmic women tended to indicate that they could depend on and trust their fathers. In contrast, most of the women who rarely reached orgasm described their fathers as having been psychologically unavailable for them. Some of the women who had difficulty achieving orgasm did not form a strong relationship with their father either because he had died early in their lives or he was frequently away from home for long periods of time because of work commitments. Surprisingly, this study revealed no evidence as to the special significance of the mother-daughter relationship with respect to the female's orgasmic capacity.

The father being involved and having high expectations for his daughter shows that he cares about her development and that she can rely upon him. Such a perception of the father makes it easier for the female to trust another man and to expect him to be considerate and caring toward her.

Acting Responsibly

Assuming they become aware of it, many parents feel quite unprepared to deal with their adolescent becoming involved in a sexual relationship, especially if it is their daughter. If there has been a good prior family atmosphere, although it may be difficult for them, the father and mother should continue to be supportive during the time of their child's first serious sexual involvement. Even prior to adolescence children usually have some idea of parental feelings about sexual relationships. There is a good chance that the child's initial sexual encounter will come during the high school years. The child should have a clear conception about parental feelings concerning premarital sexuality.

While parents may be very explicit about their expectations, they must realize that their children will, at some point during adolescence, begin to take more charge of their own lives. Constructive parenting involves being a concerned and loving adviser but not a controller of the child's personal decisions. High expectations will be much more effective in the long run than any attempts at ultimatums or intimidation. Some parents virtually lock their daughters up in an attempt to restrict their opportunity for any sexual involvement. However, this is likely to have very negative implications for long-term family relations. Parents should set reasonable time limits for the adolescent to be home at night and for notification of change in plans. They should make it clear that they will respond in a protective way if the child needs help in being extricated from a difficult situation.

Premarital sex can be more of a problem for females than males. Should a daughter become pregnant, she will most likely be left with the responsibility of making the major decisions relating to the pregnancy. She will probably have to decide whether she is willing to have the baby and if so, whether or not she will give it up for adoption. Fortunately, a growing trend in our society is for unwed fathers to share responsibility for such decisions and to be involved with their infants. Part of effective sex education is for the son as well as the daughter to develop a responsible attitude. Such an attitude involves exercising self-control, not being manipulative of another person and, if there is mutual consent for sexual relations, to assume responsibility jointly for appropriate birth-control techniques. Parent and child perspectives on these issues often differ, but as with other areas it is very important that the mother and father be explicit about their values and expectations.

If parents have some clear indications that their teenager is involved in a negative relationship, they can try to assume a concerned advisory role rather than an authoritarian one. If, for example, a daughter has been dating a young man who is insensitive and irresponsible, her parents should try to help her to end the relationship supportively without issuing any ultimatums. As most parents discover sooner or later, attempts to control their adolescent's behavior are doomed to failure. But if a positive history of family communication exists, parental values will most likely have a significant impact on the child's development. While parents can always have a role in being emotionally supportive and understanding, they must accept the fact that their children need to take responsibility for their own relationships.

The father and daughter need to acknowledge each other's sexuality in a safe manner without being incestuous. The healthy father is warm, patient and responsive to his daughter without being seductive. He helps to provide her with the emotional security to expand her experiences beyond the family gradually and confidently. When she enters adolescence he accepts her sexual development without becoming a rival with her boyfriends. The father should maintain a supportive relationship with his daughter without hindering her ability to form positive attachments with other males. He should encourage her to take responsibility for her actions whether they involve social encounters with male peers or decisions relating to education or career. A positive father-daughter relationship provides the young woman with a firm foundation for becoming close and intimate with another male as well as the confidence to pursue further educational and career development.

SOCIAL COMPETENCE

Children who have the benefit of being exposed to kind, considerate interactions between their parents are more apt to demonstrate respect for the rights of others. By expressing affection and caring toward each other, the father and mother are vividly presenting themselves as constructive role models. Both boys and girls need to develop effective modes of social interaction with males as well as females. The father's positive family involvement assumes special significance in fostering social competence because he is apt to be the only salient male adult the young child will encounter on a day-to-day basis.

Parental Example

Siblings are much more likely to respect one another when each child has the benefit of a positive relationship with both the mother and the father. Interactions between siblings can also be particularly significant in influencing relationships outside of the family. In some families, an older sibling may actually be more influential in socializing a child than either parent is. However, in most families, how the parents relate to one another as well as to each of their children sets the tone for both sibling and peer relationships.

Within the same family, children may vary greatly in their temperamental predispositions toward being socially active. One child may be quite shy while another may try to play and interact with everyone. Parents do much to encourage assertiveness and independence, but they must also accept the reality of individual differences in levels of sociability. At the most fundamental level parents need to be accepting of each child's individuality. Nevertheless, even as infants and toddlers, those children who have close, stimulating relationships with their fathers tend to be more socially competent with both adults and age-mates.

Ross Parke and his colleagues have conducted an extensive series of observational and experimental studies illustrating how play patterns with parents may influence the quality of the child's relationships with peers. This research has yielded a vast array of complex findings but, in general, young children who have parents who are engaging and expressive of positive effect while playing with them tend to do well in peer relationships. The most clear-cut results involved an association between the ability of the father to engage reciprocally in positively playful physical interactions with his son or daughter and the child's popularity. The father's ability to be responsive to the child's initiative, allowing for a nurturant give-and-take in their play, is especially important. However, when the father is dominating and controlling, the child is not learning effective social skills. Not surprisingly, Parke's research program has also revealed a linkage between paternal intrusiveness and over-directedness during play and the child, especially the son, being rejected or neglected by peers.

The capacity to express positive concern for the feelings of others is an important dimension of successful intimate relationships. Longitudinal data analyzed by psychologist Richard Koestner and his colleagues suggest that a major early family predictor of both men's and women's capacity for empathy toward others is the extent of positive father involvement experienced during the preschool years. Father participation in child care (assessed from maternal interview data) when the subjects were age five was strongly related to a measure of empathic concern (derived from a complex self-report measure) when they were age thirty-one. Other data indicate that a secure attachment to the father during infancy is predictive of the child's capacity for empathy and positive emotional responsivity during later phases of development.

Expanding Perspectives

Interactions with peers are a vital part of the child's development; they provide the opportunity to increase social knowledge as well as to test out patterns of reacting acquired within the family. Friendships can stimulate further cognitive and emotional development and expand the child's social competence. Fathers have a significant role to play in encouraging their children's positive peer relationships. Family experiences not only affect the young child but also have continuing ramifications throughout adolescence and adulthood. Although the older child may prefer being with friends much of the time, this does not mean that the family is no longer influential. For most children, even during adolescence and early adulthood, parents' opinions remain at least as significant as those of peers in matters ranging from self-discipline to personal grooming.

Assuming a background of relatively positive family relationships during earlier childhood, the teenager can still value fair and sensitively communicated parental opinions. Even when in phases of seeming adolescent rebelliousness, most children are affected by their parents' views in making major decisions.

Adolescents may publicly disavow parental influence, but at the same time they usually are still quite influenced by the values they were exposed to at home.

During later childhood and adolescence, children often become members of cliques or other types of peer groups. Being part of an informal peer group can have a valuable function as it allows a child to practice new ideas and social skills with others at a similar phase in their development. However, a weak self-concept may lead the individual to rely too heavily on friends when making decisions even after marriage and parenthood. To develop a mature sense of individuality, children must eventually acquire a sense of inner-directedness, considering the views of others but taking responsibility for their own lives. Parents can encourage children to realize that the quality of relationships is more significant than the quantity. They can emphasize the temporary nature of social cliques and the importance of making one's own decisions, helping the child to gain self-confidence regardless of the opinion of peers. Those children who have a close relationship with their father as well as with their mother are much more likely to have developed the self-discipline and moral judgment to resist peer pressure.

The child who has a supportive father and mother is likely to have the chance to experience a more diverse range of interpersonal relations with socially competent adults outside the family than is the boy or girl growing up with only an involved mother. Because of their differing interests and responsibilities, each parent has opportunities to help broaden the child's social knowledge. The father, for example, probably has social and work relationships with more men than the mother does. Constructive encounters with other men in the community are more likely for the child who has an involved father. However, the paternally neglected child is at risk to miss out on important social learning experiences, both inside and outside of the home.

Paternal Deprivation

Young children generally have ample opportunity to interact with women but typically have much more restricted experiences with men. Their mothers are usually highly available to them, and they encounter many women in other situations including female caretakers, teachers and family friends. However, if the father is not an available and caring parent, the young child may be at a long-term disadvantage with respect to learning how to relate positively to other males including peers.

Inadequately fathered children, particularly boys, tend to be less popular and have less satisfying peer relationships than children with highly involved fathers. Many father-absent or otherwise paternally deprived boys and girls have trouble maintaining friendships because they do not feel good about themselves and lack a sense of social confidence. Inadequately fathered children often have difficulty in constructively asserting themselves with peers, being more apt to be either overly passive or excessively demanding as compared to those who have been the recipients of positive involvement from both parents.

Paternal deprivation, including father-absence or neglect, may make a boy's relationship with females much more problematic. Without a solid gender identity the boy is less likely to feel secure with females. As he matures, the paternally deprived male may lack confidence in asserting his romantic intentions or may go to the other extreme of adopting a ''Don Juan'' mode of behavior, desperately trying to make himself feel masculine by attempting to add continually to his list of sexual conquests. Compared to those who are well fathered, paternally deprived males are more apt to have less satisfying sexual relationships and more unstable marriages. Research with unwed fathers indicates that they are likely themselves to have been members of paternally deprived families. It is relevant to note that a very high proportion of unwed mothers also grew up in families suffering from father-absence or other types of paternal inadequacy.

Father deprivation can greatly interfere with the daughter's interpersonal and sexual adjustment. Some paternally deprived girls become obsessed with heterosexual relationships as they desperately seek some form of substitute male affection. Others may idealize absent fathers and spend their lives in a futile search for a male who fits their unrealistic fantasy. Some women constructively overcome their childhood backgrounds of inadequate fathering, but for many the consequences of paternal deprivation have long-term implications. Women who reject the role of mother, or who are insecure in their basic femininity, are likely to come from father-deprived backgrounds. Delinquent girls and those who become pregnant out of wedlock are also more apt to have grown up in families lacking in positive father involvement.

When the father is absent because of divorce or desertion, the mother may bequeath derogatory attitudes toward males to her children. A female is very likely to grow up with the perception that men are irresponsible and untrustworthy. This seems to be a particular danger in economically impoverished communities where girls are less likely to be exposed to involved adult males inside or outside the family.

Paternal deprivation also has an impact on the quality of the mother-child relationship. When the father is absent, the child is more at risk to become overdependent on the mother. Maternal overdependence may injure girls more than boys because traditionally girls are not as socially encouraged to be assertive and independent. The result may be a girl who is excessively dependent on females and at the same time not able to trust males fully.

Mavis Hetherington conducted an extensive study illustrating some of the problems that father-absent females may have in dealing with males. Hetherington compared the behavior of adolescent girls from intact, widowed and divorced families in different situations. An important part of the research involved observations of each girl individually responding to questions posed by a male interviewer seated in a room with a desk and three other chairs. One chair was very near the interviewer, another was on the other side of the desk and the third was about three feet away.

Definite differences were revealed among the girls in terms of which chair they took and their other behaviors during the interview process. The girls from father-present families usually took the chair that was a medium distance away from the male interviewer, and they were fairly at ease with him. The girls whose parents had divorced tended to take the chair closest to the interviewer and to assume a more seductive, sprawling, open posture. They typically sat closer, leaned further forward and talked and smiled more than the girls from the other two groups. The girls whose fathers had died more often took the chair farthest away from the interviewer. They tended to sit, stiffly upright, looking away from the interviewer and speaking very little. Both groups of father-absent girls exhibited greater anxiety during the interview than those from intact families, more frequently pulling or tugging at their clothes, fingers or hair.

Differences among the groups of girls were also apparent in other social situations. Girls with divorced parents sought out boys more and tended to be seductive toward them. Observations made at a dance revealed that the daughters with divorced parents were usually found near the boys' stag lines, constantly trying to get their attention. Such girls also tended to be promiscuous, engaging in more and earlier sexual relationships than their father-present counterparts. In contrast, the girls whose fathers had died generally avoided boys and remained very inhibited around them. At the dance these girls kept away from the more male-populated areas of the dance floor. Two girls in this group even hid in the ladies' room for the entire evening.

Continuing Implications

Hetherington's research indicated that a girl's attitude toward males is influenced significantly by the context of her father deprivation. Interview responses revealed that the daughters in divorced families had very negative perceptions of their fathers, often mirroring their mothers' attitudes. In contrast, the girls whose fathers had died were more likely to remember them as idealized images that no other man could equal. Although they expressed it quite differently, both groups of father-absent girls had little self-confidence in dealing with males. Insecurity in relating to males was greater among those girls who became father-absent before the age of five. Such findings suggest that the early father-daughter relationship may be especially important in the female's later development.

Difficulties in dealing with men are not restricted to those females who grow up in father-absent homes. Females who have available but neglectful fathers can have very serious difficulties relating to males. For example, a study conducted by Kathleen Fish and me revealed the strong association between perceived father neglect during earlier childhood and the poor personal and social adjustment of females during late adolescence and early adulthood. When father-deprived girls become mothers themselves, they are more likely to be "carriers" of psychologically unhealthy attitudes about men, passing them on to both their sons and their daughters. Because of their own frustrating experiences, divorced and unmarried mothers are likely to communicate very negative attitudes about men to their children. Although it may be very difficult, it is important for mothers in single-parent families to give their children a more balanced view of men. Much needs to be done in our society to provide paternally deprived children with the opportunity to interact with caring adult males.

Hetherington presented evidence that suggests the continuing influence of early father-absence on adolescent and adult development. The daughters of divorced mothers generally had especially troubled heterosexual relationships. They were likely to marry at an earlier age than the other females and also to be pregnant before marriage. In addition, after a relatively brief period of time, some of these women were separated or divorced from their husbands. The daughters of divorced mothers tended to marry less adequate men than the other women did. Their husbands typically had a lower level of educational and vocational accomplishment and more often had been involved in difficulties with the law. Compared to the husbands of women in the other groups, these men also had more negative feelings toward their wives and infants and had greater difficulty controlling their impulses and behaving in an emotionally mature manner.

Daughters of widows tended to marry men who were vocationally successful and ambitious but who were overly controlled and inhibited in their social interactions. In general, the results of Hetherington's follow-up study suggested that women who grew up in two-parent households tended to make the most realistic and successful marital choices. These women also reported more satisfaction in their sexual relationships with their husbands than did the two groups of women who grew up in father-absent homes.

Hetherington's research must be viewed in the context of particular family-development issues. The divorced and widowed mothers of the father-absent girls had remained unmarried for a very lengthy period of time and were from working- and lower-middle-class backgrounds. Research involving more affluent previously divorced mothers who achieved happy second marriages while still relatively young does not suggest the same degree of social and psychological disablement for their children.

Sexual Adaptations

Individuals vary tremendously in the quality of their relationships and sexual adjustments. The development of sexual preferences and life-styles is a very complex process. Much controversy exists as to how much of a role early experience and family interactions play in determining an individual's proclivity toward heterosexuality or homosexuality. For example, some argue that genetic and prenatal factors largely determine which individuals will become homosexual, while others view this process largely in terms of social learning within the family. Homosexuals are indeed diverse in their early family backgrounds. However, some parent-child relationship patterns are quite prevalent though certainly not exclusive to them. Paternal absence, abuse or neglect can be at least a contributing factor in the development of homosexuality.

The close-binding mother-son relationship that sometimes precedes the expression of homosexuality in males frequently takes place in the context of a distant or otherwise inappropriate father-son relationship. In such a family situation, the father typically either ignores, rejects or abuses the boy, discouraging the development of self-esteem, assertiveness and independence. In addition to depriving the boy of an appropriate source of support, the indifferent or hostile father may thrust his son into a continuing search for a more loving male role model. This search together with the lack of a secure inner sense of masculinity makes the boy especially vulnerable to becoming involved in a relationship with an older, seemingly nurturant, male homosexual.

Some clinicians insist they have never dealt with a homosexual who had a close and warm relationship with his father. In a pioneering nine-year study of homosexuals undergoing psychotherapy, psychiatrist Irving Bieber and his colleagues found that most had hostile, indifferent or absent fathers. The mere absence of paternal hostility, however, was not enough to insulate sons from a homosexual adaptation. Some fathers of homosexuals were described as weak and ineffectual though not rejecting of their child.

Inadequacies in the father-child relationship have also been linked with female homosexuality. Compared to heterosexual women, lesbians are much more likely to view their fathers as weak and incompetent. But a variety of negative family and father-child relationships have been found in the backgrounds of lesbians. Some lesbians describe their fathers as having been puritanical, exploitative and fear-inducing, while others perceive them as overly possessive and infantilizing. A very high incidence of incestuous father-daughter relationships has been reported for lesbians. Incest victims may come to fear men and to reject heterosexuality because of their devastating early experiences. More relatively passive female homosexuals appear to have been incest victims as compared to those who possess a more stereotyped masculinized style.

Psychiatrist Harvey Kaye and his colleagues did a clinical research study comparing a group of female homosexuals and a group of female heterosexuals. Female homosexuals seemed to have had much the same type of family relationships as male homosexuals, except with the sexes of their parents reversed. While the fathers of male homosexuals were hostile and aloof, the mothers of lesbians were reported to be cold and distant from their daughters. Similar to the mothers of male homosexuals, the fathers of lesbians were close-binding, babying and unencouraging of normal gender development, many of them belittling their child's friends and communicating exaggerated fears and anxieties concerning health-related issues.

A major criticism of much of the research on homosexuality has been that it focuses on individuals with psychological problems. However, other investigators have found that even relatively well-adjusted homosexuals usually describe their fathers as having had little to do with them during childhood, being either ineffectual, neglectful or hostile. A study by psychologists Norman Thompson and Boyd McCandless with a nonclinical sample revealed that, compared to heterosexuals, both male and female homosexuals were more likely to come from homes with close-binding mothers and relatively uninvolved fathers.

Inadequate parent-child relations can play a role in the etiology of female as well as male homosexuality. However, there is a need to point out that the individual child's characteristics such as body-build and temperament can have a major impact on the quality of parenting behavior. Within the same family one child may benefit from what appears to be very positive paternal and maternal support while another receives very inadequate parenting. Nevertheless, most individuals who are the recipients of poor parenting still retain a heterosexual orientation even though they are at risk to experience much frustration and conflict in their relationships.

Complex Influences

Despite the indictment of inadequate parenting as a potential factor in the development of homosexuality, it is important to underscore the interactive nature of family influences. The child's temperament, appearance and interests affect the perceptions and reactions of parents. For example, the athletic, well-built father may not value his frail son because the boy does not live up to his concept of masculinity. The parent's rejecting or indifferent attitude may result in the child's lack of gender security and increase vulnerability to a homosexual pattern of behavior. But the same parent can have a relatively positive relationship with another child whose behavior more clearly fits family sex-role expectations.

Disagreement persists as to how much homosexuality is based upon early experiences and how much it is a function of subtle biological predispositions. Examples of homosexual development, at least on the surface, can be used to support either view, but in my opinion, more examples fit an interactional perspective. Many individuals are vulnerable to manifest somewhat gender-atypical behavior as a function of biological predispositions, but in most cases, high-quality involvement by both parents can counter the development of a homosexual pattern of behavior.

Hormonal irregularities during the prenatal period may influence subtle changes in brain chemistry, which in turn may make it more likely that an individual will gravitate toward interests at an early age that are inconsistent with gender stereotypes. A boy may be uncomfortable in rough-and-tumble endeavors, preferring sedentary activities. A young girl who is especially active and assertive may develop a strong preference for play with boys. Nevertheless, most children who are interested in activities more common to the other sex in early childhood do not later end up making a homosexual adaptation.

Children are not merely passive recipients of the behavior modeled by parents. In fact, most homosexuals have heterosexual parents. Some data presented by psychiatrist Richard Green also do not support the simplistic notion that homosexual or transsexual parents are likely to produce children who develop similar sexual adaptations. For instance, children who have lesbian mothers do not seem to be particularly programmed to become homosexual. The vast majority of boys and girls have a natural, innate tendency toward heterosexuality. Except in unusual cases, the predisposition to respond in an erotically aroused fashion to the other sex is inborn. On the other hand, the specifics of interpersonal relations between males and females are greatly influenced by learning within the family.

A homosexual pattern of behavior is often developed as a defense against a fear of being dominated or abused in the context of intimacy with the other sex.

Homosexuality refers to a consistent preference for sexual activity with individuals of the same gender. Parents should not stereotype a child who has a homosexual episode before or during adolescence. Some children go through such experiences while experimenting in peer relationships but later adopt a consistent preference for a heterosexual life-style.

Despite the likelihood of earlier family development difficulties, many homosexuals have been able during adulthood to live relatively happy and productive lives. Just as individuals are not necessarily well-adjusted as a function of being heterosexual, they are not maladjusted simply because they are homosexual. Tremendous individual differences are evident among homosexuals as well as among heterosexuals.

Children who have a homosexual father or mother are more at risk to develop sexual conflicts and problems than those with two positively heterosexual parents. But so are children with heterosexual parents who have very inadequate marriages. Whether heterosexual or homosexual, parents with serious relationship difficulties are likely to contribute to their children's long-term vulnerability to sexually related problems.

Adult Functioning

Psychiatrist William Appleton has argued that the father remains a highly significant influence throughout his daughter's development. Using in-depth clinical interviews, he intensively studied the life histories and functioning of eighty-one middle-class women. These individuals, as compared to the hundreds he had dealt with in therapy, were not in treatment, but nevertheless were willing to delve into their relationships with their fathers and other men in their lives. From these interviews as well as his clinical practice, Appleton emphasizes how the earlier father-daughter relationship may have a continuing impact on the development of adult women.

The father's attentiveness and support are crucial for the daughter's feelings of self-worth during childhood and for her potential to develop positive relationships with other men during adulthood. Unfortunately, fewer than 20 percent (only 15 of 81) of the women that Appleton interviewed reported having fathers who were able to be loving and supportive in a way that also enhanced their daughter's sense of individuality, competence and ability to engage in mature intimate relationships with other men. Most of the women reported having experienced very inadequate relationships with their fathers. Almost 60 percent (48 of 81) described distant or nonexistent relationships with their fathers. Half of these (24) women had fathers who were very aloof, and a similar number (24) suffered from childhood paternal deprivation due to their father's death (12) or their parents' divorce (12). The remaining 22 percent (18 of 81) had overly intrusive, controlling or restrictive fathers who enmeshed them in rather symbiotic relationships.

Whereas 60 percent (9 of 15) of the women who had positive relationships with their fathers during childhood reported healthy, satisfying marriages or attachments with men, this was true for less than 10 percent (6 of 61) of those who had suffered from inadequate or symbiotic paternal influence. For example, none of the women with symbiotic paternal relationships or divorced parents, and only three each in the deceased or aloof father groups, had yet achieved what Appleton considered a healthy heterosexual adjustment.

Appleton also reported other interview findings that supported a connection between a woman's perception of her childhood relationship with her father and her adult adjustment. More than 75 percent of the women who described their fathers as having been gentle to them considered themselves to be generally happy individuals. In contrast, among those who had viewed their fathers as stern, harsh or cruel, more than 60 percent communicated a pervasive sense of unhappiness. Among women who felt emotionally distanced from their husbands or lovers, 80 percent had experienced some form of paternal deprivation during childhood whereas only 20 percent viewed their relationship with their father as having been positive.

Appleton's interview and clinical observations are quite provocative, but the richness of his speculations must be tempered with an awareness of the uncontrolled nature of his data collection. For example, he gives no detailed report of his subjects' characteristics or any objective assessment of their functioning— in fact, all observations and interpretations were made directly by him. Nevertheless, other researchers' more systematic investigations support the notion that the quality of the early father-daughter relationship has a significant impact on the long-term adjustment of women.

Multiple Accomplishments

Longitudinal data analyzed by psychologist Carol Franz and her colleagues uncovered a linkage between paternal warmth experienced at age five and mid-life success at age forty-one for both men and women. Those individuals who were rated as having warm and affectionate fathers when they were in kindergarten were more likely at mid-life to have achieved long-term marriages, parenthood and close friendships. The measure of paternal warmth at age five was garnered from the mother's interview responses and was positively associated with her general agreement with her husband's discipline techniques and her overall respect for him. Although the measure of maternal warmth was also positively associated with the child's accomplishments at mid-life, the findings were not as strong as those involving the paternal warmth measure.

Sociologists Frank Furstenberg and Kathleen Harris provide evidence that nurturant fathering can help individuals to overcome difficult life circumstances. They found that the quality of paternal relationships was especially important for economically disadvantaged black children. In two-parent families, compared to those with less adequate paternal relationships, those who reported close attachments and feelings of identification with their fathers (or stepfathers) during adolescence were twice as likely as young adults to have found a stable job or to have entered college and were 75 percent less likely to have become unwed parents, 80 percent less likely to have been in jail and 50 percent less likely to have suffered from multiple symptoms of depression.

Having a close relationship with the nonresidential biological father also was somewhat associated with an increased likelihood for high attainment and less risk for imprisonment or depression, but the advantages for such children were considerably less than they appeared to be for those who lived with both parents. Furthermore, children's perceived closeness to their biological mothers, whether in one-parent or two-parent families, it generally seemed to have much *less* impact on their well-being during early adulthood than the quality of their relationship with their fathers.

As Furstenberg and Harris emphasize, however, only a small minority, less than 10 percent of the economically disadvantaged children they studied, experienced a stable and close relationship with a residential father (or stepfather) during childhood and adolescence. Although daughters were less likely than sons to form strong attachments to their fathers, those who developed close paternal bonds functioned especially well in early adulthood. This research indicates that children generally thrive better in families with two stable parenting figures. The data are consistent with the supposition that the child is a great deal more likely to experience high-quality parental involvement in a two-parent family than when the father does not reside in the household.

Life Satisfaction

The quality of paternal involvement that individuals receive during childhood tends to be associated with their social competence and life satisfaction in later development. Mark Reuter and I found that the personal and social adjustment of college males was positively related to their perceptions of having been exposed to at least moderate amounts of father nurturance and availability during childhood. Kathleen Fish and I collected data that indicated that the father also plays a particularly important role in the girl's personality development. College females who perceived their fathers as having been very nurturant and positively interested in them during childhood scored much higher on measures of self-acceptance and personal and social adjustment than those who viewed their fathers as having been negligent and rejecting toward them.

Michael Hansen and I investigated the father-related perceptions of young adult children and their parents. Middle-aged fathers who viewed themselves as having been the recipients of a high level of paternal nurturance during childhood tended to have sons and daughters who perceived them as being attentive and affectionate parents. Moreover, among the young adult sons and daughters, perceived nurturant father involvement during childhood was positively associated with self-reports of personal adjustment, emotional stability and social competence. Our findings were consistent with the notion that the earlier father-child relationship is a significant factor in the adult's personality functioning and potential to be an effective parent.

Using family data collected decades earlier, psychologist Jack Block analyzed the connection between parenting during childhood and personal and social adjustment in adulthood. He found that both fathers and mothers were highly involved in the upbringing of males who achieved a successful adjustment in adulthood. Those adult males who were poorly adjusted, however, had fathers who were typically neglectful and uninvolved in child rearing and mothers who tended to be anxious and insecure. Females who were the best adjusted as adults grew up in homes with two positively involved parents. Their mothers were described as affectionate, personable and resourceful and their fathers as warm, competent and firm. A second group of relatively well-adjusted females came from homes with extremely bright, capable and ambitious mothers but rather passive yet warm fathers. In contrast, most of the less well-adjusted females had been reared in homes where either one or both parents demonstrated inadequate social relations skills within the family.

In a related research project, Block and his coworkers found that well-socialized and successful adult males typically had grown up in households with highly involved fathers and parents who had compatible relationships. In contrast, adult males who were relatively low in social skills and personal adjustment typically grew up in families in which the parents were incompatible and the fathers were either uninvolved, weak or emotionally conflicted. The most well-adjusted females tended to come from families in which both parents had been positively involved with them. Their fathers were described as warm and accepting, and their mothers appeared to have been excellent role models with respect to intellectual competence. A variety of family patterns emerged among the less well-adjusted females, but it was clear that few if any had family backgrounds marked by a combination of a compatible father-mother relationship and a positively involved father.

Psychologist Margery Lozoff's findings from a study with upper-middle-class individuals strongly suggest that positive father-daughter relationships are crucial in the development of women who are able to be successful in their heterosexual relationships as well as in their career endeavors. These unusually competent women had accomplished fathers who had treated them with respect. They valued their daughters' basic femininity but at the same time encouraged and expected them to develop their competencies. The women exposed to a basic compatibility between their fathers and mothers developed positive identifications with both parents and comfortably feminine gender identities.

Inadequate father-child relationships were evident for a second group of women who displayed autonomy but had much personal conflict. Their fathers tended to be aloof perfectionists who had very high expectations for their daughters but did not provide enough emotional support for them to develop solid self-confidence. A third group of women who were very low in autonomy came from economically privileged but highly sex-typed family situations. The father in such a family seemed to offer his daughter little encouragement for intellectual competence, leaving her socialization mainly up to his wife. In contrast, women who had achieved a high level of success in intellectual and occupational endeavors were much more likely to have had a strong relationship with a father who accepted their femininity but expected them to be persistent and competent.

It is not easy for a female to get the necessary family support to develop into a well-rounded, secure and competent adult. It is striking that so few fathers are adequately involved with their daughters. Not many females receive paternal encouragement for both a strong feminine self-concept and intellectual competence. The female's ability to have both a successful marriage and a career is increased when she has experienced a supportive relationship with her father. On the other hand, chronic marital and career dissatisfaction occurs at a much higher rate among women who have grown up in families with an uninvolved, inadequate or abusive father. Exposure to positive paternal and maternal influence during childhood increases the likelihood that females as well as males will be socially and vocationally successful during adulthood, able happily to pursue their personal, family and career interests.

SUMMARY

The child's social and sexual development can be greatly facilitated by a caring, accessible and dependable father who fosters a sense of closeness, sharing and trust. The father's positive family involvement assumes special significance in fostering social competence because he is apt to be the only salient male adult the child encounters on a day-to-day basis. Both boys and girls need to develop effective modes of social interaction with males as well as females.

Children who have the benefit of being exposed to kind, considerate interactions between their parents are likely to have a solid basis for constructive male-female relationships. By conveying positive values about male-female relationships, the nurturant father can have an especially crucial role in supporting his son's and daughter's capacity for intimacy. His encouragement of assertiveness, body pride and basic self-esteem increases the likelihood of his child having constructive relationships both inside and outside of the family.

Although many interacting biopsychosocial influences are involved, the quality of fathering that individuals receive during childhood tends to be associated with their social competence, sexual adjustment and life satisfaction in adulthood. The earlier father-mother-child relationship is a significant factor in the adult's personality functioning and capacity for success in marriage, parenting and work. Exposure to positive paternal and maternal influence during childhood increases the likelihood that females as well as males will be socially and vocationally successful during adulthood, able happily to pursue their personal, family and career interests.

FURTHER READING

Intimate Relationships

Family Dynamics

Concerning basic psychoanalytic conceptions of early sexual development and the Oedipal complex, see Freud (1950, 1962), Machtlinger (1981) and Viorst (1986). For reviews of psychodynamic and other theories and research emphasizing particular aspects of parental behavior in fostering a positive identification with the same-sex parent, see Biller (1971a, 1974c).

With respect to research relating parental sexual anxiety and discomfort in certain aspects of child care, see Sears, Rau and Alpert (1965).

For suggestions for differentiating between constructive and destructive parent-child intimacy, see Biller and Meredith (1974), Biller and Solomon (1986), Katchadourian (1985), Rosen and Hall (1984) and Sgroi (1981).

Sharing Values

On children's learning about sexuality and reproduction, see Bernstein and Cowan (1975), Goldman and Goldman (1982) and Rosen and Hall (1984). For detailed information regarding human sexual behavior, see Katchadourian (1985), Masters and Johnson (1966, 1970) and Rosen and Hall (1984).

For value-related issues and parent-child communication relevant to sexuality, see Brooks (1991), Brooks-Gunn and Furstenberg (1989) and Schulman and Mekler (1985).

Fostering Trust

About the father's role in the child's sexual development, see Biller (1971a, 1971b, 1981a) and Biller and Solomon (1986). For the mother's influence on the daughter's sexual behavior, see Hetherington (1972) and Inazu and Fox (1980).

Concerning orgasm among females, see Fisher (1973). For other research emphasizing the significance of early paternal influence on the daughter's later sexual and marital functioning, see Biller (1971a, 1981b), Biller and Solomon (1986), Fleck et al. (1980), Hetherington (1972, 1977) and Hetherington and Parke (1986).

Acting Responsibly

With regard to guidelines for responsible sexual behavior, see Brooks (1991), Katchadourian (1985) and Rosen and Hall (1984). About sexual responsibility in adolescence and long-term issues involved in teenaged pregnancy and childbearing, see Furstenberg, Brooks-Gunn and Chase-Landsdale (1989) and Furstenberg, Brooks-Gunn and Morgan (1987).

Social Competence

Parental Example

On friendship patterns and peer influences in the child's socialization, see Brooks (1991), Hartup (1989), Hay (1985), MacDonald (1987) and Parke et al. (1988).

For sibling influences, see Bank and Kahn (1982), Cicirelli (1982), Dunn (1985), Dunn and Kendrick (1982), Lamb and Sutton-Smith (1982), Minett, Vandell and Santrock (1983), Sutton-Smith and Rosenberg (1970) and Taylor and Kogan (1973). For research on only children, see Falbo (1982) and Glenn and Hoppe (1984). For the typically greater influence of parents as compared to siblings in the child's development, see Baskett and Johnston (1982) and Biller (1968a).

About temperamentally related individual differences and parenting issues in dealing with the socially inhibited and shy child, see Belsky and Rovine (1987), Chess and Thomas (1986, 1987), Kagan (1984, 1989) and Zimbardo and Radl (1981).

Expanding Perspectives

Concerning the importance of the child being able to relate well to both the father and the mother, and how such experiences can positively generalize to social relations beyond the family, see Biller (1971a, 1974c, 1981c), Biller and Meredith (1974), Biller and Solomon (1986), Hartup (1983, 1989), Pettit, Dodge and Brown (1988) and Steinberg et al. (1991). For the relationship between parental occupation and child's social experiences, see Barclay, Stillwell and Barclay (1972), Biller (1971a), Kohn (1979) and Kohn and Schooler (1978).

Paternal Deprivation

On the general quality of male-female relationships in the family being a major factor in the child's later sexual and marital adjustment, see Biller (1971a, 1971c, 1981c, 1982a), Biller and Meredith (1974), Biller and Solomon (1986), Block (1971) and Block, von der Lippe and Block (1973).

For the impact of father-absence on the daughter's sexual adjustment, see Hetherington (1972) and Hetherington and Parke (1986). See also Fisher (1973) and Fleck et al. (1980).

Continuing Implications

About patterns of adult female development often associated with early paternal deprivation, see Biller (1982a), Biller and Solomon (1986), Fish and Biller (1973), Hetherington (1977), Hetherington and Parke (1986) and Wallerstein and Blakeslee (1989).

Sexual Adaptations

Regarding research focusing on parenting factors associated with homosexuality, see Bieber et al. (1962), Green (1987), Kaye et al. (1967), Thompson and McCandless (1976) and Thompson et al. (1973). See also Apperson and McAdoo (1968) and Evans (1969).

Complex Influences

For biosocial factors involved in the development of sexual preferences, see Bell, Weinberg and Mannersmith (1981), Biller (1975b), Green (1978, 1987), Money (1987) and Money and Ehrhardt (1972). For research on homosexual parents and their children, see Bozett (1988) and Robinson and Barrett (1986).

Adult Functioning

With respect to interview study of adult women, see Appleton (1981). For more systematically collected data, see Block (1971), Block, von der Lippe and Block (1973), Hetherington, Cox and Cox (1985) and Wallerstein and Blakeslee (1989).

Multiple Accomplishments

Concerning studies linking paternal involvement during childhood with adult success, see Franz, McClelland and Weinberger (1991) and Furstenberg and Harris (1992). For other relevant longitudinal research see Block (1971), Block, von der Lippe and Block (1973), Heath and Heath (1991), Koestner, Franz and Weinberger (1990), Koestner, Zuroff and Powers (1991), Snarey (1992) and Snarey, Maier and Pleck (1987).

Life Satisfaction

For data relating to fathering factors involved in college students' adjustment, see Fish and Biller (1973), Hansen and Biller (1992) and Reuter and Biller (1973). For reviews of early parenting antecedents of adult adjustment, see Biller (1981b, 1981c, 1982a) and Biller and Solomon (1986).

Concerning research linking the behavior of both parents during childhood and the quality of adult functioning, see Block (1971), Block, von der Lippe and Block (1973) and Lozoff (1974). See also Barnett and Baruch (1978) and McClelland et al. (1978).

About individuals who function extremely well as adults despite having had quite limited parental or family support as children, see Berlinsky and Biller (1982), Gordon and Braitwaite (1986), Kagan (1984) and Werner and Smith (1982).

11

Child and Family Problems

In this chapter, an emphasis is placed on circumstances that may make family life especially difficult for parents and children. The first half addresses divorce-related topics, but it is relevant for individuals in a variety of family situations. The second half focuses on the development of troubled and maltreated children. Many family and child problems are associated with inadequate father participation and an overburdened mother.

MARITAL SEPARATION

Maintaining an effective sense of parenthood becomes particularly complicated for most divorced fathers and mothers. Over one million couples in this country get divorced each year, and almost two-thirds of them have children. The divorce process may initially only directly involve the father and mother, but children are the family members who may ultimately be most influenced by parental separation. Children are particularly vulnerable to suffering from a lack of paternal involvement since almost 90 percent of them do not live with their father subsequent to the divorce.

Proceeding Cautiously

Although a growing recognition of problems relating to paternal deprivation exists, the divorced father's role is in great need of more positive definition and social support. Even in divorced families, the general expectation should be that men as well as women have an enduring responsibility to their children. A father who is chronically out of the home because of the nature of his employment may still be perceived as trying to provide economically for his family. In the event of paternal death, the child realizes that it is not the father's fault that he is absent from the family. However, children from divorced families who have a noninvolved father have a much more difficult time trying to rationalize their paternal deprivation. In such circumstances, the child is likely to feel a profound sense of being rejected by the father.

Parents can help their children better cope with divorce in many ways. Except in extreme cases of family violence, every consideration should be given to slowing down the separation and divorce process. This should be done not only to provide for a greater possibility of successful reconciliation but also to allow more time for both adults and children to adjust to new family living arrangements.

In the past, a greater proportion of parents remained in unsatisfactory marriages for many reasons including their belief that divorce would be harmful to their children. No doubt, in previous generations, many parents and children would have been better off if divorce was considered a viable alternative. However, in contemporary American society, divorce has typically become so legally simplified that far too often parents do not give enough consideration to long-term or even short-term ramifications of such a decision. Some parents, although they do not hurry into a divorce, rather quickly seek a legal separation, which may inadvertently hasten a permanent family breakup, or at least drastically change the nature of parent-child relationships. Parents and mental health professionals need to be just as fully cognizant of the long-term risks associated with a premature separation as they are of the implications of being chronically locked into an unsatisfying marriage. A thorough analysis should be undertaken as to whether the marriage might, with time and effort, be revitalized, and if not, how it can be terminated in a way that minimizes the negative impact on each family member.

Divorce affects the development of parents as well as children. Typically it takes fathers and mothers a period of at least a year or two, and more often three to five years, to regain a consistent sense of emotional well-being. Some adults, unfortunately, never really deal constructively with the aftermath of divorce. Because of the psychological difficulties that adults may be experiencing in the divorce process, the quality of parenting may greatly suffer at a time when children are in particular need of both positive paternal and maternal involvement.

Exhibiting Commitment

In families where both the father and the mother were positively involved parents before the divorce, the child is likely to have a sound basis for a continuing sense of security. However, the child's emotional security can be greatly threatened if a previously involved parent becomes relatively inaccessible, so often the case for the postdivorce father. The idea of a parent no longer being part of the family is very frightening for a child. The best way to allay these fears is for both parents to spend individualized quality time with their child on a regular basis. Divorce may actually lead parents in certain circumstances to become more constructively involved with their children. Although in the minority, some noncustodial fathers actually spend more one-to-one time with their children than they did prior to the divorce. Some heretofore relatively uninvolved fathers now make sure that they devote at least a limited amount of individualized time to seeing their children.

A major issue in the child's adjustment to divorce relates to the degree to which some positive sense of connectedness and continuity remains in the relationship with each parent. For this reason, postdivorce, significant advantages often emerge for some sort of joint or shared custody arrangement, ensuring regular child-rearing responsibilities for each parent.

The findings of family development researchers Kristen Rosenthal and Harry Keshet vividly illustrate how separated and divorced fathers tend to feel better about themselves and their relationships with their children when they have regularly shared child-rearing responsibilities. Quarter-time and half-time fathers generally felt much more satisfied than either traditional divorced fathers who had limited visitation with their offspring or those who had ended up with total child-rearing responsibilities. From the perspective of most quarter-time and half-time fathers, shared parenting responsibilities allow for a relatively positive balance of time to pursue their personal interests and to have high-quality individualized involvement with their children. A frequent and somewhat wistful sentiment expressed by many such fathers was that they may have had much bette: marriages if they could have as effectively shared parenting responsibilities before the separation or divorce.

A particular problem with traditional mother-custody is that it tends to circumscribe greatly the father's role in child rearing, reducing him in many cases to an occasional provider of entertainment. The father who has only Saturday or Sunday visitation, for example, may find it very difficult to feel any real sense of effectiveness. On the other hand, the mother is put in the role of assuming all parental decision making on a day-to-day basis, making her a likely target for the child's frustration and resentment.

In the traditional custody situation, the mother has to see to it that the child's teeth are brushed, take care of doctor's visits and try to enforce household rules. In contrast the father, if he does follow through with visitation opportunities, probably just takes the child for a fun afternoon and evening, perhaps going to a movie and out for dinner. In such a situation the father is likely to be cast in the role of an overly permissive parent. Nevertheless, noncustodial parents who regularly interact with their children can become positive examples of dependability, caring and sensitivity. For instance, the responsible noncustodial father who does not abandon his children but makes the most out of opportunities to interact with them can indeed be a very salient model of adult adaptation under difficult circumstances.

When either parent is perceived to be neglectful, the child may develop a "quitting syndrome." This type of predilection does not apply only to a child's future love relationships but also to school, friendships and other areas of life. Divorced fathers, as well as those in intact families, can guard against a family pattern of irresponsibility by maintaining a close relationship with each of their children.

Sharing Custody

In most cases, ramifications of custody decisions that exclude or narrowly limit the participation of either parent tend ultimately to have a negative impact on children. The majority of custody decisions giving exclusive or primary responsibility to mothers parallels the more general social attitude concerning the alleged primacy of maternal influence in the lives of children. Such an unbalanced perspective is potentially damaging to children, whether it is related to families of divorce or to households where the parents live together.

Although definite signs of change have become evident, especially during the past decade, discrimination against the father remains an issue in the divorce court. Just as society tends to treat fatherhood as a second-class role, so does the law. Many judges today still assume, despite the legal concept of joint custody, that a mother is naturally more fit to be the primary parent and to raise the child than is the father. This is not to say that unfit fathers do not exist but that every custody situation should be carefully assessed without reliance on outmoded stereotypes. Whether the parents are married or divorced, each should be assumed to have equally important responsibilities in child rearing. By beginning the division of child-care responsibilities from a basis of legal equality, the divorced father who wants to have an active role will really have a chance to behave in a committed manner. The divorced father should have a solid basis from which to assert his rights and responsibilities. He should not be considered guilty of incompetence as a parent just because he is a man.

The expectation of mother-custody as the norm is outdated in today's society. Given the greater opportunities for women in the working world today, it is an anachronism for a court simply to award support payments to a woman so that she can stay home to be a full-time mother while at the same time severely restricting the father's access to the child. Neither parent should be expected to assume all the economic or emotional responsibilities of child rearing. Although much deep-seated resistance still persists, the importance of fathers has received increased attention in divorce settlements. A slowly growing percentage of fathers are being granted custody, one hopes when it is clearly in the best interests of the child. No general policy should automatically favor either fathers or mothers in the awarding of physical custody. Each case should be considered on an individual basis with many different factors being taken into account.

Predivorce discussions can lead to more situations where both parents remain actively involved with their children. When custody is awarded to the mother, most judges are making attempts to ensure more equitable visitation privileges for fathers than was the case in past decades. A marked increase has occurred in the consideration of joint-custody provisions that relate to shared child-rearing responsibilities beyond each parent's basic legal right to have a say in major educational and medical decisions. A mutually agreeable visitation arrangement may defuse custody as a major issue. In one case in which I was involved as a consultant, although the mother had physical custody of the child, the father was guaranteed very frequent and regular visiting privileges. This father has remained particularly involved and effective with his child even though he has a very demanding career and the child was less than two at the time of the divorce. The father does something with his young daughter four or five times a week in the late afternoon for at least an hour, keeps in contact with her by phone on days they do not see each other, and they have bimonthly overnight weekend visits together.

During the last twenty years, I have received hundreds of inquiries from parents, mostly fathers but also some mothers, concerning custody and visitation issues. Some of the parents merely wanted information but most were interested in having me participate in more direct consultation or as an expert witness. Perhaps the most important sign of progress is the more careful consideration of the child's perspective in custody decisions. In an increasing proportion of cases, the court appoints a specific lawyer or advocate to represent the rights of the child.

Maintaining Stability

In making custody arrangements, it is important to realize that family life is not static, and situations change. However, it is the responsibility of both parents to provide stability for their children. It is exceedingly stressful when young children from divorced families are put in the position where they are faced with a marked reduction of contact with one of their parents because either their mother or their father has chosen to move to another area.

In a very large proportion of the cases where I am contacted, the precipitating factor for the divorced parents waging a battle over custody has been related to the mother's decision to move to another locality. The mother's decision usually occurs within the first few years following the divorce. In most of these situations, the mother has had primary custody, but the father often has had liberal visitation privileges or even, in some instances, has had joint physical custody. Because of social or employment opportunities, or because of remarriage, the mother may decide to move with the children to another part of the country. After the divorce, for similar reasons, the father may also decide to move out of state, but typically he does not expect to take his children with him. Prior to the mother's decision to move, the father usually has not even considered primary physical custody. However, he now feels compelled to fight for custody when faced with losing the continuity of his contact with his children, and he is likely to be further motivated because of their reluctance to move away from friends, relatives and classmates as well as from him.

Whatever the reasons for a decision to move, significant geographical distance between the parents usually creates problems for the children. In the case of young children, even one or two hours of travel time can make easy access to both parents difficult. When children are older or reach adolescence this may not be as much of an issue. On the other hand, a large amount of traveling distance between the divorced spouses may increase the likelihood of the child choosing to leave the residence of the custodial parent. Living with the previously noncustodial parent may begin to appear preferable to the child when much conflict occurs at home. Children usually do not have as much of a need to run away when they have easy access to both parents. They do not have to move out of a household just to get contact with the other parent.

When divorced parents live relatively close to one another, children are more likely to feel comfortable at both residences. Such proximity may be difficult for some divorced parents, but over time it fosters the child's security to see the mother and father cooperate and share responsibility. In the shared custody arrangement, both parents can take turns in necessary transportation. When both residences are nearby, and as children become more mobile, divorced parents may have little need to have face-to-face interactions.

How divorced parents communicate about each other to the child continues to be of great importance, perhaps even more so than during the marriage. Denouncing the ex-spouse to the children is an all-too-common problem in divorced families. The stress that typically accompanies divorce, even in many cases where it began as a relatively amicable process, can negatively impact all members of the family. To maintain sensitivity toward the needs of children when the emotional world of one and probably both parents is in turmoil is at best an extremely difficult task.

Parent Loss

Individuals who spend a significant part of their childhoods in single-parent families are extremely varied in the quality of their later development: some have highly successful personality adaptations while others have long-term problems. Ellen Berlinsky and I reviewed research concerning the impact of loss of a parent during childhood. Father-loss was found to be at least as predictive of later developmental problems as mother-loss. However, our analysis emphasized the importance of examining the total context of parental loss including consideration of the child's personal characteristics, the reason for the loss and the quality of the remaining family support system.

Although children were at risk to suffer from paternal deprivation associated either with the father's death or with divorce, the type of personality difficulties tended to be different. Paternal deprivation as a result of divorce was more likely to be associated with impulse control problems and with lessened intellectual abilities. Though at risk to suffer from self-doubt and passivity, father-bereaved individuals were more often viewed as having made a socially appropriate adjustment than those who suffered from father-loss due to divorce.

In any case, a large proportion of individuals do develop quite well despite experiencing parental loss during childhood. In the face of coping with the loss of a parent whether through death or divorce, the adaptive capacities and family resources of children vary greatly. Under some circumstances, losing a parent during childhood may even be related to positive consequences. A child may actually benefit from the loss of a relationship with a physically or sexually abusive parent. Children from competent single-parent families are less handicapped in their personality development than those from two-parent households excessively dominated by either a mother or a father or marked by a severely dysfunctional husband-wife relationship. For example, maternally dominated children are likely to develop a perception of men as ineffectual, especially if their father is continually being denigrated or controlled by their mother. In contrast, father-absent children with competent mothers may evolve a much more positive view of adult male behavior.

A broad-based view of development allows for the possibility that a parent's absence from the household could have varying consequences. A parent's death could, for example, lead a child to search continually for someone else to take responsibility. The overprotective reactions of other family members could encourage a sense of helplessness in the child. In contrast, another child who has lost a parent may have similar feelings of deprivation yet have the personal and family resources to develop in a much more constructive direction. Such an individual may become extremely self-reliant and assertive, in marked contrast to the child who develops depressive tendencies after losing a parent through death or divorce. Under certain circumstances, some individuals may even react to the early loss of a parent with unusual creative achievements.

Developmental Findings

Mavis Hetherington and her colleagues Roger and Martha Cox conducted a multifaceted research project on the effects of divorce and single parenting on young children. Because this study offers better comparisons with nondivorced families than does other research, it deserves special consideration. A vast array of findings were garnered from several types of procedures. Assessments of family interactions in the home were made as well as observer, teacher and peer ratings at various points during the first two years after the divorce.

Both father-absence due to divorce and a high level of parental conflict in intact families were associated with difficulties in the personal and social adjustment of young children. Children living with their mothers postdivorce and those from homes with a high degree of father-mother conflict were generally less mature and independent in their social interactions than those from families in which there was little or only moderate marital conflict.

The relative standing of children from divorced families compared to those in high-conflict families changed over time. At one year after the divorce, the children from single parent households generally were experiencing more interpersonal difficulties at school and at home than children from high-conflict families. Two years after the divorce, however, the children from single-parent households seemed to be faring better than those from high-conflict families. The girls seemed to be less affected by both marital discord and father-absence than the boys. Decreased availability of the father during the two years postdivorce was associated with a lowered level of intellectual and social adequacy for boys. However, girls did not appear to be similarly affected by paternal deprivation. Nevertheless, the quality of mother-child interactions in the single-parent home were strongly related to boys' and girls' intellectual functioning and personal and social adjustment two years after the divorce.

Psychologist Judith Wallerstein and her colleagues have conducted an extremely important long-term project studying the effects of divorce on children. Their findings are based on extensive interviews with family members at several intervals: just after the separation and one, five, ten and fifteen years later. The depth and scope of their data relating to divorce is unparalleled, but unfortunately they did not have a nondivorced comparison group in their study. A comparison with children from nondivorced families could give a much clearer frame of reference concerning the relative severity of difficulties associated with divorce. Despite its limitations, this research has been the most extensive in terms of number and variety of children at different ages and the span of years covered.

In order to assess the effects of divorce on children at different developmental levels, Wallerstein and psychologist Joan Kelly divided the children into several different groups on the basis of their age at the time of the initial separation. It is important to emphasize that whatever their age or the nature of particular family circumstances, the children did not initially respond well to the reality of the divorce. Without exception all the children indicated a desire for their parents to stay together, and even after the divorce, most fantasized that their parents would remarry. However, the relative adequacy of the children's subsequent adjustments, both short- and long-term, was influenced by a variety of factors in addition to the divorce.

Diverse Reactions

Two- and three-year-olds were particularly prone to regress, express bewilderment, anger and a clinging and indiscriminate neediness toward adults in reaction to parental divorce. Regression seemed to be rather brief if children received adequate and consistent emotional involvement from adult family members. Those children who continuously experienced intense parental conflict and whose mothers were devastated by the divorce appeared very depressed and developmentally delayed even a year after the divorce.

Among the three- and four-year-olds, a poor self-image and loss of self-esteem were frequent concomitants of parental divorce. A feeling of responsibility for the parents' divorce was also common among these children. More of the five- and six-year-olds, in contrast to the younger children, seemed able to weather the divorce without manifesting clear-cut developmental setbacks. Such data are very consistent with other findings indicating that children are particularly vulnerable to early paternal deprivation beginning before the age of five.

Many of the seven- and eight-year-olds seemed intensely sad in response to parental divorce, especially about not having as much contact with their fathers. They were more likely to show regressive behaviors than the nine- and ten-year-olds, but were more directly communicative about the reason for their feelings than the younger children. The seven- and eight-year-olds appeared to be quite frightened about the consequences of the divorce, and all seemed desperately to want their parents back together again, even those exposed to particularly intense and abusive parental conflict. A year after the divorce, the modal response seemed to be more of a placid resignation than an energetic striving to make the family intact again.

Compared to the younger children, the more mature cognitive development of the nine- and ten-year-olds enabled them to deal with divorce in a relatively controlled and realistic fashion. They were more likely to use a variety of coping patterns so that their everyday lives seemed less disrupted than those of the younger children. However, loneliness, physical symptoms, feelings of shame and an intense conscious anger toward the parents were still quite common. About half of the nine- and ten-year-olds appeared to be coping adequately a year after the divorce, although they were still dealing with feelings of sadness and bitterness. In contrast, the rest of the children in this age group were severely handicapped by feelings of low self-esteem and depression, and difficulties in peer relationships and academic functioning. Approximately one-quarter of the children were clearly more psychologically disabled one year after the divorce than they had been prior to the marital separation.

For adolescents, the divorce was characterized by much pain, anger, sadness and often conflicts concerning their parents' sexual behavior. Those adolescents who were relatively mature at the time of the divorce and were able to maintain some distance from their parents' conflicts seemed to be doing better by the end of the first year after the divorce. They had developed a strikingly realistic perception of their parents. In contrast, those adolescents who had emotional and social problems before the divorce tended to manifest even more serious difficulties afterward.

Later Adjustment

At the five-year follow-up, many different patterns of adaptation were evident. In general, about one-third of the children appeared to be doing quite well personally, socially, and educationally. They had very positive self-concepts and showed generally high levels of competence. A slightly greater proportion (37 percent) had rather severe adjustment problems, including personal and social difficulties, with many having intense feelings of loneliness, alienation and depression. They were extremely dissatisfied with their lives, though even among this group about half were able to do adequately in some areas, such as their schoolwork. The remaining children (30 percent) made what could be termed mixed adjustments, showing typical ups and downs in coping with their life situations. Although these children appeared to be making what might be called an average adaptation to school and social demands, evidence indicated that feelings about the divorce sometimes still had negative effects on their self-esteem and overall competence.

Many different types of factors were involved in the successful adjustments of particular children, but in the majority of cases the most crucial variable was the continuing positive involvement of the father. At the five-year postdivorce assessment, almost one-third (30 percent) of the children had an emotionally meaningful and warm relationship with their father. A close relationship with the father was strongly associated with a healthy adjustment for both boys and girls. Frequent but flexible father-child visiting patterns were very important for children who lived with their mothers. Even when divorce results in children living with their mother it does not mean that they must be "father-absent" in a general way. Some children who reside with their mothers still enjoy much better relationships with their fathers than do many of those from nondivorced two-parent families.

In the context of single-parent custody the findings underscored the importance of the child's continuing relationship with both the father and the mother. The support that the custodial parent provides to the former partner and the ability of the divorced parents to develop ways to coparent are especially significant for the long-term adjustment and sense of well-being of their children. Only in the relatively rare instances where a parent was seriously disturbed or extremely abusive did it seem better that a complete termination of contact with the child occur.

Results from Wallerstein's ten-year follow-up study are very provocative. Interview data suggest that children who were the youngest at the time of the divorce were doing better a decade later than many of their older siblings, at least with respect to dealing with memories of family conflict and being relatively optimistic about their own futures. The eleven- to seventeen-year-olds were not as negatively preoccupied with troubled memories of family life as the nineteen- to twenty-eight-year-olds. Younger children typically had emotional and social difficulties in their initial adjustment to the divorce but now, as a group, seemed to have more psychological equilibrium than their older siblings.

What was especially disheartening to Wallerstein was that many young adults who had seemed previously to cope well with their parents' divorce were now having serious difficulties in their attempts to establish meaningful love relationships and career commitments. In particular, some of the females who were in their early and mid-twenties seemed haunted by divorce-related issues even though they had functioned extremely well in their earlier development.

The younger siblings seemed to be doing surprisingly well, especially when their earlier problems and the current conflicts of their older siblings were taken into consideration. However, many of these younger siblings were still quite obsessed with the persistence of parent reconciliation fantasies and with holding on to small details of very unsatisfactory relationships with elusive fathers. Some of the adolescent females, in particular, were making energetic attempts to have relationships with their previously neglectful fathers.

As the younger children enter their later adolescent years, they may also experience some of the same divorce-related problems as their older siblings. When they have to deal with more serious relationship issues, personal conflicts may resurge that were relatively quiescent during the previous several years. For both children and adults, long-term implications are associated with divorce. Compared to children who grew up with parents who stayed together in a positive marriage, those from divorced families are more likely themselves to have unstable marital relationships. They may continue to feel that their parents let them down by getting a divorce, and it may be particularly difficult for them to develop a sense of security and trust in their own marital relationship. However, it can be a far different experience when children from divorced families are aware that their fathers and mothers each made strong efforts to make the marriage work and, moreover, that they remained committed parents after the marital separation.

Family Resources

Many factors can affect the way the child is influenced by growing up in a single-parent household. The emphasis here is on the way that variations in the parenting styles of single mothers may be related to the adjustment of their children. The focus is on mothers who are single parents and have no consistent help from fathers. Maternal attitudes toward men and masculine behavior attain special significance when a child grows up in a single-parent family. The mother's derogatory comments about the absent father can contribute to the development of a poor self-concept and maladaptive behavior in the child. When mothers are very critical about absent fathers, male children in particular are more at risk for adjustment problems including academic and behavioral difficulties.

The mother's feelings of resentment can be associated with many different types of husband loss, but it is usually easier for her to talk positively about a former mate who has died than about one who has left because of divorce or desertion. Discussing the absent father with her child may be very frustrating, but when her husband is not there because he has abandoned her, it is likely to be even more painful. It is extremely difficult for a mother to maintain a balanced image of the father in the face of the conflict that often takes place before, during and after a divorce. However, single mothers who have constructive attitudes toward their ex-partners can facilitate the child's personality development. For instance, by praising the absent father's particular areas of competence she can encourage her son to learn to value his own maleness. On the other hand, chronic maternal deprecation of the father can undermine the boy's sense of self-acceptance.

Developmental status at the onset of father absence is an important factor influencing the child's adjustment. Father deprivation during the preschool years has been found to be associated with the child's dependence on the mother. For instance, a large proportion of kindergarten and first-grade children who display immature behavior at school have been father-absent or otherwise paternally deprived during their preschool years. If father-absence begins during the elementary school years, or later, the single mother usually expects the child to assume more adultlike responsibilities.

The relative availability of social and economic resources has a great impact on the functioning of the single-parent family. A major difficulty in the economically disadvantaged father-absent home is that the mother is flooded with responsibilities and often has no other adult to help her. Among poor children, those in single-mother-headed families are much more at risk for social and personal maladjustment than those who reside in cooperative two-parent households. But having a grandparent or a competent older sibling also living in the single-parent household may decrease developmental risks for children.

Consistent economic deprivation makes it easy for single parents to develop a defeatist attitude about their potential impact on their children. Poor single mothers, alone in dealing with parenting responsibilities, are more likely to feel overwhelmed and neglect their children than are parents with more adequate social and economic support systems. Compared to those who are unemployed, single mothers who are able to find relatively stable jobs feel better about themselves and are more positive role models for their children. When a mother is happy about her employment, she is more apt to have effective interactions with her family than if she considers her job unfulfilling or demeaning. If a mother feels satisfied with her career, she is also much less likely to become overly focused on her children. A satisfying career may be especially beneficial in allowing the single mother to accept the child's growing needs for independence and autonomy.

Most never-married parents had unplanned pregnancies but there are also those who intentionally chose to have a child out of wedlock. In some cases unwed couples with children live together but in most the mother assumes the responsibility of being a single parent. There is a stereotype that unwed fathers are usually considerably older or from higher socioeconomic backgrounds than are unwed mothers, with the assumption that the male has taken advantage of the female. In fact, in most situations the unwed father and mother have been closely involved prior to the pregnancy and are similar to one another in terms of age, education, and social class. Much more attention needs to be given to the role of the unwed father. Even if the unwed parents do not live together, the child can profit when there is continuing contact with both parents. There are unwed fathers and mothers who live separately yet do have reliable relationships and cooperate in parenting. These situations usually involve unwed parents who were committed to one another prior to the pregnancy.

There has been an increase in the number of relatively mature unmarried women, in their mid-thirties or older, who decide to have a child with the expectation of being single parents. Because of the inevitability of approaching biological infertility, they may perceive it as now or never if they are going to go through the pregnancy process and have a child of their own. Most of these single women are well-educated, have enjoyed successful careers, and are financially independent. They may have once been married, or in relationships that did not work out, but have decided that they want the experience of being a mother despite the prospect of remaining a single parent. In fact, some fervently are against considering a future marital relationship, claiming that they prefer to be single parents rather than having to compromise their child rearing expectations by sharing responsibility with a partner.

On the positive side, there is no doubt that most mature women who decide to give birth to a baby without being married are sincerely committed to being good parents, will be very adequate economic providers, and will look for ways to intellectually and educationally stimulate their children. What I find disconcerting is the belief of many such women that children just need an involved mother to ensure successful development. The argument that children from female-headed single parent homes typically suffer only from an economic disadvantage is questionable. All single parents should realize the importance of their children having regular quality contact with adult males as well as females. Individuals certainly have a right to choose to be single parents. However, the implication that children can get along without there being any concern for the importance of paternal influence is extremely troubling when taken in the context of the realities of individual and family development.

Parental Competence

The parent-child relationship in the single-mother family can either stimulate or hinder the child's development. For the paternally deprived boy or girl, the mother-child relationship assumes even greater importance. The mother's self-esteem and overall competence, more than her warmth or tenderness, are major factors contributing to her child's adjustment.

Maternal encouragement of assertive behavior seems particularly important for the father-absent child. In a research project I did with kindergarten children from single-parent families, boys whose mothers accepted and reinforced assertive and independent behavior were more socially competent than those boys whose mothers discouraged such behavior. Assessing junior high school students, Robert Bahm and I found evidence suggesting that the single mother's support of socially assertive behavior also had a beneficial impact on her son's self-concept. Among those boys who had been father-absent since before the age of five, there was a positive relationship between perceived maternal encouragement for assertive behavior and the masculinity of their self-concepts.

The way that the single mother deals with the reality of her family situation can impact greatly on her child's development. The emotional health of the single mother is highly related to her ability realistically to cope with her family responsibilities. Family development expert Pauline Boss, studying families of men who were missing in military action, found that the mother's ability to strive for personal growth, have close relations with others, seek further education and develop plans to remarry were all strongly related to her child's emotional adjustment. Of course, such data should not be seen as inconsistent with the mother supporting a positive image of the absent father by sharing her memories and describing his accomplishments. However, a major implication of this research is that the mother should not encourage unrealistic expectations concerning the father who is not going to be involved with his family again.

The research of Mavis Hetherington and her coworkers has supplied a wealth of data highlighting the significance of the mother-child relationship in the single-parent family. In their study assessing the impact of divorce, they found that a positive relationship with the custodial mother was likely to be associated with a healthy social and emotional adjustment for the young child. Even where the parents were experiencing much postdivorce conflict, a good mother-child relationship seemed capable of serving as a buffer for the child. Single mothers who had clear expectations and presented an orderly environment seemed to facilitate the child's intellectual functioning and ability to develop self-control. Mothers who reinforced sex-typed behavior and encouraged independence, who were low in anxiety and had a positive view of the child's father, seemed particularly likely to facilitate the boy's masculine development. In contrast, a combination of maternal fearfulness and inhibition, discouragement of independence and disapproval of the father were found to be associated with anxious dependency and a feminine pattern of behavior in some of the boys.

Despite their increasing numbers, men still represent only about 10 percent of single custodial parents. Those men who seek primary or shared custody generally have been especially committed parents. The success of men as single custodial fathers tends to be associated with the close relationships they had established with their children prior to the divorce or marital separation. A key factor common to successful single fathers is the continuing motivation to maintain a supportive involvement in their children's daily activities. In contrast, those men who feel trapped with the responsibility of custody are likely to have a much more difficult time serving in a primary parenting role. Although even highly motivated custodial fathers face difficult challenges, they are usually able to cope effectively with basic child-rearing and domestic tasks.

Psychologists John Santrock and Richard Warshak have found that among elementary school-age children living in single-parent households, boys generally do better with their fathers and girls with their mothers. The same-sex parent and child are more likely to share a sense of mutual understanding and common interests. Single parents usually find it is easier to communicate with children of the same sex and have fewer discipline-related problems with them. However, the research of Santrock and Warshak also indicates that the single father's or mother's relative ability to communicate and provide adequate structure and security for the child, over and above the parent's gender, is the most crucial factor in the family's adjustment.

Nevertheless, family relationships in single-adult households are not just a function of parental competence. The child's characteristics have much impact on parenting styles. For instance, mothers in single-parent families generally have much more difficulty dealing with sons than daughters, especially with regard to limit setting. Research indicates that young children who are highly competent prior to the divorce are not as handicapped by parent loss as those who are average or below in their developmental level. Similarly, some children are much more temperamentally adaptive and resilient than others.

Remarriage Issues

Most single parents of young children who have been divorced or widowed remarry well before their offspring reach adulthood. Remarriage has very significant child-rearing implications, and the quality of stepparent-stepchild relationships can be a major factor in the viability of the reconstituted family. Many a second marriage has ended because the stepparent and children had chronic conflicts, with the parent often placed in the middle in an untenable position.

The situation is even more complicated when both adults have children from previous marriages. Time, patience and acceptance of individual differences are crucial if the new family system is to be reasonably positive for all the participants. It may in the short run be very difficult for all family members, but it is also important for the children to see that the adults are committed to balancing parental and marital responsibilities constructively.

Because of the likelihood of continuing conflicts between ex-spouses as well as the complex adaptations required in remarriage, typically difficult challenges present themselves for both parents and stepparents. It takes a great deal of insight and maturity to keep feelings of jealousy and bitterness from interfering with constructive family relationships. It is not easy for adults in these situations to maintain a focus on the child's best interests when they are simultaneously dealing with intense issues of their own.

Since most divorced fathers do not have physical custody of their children, it is common for them to have to adjust to a situation where, if their ex-spouse remarries, a stepfather may become a very prominent figure in their child's life. From a positive perspective, if both the father and the stepfather are attached to the child, a type of shared and cooperative fatherhood is feasible. It is certainly possible for both men to feel comfortable in a nurturing role with a particular child. When the single father decides to remarry, the situation is usually somewhat different with respect to child rearing and other issues than when the single mother makes a similar commitment. Since the mother typically has physical custody, the stepmother will not likely become the child's major maternal influence. Nevertheless, the father should be careful not to behave in a way that increases the chances that the mother will feel that he is trying to lure the child away from her by marrying another woman.

As with other gender-related expectations for parents, the female stepparent usually assumes a different role vis-à-vis the child than the male stepparent does. Compared to the typical stepfather, the stepmother will probably feel more pressure to become involved in some direct care activities when the child is in her home. For example, even if her spouse only sees his children periodically, she is likely to assume some parenting responsibilities involving meal preparation. The stepmother is often put in a position where her direct contact with the child makes comparisons with the mother inevitable. In contrast, many aspects of the role of the stepfather are generally less clear. This allows him, if he so desires, to be more peripheral in the child's life. This may be advantageous for him and the child if it facilitates a gradual building of a relationship at a mutually comfortable pace.

Usually more opportunities arise for angry confrontations concerning parenting issues between the mother and the stepmother than between the father and the stepfather. In some families, in fact, neither the father nor the stepfather are very involved in child care. The mother and stepmother are often placed in situations where they are likely to feel quite competitive with respect to their ability to assume traditionally maternal responsibilities. Power struggles between the mother and stepmother are often fueled by childrens' ambivalent feelings toward the divorce and each of the parents. The mother and stepmother may find themselves arguing over child-care issues while the father and stepfather are seemingly more passive observers. The divorced parents also may have their most intense arguments centered around differences in the mother's and step-mother's child-rearing approaches. Over time, greater cooperation between the two households is possible if the adults try to be sensitive to the difficult roles each has in the family and focus on the well-being of the children. The more the father and stepfather take supportive coparenting roles, the less likely an overfocus on mother-stepmother conflicts will happen.

Stepparenting Challenges

Most divorced parents eventually have to deal with stepparenting issues, both when becoming remarried themselves and in having to adjust to their ex-spouse acquiring a new marriage partner. Sometimes, as in blended families, divorced parents are dealing with a new stepparent for their children as well as being in the role themselves vis-à-vis their new spouse's children.

The stepfather's role is often shortchanged in discussions concerning parenting issues. Becoming a stepfather is perhaps one of the most difficult yet potentially rewarding types of parenthood. A stepfather is entering an established family, usually one in which the natural father is still involved to some extent. The stepfather's parenting efforts may meet with ambivalence from his new wife, as well as with considerable resentment from her children and from their father. Despite such barriers, a patient and positively involved stepfather can have a constructive impact in a child's life. In some cases, children who have been paternally deprived change from being unhappy and insecure to being self-assured and competent after a few years of an active relationship with a caring stepfather.

Significant life changes, even if they appear to be quite positive, require learning new adaptations, which can be highly stressful. Moreover, difficulties can be greater when an individual does not have a feeling of control or choice, typically the case for the child being confronted with a parent's remarriage. Whenever possible, the stepparent should join the already established household. In this way the child will not have to get used to a new home, school and friends in addition to adjusting to a stepparent.

The child's developmental level influences greatly the nature of stepparenting relationships. During the preschool years a child will usually rather easily become attached to a supportive stepparent. It is typically much more difficult for an older child to accept another adult in a parenting role. It is very important to give the child time to adjust to changes in family structure. Stepparents should try to be patient and not expect children to conform immediately to their ex-pectations. As much as possible, they should be available and accessible but allow their stepchildren to take the initiative. They can encourage a closer re-lationship but at the same time they should not insist that their stepchildren treat them as if they were their parents.

Beginning a stepparenting relationship with a teenager can be particularly difficult. The adolescent has probably already established some degree of independence from the family, having firm ties with friends and others outside the home. The adolescent is also still likely to be struggling for autonomy from the parent and is not apt to welcome any additional source of family authority. Vigorous attempts by the stepparent to break through a generalized barrier of resentment may contribute to much frustration for both the adult and the child. Many times about the most a stepparent can expect from an adolescent stepchild is a cordial but somewhat distanced relationship. These are, of course, generalities. In some families an involved stepparent has contributed a great deal to the teenager's life, but such positive outcomes are typically the result of much time and patience on the adult's part.

The key is not that stepparents necessarily love their stepchildren or that they play a direct parenting role. But what is essential for adequate family functioning is that stepparents and stepchildren are able to develop an acceptance and tolerance of one another. In many families this may mean more of a peaceful coexistence than anything resembling an active parent-child relationship. The best general advice for both parents and stepparents is to remember that successful family adjustments usually take a great deal of time and patience.

TROUBLED CHILDREN

Social expectations usually increase the mother's involvement with her troubled child. However, all too often the father withdraws his support forcing the mother into a solitary parenting role. This kind of emotional desertion typically aggravates the child's and family's problems. In most situations, the father must share more of the parenting responsibility if the family is to cope constructively with the child's problem.

Diagnostic Complexities

There is always a need to view the child's behavior in an appropriate developmental context. Parents may, for example, overreact to a young child's behavior because of unrealistic expectations. Just because a three-year-old is a thumb sucker or a four-year-old is a bed wetter is not necessarily evidence of chronic psychological problems. An isolated difficulty is likely to give way to more mature behavior if parents have reasonable expectations and treat the child with love and respect.

As psychiatrists Stella Chess and Alexander Thomas emphasize so well, many children who are viewed as deviant or emotionally disturbed in actuality have difficult temperaments rather than some underlying pathology. The individual behavioral styles of such children may lead to much family conflict because a good fit with parental expectations or with the father's or mother's own temperament is missing. An experienced clinician may be able to counsel the parents toward a more appropriate way of dealing with their particular child. In time, most children with difficult temperaments are likely to achieve quite positive social adjustments if they are the beneficiaries of patience, support and reasonable expectations from both their father and their mother.

The child's seeming symptoms may not be the result of an underlying deficit in adaptive capacity and, in fact, may be well within the normal range of behavior for individuals in his or her age group. A child's behavior may also appear very aberrant but in actuality be merely a potentially short-term reaction to a family conflict. In some cases the child's problems may be more a reflection of a learning disability or even a dietary deficiency than the result of chronic emotional difficulties. On the other hand, the child may have multiple deficits, for example, being learning disabled as well as suffering from a depressive disorder. A meaningful diagnosis as to what may be a primary or secondary problem may require a very thorough assessment by several different professionals. The seemingly bizarre behaviors and poor impulse control of some children are basically symptoms of brain damage. Neurological handicaps can themselves be the result of varying factors. Genetic or prenatal influences may have been involved as well as early childhood illnesses or accidents involving serious head injuries. Mental retardation, whatever its origins, may put a child at particular risk to develop emotional and social problems.

Family assessment is usually critical for adequately dealing with children's psychological difficulties, although serious emotional and behavioral handicaps are, in most cases, not simply a function of inadequate parenting. Most often, child-specific ingredients combine to interact with family factors. However, whether or not they have directly contributed to the child's problems, parents are certainly responsible for seeking professional consultation.

If the child has had serious handicaps dating back to infancy, they are likely primarily of a genetic or prenatal origin. The parents could have done little to prevent the basic problem. But some guidelines can still be applied to help determine whether the father's or mother's behavior may be contributing to an intensification of the child's problems. Perhaps most important, such guidelines can be used to help decrease the likelihood or severity of future difficulties.

Parents must confront what the child's handicap means in terms of their own values and interests. For example, an intellectually oriented father may find it easier to be supportive toward a somewhat physically handicapped child but have much more difficulty relating to a learning disabled offspring. Handicapped children, like other boys and girls, have their areas of strength as well as weakness. Parents may erroneously define the handicap in terms of what the child cannot do rather than what he or she can accomplish. One father was so concerned that his partially paralyzed son could not play baseball that he was oblivious to the boy's impressive verbal and artistic abilities. As in any family, parents need to be cognizant of the child's resources and interests, taking a positive view rather than just focusing on limitations.

Basic personality attributes such as nurturance, self-confidence, assertiveness, sensitivity and creativity do not necessarily have to be limited because of physical appearance or bodily deficits. In a very general sense, the role of parents with a handicapped child is not inherently different. All parents should encourage their child's independence, responsibility, competence and self-reliance. Parents should not contribute to making a disability a disabling condition, unnecessarily restricting the child's or their own development. When a child has a handicap, a positive developmental outcome is much more likely when the father as well as the mother has an active role in the family.

Although the focus here is on dealing with children's handicaps, the handicaps of parents also deserve some attention. Families differ greatly in coping with ostensibly similar problems. The physical handicaps of some adults undermine their parenting effectiveness while others are somehow able to turn a disadvantage into a very positive example of courage and fortitude for their children.

Individuals who are handicapped may feel that they will fail as parents because they perceive that they lack the necessary requisites for child rearing competence. However, effective child rearing is based not so much on overall abilities as it is on the capacity of parents to present positively what strengths they have to the child. Their primary responsibility is to help the child develop self-acceptance and consideration for others through the communication of solid values. The foundation of parenting competence is built on kindness and acceptance of individuality, not on the adult or child being free from medical, physical or other types of disabilities. Children can benefit from observing parents constructively adapt to difficult situations. Positive psychological development is not a result of always avoiding frustrating conditions but also involves the individual's capacity to confront challenging life circumstances.

Antisocial Patterns

One child may be viewed as delinquent and another as having a severe adjustment disorder, but both may manifest a very similar set of underlying problems. For example, depression in some children leads to aloofness and withdrawal, and in others to aggressive acting out. The child's basic temperament can have much to do with the way psychological problems are expressed. The major issue should not be the diagnostic label but whether or not the child and family receive adequate professional help.

A multitude of factors can be involved in the development of antisocial behavior patterns. First of all, many so-called delinquents have subtle learning disabilities and difficulties focusing their attention. A child may lash out at others because of frustration at not being able to keep up with classmates in school or in other situations. Peer-group pressure is often a contributing factor to delinquency. However, parents may use the reality of negative peer influence as an excuse to absolve themselves or their children of irresponsible behavior. In many cases, children show poor judgment in choosing friends because of a desperate need for acceptance based, in part, on a lack of positive family communication and support.

Father deprivation, especially when it begins early in the child's life, is often associated with delinquent behavior among both boys and girls. When a basically adequate mother takes all the responsibility for nurturing children, whether in a two-parent family or as a single adult, she is likely to feel overwhelmed in her attempts to set constructive limits. While it must be emphasized that delinquency typically stems from multiple factors, fathers should carefully reflect about the extent of their child-rearing commitments. Certainly some mothers' inappropriate behavior is a major negative influence contributing to their children's delinquent behavior patterns, but the lack of an adequate father-child relationship is a far more common factor in the backgrounds of troubled and acting-out sons and daughters.

Among delinquents, even more common than an obviously abusive father is one who has been chronically neglectful. Delinquents have usually received very little positive attention or guidance from their fathers. Compared to fathers of nondelinquents, fathers of delinquents typically give little direction and share fewer plans, activities and interests with their children. A more general pattern of paternal neglect may be accompanied by the father's intermittent verbal abuse and ridicule of the child.

There tend to be marked gender differences in the expression of behavior problems. Delinquency in boys is frequently associated with physical aggressiveness while in girls it is more often socially defined in terms of running away or sexual promiscuity. Delinquent girls are sometimes physically abusive toward others, but they seem to be more often accomplices to criminal acts rather than the primary protagonists. Girls, usually being smaller and less muscular than boys, are not as apt to use physical intimidation to meet their needs.

During the last few decades, much more tolerance, if not acceptance, has been shown toward active sexual expression among adolescent females. Nevertheless, certain styles of adolescent sexual behavior are clearly indicative of maladjustment. Engaging in promiscuous sexual behavior is often a symptom of a poor self-image and serious psychological problems, even if the label of delinquency is not justifiable.

Inadequate father-child relationships are a primary contributor to various types of acting out among females as well as males. Fathers of sexually promiscuous daughters are likely to have been cold, rejecting and hostile toward them. They may be rigidly restrictive because they are obsessed about their daughter's potential for sexual misconduct. Fathers and stepfathers who have themselves engaged in sexually abusive relationships may perceive that other males will treat adolescent females in a similar fashion. A maltreating father may become distrustful and preoccupied with his daughter's relationships with male peers long before she becomes involved in an overtly sexual relationship. In some cases, this may be because of the father's conflicts over his own sexual attraction to his daughter. Frustrated with her father's behavior, the daughter may have sexual relations to get back at him or as an attempt to develop a relationship that she hopes will free her from an abusive family situation.

Multiple Influences

Inadequate fathering is frequently a major factor, but the development of delinquent behavior patterns often includes a constellation of other influences.

Most delinquents, and for that matter most career criminals, do indeed come from father-deprived backgrounds, but in addition they are likely to grow up in economically disadvantaged neighborhoods with a generally low level of family support. Furthermore, a high proportion of males who are incarcerated for serious crimes displayed behavior as young children that was indicative (although usually undiagnosed at the time) of an attention-deficit disorder or other learning disability. Given economic, family and learning handicaps, it is not surprising that an early history of academic and conduct problems is often prominent in the elementary school records of criminals.

A definite association can be made between antisocial behavior and poverty. Most children who get involved in the family court system because of delinquent behavior are from relatively poor families, but some are also from affluent homes. A rather classic case of a negative middle-class family situation contributing to delinquent behavior involves the occupationally successful father who in a material sense provided well for his children but has emotionally neglected them. To his puzzlement, his children are caught stealing, get hooked on drugs or do not respect the property of other people. The paternally deprived child may interpret the father's lack of positive interest as a personal devaluation. Many delinquents seem to extend their perception of paternal neglect to a more generalized view that no one really cares about them. Whether or not they are viewed as delinquent, the acting out of many adolescents is often a desperate attempt to get paternal attention as much as an effort to gain acceptance from peers.

To some extent, a caring mother can act as a buffer against father neglect, but she is usually limited in her ability to compensate for paternal deprivation. Whether the family is rich or poor, one responsible adult simply cannot give as much positive attention and guidance as two involved parents. Children are in need of a sense of consensual validity of their basic worthiness that is much more readily provided with the active support of both parents.

When parents are neglectful, the vacuum in children's lives may be filled by a peer group that supplies overly rigid and potentially destructive views of acceptable behavior. The paternally deprived child, whether from a ghetto or an affluent suburb, is especially vulnerable to peer group pressures. Other children, who themselves are likely to suffer from inadequate parenting, become influential in providing the paternally deprived boy or girl with emotional support. In an effort to gain and maintain peer acceptance, father-neglected children are at particular risk to become involved in alcohol and other forms of drug abuse.

Disadvantaged Families

Paternal deprivation occurs at all socioeconomic levels, but it is especially common among poor families. Although the problems encountered by poor families are quite complex, they typically illustrate the combined costs of poverty and lack of positive father involvement. Poor white and black families often share many of the same disadvantages including a multigenerational history of paternal deprivation. However, the still-lingering aftereffects of slavery and continuing racial prejudice make the plight of most poor black families particularly difficult. Without a clear heritage of paternal influence, a very high proportion of black fathers are unsure of their parental role. Social and economic discrimination has severely handicapped black males attempting to be responsible fathers. The welfare system can also indirectly contribute to undermining the father's role. By giving aid more easily to families without fathers, welfare departments, in essence, often make the judgment that the man who is unemployed does not deserve to remain in the household.

Single mothers head over 50 percent of black families, as compared to about 20 percent of white households with children. But despite the generally serious problems of poverty and paternal deprivation, care must be taken not to overgeneralize about black families. Many black fathers are poor but committed, as well as those who are both economically successful and deeply involved with their families. Although one-third of black families live in poverty, as many have achieved a basically adequate financial status.

As a group, however, black children are especially at risk to suffer from economic disadvantages as well as inadequate paternal influence. Father-deprived children, particularly those who live in economically impoverished conditions, are more vulnerable to intellectual deficits and are more likely to have emotional and social problems than their well-fathered counterparts. Poor and paternally deprived males also grow up exposed to a peer-oriented value system that makes them highly susceptible to conflicts with authority in school and on the job. Peers typically do not support values that are conducive to self-discipline.

It has been more than a quarter of a century since the publication of the government-sponsored Moynihan Report, which focused on issues confronting the black family. This report emphasized that children growing up in female-headed black families were likely to suffer from a multitude of social problems including educational failure, unemployment and poor health. Daniel Moynihan and his colleagues were far from the first to suggest such relationships, but their data presentation was quite provocative. Critics of the Moynihan Report pointed out the need to emphasize the adaptability of the black female-centered family despite severe social and economic discrimination. Moynihan and others were assailed for viewing the black family as a broken unit rather than recognizing the strong intergenerational female support system.

In the summer of 1965, at that point not aware of the Moynihan Report, I conducted research with preschool-age black and white children from very low-income families. The data suggested that most of the boys were disadvantaged in self-concept because of the additive effects of father-absence and an economically unsupportive background. In particular, father-absent boys, both black and white, responded in ways indicating that they had less secure masculine self-concepts than those from father-present families. Although there were some exceptions, the black father-absent boys seemed to have especially insecure gender identities. Compared to girls, boys in poor one-parent families generally receive less positive maternal support. Black mothers pass on their legacy of competence to their daughters, but frequently have much lower expectations for their sons. Black women tend to be more comfortable with female offspring and view male children as much less responsible and dependable. Females in poor black families usually have higher educational aspirations and attainments than their male counterparts.

The relative competence of females as compared to males among poor families may also stem, in part, from the aftermath of inadequate prenatal care. Male fetuses are generally more vulnerable to negative influences in the prenatal environment than female fetuses. The fact that males are more likely to be affected negatively by inadequate prenatal care also contributes to the greater postbirth incidence among boys of academic impulse control and conduct problems. Their handicaps are often the unfortunate consequence of the combined effects of biological, paternal and socioeconomic disadvantagement.

By school age, the insecurity of paternally deprived boys is likely to contribute to conflicts with their mothers and other females. Female-dominated elementary schools can greatly intensify the discomfort of boys who are already at risk for academic failure. Paternally deprived boys growing up in poverty are also apt to have values very discrepant from those of their middle-class female teachers. In their desperate attempts to prove their masculinity, such boys are likely to be much more influenced by older male peers than their female teachers. A very high proportion of boys from economically disadvantaged single-mother households have serious academic problems. Black and white boys who are from lower-class, father-absent households often have particular difficulty coping with the female-dominated early educational environment. Add to this the possibility of learning and attention deficiencies related to inadequate prenatal care, and it is not surprising that very few of them develop positive attitudes about education.

Although positive paternal involvement cannot prevent all school-related or other types of problems, children with initial handicaps have much more of a chance to cope constructively if they are the beneficiaries of close supportive relationships with their fathers. Among children who have temperamental difficulties or learning disabilities, those with involved fathers are still much more likely than those from paternally-deprived families to develop self-esteem and a sense of well being. In most cases, whatever the nature of their initial disadvantage (whether it be primarily intellectual, physical, emotional, or social), there is a much greater likelihood that children with attentive, encouraging fathers will eventually make relatively successful adjustments as compared to those who, additionally, suffer from a lack of paternal involvement.

Parental Accountability

Children are influenced by many factors including their own biological individuality, but the way that parents treat them can have an especially significant impact. This is not to suggest that children need all-perfect parents. However, if parents are not being constructive models of kind and considerate behavior, they may be a contributing source to their child's emotional and behavioral difficulties or at the least be increasing the likelihood of future family problems.

An important step in preventing a child from having emotional problems is for parents to assess their own behavior realistically. Even if parents are not directly abusive toward their offspring, a high level of father-mother conflict can undermine the emotional security of children and increase the risk that they will suffer from serious adjustment problems. Parents do not have to be physically abusive to one another to create a negative family situation. Parents who constantly criticize and demean each other are presenting very poor models of intimacy to their children.

Children cannot be expected to treat themselves and others with respect if they are not responded to as valued individuals by their parents. Parents who are frequently hostile, restrictive or neglectful may be undermining their child's mental health. Even very adequate parents are occasionally thoughtless or insensitive, but a chronic pattern of abuse or neglect is likely to damage the child's sense of emotional well-being.

Not only is the incidence of emotional disturbance higher among inadequately fathered boys and girls, but the earlier and the more prolonged the paternal deprivation, the more likely the problems will be severe and long-lasting. Paternal deprivation because of marital separation, divorce or desertion has generally been linked with more serious psychological handicaps than has the death of the father. Among severely emotionally disabled and psychotic patients the incidence of father-absence due to divorce or separation is very high in childhood. An unusually large proportion of patients hospitalized for severe depression and attempted suicide were father-absent or otherwise paternally neglected or abused during childhood.

Not surprisingly, researchers have discovered that fathers of adult schizophrenics typically did not display effective paternal behavior toward them during childhood. Many of the fathers had severe conflicts with their wives, often undercutting their attempts to set limits for their children and generally showing them little respect. Some parents of schizophrenics have also themselves been found to be severely disturbed or to have displayed extremely limited adaptive skills. However, such evidence can be interpreted as suggesting that parent and child share a similar genetic or temperamental predisposition toward disordered behavior rather than indicating that inadequate paternal or maternal behavior is a singular causal factor.

It must be emphasized that parental behavior may have no direct connection to the development of certain types of severe childhood disorders. In fact, many psychologically healthy and effective parents have emotionally disturbed or mentally ill children. The child may have a genetically related inadequacy or some other type of constitutional vulnerability that is a predisposing factor toward extremely disordered behavior. Mental illness is often the result of a combination of factors, which may or may not include inadequate parenting.

A rapid increase has been noted in data that point to biological predispositions for many serious psychiatric disabilities including manic-depressive disorders and some forms of schizophrenia. Recent research has shown linkages between the so-called fragile y chromosome and diverse behavioral phenomena including some types of autistic behavior, severe shyness and specific forms of intellectual retardation. Evidence also suggests that, for a large proportion of individuals, a combination of inadequate parenting along with a genetic predisposition is necessary for the emergence of schizophrenia.

Individual Vulnerability

Although many types of parental inadequacy can contribute to emotional problems among children, the complexity of factors involved in the development of what can be viewed as severe mental illness needs to be emphasized. For example, most schizophrenics, particularly those with problems that first surfaced during their early life, suffer from a biological vulnerability that leads to distorted child-parent relationships as well as to many of their specific symptoms.

Inadequate parenting can, of course, contribute to the development of mental illness in children, but even in these instances, it may be only one of many factors. Various forms of mental illness are the result of complex interactions among many types of influence. In most cases it is uncertain how much a son's or daughter's maladjustment is directly attributable to the father or mother, or how much of the parents' behavior is a reaction to biologically predisposed problems in the child.

Robert Kayton and I collected data that supported the notion that the adjustment of children may be facilitated if they perceive their parents as fitting positive family roles. However, our findings indicated that degree of serious psychopathology is relatively independent of the individual's paternal and maternal images. Adults who appeared to be relatively well adjusted tended to view their fathers as possessing masculine-instrumental traits and their mothers as having feminine-expressive characteristics, while a much smaller proportion of psychiatrically troubled subjects reported such perceptions. Nevertheless, clear-cut differences regarding perceptions of paternal and maternal behavior were not found among groups of subjects exhibiting different levels of problems, suggesting that their degree of pathology was probably more a function of constitutional predispositions than a reflection of the quality of parenting available to them as children.

Parents may engage in inconsistent or negative disciplinary techniques because their child is developing and behaving in a very atypical manner. In some cases, inappropriate parenting is a consequence rather than an antecedent of the child's maladaptive behavior patterns. It may be, for example, that a parent was quite successful in interacting with an older son or daughter but became disorganized to a large extent as a result of dealing with a younger developmentally handicapped child. A child's problem behavior can be a precipitating factor in parental psychological difficulties. This is especially the case for younger, first-time parents or those who are already under much stress, such as single mothers with several preschool-age children. New parents may be particularly unprepared to deal with an infant who does not respond to affection or one who seems hypersensitive to even the slightest environmental changes. A young child who is emotionally unresponsive can do much to undermine the parents' self-confidence and sense of well-being.

The atypical infant or young child can put much additional pressure on an already problem-filled marital relationship or on a family with very limited social and financial resources. Unfortunately, child-specific risk factors and parental problems have a way of compounding one another. On the other hand, parents who have a relatively positive marital relationship, adequate financial security and some established success in rearing children are much more likely to be able to cope with an atypical son or daughter. Any parent with a child suffering from some type of obvious handicap is going to have initial feelings of depression and anger, but with time and a positive support system, the outlook for all family members is generally much brighter. When the parents work together to help the child, constructive family adaptation is much more probable. Unfortunately, the father too often avoids taking an active role. The parents should have a joint commitment rather than reverting to the traditional stereotype of the child being the mother's responsibility.

Family Interventions

Parents should seek help if they perceive that their child has an emotional, learning or behavioral problem. A first step for parents is to discuss their concerns with their pediatrician and then, if necessary, consult with other professionals. A child's problem has implications for the whole family.

When a child requires clinical services, both parents should be encouraged to participate constructively in the assessment and treatment process. In many cases, in fact, the father's as well as the mother's participation can be made a condition for helping the family. The importance of the father to the family and his potential for positively affecting his child should be stressed in putting forth such expectations. Even if the child's difficulties do not stem from paternal neglect, the father's increased involvement may do much to improve the situation. The child's problems may offer the opportunity for getting the father better integrated into the family. Many difficulties that children and mothers experience can be mitigated if clear communication occurs about ways that the father can become a more active and positive family participant.

Much of the success of family therapy is due to the inclusion of the father. A child's problems, even if not directly a result of parental behaviors, can be exacerbated by the family's reaction to them. Treating family members as a group allows the therapist to observe both strengths and difficulties in their interactions. Parents should not enter the assessment process assuming that the problem is just isolated to the child. Unfortunately, many parents expect the professional to treat the child without dealing with the whole family system. On the other hand, in many cases, parental counseling may be very effective without any direct clinical intervention with the child.

The probability of successful treatment can be greatly increased if knowledge concerning positive child-rearing techniques is incorporated into the family therapy process. For example, the therapist can role play appropriate parenting behaviors in interacting with the family. However, the therapist must be careful to support the parents' strengths and not undermine their effectiveness by unwittingly competing with them. Observing the family's behavior is often more meaningful when it is done in their own home rather than in the therapist's office.

Although it is not always feasible, having male and female cotherapists can provide even more explicit examples of appropriate interactions for the family to observe. Role-playing procedures for family members also can be very helpful in teaching and reinforcing effective behavior patterns and communication. Any attempt to modify the family's functioning, however, should take into account their previous modes of interaction and their cultural background.

Family therapy can help fathers and mothers to gain a better perspective on their own childhood experiences. Mothers and fathers confronting their feelings about their own parents often find that the therapy process allows them to increase their child-rearing effectiveness. A great need also exists to provide parent education programs for dealing with specific types of child-related problems. In addition, fathers and mothers who have children with serious handicaps may derive much from participation in parent support groups.

Child Maltreatment

Most researchers and clinicians began by using the term *child abuse* to refer only to inappropriate physical actions on the part of a parent or caregiver. Pioneering investigations of the so-called battered-child syndrome focused on severe injury, but gradually, definitions of child abuse were extended to include parental neglect of children's physical or emotional needs. In our book, *Child Maltreatment and Paternal Deprivation*, Richard Solomon and I emphasized the importance of preventing various patterns of negative parenting including emotional neglect and verbal harassment as well as physical and sexual abuse.

Inadequate fathering is an especially prominent factor associated with child maltreatment. Paternal deprivation and child maltreatment are strongly associated even when the father is not directly abusive. The most common type of maltreatment is father neglect, but the mother is also much more likely to be abusive or to allow others to mistreat her child when she does not have the support of an actively involved partner. In both one-parent and two-parent families, the mother is more at risk to abuse or otherwise inappropriately socialize her child when the father does not adequately share parenting responsibilities.

The relatively high incidence of child abuse by single mothers can be viewed, at least in part, as being related to a social system that tends to put too much pressure on maternal accountability and not enough on the father's positive participation in child rearing. Upwards of 25 percent of children in our society do not have a father living at home. Children in single-mother families are overrepresented in terms of reported cases of physical abuse and other forms of child maltreatment. When statistics for physical abuse for both single-parent and two-parent families are combined, mothers are identified more often than fathers as physically abusing parents.

Neglectful fathers in two-parent families, as well as uninvolved fathers who do not live with their children, are a major factor in the incidence of mothers abusing their children. The quality of the father-mother relationship and the father's behavior toward the child must be taken into account in deciphering the roots of abusive maternal behavior. From a statistical perspective, I would argue that more than 80 percent of incidents involving family-related physical abuse toward children are associated with inadequate fathering, either with the father as the specific perpetrator or with his relative noninvolvement in child rearing as a stress factor connected to the mother's abusive behavior.

In the social work and child welfare literature, relatively little mention has been made of the quality of fathering behavior as a factor in the neglect of children's nutritional, medical or other physical needs. If she is in the home, the mother is assumed to be the exclusive caretaker of the child. Researchers focusing on neglect rarely inquire as to the nature of the father-child relationship except to note whether or not the father is living in the home. However, the absence of the father in the family can also be viewed as a major risk factor relating to physical neglect. The presence of the father in the household tends to be associated with additional family financial and social resources even if he himself is not an active participant in child rearing. Among poor children, those with fathers living with them are less likely to suffer from physical neglect than those whose fathers are absent; the presence of the father tends to be positively related to the level of overall child care and the general condition of the household.

Assessing Abuse

In excess of two million cases of child abuse will be reported in the United States this year. More than one-quarter of these cases will center on actual or intended physical injury to children. However, reported cases of child abuse represent only those incidents that are brought to the attention of agencies responsible for record keeping. Although reported cases may not turn out on further examination to qualify as maltreatment, it is estimated that more than one million cases of physically abused children go unreported every year.

Physically abusive acts represent only one dimension of the problem of child maltreatment. In addition to direct physical maltreatment, other forms of inappropriate parenting involve chronic verbal abuse and various forms of neglect and insensitivity to children. Very damaging acts of child maltreatment also take place in day-care centers, schools and other social institutions. Greater recognition must be given to children's rights both inside and outside of the family.

Because of differing value judgments and social standards, it is difficult to define physical abuse precisely, but a general consensus exists regarding intentional parental acts that result in serious injury to a child. From a developmental perspective, inappropriately aggressive behavior by parents can be viewed as abusive even if no discernible bodily damage is done to the child. However, regardless of parental intent, most abusive situations are not reported unless someone perceives that a child has been purposely injured in some explicit manner.

Physical aggression as a response to perceived child misbehavior is all too common in the American family. More than half of parents at least occasionally spank, slap or hit a child. In a legal sense, physical punishment involving the use of slapping or spanking by hand, belt or other means is typically not considered to constitute abuse unless it is so severe that it results in bodily injury to the child. However, physical abuse and other forms of maltreatment should be viewed on a continuum. A social attitude that condones physical aggression as an appropriate means of discipline puts children at great risk for being the victims of abuse. Physical abuse occurs at every social class level. Some parents who are very well educated, have prestigious jobs and are highly respected members of their community physically abuse their children. Nevertheless, the incidence of physical abuse, especially cases involving severe battering, is much higher among families living in economically disadvantaged circumstances.

Almost half of the children who are physically abused come from families receiving public assistance, and in most of these there is no regularly employed adult. However, it must be emphasized that the majority of economically disadvantaged parents do not physically abuse their children. More than just the presence of social and economic pressures is involved in parental tendencies to abuse children. Some parents, even under especially adverse conditions, have the capacity to maintain their self-control whereas others are quite abusive even when stress factors appear minimal.

Determining the antecedents of child abuse is a very complex matter involving consideration of the intermix of a wide variety of individual, family and social factors. No particular personality pattern is common to all abusive parents. As a group, parents who abuse their children do not fit neatly into any specific diagnostic or psychiatric category. Although they do not fit a particular personality style, abusive parents typically have low self-esteem and perceive others as being critical or nonaccepting of them. Under stress when with their children, they tend to respond in a rather impulsive and aggressive fashion. Parental alcohol or other drug use is sometimes a factor in impulsively aggressive punishment of the child.

Many abusive fathers and mothers were themselves targets of inappropriate parental aggression and violence when they were children. But it is important to emphasize that many individuals who have been abused do not as adults physically maltreat their own children. Many, in fact, conscientiously avoid subjecting their children to the kinds of abuse that they were exposed to in their own earlier family backgrounds.

Diverse Patterns

Child abuse comes in many forms and occurs in a variety of social contexts. Incidents of the sexual and physical abuse of children can be found in families at all socioeconomic levels. However, children from economically impoverished single-parent households and those who suffer from other forms of paternal inadequacy are overrepresented in most types of abuse statistics.

In incestuous families adults are more apt to use emotional manipulation rather than violent power to seduce the child. An all-too-common example of incest is the father or stepfather who, with the mother's tacit approval, gives the daughter a special wifelike role within the family structure. Father-daughter and stepfather-stepdaughter incest accounts for approximately three-quarters of reported cases. The remaining cases involve mother-son, mother-daughter, father-son and sibling incest, but few researchers have investigated these forms of family sexual abuse.

Most typical, an immature and emotionally needy husband, involved in a relationship with an indifferent, rejecting or unavailable wife, displaces his needs onto a child, usually the eldest daughter. The abuse most often remains undetected or denied by others within the family, but if exposed, it is usually through a crisis precipitated by the daughter's desire for independence and separation from the family. Since fathers and stepfathers are typically the perpetrators of incest, it seems ironic that so much emphasis has been placed on the mother's responsibility. Some literature even casts the father as a covictim while blaming the mother for not providing an adequate affectional and parental structure within the family. In most cases, both parents contribute without question to the incestuous situation, but some of the focus on the mother's culpability is also, in part, a function of our social values deemphasizing paternal responsibility for children.

Poorly fathered children are more susceptible to sexual abuse both inside and outside of the family. Children who do not receive positive nurturance from adult males within their family are more vulnerable to respond to inappropriate sexual advances by others, whether they be family members, neighbors, teachers or strangers. Inadequately fathered children are likely to feel deprived of male attention and to be overly receptive to adolescents or adults who want to sexually, or otherwise, manipulate them.

Serious concern needs to be directed at more subtle forms of sexually related abuse. For example, the father who, while not physically accosting his daughter, states that she is inferior and much less capable than her brother because she is a female is, in my view, sexually maltreating her. The little boy who is constantly berated by his parents because he is not "masculine" could also be viewed as a victim of verbal-sexual maltreatment. The principal issue is that the child's healthy self-concept development may be seriously impeded through continuous verbal assault by a parent. Verbal derogation of the child's body or active discouragement of positive gender development can be considered to be part of a broad definition of sexual maltreatment. Failure to acknowledge these more subtle types of maltreatment offers passive condonement of parental, institutional and other forms of caretaking abuse that, though not directly physical, continue to interfere with the positive emotional and social development of children.

Developmental Implications

A formidable literature deals with the behavior of children who have been identified by clinicians or social agencies as being the victims of abuse or neglect. Extensive data underscore the negative impact that severe abuse has on various aspects of children's psychological and social functioning. Abused or neglected children are at risk to develop low self-esteem, a limited capacity for experiencing pleasure and depressive or hyperaggressive tendencies. An impaired capacity to maintain a healthy reciprocity in intimate relationships is common among severely abused children.

Inadequately parented children may not be clinically labeled as maltreated, but their behavior often bears a striking similarity to that of chronically abused individuals. Children whose parents are rejecting, neglecting, hostile, punitive or overcontrolling generally fare much worse in their personal and social development than those whose parents are high in acceptance and nurturance while encouraging independence and responsibility. Even when there is no lasting physical damage, a great cost in emotional suffering is usually experienced by the victims of child abuse. Children who are physically abused tend to have serious difficulties dealing with aggressive impulses and responding in a sensitive, supportive way to others. However, no distinct pattern of behavior consistently differentiates physically abused children from those who suffer from other types of inadequate parenting. Despite being severely abused by their parents, some individuals have so much resilience that they are able to achieve a surprisingly positive adjustment.

The effects of abuse have to be considered within a total pattern of family interactions and resources. Children who have a positive relationship with one parent usually fare much better than those who are abused by both their father and their mother. It is far different to have suffered short-term or occasional physical abuse than to be a chronically targeted scapegoat for parents throughout childhood.

Children who are rejected and neglected as well as physically abused are especially likely to have very serious psychological and social problems. Children who are not ever physically abused but are constant targets for parental verbal maltreatment and emotional deprivation are much more at risk than those who are sometimes physically abused but are also the recipients of considerable family love and acceptance. A pattern of paternal neglect and rejection is, in fact, a far more pervasive factor associated with later psychological difficulties than is occasional physical abuse.

Risk Factors

The presence of characteristics in the child that relate to abusive parenting should in no way be construed as lessening the adult's accountability. Nevertheless, the developmental status of some children puts them at significant risk for maltreatment. For example, the premature infant is more likely than a full-term baby to be restless, distractible and difficult to soothe—characteristics that, in turn, can lead to considerable stress and frustration for parents. The cause-and-effect dilemma is clear when evaluating the role of prematurity in maltreatment. Although sometimes a correlation exists, prematurity does not operate in isolation from other factors to product maltreatment. Family influences that increase the risk of prematurity (inadequate prenatal care, maternal alcoholism and the like) are also potential factors that may reflect a parent's more general disposition to be insensitive to the needs of an infant.

Children who are retarded or who have a learning disability or severe attention disorder may also be at increased risk for suffering from parental maltreatment. For example, brain-damaged children tend to be anxious, tense and difficult to appease—behavior that increases parental frustration and the likelihood of maltreatment.

The work of psychiatrists Stella Chess and Alexander Thomas concerning enduring patterns of temperament is quite relevant in identifying children who may be particularly at risk for maltreatment. The difficult child is characterized by irregularity in biological functions, nonadaptability, withdrawal from new situations, frequent negative moods and irritability. The slow-to-warm-up child has very inconsistent mood patterns and takes much time to adapt to new situations. Such children are at greater risk to be maltreated when compared to those who are socially responsive and easily adapt to new situations. Moreover, temperamental styles and expectations of parents interact with the child's unique characteristics in ways that may increase or decrease the probability of maltreatment.

Low income levels, single-parent households and temperamentally difficult children are factors that can combine to heighten family stress and increase the likelihood of maltreatment. Research by psychologist Joseph Garbarino and others has also suggested that economically disadvantaged families may be in particular need of neighborhood supports if they are to avoid child maltreatment. Neighborhoods where the risk of child maltreatment is especially great are characterized by social as well as economic deprivation. In such neighborhoods, single mothers have little communication with one another and tend to be relatively young, inexperienced and have few provisions for alternative child care. Neighborhoods that offer little sense of social connectedness exacerbate the already existing negative effects of poverty. The financially and socially impoverished family suffers from a sense of isolation from potential support networks. Single mothers are often left completely to their own individual resources to solve serious family problems.

A family's sense of community isolation can be a decisive factor in the chain of events leading to child maltreatment. Parents in at-risk neighborhoods could greatly benefit from the availability of social support programs including community day-care facilities. Increasing the involvement of male adults in taking more responsibility for young children should be one of the priorities.

Constructive Approaches

The most promising approaches for preventing maltreatment include not only educating parents in the use of appropriate child-rearing techniques but also additional services to help them more effectively deal with other aspects of their lives. For example, depending on the specific needs of parents, a successful program may involve workshops in stress reduction, assertiveness training, financial management and job placement as well as clinical interventions relating to marital counseling and alcohol and other drug problems. In some cases, more intensive family treatment may be needed, and parents and children may also require individual psychotherapy. However, social casework and psychotherapy in isolation from other interventions have not been found to be very successful with most abusive families.

In their efforts to help abusive parents, clinicians typically find it necessary to utilize a wide variety of methods beyond traditional therapy approaches. Volunteer-friends and participation in self-help groups, particularly Parents Anonymous, have helped many abusive adults to lessen their feelings of isolation and powerlessness. Providing more adequate community services can be a major factor in alleviating stress for parents who feel overwhelmed with total responsibility for their children. Important services for families in low-income neighborhoods include the development of day-care programs, cooperative babysitting arrangements, community support groups, transportation networks and recreational facilities.

Since physical abuse and other forms of child maltreatment are so often linked with paternal deprivation, both treatment and preventative programs need to focus on ways to get men as well as women more constructively involved in the child-rearing process. Opportunities for expectant fathers and new fathers to practice effective caretaking activities and to learn about infant and child development are particularly important. To prevent child maltreatment and paternal deprivation, preparation for parenthood should be part of the educational curriculum even during the elementary school years. Involving schools in positive family-life educational efforts can be especially helpful in preventing child maltreatment and paternal deprivation. Parent preparation classes for both male and female students and direct counseling and referral of abusive families can be organized within the school. Child maltreatment is a school and social problem as well as a family issue.

The greater availability of preventative programs emphasizing parent training may greatly reduce the incidence of maltreatment. Clinicians and other human service personnel need to help fathers and mothers develop community resources supporting positive family functioning. Interventions with maltreating parents can be better accomplished within a more holistic community perspective, especially if there is a greater focus on the total family system and the quality of father-mother-child interactions.

Family stress and the likelihood of maltreatment may also be influenced by the child's characteristics and biologically related problems. Public health preventative programs can lessen the incidence of negative prenatal factors and, along with accessible high-quality pediatric services, reduce the stressful impact of early childhood medical difficulties. Educating potential parents as to the risks of poor prenatal care and the importance of the expectant father-mother relationship can do much to decrease the probability of later child maltreatment and paternal deprivation.

SUMMARY

Many family and child problems are associated with inadequate father participation and an overburdened mother. The divorce process may initially only involve the father and mother, but children are the family members who may ultimately be most influenced by parental separation. Children from divorced families are particularly vulnerable to suffering from a lack of paternal involvement since almost 90 percent of them do not live with their fathers. Many interacting influences impact on the child's adjustment subsequent to divorce, but generally none is more important than having continuous positive involvement with the father as well as the mother, whatever the specific custody arrangements.

Nevertheless, great variations occur with respect to the development of children from divorced and other types of families. Children from households with very high father-mother conflict, for example, are generally more disadvantaged than those whose parents have more compatible relationships, whether or not they are divorced. Children with competent single parents generally function better than those from paternally deprived two-parent families. But family relationships always should be viewed in a biopsychosocial context with child-specific characteristics and social system factors having much reciprocal impact on parenting styles.

A history of paternal deprivation during childhood puts individuals at greater risk for later developmental difficulties, including poor self-esteem, depressive tendencies and relationship problems. However, the child's characteristics and other earlier experiences also have much to do with adjustment outcomes during various phases of development. For example, serious behavior problems are especially common among adolescent males who not only have been paternally deprived but who, in addition, have experienced early learning-related deficits in school and grown up in an economically impoverished household.

Paternal deprivation and child maltreatment are strongly associated even when the father is not directly abusive. The most common type of maltreatment is father neglect, but the mother is also much more likely to be abusive, or to allow others to mistreat her child, when she does not have the support of an actively involved partner. In both one-parent and two-parent families, the mother is more at risk to abuse or otherwise inappropriately socialize her child when the father does not adequately share parenting responsibilities. Preventative and treatment programs designed to help families and children must recognize the importance of men and women becoming partners in parenting.

FURTHER READING

Marital Separation

Proceeding Cautiously

For reviews of research underscoring the risks of paternal deprivation for children from divorced families, see Biller (1974c), Biller and Solomon (1986), Hetherington and Arasteh (1988), Hodges (1986), Santrock and Warshak (1986), Thompson (1983) and Warshak (1992).

Regarding long-term consequences of divorce for parents as well as children, see especially Hetherington and Arasteh (1988), Hetherington, Stanley-Hagan and Anderson (1989), Kalter (1990), Raschke (1987), Wallerstein and Blakeslee (1989) and Weitzman (1985). For practical advice for parents communicating about divorce to children, see Brown (1988b), Hodges (1986) and Kalter (1990).

Exhibiting Commitment

For research on different levels of father participation postdivorce, see Keshet and Rosenthal (1978) and Rosenthal and Keshet (1981). For varied patterns of paternal involvement postdivorce, especially in mother-custody families, see Arbarbanel (1979), Biller (1981b, 1982c), Biller and Salter (1986), Biller and Solomon (1986), Hetherington and Arasteh (1988) and Warshak (1992).

Concerning the importance of the divorced father's continuing involvement with the child even in the traditional mother-custody situation, see Biller (1981b), Biller and Meredith (1974), Furstenberg, Morgan and Allison (1987), Hetherington, Cox and Cox (1978, 1982), Hetherington, Stanley-Hagan and Anderson (1989), Kalter (1990), Wallerstein and Blakeslee (1989), Wallerstein and Kelly (1980a, 1980b) and Warshak (1992).

Sharing Custody

For custody-related issues and problems, see Biller (1981b), Chesler (1986), Hetherington, Stanley-Hagan and Anderson (1989), Liss (1987), Santrock and Warshak (1986), Steinman, Zemmelman and Knoblauch (1985), Thompson (1983), Wallerstein and Blakeslee (1989) and Warshak (1992).

With respect to research supporting primary custody by the same-sex parent for school-aged children, see Camara and Resnick (1988), Warshak (1992), Warshak and Santrock (1983) and Zill (1988).

For data indicating that positive relationships with both parents are more important in the adjustment of children postdivorce than the specific type or form of custody arrangement, see Biller (1981b), Camara and Resnick (1988), Clingempeel and Repucci (1982), Derdeyn and Scott (1984), Furstenberg, Morgan and Allison (1987), Hess and Camara (1979), Hetherington, Cox and Cox (1978, 1982), Kalter (1990), Peterson and Zill (1986), Santrock and Warshak (1986), Wallerstein and Blakeslee (1989) and Warshak (1992).

Maintaining Stability

On the relative advantages of stable living arrangements and continuity in social supports for children following divorce, see Biller (1981b), Biller and Meredith (1974), Biller and Salter (1982), Brown (1988b), Camara and Resnick (1988), Furstenberg (1988), Furstenberg, Morgan and Allison (1987), Hetherington, Cox and Cox (1982, 1985), Hodges (1986), Kalter (1990), Santrock and Warshak (1986), Wallerstein and Blakeslee (1989) and Warshak (1992).

For emphasis on the child's characteristics including temperament and developmental level as factors that are important to consider in dealing with divorce-related changes in family living arrangements, see Block, Block and Gjerde (1986), Hetherington, Stanley-Hagan and Anderson (1989) and Wallerstein and Blakeslee (1989).

Concerning various issues and perspectives involved in the scheduling of postdivorce parent-child interactions, especially with regard to the noncustodial parent, see Biller and Meredith (1974), Camara and Resnick (1988), Hetherington and Arasteh (1988), Hodges (1986), Kalter (1990),

Santrock and Warshak (1986), Thompson (1983), Wallerstein and Blakeslee (1989) and Warshak (1992).

Parent Loss

Regarding parent loss and the varied factors involved in the quality of different children's adjustment to changing family circumstances, see Berlinsky and Biller (1982), Biller (1971c, 1974c, 1981b) and Biller and Solomon (1986). For children's diverse adaptations to loss of a parent through death or divorce, see also Block, Block and Gjerde (1986), Boss (1977), Brown (1988a), Eisenstadt (1978), Emery (1988), Hetherington and Arasteh (1988), Kalter (1990) and Raschke (1987).

For evidence that competence in interpersonal reasoning, a strongly internal locus of control and a general sense of self-determination tend to enable some children to cope successfully with divorce and parent loss, see Biller (1971a, 1974c), Biller and Salter (1989), Biller and Solomon (1986), Ferrante and Biller (1986) and Hetherington, Stanley-Hagan and Anderson (1989).

Developmental Findings

For longitudinal research on the impact of divorce and family conflict on children, see Hetherington, Cox and Cox (1978a, 1978b, 1982, 1985). For reviews of other relevant research, see Biller (1981b), Emery (1988), Hetherington (1989, 1991), Hetherington and Arasteh (1988), Raschke (1987) and Warshak (1992).

For overviews of five-year follow-up, see Wallerstein and Kelly (1980a, b). For ten-year follow-up, see Wallerstein and Blakeslee (1989).

Diverse Reactions

With regard to data relating to the short-term effects of divorce for children at particular developmental levels, see Wallerstein and Kelly (1980b). For reviews of other relevant research, see Biller (1981b), Emery (1988), Hetherington and Arasteh (1988) and Hetherington and Stanley-Hagan (1989).

Later Adjustment

For details of the five-year follow-up study, see Wallerstein and Kelly (1980a, 1980b). For details of the ten-year follow-up study, see Wallerstein and Blakeslee (1989). For preliminary data on the fifteen-year follow-up study, see also Wallerstein and Blakeslee (1989).

Concerning discussions of various other data suggesting long-term adult consequences associated with divorce and parent loss during childhood, see Berlinsky and Biller (1982), Biller (1970, 1971a, 1974c, 1981b), Biller and Solomon (1986), Eisenstadt (1978), Emery (1988), Furstenberg, Brooks-Gunn and Morgan (1987), Hetherington and Arasteh (1988), Huttunen and Niskanen (1978), Kalter (1990), Raschke (1987), Rubenstein (1980), Warshak (1992) and Weiss (1979b).

Family Resources

Regarding a transactional view of socioeconomic status, maternal attitudes, paternal deprivation, developmental phase and the young child's level of functioning, see Berlinsky and Biller (1982), Biller (1971c, 1974c, 1981b) and Biller and Solomon (1986). For other data supporting the importance of overall family resources in the adaptation of single parents and their children, see Adams, Milner and Schrepf (1984), Furstenberg, Brooks-Gunn and Morgan (1987), Hetherington and Arasteh (1988) and Kellam, Ensminger and Turner (1977).

About unwed parents and their children, see Adams, Milner and Schrepf (1984), Berlinsky and Biller (1982), Biller (1974c, 1981b), Biller and Salter (1982), Biller and Smith (1972), Elster and Lamb (1986), Furstenberg, Brooks-Gunn and Chase-Lansdale (1989), Lamb and Elster (1985) and Weitzman (1985). For research relating to adolescent unwed fathers and mothers, see Biller and Salter (1982), Furstenberg, Brooks-Gunn and Morgan (1987), Lamb and Elster (1985) and Robinson and Barrett (1986).

Parental Competence

For research relating to maternal support of positive self-concept and gender development in boys from single-mother families, see Biller (1969a), Biller and Bahm (1971), Biller and Salter (1989) and Biller and Solomon (1986). For other research stressing the relationship between individual differences in parenting competence and the adaptations of children from single-parent households, see Hetherington, Cox and Cox (1978, 1982, 1985), Hetherington, Stanley-Hagan and Anderson (1989), Pedersen (1966), Santrock and Warshak (1979, 1986) and Warshak (1992).

On single fathers and their diverse situations, see Furstenberg (1988), Gongla and Thompson (1987), Greif (1985), Hanson (1988), Hetherington and Stanley-Hagan (1986), Keshet and Rosenthal (1978), LeMasters and DeFrain (1983), Lewis (1978), Rosenthal and Keshet (1981), Santrock and Warshak (1983), Santrock, Warshak and Elliot (1982) and Wallerstein and Kelly (1982). For research focusing on the varied circumstances and adaptations among single mothers, see Berlinsky and Biller (1982), Biller (1971c), Chesler (1986), Furstenberg, Brooks-Gunn and Morgan (1987), LeMasters and DeFrain (1983), Levy-Shiff (1982) and Weitzman (1985).

For details of research relating parenting competency to the adjustment of children in divorced families, see Hetherington, Cox and Cox (1978, 1982, 1985). See also Hetherington and Arasteh (1988) and Santrock and Warshak (1979, 1986).

On the significance of positive mother-child relationships as buffers in the face of severe family stressors including divorce, the father's death or long-term unemployment, see Berlinsky and Biller (1982), Elder (1979), Elder et al. (1986), Hetherington, Cox and Cox (1982) and Ray and McLoyd (1986).

Concerning the coping styles of mothers from families where fathers are declared missing in action, see Boss (1977, 1987). For other research relevant to mothers coping with husband separation related to military service or other forms of employment, see Boss, McCubbin and Lester (1979), Farley and Werkman (1986), Hillenbrand (1976) and Hunter (1978, 1982).

Remarriage Issues

For complex issues involved in remarriage and stepparenting, see Brand, Clingempeel and Bowen-Woodward (1988), Bray (1988), Duberman (1975), Einstein (1982), Furstenberg (1988), Gamong and Coleman (1984), Hetherington and Arasteh (1988), Hetherington, Stanley-Hagan and Anderson (1989), McGoldrick and Carter (1988), Robinson (1984), Spanier and Furstenberg (1987), Visher and Visher (1982) and Wallerstein and Blakeslee (1989).

Concerning parent-stepparent-child issues, see especially Bray (1988), Brown (1988b), Einstein (1982), Hetherington and Arasteh (1988), Hodges (1986), McGoldrick and Carter (1988), Pasley and Ihinger-Tallman (1987), Robinson and Barrett (1986) and Visher and Visher (1982).

Stepparenting Challenges

For research supporting the potentially positive impact that the presence of a stepfather can have on a young boy, see Chapman (1977), Einstein (1982), Hetherington, Cox and Cox (1985), Parish and Dostal (1980a), Robinson and Barrett (1986), Santrock (1972) and Wallerstein and Blakeslee (1989). For data suggesting that among young children, girls may have more difficulty adjusting to their divorced mother's remarriage than do boys, see Brand, Clingempeel and Bowen-Woodward (1988).

Regarding findings that older children and adolescents may experience much more difficulty accepting a new stepparent, especially one who attempts immediately to become highly involved with them in an authority role, see Biller and Solomon (1986), Hetherington (1987), Parker and Parker (1986) and Wallerstein and Blakeslee (1989).

On data underscoring the problems involved in parent-child relationships when there are abrupt changes in the custodial parent's marital status and/or a stepparent attempts to assume a very directive role with a stepchild, see Brand, Clingempeel and Bowen-Woodward (1988), Bray (1988), Hetherington (1987), Hetherington and Arasteh (1988), Nelson and Nelson (1982) and Wallerstein and Blakeslee (1989). About the increased difficulty that children are likely to have in adjusting to blended family situations, see Hetherington, Cox and Cox (1982), Hobart (1987), Santrock and Sitterlee (1987) and Zill (1988).

For guidelines relative to coping constructively with remarriage and stepparenting issues, see Hetherington and Arasteh (1988), Hodges (1986), McGoldrick and Carter (1988) and Visher and Visher (1982).

Troubled Children

Diagnostic Complexities

For more detailed discussions of difficulties in the differential diagnosis of various developmental problems, see Chess and Thomas (1986, 1987), Elliot (1988), Henker and Whalen (1989), Kazdin (1989), Kovacs (1989) and Tuma (1989).

Concerning the relationship between mental and physical handicaps and the child's emotional and social development, see Biller and Borstelmann (1965, 1967), Gallagher, Cross and Scharfman (1981), Lamb (1983) and Meyer (1986). With respect to adults constructively coping with various types of disabilities, see Biller and Meredith (1974), Taylor (1986), Telford and Sawrey (1986) and Wright (1983).

Antisocial Patterns

About attention-deficit problems and learning disabilities and how they are sometimes associated with acting out and other behavioral problems, see Berman and Siegal (1976), Davids (1976), Elliot (1988), Levinson (1984) and Silver (1984).

Regarding parenting factors associated with delinquent and criminal behavior, see Biller (1971a, 1974c, 1974d, 1981c), Biller and Davids (1973), Biller and Salter (1989), Biller and Solomon (1986), Bourdin and Henggeler (1982), Dornbusch, et al. (1985), Kazdin (1987), McCord (1979) and Patterson, DeBaryshe and Ramsey (1989). For a sampling of relevant research studies linking inadequate fathering and antisocial behavior, see Bandura and Walters (1959), Barnes (1984), Kelly and Baer (1969), McCord (1979), McCord, McCord and Thurber (1962), Patterson and Stouthamer-Loeber (1984) and Stern, Northman and Van Slyk (1984).

On individual and family factors involved in alcohol abuse and other drug problems, see Barnes (1984), Elkin (1984), Krestan and Bepko (1988), Phares and Compas (1992), Stern, Northman and Van Slyk (1984) and Willoughby (1979).

Multiple Influences

For transactional perspectives on delinquency and other types of behavior problems, see Biller (1971a, 1974c), Biller and Davids (1973), Biller and Solomon (1986), Lytton (1990a, b) and Patterson, DeBaryshe and Ramsey (1989). For an emphasis on the interaction of biosocial factors underlying delinquent and abusive behavior, see Berman and Siegal (1976a, 1976b), Elliot (1988), Hutchings and Mednick (1977), Kazdin (1987, 1988a, b) and Thomas and Chess (1977).

For perspectives on childhood depression and its complex relationship with other behavior problems including suicidal tendencies, see Kazdin (1988a), Kovacs (1989), Phares and Compas (1992) and Rutter (1986).

Disadvantaged Families

With respect to the need for social welfare agencies to be more responsive to the father's role, see Biller (1971a, 1974c), Biller and Meredith (1974), Bolton (1986), Jaffee (1983) and Wolins (1983). For research relating economic deprivation, job loss and unemployment to inadequate parenting, see Elder et al. (1985, 1986), McLoyd (1989), Ray and McLoyd (1986) and Voydanoff (1983).

For data underscoring the difficulties of poor families, especially those headed by single mothers, see Adams, Milner and Schrepf (1984), Furstenberg, Brooks-Gunn and Morgan (1987), Hetherington and Arasteh (1988), Rutter and Madge (1976) and Weitzman (1985). For the details and controversy surrounding the publication of the Moynihan Report, see Moynihan (1965) and Rainwater and Yancey (1967). For more recent discussions relevant for both poor black and white families and their children, see also Hines (1988), McAdoo (1978, 1981), Sciara (1975), Wilson (1989) and Zigler (1985).

Regarding the study concerning masculinity of self-concept and father-absence among economically disadvantaged children, see Biller (1968b). For research relating to the long-term impact of paternal deprivation on children growing up in economically disadvantaged, single-mother-headed black families, see Barclay and Cusumano (1967), Biller (1971a, 1974c), Biller and Solomon (1986), Bronfenbrenner (1967), Hines (1988), Moran and Barclay (1988) and Nelsen and Vangen (1971).

Concerning research indicating that constructive paternal involvement can help children cope relatively well with various types of initial handicaps and disadvantages, see Baldwin, Cole and Baldwin (1982), Biller (1974c), Biller and Solomon (1986), Furstenberg and Harris (1992), Gallagher, Cross and Scharfman (1981), Lamb (1983), Meyer (1986), Phares and Compas (1992) and Vadasy et al. (1985). Regarding the importance of supportive fathering during the child's early school-related difficulties, see especially Elizur (1986) and Margalit (1985).

Parental Accountability

Regarding negative or negligent parenting that may contribute to provoking a child to behave in a socially maladaptive and emotionally disturbed manner, see Biller and Davids (1973), Biller and Meredith (1974), Biller and Solomon (1986), Chess and Thomas (1986, 1987), Lefkowitz and Tesiny (1984) and Phares and Compas (1992). (But note the emphasis that family factors usually interact with other influences, including the child's particular temperament, in the development of severe psychopathology.)

With regard to the frequent association of neglectful or abusive fathering and other forms of paternal deprivation as common risk factors in the development of emotional disturbance and other psychological difficulties in children, see Biller (1971a, 1974c, 1974d, 1981c), Biller and Davids (1973), Biller and Solomon (1986) and Cath, Gurwitt and Ross (1982). For some specific research projects indicating a link between paternal inadequacy, family problems and child maladjustment, see Block (1971), Fish and Biller (1973), Gasser and Murray (1969), Kayton and Biller (1971), Kellam, Ensminger and Turner (1977), Mishler and Waxler (1968), Phares (1992), Phares and Compas (1992), Reuter and Biller (1973), Stern, Northman and Van Slyk (1984) and Westley and Epstein (1970).

Individual Vulnerability

For perspectives emphasizing child-based risk factors in the development of severe psychopathology, see Biller (1974c), Biller and Solomon (1986), Chess and Thomas (1986, 1987), Frodi and Lamb (1980), Garmezy and Rutter (1988), Kazdin (1989), Kopp (1987), Kopp and Kaler (1989), Kovacs (1989), Mednick (1973), Rutter (1986), Talovic et al. (1981), Tuma (1989) and Wender et al. (1986).

Regarding the parental images of psychiatric patients, see Kayton and Biller (1971, 1972). Concerning the special needs of families with a mentally ill individual, see Hatfield and Lefley (1987) and Lefley (1989).

Family Interventions

About approaches stressing the inclusion of the father in child and family therapy, see Atkins and Lansky (1986), Biller (1974c, 1984b), Biller and Meredith (1974), Biller and Solomon (1986), Bowen (1978), Ferholt and Gurwitt (1982), Hatfield and Lefley (1987) and Kaslow (1981). For various other perspectives on family therapy, which include working conjointly with parents and children, see also Carter and McGoldrick (1988), Grebstein (1986), Gurman and Kniskeon (1981), Hubeck, Watson and Russell (1986), Kaslow (1987), Minuchin (1974) and Nichols (1984).

Child Maltreatment

On father neglect and other forms of paternal inadequacy being highly associated with various types of child maltreatment and family problems, see Biller (1974c, 1974d, 1989b, 1989c), Biller and Meredith (1974) and Biller and Solomon (1986).

Assessing Abuse

For the classic article on battered children, see Kempe et al. (1962). For reviews of the child maltreatment literature, including considerations of the multidimensional nature of abuse and neglect, see Biller (1989b), Biller and Solomon (1986), Egeland, Jacobvitz and Sroufe (1987), Emery (1989), Garbarino, Guttman and Seeley (1988), Gelles and Strauss (1988), Parke (1982), Starr (1988), Steinmetz (1987) and Van Hasselt et al. (1988).

Diverse Patterns

Regarding incest and the sexual maltreatment of children, see Biller and Solomon (1986), Browne and Finkelhor (1986), Finkelhor (1984), Forward and Buck (1978), Harter, Alexander and Neimeyer (1988), Herman (1981), Parker and Parker (1986), Sgroi (1981) and Van Hasselt et al. (1988).

For data emphasizing sociocultural influences, including poverty, as risk factors associated with various forms of child and family maltreatment, see Biller and Solomon (1986), Breton (1980), Garbarino (1981), Gelles and Strauss (1988), Parke (1982), Pelton (1981), Steinberg, Catalano and Dooley (1981) and Steinmetz (1987).

Developmental Implications

For the varied developmental consequences of different forms of child maltreatment, see Biller (1989b), Biller and Solomon (1986), Biller and Zung (1972), Egeland, Jacobvitz and Papatola (1988), Emery (1989), Faretra (1981), Forward and Buck (1978), Gelles and Strauss (1988), Heilbrun (1973), Huckel (1984), Martin (1980), Parke (1982), Parker (1983), and Van Hasselt et al. (1988). For relating the general socialization literature with the clinical child-abuse literature viewing parenting competence on various continua ranging from outstanding child rearing to severe maltreatment, see especially Biller and Solomon (1986).

Risk Factors

About child temperament and parenting difficulties, see Chess and Thomas (1986, 1987) and Thomas and Chess (1977). For the association between particular child characteristics and maltreatment, see Biller and Solomon (1986), Elder et al. (1985, 1986), Elliot (1988), Frodi and Lamb (1980) and Parke (1982).

Regarding ecological and neighborhood factors increasing the likelihood of child abuse, see Garbarino (1981), and Garbarino, Sebes and Schellenbach (1984). For social and economic risk factors associated with child maltreatment and family violence, see Belsky (1980a), Biller and Solomon (1986), Gelles and Strauss (1988), Parke (1982), Pelton (1981), Ray and McLoyd (1986) and Steinberg, Catalano and Dooley (1981).

Constructive Approaches

Concerning various perspectives on preventing parents from maltreating children, see Biller (1986, 1989a, 1989b), Biller and Solomon (1986), Breton (1980), Egeland, Jacobvitz and Sroufe (1987), Emery (1989), Gelles and Strauss (1988), Kempe and Kempe (1984), Rosenberg and Repucci (1985), Starr (1988) and Van Hasselt et al. (1988).

12

Family, Community and Society

Quality family life is the basic ingredient for the success of a society. But at the same time social factors have an ongoing influence on family functioning. Schools, churches, social service agencies, media, industry and government can in varying degrees be supportive or unsupportive with respect to the needs of parents and children. This chapter focuses on some contemporary social concerns and ways to strengthen positive connections between the family and society, with a particular emphasis on giving greater support to the role of the father.

CONTEMPORARY CONCERNS

Technological advances can be used to help parents and children spend more time together, but they often have the opposite influence. For instance, modern high-speed transportation systems can have the effect of keeping family members apart if parents decide to work greater distances from home. Whatever their family's socioeconomic status, a large proportion of young children have very little opportunity to spend quality time with their parents, especially their fathers.

Hurried Pace

Increased mobility has contributed to a decline in the sense of community in our society. Families may have friends at the other end of the city yet be strangers to the neighbors next door. They are likely to live a considerable distance away from grandparents, uncles, aunts, cousins and other relatives. More than 20 percent of American families move every year, often because of a parent's employment or because of divorce-related issues. Though children may learn a great deal from moving to another area, a family's connectedness to the community lessens. Changing neighborhoods can also disrupt social support systems, increasing parent and child stress and the probability of family problems. For example, moving only a few miles away may interfere with the young child's feeling of peer stability.

In many families, much of the time parents and children spend together seems to revolve around car pools. During a particular week, suburban parents may end up chauffeuring children back and forth to team practices, music or tennis lessons, religion classes or scout or other organized activities. Many fathers, for example, do things for their children, but in the process may have very little individualized contact with them. A father and child may be so immersed in a whirl of activities that they seldom have the opportunity simply to have a quiet talk or enjoy one-to-one time together. Although the particular activities may be quite different, weekends may be a continuation of the hurried pace during the week. The overall quality of family relationships is ultimately much more important than the specific activities that parents and children do together. Parents can do much to slow down their pace and increase quality family time if they are willing to take a hard look at their own schedules and priorities.

Although all fathers have some restrictions in the use of their time, most have much more potential control over their schedules than would have been the case if they had lived in an earlier historical period. They have more choice in setting time priorities because, in part, modern technology has allowed us more leisure time. This may be very difficult for many career-oriented fathers to comprehend, because if work gets done more efficiently, the tendency is to set higher job expectations rather than use potential free time for family pursuits.

Many fathers work much more than forty hours a week. They may do this for a variety of reasons including economic need, professional demands or even because they feel more comfortable away from their children and families. It is common for those parents with demanding careers to expand job-related commitments beyond the modal eight-to-four or nine-to-five workday. Evening and weekend work activities are quite typical for many self-employed professionals and for those in competitive positions in various organizational settings. However, working fifty, sixty or seventy hours a week is not conducive to quality family relationships. When considering very extended time commitments at work, fathers should take their parenting responsibilities into account. For example, if a father works unusual hours, the parents may find it worthwhile to adjust the family schedule of eating and sleeping somewhat so that he will have more time to spend with his child.

If the parents work long hours, the preschool child can be up to see them when they get home, sleeping later in the morning or taking a nap during the day. The school-age child may be able to take a nap in the late afternoon in order to stay up and spend time with parents who work late. Such scheduling arrangements are easier in some families than others, but it is important to have regular opportunities for the child to interact with each parent. Alternative strategies can involve family interactions in the early morning hours. For example, nothing prevents a father and child from having just as meaningful a time together between 5:00 A.M. and 6:00 A.M. as they could between 5:00 P.M. and 6:00 P.M. In fact, they may find early morning times especially conducive for enjoying relaxed activities together.

Many men believe that in order to be very successful in a career, one cannot be a highly involved parent on a day-to-day basis. It is certainly not easy to come home exhausted from a twelve-hour workday and be an effective parent. Conversely, it may be just as difficult to spend a great deal of time with the family and still be successful in a highly competitive career. However, many extremely competent career women find the day-to-day time to be involved with their children, although fathers in a similar employment track may insist that they cannot regularly share parenting responsibilities.

A major dimension of adjustment in adulthood is the ability to be in control of one's schedule. Making meaningful choices relating to time priorities is a very important ingredient in personal happiness. Workaholics are controlled by their jobs and the demands of other people. Ironically, most workaholics are not particularly successful in their careers because they get caught up in superfluous details and obsess about minor decisions. Workaholic fathers can endanger their own health as well as the general well-being of their families. In contrast, individuals with a sense of reasonable boundaries between work and nonwork activities are likely to be successful in their careers and, most important, to feel fulfilled in their personal and family endeavors.

It is much easier to combine competent parenting and career success when one has a supportive partner. When the mother and father can effectively share parenting responsibilities and be encouraging of each other's career goals, a much greater chance occurs for both of them to be able to balance meaningfully family and work commitments. The married career woman who jokes that what she really needs is a wife rather than a husband is not being totally facetious. Even in most families where both parents are working, the mother still is likely to assume the bulk of child-rearing responsibilities.

Informational Sources

In contrast to technological advances involving transportation, those relating to television, video and computer technology have increased certain home-based activities. However, the impact has not generally been in the form of stimulating positive family interaction. The most heated discussions in many contemporary families do not concern morals or politics but revolve around which television programs to watch or which videotapes or computer programs to rent. In some families, television is treated almost as if it represents a superparent benignly and authoritatively presenting news and entertainment. In such households, discussions at the family dinner table have been replaced by the TV-tray supper with a network commentator providing one-sided conversation.

However, television too can be used in a positive individual and family context. As with other technology-related advances, the impact of television on the family is greatly influenced by the degree to which parents simply allow external factors to control their lives. Being an active critic and selective user, for instance, is far different than indiscriminately depending on television for one's source of entertainment and stimulation.

Intermittently some 1950s and 1960s situation comedies such as "Father Knows Best," "Leave It to Beaver" and the "Donna Reed Show" are revived on local and cable television channels. These shows generally present both fathers and mothers in a positive light, but little consideration is given to how adults grapple with conflicts between work and parenting. Although such shows may be perceived as unrealistic, they do connect with the basic need of so many in our society to experience at least vicariously what seems to be a constructive two-parent family situation. "Little House on the Prairie" and "The Waltons" also touched a core of positive feelings about family life.

Some of the most nurturant adult males can be found on public or cable television. While the real father is away from his children at work, father figures such as Fred Rogers and Bob Kutchen, the genial host of "The Captain Kangaroo Show," both entertain and teach children important values. Science experiments are still patiently demonstrated to children by Don Herbert, who originated the title role in the 1950s television program "Watch Mr. Wizard." Perhaps most important, these talented men present themselves as kindly and sensitively interested in the welfare of children. The popularity of the "Bill Cosby Show" certainly suggested that the general public is also eager for more complex portrayals of sensitive fathers coping with family issues. To a great extent, Cosby has become a paternal role model not just for many African Americans but for many of those in the white middle class as well. He is a kind of hero for our times, an extremely successful entertainer, businessman and, not least of all, a concerned father. Some criticized his show as unrealistic, but our society is in need of a variety of positive family life images. The public will continue to respond with interest to vital depictions of active paternal involvement in family-oriented television programming.

In the last decade a proliferation of newspaper and magazine articles as well as books have been devoted to parenting issues. However, for the most part, publications that deal with parenting do not include a focus on the father's role. They tend to reflect the still pervasive stereotype that the only persons really interested in day-to-day child rearing are mothers.

The behavioral or social scientist can be a catalyst in sensitizing both men and women to father-related issues. Unfortunately, less than 10 percent of scientific investigations proporting to study parental influence and child-rearing techniques have taken the father's role into account. Scientists are, despite their so-called objectivity, still subject to some of the same prevailing cultural attitudes concerning the family as are their contemporaries in other fields.

Ironically, the relative lack of research including the father also stems from the fact that in our male-dominated society most behavioral and social scientists are men. Many social scientists, for example, have been quite focused on studying career development, but they have not been as interested in pursuing what they have perceived as a more secondary male role. The degree of career commitment shared by many scientists may, in fact, leave them little time to spend with their own children. However, it is noteworthy that female scientists who are parents appear much less likely to neglect their child-rearing responsibilities than do their male counterparts.

The priority of career over family is all too often reflected in the value systems of fathers in various professions. When professionals have a constricted view of fatherhood, it is difficult for them to be supportive of men sharing child-rearing responsibilities. For example, many male lawyers are especially resistant to the notion of divorced fathers participating in the care of children on a daily basis because it makes little sense to them on a personal level. Paternal deprivation may be more obvious among economically disadvantaged families, but it is a pervasive problem regardless of social class.

Whatever their occupational status, men should not abdicate their child-rearing responsibilities. The old cliché of the cobbler whose children go without shoes is an all too frequent and telling analogy in our society. All too many physicians do not take care of their own health, and all too many human service professionals do not give enough attention to their own families. Although it may be quite difficult, all parents should make a concerted effort to balance their occupational and social aspirations with what they need to provide for their own children. Many men make significant contributions to their community but in the process neglect their own families. By serving others, parents can indeed set a positive example, but it is important for them to be vigilant in order to ensure that their own family connections are not damaged in the process. Being an effective parent is, in itself, a highly significant way to help one's community.

Organizational Supports

Business, industry and government can develop policies that are more supportive of families. For example, large companies may find it financially advantageous to provide day care, especially when they are trying to recruit and retain employees with special skills. Some hospitals and other medical facilities, attempting to attract hard-to-find nursing personnel, are using on-the-premises day care as a recruiting and retention inducement. Some organizations are providing day-care services as part of a package of employee benefits. When both parents are working, company-operated day-care centers have particularly salient advantages for families with preschool-age children. For instance, it may be possible for a father to spend time with his child when commuting, during work breaks and at lunchtime.

There should be increased availability of paternity leaves as well as maternity leaves, granted at the birth or adoption of an infant or during a child's illness. Employee benefits can also include giving the parent a certain number of days off a year for the purpose of visiting the child's school to share work-related information or to participate in other educationally relevant endeavors.

Large corporations can be supportive of families in additional ways. Business, industry and government can sponsor more courses for employees concerning family relations. The curriculum can cover general parenting issues and also the special kinds of family problems that may be encountered by employees with particular types of responsibilities. Because of the increased awareness of the costs of alcohol-related problems and other forms of drug abuse, more companies are offering employee assistance programs that include some attention to family and parenting issues.

Families may face particular disadvantages when the father's outside commitments conflict with his consistent sharing of child-rearing responsibilities. Most of the early research on father-absence related to concerns for the plight of children and families during World War II when so many men were shipped overseas for military duty. Wartime situations may make parent-child separations inevitable, but awareness has also been growing about the effects of family disruption related to military service during peacetime.

I recall a conversation with a psychiatrist who, in the late 1950s, had fulfilled his military obligation by working at a large service-connected mental health center. He found an extremely high percentage of psychological problems among military dependents, seemingly related to father-absence. However, he claimed that he was told by his commanding officer not to write up his findings or discuss them at professional meetings. At that time, the military establishment seemed to be extremely defensive about the impact of service-connected family separations on children and spouses.

The 1970s and 1980s witnessed increasing acknowledgment that frequent and lengthy separations of fathers from their wives and children can cause great psychological and social hardship for all family members. Military and government leaders have sought to deal more directly with family problems and have supported much important research and preventative programming. For example, the First Annual Military Family Research Conference, sponsored by the navy but featuring representatives from all branches of the armed services, took place in September 1977 in San Diego. I was invited to be the keynote speaker and gave an overview of research on the effects of father-separation.

In November 1983, the House of Representatives Select Committee on Children, Youth and Families held hearings relating to the impact of the father's role and paternal deprivation, targeting military family issues as one of the four primary areas for consideration. My presentation was in the more general research-oriented session, but the data and preventative programs described by military personnel were especially impressive. Various branches of the military have given increasing attention to family needs including minimizing the frequency and length of parental separations as well as providing greater community support systems for spouses and children.

Voluntary Efforts

Children who are paternally deprived are in special need of positive contact with caring men. George Bahlmann, executive director of Big Brothers, has described the coordinated efforts of several service organizations directed at helping children in fatherless families. A major thrust is to recruit effective volunteers who are committed to developing individualized relationships with paternally deprived children. Many opportunities exist for men to do volunteer work with children who are served by various community centers and charitable organizations. Scouting and sports organizations attract many dedicated volunteers, but such endeavors may lack some of the prerequisites for supporting an individualized type of "social fatherhood." In scouting, Little League and other youth organizations, the emphasis is heavily on group endeavors, and it may be difficult to provide individualized personal guidance to children.

In most youth-oriented organizations, more emphasis tends to be on productivity and achievement than on one-to-one interactions between adult and child. For children receiving adequate parenting at home this may not be a problem, but many boys and girls have little opportunity within their families for close relationships with men. I have consulted with the Los Angeles chapter of the Boy Scouts of America, which has developed programs geared toward children who have grown up in female-headed households. A special emphasis is placed on the needs of father-absent boys for positive individualized attention from caring adult males. However, there is generally a lack of organized community programs directed toward younger paternally deprived children.

Our educational system could also do much to mitigate the effects of father neglect if more male teachers and volunteers were available, particularly in nursery school, kindergarten and the lower elementary school grades. More incentives should be developed to encourage males to become involved in early childhood education. We generally need to make our schools more a part of the community and to invite fuller participation from fathers as well as mothers. A concerted effort must be made to devote greater social and economic resources to schools serving children from financially disadvantaged families so that all boys and girls will have a fair chance to develop their intellectual and academic potential.

In addition, business and industry can cooperate in giving men more opportunities to become involved with school-related activities. Children, as part of their education, should be encouraged to visit various work settings in the community. Such visits can provide children with more experiences interacting with competent men and women. A reduction of the general segregation of children and adults in our society should occur.

Although they can be very helpful, organizational supports are not always needed to provide a basis for adults to have a positive influence on children. Many men and women, informally, take a special interest in children in their extended family or in their neighborhood. Such caring does not have to be time consuming, but it can be very gratifying for both the adult and the child. I have tried, as an adult, to give some special attention to children who live in mother-only families or to those whose fathers are not very involved with them. I hoped by doing this also to set a positive example of caring for my own children. It is a great feeling to provide others with the kind of attention that I appreciated as a child and wished was much more frequent after the premature deaths of my grandfather and father. I vividly remember the occasions when the father of another child would include me in an athletic activity or just take a few minutes for a brief conversation.

Parenthood Training

Unfortunately, many men and women are relatively unprepared for parenthood. The expectant father and mother who are able to be positively involved with one another during the pregnancy are more likely to share child-rearing responsibilities effectively. Childbirth education, especially if accompanied by some guidelines for taking care of the newborn, can provide good preparation for both expectant parents.

Psychologist Ross Parke and his coworkers designed a hospital-based intervention program for fathers. In the initial phase, during their wives' postdelivery hospitalization, husbands were shown an educational videotapes focusing on father-infant interactions, specific caretaking activities and babies' learning and social capacities. An emphasis was made on fathers becoming active participants in the care and stimulation of even newborn infants. A clear-cut impact on the behavior and attitudes of fathers who had the opportunity to view the videotape was observed. Fathers who watched the videotape, compared to those who did not, were more willing to take care of their infants and to stimulate them actively. Viewing the videotape was also correlated with fathers' diary reports of frequency of feeding and changing diapers of their three-month-old sons. According to observational data, those fathers who were exposed to the videotape engaged in more feeding-related caretaking when their infants were three months old as well as when they were newborns. Perhaps most significant was the fact that the fathers who viewed the videotape were more likely to connect their stimulating and affectionate behavior with their infants' overtures and generally seemed more sensitive and attuned to their infants' needs.

In addition to Parke's pioneering program, several other constructive projects have been directed at increasing father-child involvement. Psychologist Milton Kotelchuck and his colleagues trained previously low-interacting fathers to play at home with their infants on a regular basis for thirty minutes a day over a four-week period. The opportunity to view another man skillfully playing with an infant as well as direct coaching was provided for the fathers. Compared to untrained fathers, those who were trained became more active with their infants. Moreover, their infants took more social initiative with them.

Developmental psychologists Jane Dickie and Sharon Gerber trained both fathers and mothers to become more responsive and effective in interacting with their four-to-twelve-month-old infants. Over a two-month period, parents participated in eight two-hour sessions focusing on information on individual differences in babies and ways in which parents and infants stimulated one another. Similar to the findings of Kotelchuck, infants of parents who participated in the training sessions initiated more social interaction with their fathers than did those whose parents were in the nontrained comparison group. Dickie and Gerber also found that, among the trained couples, mothers supported father-child interactions while at the same time decreasing their own direct level of involvement, thus helping to provide their infants with what could perhaps be viewed as a more balanced type of parental influence.

A promising parent education program for married fathers of school-aged children has been developed by psychologist Ronald Levant. His training format included eight three-hour sessions with an emphasis on helping the men pay more attention to their own and others' feelings, as well as including homework exercises involving father-child interactions. Self-report paper-and-pencil measures indicated a significant positive gain in the father's overall sensitivity to children. As reflected both in structured interviews and in their family drawings, the children themselves perceived improvement in their relationships with their fathers.

Family education specialist James Levine and his colleagues developed The Fatherhood Project. This project was an innovative attempt to coordinate research and demonstration programs concerning the paternal role. The project had many and varied functions, including providing a countrywide clearinghouse for information, weekend group programs for fathers and their preschool-age children, courses for both male and female preadolescents on infant care and a national series of Fatherhood Forums. The staff prepared valuable resource materials, including a comprehensive guide to programs and services across the country, and manuals on *How to Start a Father-Child Group* and *How to Start a Babycare Program for Boys and Girls*. Efforts such as those provided by The Fatherhood Project can do much to increase social awareness about the importance of men and women sharing parenting responsibilities.

Effective Programs

Unfortunately, parent and family education programs have traditionally focused only on mothers, and the rate of father participation has been extremely low. More parent training should include a special emphasis on fatherhood along with a greater acknowledgment of the importance of the father-mother relationship. Thomas Gordon's Parent Effectiveness Training (P.E.T.) has been the most widespread program designed to improve parent-child relationships. But relatively few fathers participate, and Gordon has also commented that all too many mothers in the program feel frustrated because their untrained husbands are not supportive of P.E.T. techniques.

Gordon has made a systematic application of well-researched communication and counseling techniques to parent-child relationships. The parenting approach encouraged in the P.E.T. program is highly compatible with the philosophy of child rearing that I have put forth in this book. For example, Gordon emphasizes the importance of parents owning their own feelings and being sensitive to differences between themselves and their children. Parents are encouraged to treat children with respect and acceptance by actively listening to their concerns. Parents are provided with practical techniques designed to facilitate family problem solving and conflict resolution.

A great advantage of P.E.T. is that it avoids the use of so-called disciplinary techniques, while teaching parents a process of communication whereby they can deal with their children in a respectful, reciprocal manner. Gordon and I share the view that traditional disciplinary techniques are not only ineffective but also actually tend to promote an adversarial relationship between parent and child. Children deserve respect just as they need to learn to be considerate of others inside and outside of their families. In addition to P.E.T., Gordon has developed other systematic training programs, including Teacher Effectiveness Training and Leadership Effectiveness Training, which are also extremely relevant for adults working with children in nonfamily settings.

As Gordon so incisively argues in his book *Teaching Children Self-Discipline*, adults need to avoid the use of power-assertive techniques, while engaging children in mutually cooperative relationships. The key is for adults to treat children in a democratic manner. It is tragic that, although we live in a supposedly democratic society, the rights of children are so often ignored within the family, school and other settings. P.E.T. can be helpful not only in dealing with current problems but also in contributing to building longer-term cooperative relationships between parents and children, thus preventing many types of later family difficulties. Gordon cites numerous studies that support the effectiveness of P.E.T. in increasing the self-esteem of both parents and children. The techniques that Gordon has advocated can also be taught to children and future parents in the context of school-based family-life education programs. Moreover, teachers, school administrators, coaches, youth leaders and all those working with children can become much more effective in carrying out their responsibilities if they master the communication skills that are promoted by Gordon and his colleagues.

As Michael Gershon and I emphasized in our book *The Other Helpers*, a major factor in the success of P.E.T. and other programs geared toward improving human relations skills is the combined use of experiential and didactic techniques. The format of P.E.T. encourages parents to reflect on their own feelings and experiences, while mastering new techniques for relating and problem solving with their children. Nevertheless, despite the contributions of P.E.T., a much more concerted effort is needed to increase the participation of fathers. Extension of the course content should include greater attention to special issues relating to fathering with a particular emphasis on the importance of effective coparenting.

Developing skills in democratically dealing with children is not just the responsibility of mothers and other females. When both parents take a P.E.T. course together, the potential exists not only to learn better individual child-rearing skills but also to develop communication techniques that can contribute to the parents' relationship with one another and to their ability to coparent. More fathers need to become involved in P.E.T., and more male teachers and administrators should enroll in Gordon's Teacher Effectiveness Training program. Both men and women must be committed to the welfare of children.

Any discussion of programs designed to improve parenting skills should also take into account ways to enhance father-mother communication. Children thrive best in an atmosphere where their father and mother cooperatively share parenting responsibilities. When parents have chronic marital problems, or are separated or divorced, children are more at risk for later emotional and relationship problems. Solution-oriented brief therapy is an especially promising approach applicable to marriage enhancement and divorce prevention. Social worker Michele Weiner-Davis has written *Divorce Busting: A Revolutionary and Rapid Program for Staying Together*. Her present- and future-oriented focus helps couples build on their relationship strengths—what has previously worked for them—to improve their marriages even if they are contemplating divorce. The emphasis is on harnessing the couples' ability to change, actively and creatively, those current patterns of behavior that are dysfunctional in their relationships. Improving the marital partnership is likely to have very positive benefits for the quality of parenting and the child's development. Weiner-Davis is highly sensitive to individual variations and the reality that men and women may sometimes express similar underlying needs in quite different ways.

Men's Issues

Even in the late 1960s and early 1970s, clear, but generally ignored evidence was available concerning the importance of paternal involvement. In my first two books, *Father, Child and Sex Role* (1971) and *Paternal Deprivation* (1974), I reviewed a surprising amount of then available data underscoring the impact of fathers in the development of both sons and daughters. However, much cultural resistance still remains to acknowledging the special contributions of paternal participation in the daily lives of children. During the 1980s and 1990s, along with the continuing influence of the women's movement, interest has been growing in men's issues. The so-called men's movement includes a strong focus on the significance of the father's role for men and their sons.

In his provocative book *Iron John: A Book About Men*, poet Robert Bly emphasizes the profound importance of men being nurturant mentors for younger males. He elaborates on the responsibility of men to model an active, expressive masculinity and decries the lack of meaningful rituals marking phases of male development in our society. He analyzes ancient stories and legends to remind us of the crucial role of men in helping to promote an inner sense of masculine resolve, decisiveness and competency in their sons. Other contributors to the men's movement such as social critic Sam Keen, who wrote *Fire in the Belly*, and Jungian analyst Guy Corneau, author of *Absent Fathers, Lost Sons*, also call for a greater paternal involvement in socializing boys. However, along with Bly, they do not give sufficient attention to the father-daughter relationship.

Men should actively share in the parenting of their daughters as well as their sons. Young women as well as young men need to have a positive sense of connectedness to their fathers. In this way both parents and children, whether male or female, can come to appreciate better the crucial role that the father has in family development. What our society most requires is more positive family cooperation between men and women, so as to provide better role models for future generations of parents.

Age does not, in itself, limit the expression of paternal effectiveness. With the increasing recognition of the significance of paternal influence, more men will have the opportunity to develop a strong sense of positive emotional connectedness with their children. Our society can greatly benefit from the motivation of men of all ages to be involved constructively with younger family members. Elderly men who have retained positive relationships with their children and grandchildren may be especially important role models for younger fathers.

Designating a clear-cut age of entry into the so-called elderly period of life is extremely difficult, particularly if it is viewed as a stage of declining competence. Automatically referring to those over the age of sixty or sixty-five as elderly can have very misleading connotations given that an increasingly greater proportion of our population remains vigorously involved in a variety of creative and social activities in their seventies, eighties and nineties. Disengagement is more a function of social circumstances, health factors and personality styles than a necessary consequence of being old in the chronological sense.

The life experience and wisdom of elderly men and women can provide significant contributions to all segments of society. Being productive members of a social unit (whether it be a family, business, professional or volunteer organization) can do much to support a sense of personal worth for individuals no matter how advanced their chronological age. In many professions requiring highly complex skills, the elderly may be particularly effective teachers and consultants. Perhaps as important as any other social function, happily involved elderly individuals can provide middle-aged and younger adults with inspiring role models of generativity. Exposure to the wisdom, caring, creativity and courage of the elderly can encourage a more profound sense of the meaningfulness of later life.

The happiest individuals in late adulthood are those who remain vigorous and connected to others including younger family members. Although there is a tendency among the elderly to associate with those of a similar age, this is not an inevitable process and often not one of choice. Age segregation at any point in development is likely to have a stifling effect. Those elderly individuals who have a feeling of connectedness to different generations of family members are much more likely to retain effective social skills than are those who are isolated into narrow age groupings. Life is enriched by a recognition of the significance of past, present and future. Intergenerational relationships can do much to keep the individual of any age in touch with varying time perspectives and social realities.

Cultural Values

Our society can support increased male participation in child rearing without necessarily expecting men to change radically their basic views of themselves. Having a strong sense of masculinity and parenting actively do not have to be incompatible. In fact, men can gain a greater sense of security with respect to their gender adequacy by being involved and successful fathers.

Most fathers retain a relatively masculine style of parenting even when their level of child-rearing involvement increases markedly. Just because a father becomes more involved in traditionally female child-care tasks does not mean that he adopts a nonmasculine manner of interacting with his son or daughter. The reasons a father may be perceived as nonmasculine or feminized by his children have much more to do with his basic personality style than with the kinds of caretaking responsibilities he assumes in the family.

Men and women can contribute to the successful development of children in many different ways. When men become parents, they should be held accountable for their level of commitment and quality of involvement. If society is really concerned about children's rights and strengthening families, men must be expected to cooperate in parenting endeavors. Much room is available for cultural and individual variation, as long as the expectation of both positive paternal and maternal involvement is clear.

Constructive participation by males and females is important in child rearing whatever the family context. Positively involved men can be successful in facilitating the development of children as divorced noncustodial parents, as single custodial parents, as married househusbands, as adoptive or foster parents or as stepparents, as well as in more traditional family situations. I am not advocating that men strive to be more influential in child rearing than women, but that they become committed to sharing parenting responsibilities.

Families with two parents and one or more children no longer represent the majority of households in the United States. Our society experienced a tremendous explosion in the rate of divorce in the 1960s and 1970s, reaching its peak in the early 1980s. More than half of the boys and girls born in the 1990s may spend part of their childhood in one-parent families. Both a high divorce rate and the increasing incidence of children born out of wedlock have contributed to the upsurge in the number of families headed by single mothers.

Although the nuclear family concept may not be actualized in a stable form for many parents and children, it will remain the type of household preferred by most fathers and mothers. A committed, monogamous marital relationship along with one or more children is still the family situation desired by the great majority of adults. Even those individuals who do not want children are likely to choose to live in a family relationship with another adult. If given the opportunity, most single adults, whether wanting to be parents or to remain childless, would prefer to be part of a family group with another man or woman of their choosing rather than to live alone. In an increasingly crowded world, the two-adult family offers the potential for a special combination of intimacy and privacy. For individuals wishing to share their lives with another adult and to have children together, the nuclear family provides definite advantages. Each parent and each child can have involved and personal contact with other family members. Moreover, the child can receive a solid base of support from two committed adults who contribute to each other's parenting competence.

The nuclear family provides parents with the opportunity to feel effective in aiding the development of their children and themselves. Most individuals, regardless of how committed they are to larger social groupings and institutions, have their own ideas of how they want to raise their children. Although the nuclear family will remain the preferred form, single-parent households will continue to be important contexts for family connections. In order to support healthy individual and family development, a growing community awareness concerning the rights of children is needed. A child without an involved father should not suffer from more generalized paternal deprivation. A sense of community commitment can strengthen the positive bonds between families and society by encouraging men to take more responsibility for meeting the needs of children.

GENERAL OVERVIEW

This final section highlights many of the key issues discussed in this book. The goal is to provide an overview that emphasizes the significance of constructive fathering and coparenting. I hope that this section further stimulates researchers, clinicians and community leaders toward an active interest in strengthening paternal involvement in the family. Our society must give much more attention to tapping the crucial role of men in child development.

Coparenting Perspectives

1. The quality of paternal behavior within a society is clearly linked to the adaptive capacities of children and families. Constructive fathering can add much to the positive functioning of both children and adults, whereas paternal deprivation may significantly handicap individuals throughout their development.

2. The father's nurturance and positive interest contribute to the successful development of his child. Constructive father involvement is advantageous for the child's self-esteem, body image and emotional, social and intellectual development. Boys and girls need to learn how to relate effectively with both males and females, and a cooperative father-mother relationship provides an especially salient example.

3. Children develop best when given the opportunity to form relationships with two positively involved parents. Fathers are as important as mothers in the overall development of children. However, given sufficient other resources, children may develop relatively well when reared by one competent parent, especially when compared with those from two-parent families where father-mother conflict is high and constructive paternal involvement is lacking.

4. Father neglect is the most prevalent form of child maltreatment in our society. Paternal deprivation in its many forms (including emotional neglect and rejection as well as father unavailability) can have a particularly negative impact on child and family development. A double standard has prevailed with relatively low-level expectations concerning the participation of men in day-to-day child-rearing activities.

5. Fathers as well as mothers must be held accountable for providing adequate parenting to their children. Children need the opportunity to interact in a positive, stimulating manner with both of their parents. In terms of the number of children affected, paternal deprivation is much more of a problem for our society than maternal deprivation. Inadequately fathered children, particularly if they are young, are unlikely to receive much compensatory male influence.

6. Mothers are also more likely to parent their children in a negative manner when fathers are relatively uninvolved in child rearing. Father neglect in both two-parent and one-parent families tends to be associated with a high incidence of maternal stress. The overburdened mother's frustrations may be expressed in a variety of inappropriate ways, including restrictiveness, overprotectiveness, physical abuse or emotional neglect of her children. Maltreatment of children can be viewed, at least in part, as being related to a set of social values that tends to put too much emphasis on mothering and not enough on fathering.

7. The cooperative involvement of the expectant father is an important factor in strengthening family relationships. Expectant mothers with supportive partners are more likely than those without such a relationship to accept their pregnancy, to go for regularly scheduled obstetrical visits and to be appropriately concerned about the effects of their own well-being on the fetus. Partner support can be crucial for the expectant mother's self-esteem and concern for her health. A positive relationship between the expectant parents bodes well for the child's and family's subsequent development.

8. Fathers, as a group, have just as great a capacity to be sensitive and responsive to their infant's needs as do mothers. Men are capable of being involved in a highly constructive manner with their children, even with their newborns, if they have the opportunity. Although paternal and maternal styles of stimulating and caring may differ, fathers can parent infants quite adequately. The infant who has both an involved father and an involved mother receives much special stimulation from each.

9. The extent to which the father and mother are supportive of each other's participation with the infant also influences the quality of parenting the child receives. Even in the first few months of life, the infant can form a very significant attachment to the father. Paternal stimulation can have a highly facilitating impact on the infant's cognitive and social development. Long-term benefits are available to children who have had close relationships with their fathers during infancy and early childhood.

10. It is important for both the father and the mother to develop a feeling of responsibility toward the child. Such a commitment can do much to energize the father's capacity for effective nurturance as well as helping him to inhibit inappropriate impulses toward the child. A strong father-infant attachment increases the probability that the child will later be positively responsive toward each parent.

11. Optimal family functioning occurs when both parents behave in the kind and caring manner that they wish their children to emulate. Children and adults develop best in families in which parents are accepting of individuality, clear about their values and democratic in their decision making. The mother and father should nurturantly model standards of fairness with an explicit concern for the rights of all family members.

12. The quality of the father-mother relationship can have much impact on the child's adjustment. A severe imbalance in the family system, typically with the mother being overinvolved and the father underinvolved, can result in problems for the parents as well as the children. The presence of several children close in age, a handicapped family member or lack of economic resources can all add to parental stress and increase the likelihood of family conflicts. However, two parents cooperating have a much better chance to deal successfully with such difficult situations.

Individual Variations

13. Children who are both well fathered and well mothered are likely to have strong self-concepts and a healthy acceptance of their biological sexuality. With the support of two positively involved parents, children are able to deal with social pressures in a relatively individualized manner. Gender security gives the boy or girl more of an opportunity to develop in a self-actualized direction. In contrast, inadequate fathering can put the child at risk for later emotional and social problems.

14. Parents who are nurturant, accepting and reasonable in their expectations are likely to have confident sons and daughters who are socially and academically successful. Well-fathered individuals typically have an advantage in intellectual achievement, social skills and sexual adjustment, and usually have high levels of self-esteem and overall mental health. The quality of the father's relationship with the mother is very important, as is his nurturance and acceptance of the child's individuality. The child with an involved father and mother is typically exposed to a much broader range of competencies than the boy or girl who has a positive relationship with only one parent.

15. Paternal deprivation tends to be associated with deficits in personal adjustment as well as with lessened competence in academic, emotional and social functioning. Fathers who are controlling, punitive, authoritarian and nonnurturant are likely to have children who are relatively timid, passive, anxious and low in self-esteem and interpersonal competence. Fathers demonstrating poor impulse control and abusive and rejecting tendencies are at risk to have children who have serious identity and relationship problems and who may engage in antisocial and delinquent behavior. Inadequate fathering is a major contributor to the development of insecure children, who are especially vulnerable to negative peer influence and to alcohol- and other drug-related difficulties.

16. Both sons and daughters are greatly influenced by the quality of fathering that they receive, but variations relating to the sex and developmental status of the child must be taken into account. Even though their overall involvement may be quite limited, fathers typically spend more individualized time with their sons than with their daughters. During early development, compared to girls, boys generally appear to be both more positively influenced by active fathering and more handicapped by paternal deprivation.

17. Nevertheless, the quality of the early father-daughter relationship has much to do with the female's psychological and social competence in adolescence and adulthood, her sense of well-being as a wife and mother and her effectiveness in dealing with various aspects of career development. Early paternal influence is important for girls but tends to manifest itself less dramatically in preadolescence than it does for boys. The influence of a particular pattern of parenting does not necessarily have an obvious and immediate impact, but the ramifications may become clearer at a later phase of development. Some of the consequences of early paternal involvement, for example, do not seem to become apparent until the individual confronts certain family and work responsibilities during adulthood.

18. Children who have two positively involved and competent parents are more likely to have generally adequate psychological functioning and are less at risk to suffer

from personal and social difficulties than those who are reared in female-headed single-parent families. However, this generalization is not the same as assuming that all father-absent children will have more difficulties in their development than all father-present children. Many children grow up in two-parent families in which one or both parents are very inadequate models of appropriate behavior.

19. In contrast, many single-parent families are highly successful. For example, children with competent single parents are less likely to have certain types of personal problems than those who live with a domineering mother and a passive, ineffectual father. Also, children whose fathers are available in terms of physical presence but are emotionally neglectful may have serious deficits in self-acceptance and social adjustment. The father-absent child may develop a more flexible image of men and at least may seek out some type of father-surrogate, whereas the child with an ineffectual or rejecting father may continue to have a very negative and ambivalent perception of adult males.

20. In order to understand the impact of family relationships, the need is always present to consider the characteristics of the child as well as those of the parents. In some cases, adults have difficulty in parenting because of their child's behavior. At one extreme are children who remain so totally unresponsive or so atypical in their behavior patterns that it is very difficult to develop a strong attachment to them. For example, many parents have a problem in developing an attachment to a child whom they perceive as very different from themselves or as unusually handicapped.

21. On the other hand, some children are particularly resilient in the face of negative parenting experiences. They may be unusually adaptable and have the capacity to relate quickly in a positive way to adults other than their parents. Such children, because they are extremely sociable, bright or perceptive may be able to decrease their susceptibility to deprivation or maltreatment within their own families. Even when subjected to very inadequate parenting, they may still have the personal resources to make a successful personality adaptation.

Practical Considerations

22. Paternal deprivation is an all too common consequence of divorce, but the amount and quality of contact that children have with their fathers varies tremendously. In some families, children whose parents are divorced may never see their fathers again; in other families children may have contact with their fathers on a regular basis and may even spend more time with them than prior to the divorce. In fact, some children whose fathers do not live with them receive more individualized paternal attention than many children in two-parent households. Clear advantages of a high level of positive father-child interaction exist even when the parents do not live together.

23. In most cases, shared custody arrangements can be more beneficial to the development of the child and parents than traditional custody arrangements, which tend to limit father-child contact and to overburden divorced mothers. Many fathers in two-parent families could learn a lot from those divorced fathers who share parenting responsibilities with their ex-wives; ironically, some fathers make more of a commitment to child rearing postdivorce. A major impetus in divorce prevention should be to strengthen the child-rearing cooperation of fathers and mothers in two-parent households.

24. Children who do not receive adequate parenting are at risk to show deficiencies in their abilities to deal constructively with their own offspring. Intergenerational patterns of child maltreatment and parental deprivation all too often appear to be like family heirlooms being passed from generation to generation. Males as well as females should be encouraged to participate in family life preparation and parent training programs aimed at increasing positive father involvement and effective coparenting. Fortunately, most men and women still have the capacity to become effective parents even if they were mistreated as children.

25. Both males and females can improve their parenting skills. For example, expectant and new fathers who are given information about child development and opportunities to talk about parenting issues, including their earlier family experiences, are typically more effective with their infants than are those who lack such exposure. Parents can learn how to relate more positively to their children and, in turn, have a constructive impact on their own development.

26. Intervention programs targeting father-child relationships can help to improve family development. Expectant and new fathers, or those who are experiencing frustrations with their children, may have particular interest in developing better parenting skills. More family life education programs stressing the advantages of paternal involvement also need to be mounted within school systems.

27. Social values supporting the active participation of men in the lives of children must be encouraged more. Community leaders need to acknowledge, by their behavior in personal relationships and in carrying out their responsibilities, that fathers should be positively involved with their children. Men and women in leadership positions should advocate social policy and legislation designed to strengthen the father's role in child and family development. To be effective, preventative programs targeting major social problems, including violence and drug addiction, must emphasize the importance of men taking a more equitable share of responsibility for child rearing.

28. Administrators in educational and other human service organizations should address more fully the needs of children and families in their communities. The segregation of men from children must be decreased in order to alleviate paternal deprivation throughout society. Major corporations can provide longer paternity leaves, more flexible work schedules and greater support for quality day care. Creative solutions are necessary for helping men as well as women better balance career and child-rearing responsibilities.

29. Readily available opportunities for individuals to acquire basic information about development and effective parenting techniques should be created. Vigorous efforts in this direction need to be encouraged within our schools and other social institutions. Incentives should be offered to involve a larger proportion of men in careers relating to early childhood education. Increased employment opportunities that are compatible with constructive coparenting are also necessary if an improvement is to occur in the quality of family life for both children and adults.

30. In order to strengthen the family and support the rights of children, we must address the rampant paternal deprivation present in our society. More attention needs to be given to single-parent families, to children and adults affected by divorce and to unwed parents. A major social focus should be on reaching out to expectant and new fathers. The concern should be not only with decreasing ob-

vious forms of paternal deprivation, but also with optimizing coparenting skills to provide adults and children with a firm basis for developing self-esteem and social competence.

SUMMARY

Whatever their socioeconomic status, a large proportion of children have very little opportunity to spend time with their fathers. The hurried pace of modern life makes it difficult for many fathers and mothers to have regular periods of relaxed and individualized contact with their children. It is important for industry and government to develop family policies supportive of positive paternal involvement in family life. Young children who are paternally deprived are in special need of community and school programs that can provide them with some positive individualized attention from nurturant men.

Parenthood training programs can be an important vehicle for sensitizing both men and women to the crucial role of the father. Childbirth education courses should put more emphasis on postdelivery issues involving the father and mother in the care of infants. Although most parent education courses give relatively little specific attention to fathering issues, some research-oriented projects have been successfully directed at increasing positive paternal involvement and effective coparenting. Family life education courses, even at the primary school level, can help to make both boys and girls aware of the significance of paternal involvement and male-female cooperation in child rearing. A child without an involved father should not have to suffer from more generalized paternal deprivation. Men as well as women need to become engaged in endeavors strengthening supportive connections between various social institutions and the family.

A general overview of paternal factors in child development emphasizes the importance of a biopsychosocial and life-span perspective. The quality of father involvement within a society is clearly linked to the adaptive capacities of children and families. Constructive fathering can add much to the positive functioning of both children and adults, whereas paternal deprivation may significantly handicap individuals throughout their development. However, in order to understand the impact of family relationships, the characteristics of the child as well as those of the parents need to be given consideration. The child, father and mother influence each other's behavior and development. Furthermore, the family system is influenced by a wide array of interacting community and sociocultural factors.

A greater valuation is needed within our society of the crucial role of the father in child development. Creative solutions are necessary to help men and women better balance career and child-rearing responsibilities. Widespread paternal deprivation must be addressed in order to strengthen the family and increase the self-esteem and social competence of children and adults.

FURTHER READING

Contemporary Concerns

Hurried Pace

About problems associated with hurried children and families, see Elkind (1981, 1984, 1987). For the combined difficulties that are likely to be encountered by children who are both hurried and paternally deprived, see Biller and Meredith (1974) and Biller and Solomon (1986).

Concerning issues relating to families moving to different locations, see Farley and Werkman (1986) and Nida (1983). For helpful perspectives on balancing work and family responsibilities, see Bohen and Viveros-Long (1981), Brooks (1991), Hughes and Galinsky (1988) and Pruett (1987).

On the importance of working parents planning ahead to ensure quality time for their children, and for specific suggestions for balancing employment and family responsibilities, see Biller and Meredith (1974), Brazelton (1985), Brooks (1991), Crouter (1984), Galinsky (1986), Grollman and Sweder (1986), Hughes and Galinsky (1988), Olds (1989) and Scarr (1984).

For guidelines that may help parents balance work and family commitments, see Bohen and Viveros-Long (1981), Brazelton (1985), Brooks (1991), Grollman and Sweder (1986), Hughes and Galinsky (1988), Loman (1984), Olds (1989) and Scarr (1984).

Informational Sources

On the impact of television and practical suggestions for parents in encouraging constructive viewing habits for their children, see Liebert and Spratkin (1988) and Singer and Singer (1987).

For discussion of the media's depiction of parenting roles, see Anderson (1982), Biller and Meredith (1974) and Giveans (1986a, b). For the importance of presenting the father's role in a positive way, see Biller (1973a, 1980a, 1987), Biller and Meredith (1972, 1974), Biller and Salter (1985), Biller et al. (1977), Cosby (1986), Klinman (1986) and Lamb (1986). Concerning the portrayal of the family on television, see Glennon and Butsch (1983) and Moore (1992).

Organizational Supports

For various ways that companies can be supportive of the parent-child relationship including the provision of parent education programs, parental leaves and flexible scheduling, see Pleck (1985, 1986) and Stipek and McCroskey (1989).

About advantages of particular types of work schedules in meeting parental responsibilities, see Bohen and Viveros-Long (1981), Hughes and Galinsky (1988), Maklan (1977) and Pleck (1986).

For research relevant to military families, see Biller (1978), Farley and Werkman (1986), Hillenbrand (1976) and Hunter (1978, 1982).

Voluntary Efforts

Regarding coordinated efforts of service organizations to help children in fatherless families, see Bahlmann (1984). For general suggestions geared to helping paternally deprived children, see Biller (1971a, 1974c), Biller and Meredith (1974), Biller and Smith (1972), Biller and Solomon (1986), and Lamb (1986). Concerning findings supporting the potential positive impact of father surrogates in a variety of situations, see Biller (1971a, 1974c) and Biller and Solomon (1986).

With respect to programs to prepare fathers and other men better in relating to children, see Klinman (1986), Klinman and Kohl (1984), Levine and Klinman (1984), and Levine, Pleck and Lamb (1983). Concerning the shortage of men sensitive to the needs of young children in volunteer and human service positions, see Biller (1971a, 1974c), Biller and Meredith (1974), Biller and Solomon (1986), Gershon and Biller (1977) and Portnoy, Biller and Davids (1972).

For suggestions to encourage greater adult male participation in the education and socialization of children, see Biller (1971a, 1973a, 1974c), Biller and Meredith (1974), Biller and Solomon (1986), Klinman (1986) and Klinman and Kohl (1984).

About the connection between the developing father's involvement with his own children and his growing awareness and empathy to the needs of others in society, see Biller and Meredith (1974), Robinson and Barrett (1986) and Snarey (1992).

Parenthood Training

For details of hospital-based intervention programs with fathers, see Parke (1985), Parke and Beitel (1986) and Parke and Tinsley (1981). For specifics of other types of programs directed at improving the parenting effectiveness of fathers, see Dickie (1987), Dickie and Gerber (1980), Klinman (1986), Klinman and Kohl (1984), Kotelchuck (1976), Levant (1987), Levant and Doyle (1983), Levant and Kelly (1989), Parke and Beitel (1986) and Robinson and Barrett (1986).

Effective Programs

On the criticism that most previous parent education programs have been focused just on mothers, see Biller and Meredith (1974), Biller and Solomon (1986), Darling (1987), Florin and Dokecki (1983), Gershon and Biller (1977), Parke and Beitel (1986) and Robinson and Barrett (1986). For the necessity of encouraging both men and women to recognize the significance of the father's role in child development, see Biller (1971a, 1974c), Biller and Meredith (1972, 1974), Biller and Solomon (1986), Lamb (1981b, 1986), Parke (1981, 1986), Pleck (1986) and Russell (1983, 1986).

For thorough discussions of Parent Effectiveness Training, see especially Gordon (1970, 1989). Gordon (1974, 1989) also presents very positive techniques directed at improving the sensitivity of school personnel to children with his program for Teacher Effectiveness Training.

Concerning Solution-Oriented Brief Therapy, see de Shazer (1982), O'Hanlon and Weiner-Davis (1989) and Weiner-Davis (1992).

Men's Issues

With respect to extensive but relatively early reviews of the paternal involvement literature, see Biller (1971a, 1974c, 1976a). Concerning references to the men's movement, see Bly (1990), Corneau (1991), Doyle (1989), Keen (1991) and Osherson (1992).

For evidence suggesting that middle-aged and older men may be more nurturing than their younger counterparts, see Duvall and Miller (1985), Radin, Oyserman and Benn (1991), Troll and Bengston (1982) and Turner (1982). Regarding research indicating that the quality of the relationships they have with their children has an important impact on men's sense of well-being during various phases of adulthood, see Barnett, Davidson and Marshall (1991), Barnett and Marshall (1991), Barnett, Marshall and Pleck (1991), Berman and Pedersen (1987), Julian, McKenry and Arnold (1990), McKenry et al. (1987), Snarey (1992) and Snarey et al. (1987).

On individual differences among ''elderly'' adults and the complex factors involved in the aging process, see Erikson (1980, 1982), Erikson, Erikson and Kivnick (1986), Kornhaber (1987), Neugarten and Neugarten (1987), Rosenfield and Stark (1987), Schiff and Biller (1976), Troll and Bengston (1982) and Turner (1982).

Cultural Values

Concerning fathering and masculinity, see Biller (1971a, 1974c, 1982a, 1987), Biller and Meredith (1974), Biller and Solomon (1986), Lamb (1981b, 1986), Lamb and Sagi (1983), Russell (1983) and Russell and Radin (1983). For viewpoints supporting the importance of fathers being positively involved with children and cooperating with mothers, see especially Biller and Meredith (1974), Biller and Solomon (1986), Cath, Gurwitt and Ginsberg (1989), Lamb (1981b, 1986), Parke and Beitel (1986), Pruett (1987), Russell (1983) and Silverstein (1991).

Bandura, A. (1986). *Social foundations of thought and action: A social cognitive theory.* Englewood Cliffs, NJ: Prentice-Hall.

Bandura, A., & Walters, R. H. (1959). *Adolescent aggression: A study of the influence of child-rearing practices and family interrelationships.* New York: Ronald Press.

Bank, S., & Kahn, M. (1982). *The sibling bond.* New York: Basic Books.

Barclay, A. G., & Cusumano, D. (1967). Father-absence, cross-sex identity, and field-dependent behavior in male adolescents. *Child Development, 38,* 243–250.

Barclay, J. R., Stillwell, W. E., & Barclay, L. K. (1972). The influence of parental occupation on social interaction measures of elementary school children. *Journal of Vocational Behavior, 2,* 433–446.

Barnes, G. M. (1984). Adolescent alcohol abuse and other problem behaviors: Their relationships and common parental influences. *Journal of Youth and Adolescence, 13,* 329–348.

Barnett, R. C., & Baruch, G. K. (1987). Determinants of father's participation in family work. *Journal of Marriage and the Family, 44,* 29–40.

Barnett, R. C., Davidson, H., & Marshall, N. L. (1991). Physical symptoms and the interplay of work and family roles. *Health Psychology, 10,* 94–101.

Barnett, R. C., & Marshall, N. L. (1991). Men, family role quality, job role quality, and physical health. Wellesley, MA: Center for Research on Women, Wellesley College.

Barnett, R. C., Marshall, N. L., & Pleck, J. H. (1991). Men's multiple roles and their relationship to men's psychological distress. Wellesley, MA: Center for Research on Women, Wellesley College.

Barnhill, L., Rubenstein, G., & Rocklin, W. (1979). From generation to generation: Fathers-to-be in transition. *The Family Coordinator, 28,* 119–235.

Barron, F. (1969). *Creative persons and creative processes.* New York: Holt, Rinehart & Winston.

Barry, W. A. (1970). Marriage research and conflict: An integrative review. *Psychological Bulletin, 73,* 41–55.

Baruch, G. K., & Barnett, R. C. (1981a). Competence-related behaviors of preschool girls. *Genetic Psychology Monographs, 103,* 80–103.

Baruch, G. K., & Barnett, R. C. (1981b). Fathers' participation in the care of their preschool children. *Sex Roles, 7,* 104–108.

Baruch, G. K., & Barnett, R. C. (1986). Consequences of fathers' participation in family work: Parents' role strain and well-being. *Journal of Personality and Social Psychology, 51,* 983–992.

Baruch, G. K., Barnett, R. C., & Rivers, C. (1983). *Lifeprints: New patterns of love and work for today's woman.* New York: McGraw-Hill.

Baskett, L. M., & Johnston, S. M. (1982). The young child's interaction with parents versus siblings. *Child Development, 53,* 643–650.

Basow, S. (1986). *Gender stereotypes: Traditions and alternatives.* Monterey, CA: Brooks/Cole.

Baucon, D., & Aiken, P. (1984). Sex-role identity, marital satisfaction, and response to behavioral marital therapy. *Journal of Consulting and Clinical Psychology, 52,* 438–444.

Baumrind, D. (1967). Child-rearing practices anteceding three patterns of pre-school behavior. *Genetic Psychology Monographs, 78,* 43–88.

Baumrind, D. (1971). Current patterns of parental authority. *Developmental Psychology Monographs, 4,* 1–103.

Bibliography

Adams, P. L., Milner, J. P., & Schrepf, N. A. (Eds.). (1984). *Fatherless children*. New York: Wiley.

Adler, A. (1956). *The individual psychology of Alfred Adler*. New York: Basic Books.

Ainsworth, M. D. S., Blehar, M. C., Waters, E., & Wall, S. (1978). *Patterns of attachment: A psychological study of the strange situation*. Hillsdale, NJ: Erlbaum.

Ames, L. B., Ilg, F. L., & Baker, S. (1988). *Your ten to fourteen year old*. New York: Doubleday.

Anderson, C. P. (1982). *Father: The figure and the force*. New York: Warner Books.

Andry, R. G. (1971). *Delinquency and parental pathology*. London: Staples Press.

Apperson, L. B., & McAdoo, W. G., Jr. (1968). Parental factors in the childhood of homosexuals. *Journal of Abnormal Psychology, 73*, 201–206.

Appleton, W. S. (1981). *Fathers and daughters*. New York: Doubleday.

Arbarbanel, A. (1979). Shared parenting after separation and divorce: A study of joint custody. *American Journal of Orthopsychiatry, 49*, 320–329.

Arnstein, H. (1972). The crisis of becoming a father. *Sexual Behavior, 2*, 42–48.

Atkins, R. N., & Lansky, M. R. (1986). The father in family therapy: Psychoanalytic perspectives. In M. E. Lamb (Ed.), *The father's role: Applied perspectives* (pp. 167–190). New York: Wiley.

Aylmer, R. C. (1988). The launching of the single young adult. In B. Carter & M. McGoldrick (Eds.), *The changing family life cycle: A framework for family therapy* (pp. 191–208). New York: Gardner Press.

Bahlmann, D. (1984). Big Brothers/Big Sisters. In G. Miller et al., *Paternal absence and fathers' roles* (pp. 106–115). Hearing before the Select Committee on Children, Youth and Families. House of Representatives, 98th Congress, 1st Session. Washington, DC: U.S. Government Printing Office.

Bahrick, L. E. (1988). Intermodal learning in infancy: Learning on the basis of two kinds of invariant relations in audible and visible events. *Child Development, 59*, 197–209.

Baldwin, A. L., Cole, R. E., & Baldwin, C. T. (1982). Parent pathology, family interaction, and the competence of the child in school. *Monographs of the Society for Research in Child Development*, Serial No. 197.

Ban, P. L., & Lewis, M. (1971, April). *Mothers and fathers, girls and boys: Attachment behavior in the one-year-old*. Paper presented at the meeting of the Eastern Psychological Association, New York.

Baumrind, D. (1982). Are androgynous individuals more effective persons and parents? *Child Development, 53,* 76–86.

Baumrind, D. (1989). Rearing competent children. In W. Damon (Ed.), *Child development today and tomorrow* (pp. 349–378). San Francisco: Jossey-Bass.

Bell, A. P. (1969). Role modeling of fathers in adolescence and adulthood. *Journal of Counseling Psychology, 16,* 30–35.

Bell, A. P., Weinberg, M. S., & Mannersmith, S. K. (1981). *Sexual preference: Its development in men and women.* New York: Simon & Schuster.

Bell, R. Q., & Harper, L. V. (Eds.). (1977). *Child effects on adults.* Hillsdale, NJ: Erlbaum.

Belsky, J. (1979a). The interrelation of parental and spousal behavior in traditional nuclear families: An exploratory analysis. *Journal of Marriage and the Family, 41,* 749–755.

Belsky, J. (1979b). Mother-father-infant interaction: A naturalistic observational study. *Developmental Psychology, 15,* 601–607.

Belsky, J. (1980a). Child abuse: An ecological integration. *American Psychologist, 35,* 320–335.

Belsky, J. (1980b). A family analysis of parental influence on infant exploratory competence. In F. A. Pedersen (Ed.), *The father-child relationship: Observational studies in the family system.* New York: Praeger.

Belsky, J. (1985). Exploring individual differences in marital change across the transition to parenthood: The role of violated expectations. *Journal of Marriage and the Family, 47,* 1037–1044.

Belsky, J., Gilstraph, B., & Rovine, M. (1984). The Pennsylvania Infant and Family Development Project: Stability and change in mother-infant and father-infant interactions in a family setting at one, three, and nine months. *Child Development, 55,* 692–705.

Belsky, J., Lang, M., & Huston, T. L. (1987). Sex typing and division of labor as determinants of marital changes across the transition to parenthood. *Journal of Personality and Social Psychology, 50,* 517–522.

Belsky, J., & Rovine, M. (1987). Temperament and attachment security in the strange situation: An empirical rapproachement. *Child Development, 58,* 787–795.

Belsky, J., & Rovine, M. J. (1988). Nonmaternal care in the first year of life and security of infant-parent attachment. *Child Development, 59,* 164–172.

Belsky, J., Steinberg, L. D., & Walker, A. (1982). The ecology of day care. In M. E. Lamb (Ed.), *Nontraditional families: Parenting and child development* (pp. 71–116). Hillsdale, NJ: Erlbaum.

Bem, S. L. (1985). Androgyny and gender schema theory: Conceptual and empirical integration. In T. B. Sonderegger (Ed.), *Nebraska symposium on motivation.* Lincoln: University of Nebraska Press.

Benbow, C. P., & Stanley, J. C. (1983). Sex differences in mathematical reasoning ability: More facts. *Science, 22,* 1029–1031.

Bené, E. (1965). On the genesis of female homosexuality. *British Journal of Psychiatry, 3,* 815–821.

Bengston, V. L., & Robertson, J. F. (Eds.). (1985). *Grandparenthood.* Beverly Hills, CA: Sage.

Benning, I. E. (1974). *How to bring up a child without spending a fortune.* New York: McKay.

Benson, L. (1968). *Fatherhood: A sociological perspective.* New York: Random House.

Berlinsky, E. B., & Biller, H. B. (1982). *Parental death and psychological development.* Lexington, MA: Lexington Books, D. C. Heath.

Berman, A., & Siegal, A. (1976). A neuropsychological approach to the etiology, prevention and treatment of juvenile delinquency. In A. Davids (Ed.), *Child personality and psychopathology, current topics, Vol. 3.* New York: Wiley.

Berman, P. W., & Pedersen, F. A. (Eds.). (1987). *Men's transitions to parenthood: Longitudinal studies of early family experiences.* New York: Erlbaum.

Bernard, J. (1982). *The future of marriage* (rev. ed.). New Haven, CT: Yale University Press.

Bernstein, A. C., & Cowan, P. A. (1975). Children's conceptions of how people get babies. *Child Development, 46,* 77–91.

Bieber, I., et al. (1962). *Homosexuality: A psychoanalytic study.* New York: Basic Books.

Biller, H. B. (1968a). A multiaspect investigation of masculine development in kindergarten-age boys. *Genetic Psychology Monographs, 76,* 89–139.

Biller, H. B. (1968b). A note on father-absence and masculine development in young lower-class Negro and white boys. *Child Development, 39,* 1001–1006.

Biller, H. B. (1969a). Father-absence, maternal encouragement, and sex-role development in kindergarten-age boys. *Child Development, 40,* 539–546. (Reprinted in R. C. Smart (Eds.), *Readings in child development and relationships.* New York: Macmillan, 1972.)

Biller, H. B. (1969b). Father dominance and sex-role development in kindergarten-age boys. *Developmental Psychology, 1,* 87–94. (Reprinted in slightly abridged form in D. R. Heise (Ed.), *Personality and socialization.* New York: Rand McNally, 1972.)

Biller, H. B. (1969c). Maternal salience and feminine development in young girls. *Proceedings of the 77th Annual Convention of the American Psychological Association, 4,* 259–260.

Biller, H. B. (1970). Father-absence and the personality development of the male child. *Development Psychology, 2,* 181–201. (Reprinted in S. Chess & A. Thomas (Eds.), *Annual progress in child psychology and child development.* New York: Brunner/Mazel, 1971; reprinted in slightly abridged form in D. R. Heise (Ed.), *Personality and socialization.* New York: Rand McNally, 1972.)

Biller, H. B. (1971a). *Father, child, and sex role.* Lexington, MA: Lexington Books, D.C. Heath.

Biller, H. B. (1971b). Fathering and female sexual development. *Medical Aspects of Human Sexuality, 5,* 116–138.

Biller, H. B. (1971c). The mother-child relationship and the father-absent boy's personality development. *Merrill-Palmer Quarterly, 17,* 227–241. (Reprinted in slightly abridged form in U. Bronfenbrenner (Ed.), *Influences on human development.* Hinsdale, IL: Dryden Press, 1972.)

Biller, H. B. (1971d). Sexual attitudes of one-parent children. (Invited commentary.) *Medical Aspects of Human Sexuality, 5*(9), 214. (Reprinted in L. Gross (Ed.), *Medical Aspects of Human Sexuality.* New York: Williams and Williams, 1975.)

Biller, H. B. (1972). Include the father in pregnancy. *Medical Aspects of Human Sexuality, 2*(4), 47. (Reprinted in L. Gross (Ed.), *Sexual issues in marriage.* New York: Spectrum, 1975.)

Biller, H. B. (1973a, February 25). The father's role. *London Sunday Times Magazine,* pp. 48–50.

Biller, H. B. (1973b). Sex-role uncertainty and psychopathology. *Journal of Individual Psychology, 29,* 24–25.

Biller, H. B. (1974a). Paternal and sex-role factors in cognitive and academic functioning. In J. K. Cole & R. Dienstbier (Eds.), *Nebraska Symposium on Motivation, 1973* (pp. 83–123). Lincoln: University of Nebraska Press.

Biller, H. B. (1974b). Paternal deprivation, cognitive functioning, and the feminized classroom. In A. Davids (Ed.), *Child personality and psychopathology: Current topics* (pp. 11–52). New York: Wiley.

Biller, H. B. (1974c). *Paternal deprivation: Family, school, sexuality and society.* Lexington, MA: Lexington Books, D.C. Heath.

Biller, H. B. (1974d). Syndromes of paternal deprivation in man. In J. H. Cullen (Ed.), *Experimental behavior: A basis for the study of mental disturbance.* Dublin: Irish University Press.

Biller, H. B. (1975a). The effects of intermittent but prolonged absence of the father. *Medical Aspects of Human Sexuality, 9,* 179.

Biller, H. B. (1975b). Review of Richard Green's *Sexual identity conflicts in children and adults. Archives of Sexual Behavior, 4,* 105–106.

Biller, H. B. (1976a). The father and personality development: Paternal deprivation and sex-role development. In M. E. Lamb (Ed.), *The role of the father in child development* (pp. 89–156). New York: Wiley.

Biller, H. B. (1976b). The father-child relationship: Some crucial issues. In V. Vaughn & B. Brazelton (Eds.), *The family—Can it be saved?* (pp. 69–76). Chicago: Year Book Medical Publishers.

Biller, H. B. (1977a). Father absence and paternal deprivation. In B. B. Wolman (Ed.), *International encyclopedia of neurology, psychiatry, psychoanalysis, and psychology* (Vol. 5, pp. 7–8). New York: Van Nostrand Reinhold.

Biller, H. B. (1977b). Fathers and children. In B. B. Wolman (Ed.), *International encyclopedia of neurology, psychiatry, psychoanalysis, and psychology* (Vol. 5, pp. 9–11). New York: Van Nostrand Reinhold.

Biller, H. B. (1977c). Sex-role learning: Some comments and complexities from a multidimensional perspective. In S. Cohen & T. J. Comiskey (Eds.), *Child development: A study of growth processes* (pp. 201–207). Ithaca, IL: Peacock.

Biller, H. B. (1978). Father-absence and military families. In E. J. Hunter (Ed.), *A report on the military family research conference* (pp. 45–48). San Diego, CA: Family Studies Branch, Naval Health Research Center.

Biller, H. B. (Featured commentator/consultant). (1980a). *Fathers* [Film]. Washington, DC: Durrin Films/ASPO/Lamaze.

Biller, H. B. (1980b). Methodologic problems in research on psychosexual differentiation. In R. Green & J. Weiner (Eds.), *Methodology of sex research* (pp. 273–278). Rockville, MD: National Institute of Mental Health.

Biller, H. B. (1981a). The effect on the boy of a passive father. In L. Gross (Ed.), *The parents' guide to teenagers* (pp. 225–226). New York: Macmillan.

Biller, H. B. (1981b). Father-absence, divorce, and personality development. In M. E. Lamb (Ed.), *The role of the father in child development* (2nd ed., pp. 489–552). New York: Wiley.

Biller, H. B. (1981c). The father and sex-role development. In M. E. Lamb (Ed.), *The role of the father in child development* (2nd ed., pp. 319–358). New York: Wiley.

Biller, H. B. (1982a). Fatherhood: Implications for child and adult development. In

B. B. Wolman (Ed.), *Handbook of developmental psychology* (pp. 702–725). Englewood Cliffs, NJ: Prentice-Hall.

Biller, H. B. (1982b). The father-infant relationship. Unpublished manuscript, University of Rhode Island.

Biller, H. B. (1982c). Review of K. M. Rosenthal and H. Keshet's *Fathers without partners. Contemporary Psychology, 27,* 25–26.

Biller, H. B. (1984a). Father-absence and paternal deprivation. In G. Miller et al., *Paternal absence and fathers' roles* (pp. 78–85). Hearing before the Select Committee on Children, Youth and Families. House of Representatives, 98th Congress, 1st Session. Washington, DC: U.S. Government Printing Office.

Biller, H. B. (1984b). Paternal deprivation, therapy, and prevention. In G. Miller et al., *Paternal absence and fathers' roles* (pp. 128–129). Hearing before the Select Committee on Children, Youth and Families. House of Representatives, 98th Congress, 1st Session. Washington, DC: U.S. Government Printing Office.

Biller, H. B. (1986). The birth of the father: An antidote to paternal deprivation. *Nurturing News, 8*(2), 6–7.

Biller, H. B. (1987). You've come a long way Dad. *Contemporary Psychology, 32,* 884–886.

Biller, H. B. (1989a). Causes of child abuse. In J. L. Gorman (Ed.), *Health and Medical Horizons* (pp. 191–193). New York: Macmillan.

Biller, H. B. (1989b). Family violence: Multidimensional perspectives. *Contemporary Psychology, 34,* 1080–1082.

Biller, H. B. (1989c). Gender development: Biopsychosocial complexities. *Contemporary Psychology, 34,* 1030–1031.

Biller, H. B., & Bahm, R. M. (1971). Father-absence, perceived maternal behavior, and masculinity of self-concept among junior high school boys. *Developmental Psychology, 4,* 178–181.

Biller, H. B., & Barry, W. (1971). Sex-role patterns, paternal similarity, and personality adjustment in college males. *Developmental Psychology, 4,* 107.

Biller, H. B., & Borstelmann, L. J. (1965). Intellectual level and sex-role development in mentally retarded children. *American Journal of Mental Deficiency, 70,* 443–447.

Biller, H. B., & Borstelmann, L. J. (1967). Masculine development: An integrative review. *Merrill-Palmer Quarterly, 13,* 253–294.

Biller, H. B., Costello, I., Dill, J. F., Hetherington, E. M., Hoffman, L. W., Laosa, L. M., McAdoo, H. P., Pedersen, F. A., Sprung, B., Stein, P. J., & Sullivan, J. (Board of Consultants.) (1977). *Mothers and fathers* [Film]. New York: Parents' Magazine Films.

Biller, H. B., & Davids, T. (1973). Parent-child relations, personality development, and psychopathology. In T. Davids (Ed.), *Issues in abnormal child psychology.* Belmont, CA: Brooks/Cole.

Biller, H. B., & Liebman, D. A. (1971). Body build, sex-role preference, and sex-role adoption in junior high school boys. *Journal of Genetic Psychology, 118,* 81–86.

Biller, H. B., & Meredith, D. L. (1972). The invisible American father. *Sexual Behavior, 2*(7), 16–22. (Reprinted in slightly abridged form in L. Gross (Ed.), *Sexual issues in marriage.* New York: Spectrum, 1975.)

Biller, H. B., & Meredith, D. L. (1974). *Father power.* New York: David McKay. (Reprinted, New York: Doubleday Anchor Books, 1975.)

Biller, H. B., & Meredith, D. L. (1982). Father power, mother power. In S. Cahill

(Ed.), *Motherhood: A reader for men and women* (pp. 170–176). New York: Avon Books.

Biller, H. B., & Poey, K. (1969). An exploratory comparison of sex-role related behavior in schizophrenics and nonschizophrenics. *Developmental Psychology 1*, 629.

Biller, H. B., & Salter, M. (1982). Adolescent unwed fathers. Unpublished manuscript, University of Rhode Island.

Biller, H. B., & Salter, M. (1985). Fathers, mothers, and infants growing together. *Lamaze Parents Magazine*, pp. 56–64. Arlington, VA: ASPO/Lamaze.

Biller, H. B., & Salter, M. (1986). Child custody: Fathers, mothers and infants. *Infant Mental Health Journal, 7*, 90–91.

Biller, H. B., & Salter, M. (1989). Father loss, cognitive and personality functioning. In D. R. Dietrich and P. Shabad (Eds.), *The problem of loss and mourning: Psychoanalytic perspectives* (pp. 337–377). New York: International Universities Press.

Biller, H. B., Singer, D. L., & Fullerton, M. (1969). Sex-role development and creative potential among kindergarten-age boys. *Developmental Psychology, 1*, 291–296.

Biller, H. B., & Smith, A. E. (1972). An AFDC mothers' group: An exploratory effort in community mental health. *Family Coordinator, 21*, 287–290.

Biller, H. B., & Solomon, R. S. (1986). *Child maltreatment and paternal deprivation: A manifesto for research, prevention, and treatment.* Lexington, MA: Lexington Books, D.C. Heath.

Biller, H. B., & Weiss, S. (1970). The father-daughter relationship and the personality development of the female. *Journal of Genetic Psychology, 114*, 79–93. (Reprinted in D. Rogers (Ed.), *Issues in adolescent psychology*. New York: Appleton-Century-Crofts, 1970.)

Biller, H. B., & Zung, B. (1972). Perceived maternal control, anxiety, and opposite sex-role preference among elementary school girls. *Journal of Psychology, 81*, 85–88.

Bittman, S., & Zalk, S. R. (1978). *Expectant fathers*. New York: Ballantine Books.

Blanchard, R. W., & Biller, H. B. (1971). Father availability and academic performance among third-grade boys. *Developmental Psychology, 4*, 301–305.

Blasi, A. (1988). Identity and the development of the self. In D. Lapsley & F. C. Power (Eds.), *Self, ego and identity: Integrative approaches*. New York: Springer.

Block, J. (1971). *Lives through time*. Berkeley, CA: Bancroft Books.

Block, J., & Block, J. H. (1988). Longitudinally foretelling drug usage in adolescence: Early childhood personality and environmental precursors. *Child Development, 59*, 336–355.

Block, J., von der Lippe, A., & Block, J. H. (1973). Sex role and socialization: Some personality concomitants and environmental antecedents. *Journal of Consulting and Clinical Psychology, 41*, 321–341.

Block, J. H. (1974). Another look at sex differentiation in the socialization behaviors of mothers and fathers. In F. Denmark (Ed.), *Psychology of women: Future directions of research*. New York: Psychological Dimensions.

Block, J. H. (1983). Differential premises arising from differential socialization of the sexes: Some conjectures. *Child Development, 54*, 1335–1354.

Block, J. H., Block, J., & Gjerde, P. F. (1986). The personality of children prior to divorce: A prospective study. *Child Development, 57*, 827–840.

Blumstein, P., & Schwartz, P. S. (1983). *American couples: Money, work, sex.* New York: Morrow.

Bly, R. (1990). *Iron John: A book about men.* Reading, MA: Addison-Wesley.

Boegold, B. D. (1984). *Getting ready to read.* New York: Ballantine Books.

Bohen, H. H., & Viveros-Long, A. (1981). *Balancing job and family life: Do flexible work schedules help?* Philadelphia: Temple University Press.

Bolton, F. G., Jr. (1986). Today's father and the social services delivery system: A false promise. In M. E. Lamb (Ed.). *The father's role: Applied perspectives* (pp. 429–441). New York: Wiley.

Boss, P. B. (1977). A clarification of the concept of psychological father presence in families experiencing ambiguity of boundary. *Journal of Marriage and the Family, 39,* 141–151.

Boss, P. B. (1987). Family stress. In M. B. Sussman & S. K. Steinmetz (Eds.), *Handbook of marriage and the family* (pp. 695–723). New York: Plenum.

Boss, P. B., McCubbin, H. I., & Lester, G. (1979). The corporate executive wife's coping patterns in response to routine husband-father absence. *Family Process, 18,* 79–86.

Bouchard, T. M., Heston, L., Ecklert, E., Keyes, M., & Resnick, S. (1981). The Minnesota study of twins reared apart: Project description and sample results in the development domain. *Twin Research, 3,* 227–233.

Bourdin, C. M., & Henggeler, S. W. (1982). Psychosocial development of father-absent children: A systems perspective. In S. W. Henggeler (Ed.), *Delinquency and adolescent psychopathology: A family-ecological systems approach.* Littleton, MA: PSG-Wright.

Bowen, M. (1978). *Family therapy in clinical practice.* New York: Jason Aronson.

Bowlby, J. (1958). The nature of the child's tie to his mother. *International Journal of Psychoanalysis, 39,* 350–375.

Bowlby, J. (1969). *Attachment and loss, Vol. 1.* London: Hogarth.

Bozett, F. W. (1988). Gay fatherhood. In P. Bronstein & C. P. Cowan (Eds.), *Contemporary fatherhood* (pp. 214–235). New York: Wiley.

Bozett, F., & Hanson, S. (Eds.). (1985). *Dimensions of fatherhood.* Beverly Hills, CA: Sage.

Bozett, F. W., & Hanson, S. M. H. (Eds.). (1991). *Fatherhood and families in cultural context.* New York: Springer.

Brachfield-Child, S. (1986). Parents as teachers: Comparisons of mothers' and fathers' instructional interactions with infants. *Infant Behavior and Development, 9,* 127–131.

Brackbill, Y., & Nevill, D. (1981). Parental expectations of achievements as affected by children's height. *Merrill-Palmer Quarterly, 27,* 429–441.

Bradley, R. (1965). *Husband-coached childbirth.* New York: Harper & Row.

Brand, E., Clingempeel, W. E., & Bowen-Woodward, K. (1988). Family relationships and children's psychological adjustment in stepmother and stepfather families: Findings and conclusions from the Philadelphia Stepfamily Research Project. In E. M. Hetherington & J. D. Arasteh (Eds.), *Impact of divorce, single-parenting, and stepparenting on children* (pp. 299–324). Hillsdale, NJ: Erlbaum.

Bray, J. H. (1988). Children's development during early remarriage. In E. M. Hetherington & J. D. Arasteh (Eds.), *Impact of divorce, single-parenting, and stepparenting on children* (pp. 279–298). Hillsdale, NJ: Erlbaum.

Brazelton, T. B. (1983). *Infants and mothers: Differences in development.* New York: Dell.

Brazelton, T. B. (1985). *Working and caring.* Reading, MA: Addison-Wesley.

Breton, M. (1980). The school's role in the coordination of child-protection efforts. In
    R. Volpe, M. Brenton, & J. Mitton (Eds.), *The maltreatment of the school-aged
    child*. Lexington, MA: Lexington Books, D.C. Heath.

Brim, O. G., Jr., & Kagan, J. (Eds.). (1980). *Constancy and change in human devel-
    opment*. Cambridge, MA: Harvard University Press.

Brim, O. G., Jr., & Riff, C. D. (1980). On the properties of life events. In P. B. Baltes
    & O. G. Brim (Eds.), *Life-span development and behavior*. New York: Academic
    Press.

Bronfenbrenner, U. (1960). Freudian theories of identification and their derivatives. *Child
    Development, 31*, 15–40.

Bronfenbrenner, U. (1961). Some familial antecedents of responsibility and leadership
    in adolescents. In L. Petrullo & B. M. Bass (Eds.), *Leadership and interpersonal
    behavior* (pp. 239–272). New York: Holt, Rinehart & Winston.

Bronfenbrenner, U. (1967). The psychological costs of quality and equality in education.
    Child Development, 38, 909–925.

Bronfenbrenner, U. (1973). Who cares for America's children? In F. Rebelsky & Z.
    Dorman (Eds.), *Child development and behavior* (2nd ed). New York: Knopf.

Bronfenbrenner, U. (1987). *The ecology of human development: Experiments by nature
    and design*. Cambridge, MA: Harvard University Press.

Bronstein, P. (1984). Differences in mothers' and fathers' behaviors toward children: A
    cross-cultural comparison. *Developmental Psychology, 20*, 995–1003.

Bronstein, P. (1988). Marital and parenting roles in transition. In P. Bronstein & C. P.
    Cowan (Eds.), *Fatherhood today: Men's changing role in the family* (pp. 3–10).
    New York: Wiley.

Bronstein, P., & Cowan, C. P. (Eds.). (1988). *Fatherhood today: Men's changing role
    in the family*. New York: Wiley.

Brooks, J. B. (1991). *The process of parenting* (3rd ed.). Mountain View, CA: Mayfield.

Brooks-Gunn, J. (1988). Antecedents and consequences of variations in girls' maturational
    timing. In M. D. Levine & E. R. McAnarney (Eds.), *Early adolescent transitions*.
    Lexington, MA: Lexington Books.

Brooks-Gunn, J., & Furstenberg, F. F., Jr. (1989). Adolescent sexual behavior. *American
    Psychologist, 44*, 249–257.

Brooks-Gunn, J., & Lewis, M. (1979). Why mama and papa? The development of social
    labels. *Child Development, 50*, 1203–1206.

Brown, F. H. (1988a). The impact of death and serious illness on the family cycle. In
    B. Carter & M. McGoldrick (Eds.), *The changing family life cycle: A framework
    for family therapy* (pp. 457–482). New York: Gardner Press.

Brown, F. H. (1988b). The postdivorce family. In B. Carter & M. McGoldrick (Eds.),
    The changing family life cycle: A framework for family therapy (pp. 375–398).
    New York: Gardner Press.

Brown, R. (1973). *A first language*. Cambridge, MA: Harvard University Press.

Browne, A., & Finkelhor, D. (1986). Impact of child sexual abuse: A review of the
    research. *Psychological Bulletin, 99*, 66–77.

Bruner, J. S. (1983). *Child's talk*. New York: Norton.

Bruner, J. S., Jolly, A., & Silva, K. (Eds.). (1976). *Play: Its role in evolution and
    development*. Harmondsworth, England: Penguin.

Bunker, L. K. (1987). What about co-ed competition? In V. Scofedlt (Ed.), *Handbook
    for youth sport coaches* (pp. 337–354). Reston, VA: American Alliance for Health,
    Physical Education, Recreation, and Dance.

Burlingham, D. (1973). The pre-oedipal infant-father relationship. *The Psychoanalytic Study of the Child, 29,* 23–47.

Busch-Rossnagel, N. A., & Vance, N. K. (1982). The impact of the school on social and emotional development. In B. B. Wolman (Ed.), *Handbook of developmental psychology* (pp. 452–467). Englewood Cliffs, NJ: Prentice-Hall.

Camara, K. A., & Resnick, G. (1988). Interparental conflict and cooperation: Factors moderating children's post-divorce adjustment. In E. M. Hetherington & J. D. Arasteh (Eds.), *Impact of divorce, single-parenting, and stepparenting on children* (pp. 169–195). Hillsdale, NJ: Erlbaum.

Carlsmith, L. (1964). Effect of early father-absence on scholastic aptitude. *Harvard Educational Review, 34,* 3–21.

Carlson, B. E. (1984). The father's contribution to child care: Effects on children's perceptions of parent roles. *American Journal of Orthopsychiatry, 54,* 123–136.

Carter, E., & McGoldrick, M. (Eds.). (1988). *The changing family life cycle: A framework for family therapy* (2nd ed.). New York: Gardner Press.

Cath, S. H., Gurwitt, A., & Ginsberg, L. (1989). *Fathers and their families.* New York: The Analytic Press.

Cath, S. H., Gurwitt, A. R., & Ross, J. M. (Eds.). (1982). *Father and child: Developmental and clinical perspectives.* Boston: Little, Brown.

Cath, S. H., & Herzog, J. M. (1982). The dying and death of a father. In S. H. Cath, A. R. Gurwitt, & J. M. Ross (Eds.), *Father and child: Developmental and clinical perspectives* (pp. 339–356). Boston: Little, Brown.

Chapman, M. (1977). Father absence, stepfathers, and the cognitive performance of college students. *Child Development, 49,* 1155–1158.

Chapman, M., Zahn-Waxler, C., Cooperman, G., & Iannotti, R. (1987). Empathy and responsibility in the motivation of children's helping. *Developmental Psychology, 23,* 140–145.

Chedd, G. (1981). Who shall be born? *Science, 81,* 32–41.

Cherlin, A. J., & Furstenberg, F. F., Jr. (1988). *The new American grandparent: A place in the family, a life apart.* New York: Basic Books.

Chernin, K. (1981). *The obsession: Reflections on the tyranny of slenderness.* New York: Harper & Row.

Chesler, P. (1986). *Mothers on trial: The battle of children and custody.* New York: McGraw-Hill.

Chess, S., & Thomas, A. (1986). *Temperament in clinical practice.* New York: Guilford.

Chess, S., & Thomas, A. (1987). *Know your child.* New York: Basic Books.

Chiraboga, D. A. (1982a). Adaptation to marital separation in later and earlier life. *Journal of Gerontology, 37,* 109–114.

Chiraboga, D. A. (1982b). An examination of life events as possible antecedents of life change. *Journal of Gerontology, 36,* 604–624.

Chiraboga, D. A., Roberts, J., & Stein, J. A. (1978). Psychological well-being during marital separation. *Journal of Divorce, 2,* 21–36.

Chodorow, N. (1978). *The reproduction of mothering: Psychoanalysis and the sociology of gender.* Berkeley: University of California Press.

Chumela, W. C. (1982). Physical growth in adolescence. In B. B. Wolman (Ed.), *Handbook of developmental psychology* (pp. 471–485). Englewood Cliffs, NJ: Prentice-Hall.

Cicchetti, C., & Rizley, R. (1981). Developmental perspectives on the etiology, intergenerational transmission, and sequelae of child maltreatment. *New Directions in Child Development, 11*, 31–55.

Cicirelli, V. G. (1982). Sibling influence throughout the life span. In M. E. Lamb & B. Sutton-Smith (Eds.), *Sibling relationships*. Hillsdale, NJ: Erlbaum.

Clark, C. A., Worthington, E. L., and Danser, D. B. (1988). The transmission of religious beliefs and practices from parents to firstborn early adolescent sons. *Journal of Marriage and the Family, 50*, 463–472.

Clark, R. W. (1971). *Einstein: The life and times*. New York: World Publishing.

Clark, S. D., Zabin, L. S., & Hardy, J. B. (1984). Sex, contraception, and parenthood: Experience and attitudes among urban black young men. *Family Planning Perspectives, 16*, 77–82.

Clarke-Stewart, K. A. (1978). And daddy makes three: The father's impact on mother and young child. *Child Development, 49*, 466–478.

Clarke-Stewart, K. A. (1980). The father's contribution to children's cognitive and social development in early childhood. In F. A. Pedersen (Ed.), *The father-infant relationship: Observational studies in a family setting*. New York: Praeger.

Clarke-Stewart, K. A. (1989). Infant day care: Maligned or malignant? *American Psychologist, 44*, 266–273.

Clary, E. G., & Miller, J. (1986). Socialization and situational influences on sustained altruism. *Child Development, 57*, 1358–1369.

Clingempeel, W. G., & Repucci, N. D. (1982). Joint custody after divorce: Major issues and goals for research. *Psychological Bulletin, 91*, 102–127.

Cohen, L. J., & Campos, J. J. (1974). Father, mother, and stranger as elicitors of attachment behaviors in infancy. *Developmental Psychology, 10*, 146–154.

Cohen, S. Z., & Gans, B. M. (1978). *The other generation gap: The middle-aged and their aging parents*. Chicago: Follett.

Coles, R. (1986). *The moral life of children*. Boston: Houghton Mifflin.

Condry, J., & Condry, S. (1976). Sex differences: A study of the eye of the beholder. *Child Development, 47*, 812–819.

Cooper, C. R., & Ayers-Lopez, S. (1985). Family and peer systems in early adolescence: New models of the role of relationships in development. *Journal of Early Adolescence, 5*, 9–22.

Cooper, K., Chassin, L., Braver, S., Zeiss, A., & Khavari, K. A. (1986). Correlates of mood and marital satisfaction among dual-worker and single-worker couples. *Social Psychology Quarterly, 49*, 322–329.

Coopersmith, S. (1967). *The antecedents of self-esteem*. San Francisco: W.H. Freeman.

Corneau, G. (1991). *Absent fathers, lost sons*. Boston: Shambhala.

Cosby, B. (1986). *Fatherhood*. New York: Dolphin/Doubleday.

Cowan, C. P., & Cowan, P. A. (1987). Men's involvement in parenthood: Identifying the antecedents and understanding the barriers. In P. Berman & F. Pedersen (Eds.), *Men's transitions to parenthood* (pp. 145–174). Hillsdale, NJ: Erlbaum.

Cowan, C. P., & Cowan, P. A. (1992). *When partners become parents: The big life change for couples*. New York: Basic Books.

Cowan, C. P., Cowan, P. A., Heming, G., Garrett, E., Coysh, W. S., Curtis-Boles, H., & Boles, A. J. (1985). Transitions to parenthood: His, hers, and theirs. *Journal of Family Issues, 6*, 451–482.

Cowan, P. A. (1988). Becoming a father: A time of change, an opportunity for development. In P. Bronstein & C. P. Cowan (Eds.), *Fatherhood today* (pp. 13–35). New York: Wiley.

Crano, W. D., & Aronoff, J. (1978). A cross-cultural study of expressive and instrumental role complementarity in the family. *American Sociological Review, 43*, 463–471.

Crockenberg, S., & Acredole, C. (1983). Infant temperament ratings: A function of infants, or mothers, or both. *Infant Behavior and Development, 6*, 61–72.

Cronenwett, L. R., & Newmark, L. L. (1974). Fathers' responses to childbirth. *Nursing Research, 23*, 210–217.

Crouter, A. C. (1984). Spillover from family to work: The neglected side of work-family interface. *Human Relations, 37*, 425–442.

Crouter, A. C., Perry-Jenkins, M., Huston, T. L., & Hale, S. M. (1987). Processes underlying father involvement in dual-career and single-earner families. *Developmental Psychology, 23*, 431–440.

Curtona, C. E., & Troutman, R. R. (1985). Social support, infant temperament, and parenting self-efficacy. *Child Development, 57*, 1507–1518.

Damon, W. (1988). *The moral child*. New York: Free Press.

Daniels, D., Dunn, J., Furstenberg, F. F., Jr., & Plomin, R. (1985). Environmental differences within the family and adjustment of differences within pairs of adolescent siblings. *Child Development, 56*, 764–774.

Daniels, D., & Plomin, R. (1985). Origins of individual differences in infant shyness. *Developmental Psychology, 21*, 118–121.

Daniels, P., & Weingarten, K. (1982). *Sooner or later: The timing of parenthood in adult lives*. New York: Norton.

Darling, C. A. (1987). Family life education. In M. B. Sussman & S. K. Steinmetz (Eds.), *Handbook of marriage and the family* (pp. 815–833). New York: Plenum.

Dauw, D. C. (1966). Life experiences of original thinkers and good elaborators. *Exceptional Children, 32*, 433–440.

Davids, A. (Ed.). (1976). *Child personality and psychopathology: Vol. 3*. New York: Wiley.

DeFleur, L. B., & Menke, B. A. (1975). Learning about the labor force: Occupational knowledge among high school males. *Sociology of Education, 48*, 324–345.

DeFries, J. C., Plomin, R., Vandenberg, S. G., & Kuse, A. R. (1981). Parent-offspring resemblance in cognitive abilities in the Colorado adoption project: Biological, adoptive, and control parents and one-year-old children. *Intelligence, 5*, 245–277.

Derdeyn, A., & Scott, E. (1984). Joint custody: A critical analysis and appraisal. *American Journal of Orthopsychiatry, 54*, 199–209.

de Shazer, S. (1982). *Patterns of brief family therapy*. New York: Guilford.

deVries, H. A. (1970). Physiological effects of an exercise training regimen upon men aged 52 to 88. *Journal of Gerontology, 25*, 325–326.

deVries, H. A. (1974). *Physiology of exercise*. Dubuque, IA: Brown.

deVries, H. A., & Hales, D. (1982). *Fitness after 50*. New York: Scribner's.

Dickie, J. R. (1987). Interrelationships within the mother-father-infant triad. In P. W. Berman & F. A. Pedersen (Eds.), *Men's transitions to parenthood* (pp. 113–143). New York: Erlbaum.

Dickie, J., & Gerber, S. C. (1980). Training in social competence: The effect on mothers, fathers, and infants. *Child Development, 51*, 1248–1251.

Dinnerstein, D. (1977). *The mermaid and the minotaur*. New York: Harper & Row.

Dion, K., & Berscheid, E. (1974). Physical attractiveness and peer perception among children. *Sociometry, 37*, 1–12.

Dodson, F. (1974). *How to father*. Los Angeles: Nash.

Doherty, W. J., & Jacobson, N. S. (1982). Marriage and the family. In B. B. Wolman

(Ed.), *Handbook of developmental psychology* (pp. 667–680). Englewood Cliffs, NJ: Prentice-Hall.

Dornbusch, S. M., Carlsmith, J. M., Bushwall, S. J., Ritter, P. L., Leiderman, H., Hastorf, A. H., & Gross, R. T. (1985). Single parents, extended households, and the control of adolescents. *Child Development, 56*, 326–341.

Dornbusch, S. M., Ritter, P., Leiderman, P. H., Roberts, D. F., & Fraleigh, M. J. (1987). The relationship of parenting style to adolescent school performance. *Child Development, 58*, 1244–1257.

Douvan, E., & Adelson, J. (1966). *The adolescent experience*. New York: Wiley.

Downs, A. C., & Langlois, J. H. (1988). Sex typing: Construct and measurement issues. *Sex Roles, 18*, 87–100.

Doyle, J. A. (1989). *The male experience* (2nd ed.). Dubuque, IA: Wm. C. Brown.

Draper, P., & Harpending, H. (1989). A sociobiological perspective on the development of human reproductive strategies. In K. B. MacDonald (Ed.), *Sociobiological perspectives in human development* (pp. 340–372). New York: Springer-Verlag.

Dreskin, W., & Dreskin, W. (1983). *The day care decision: What's best for you and your child*. New York: M. Evans.

Dreyer, P. H. (1982). Sexuality during adolescence. In B. B. Wolman (Ed.), *Handbook of developmental psychology*. Englewood Cliffs, NJ: Prentice-Hall.

Driekurs, R., Gould, S., & Corsini, R. J. (1974). *Family council*. Chicago: Regnery.

Duberman, L. (1975). *The reconstituted family: A study of remarried couples and their children*. Chicago: Nelson-Hall.

DuHamel, T. R., & Biller, H. B. (1969). Parental imitation and nonimitation in young children. *Developmental Psychology, 1*, 772.

Dunn, J. (1985). *Sisters and brothers*. Cambridge, MA: Harvard University Press.

Dunn, J., & Kendrick, C. (1982). *Siblings: Love, envy, and understanding*. Cambridge, MA: Harvard University Press.

Durrett, M. E., Richards, P., Otaki, M., Pennebaker, J. W., & Nyquist, L. (1986). Mother's involvement with infant and her perception of spousal support, Japan and America. *Journal of Marriage and the Family, 48*, 187–194.

Dusek, J. B. (Ed.). (1985). *Teacher expectancies*. Hillsdale, NJ: Erlbaum.

Duvall, E. M., & Miller, B. C. (1985). *Marriage and family development* (6th ed.). New York: Harper & Row.

Dyk, R. B., & Witkin, H. A. (1965). Family experiences related to the development of differentiation in children. *Child Development, 36*, 21–55.

Dyl, A. S., & Biller, H. B. (1973). Paternal absence, social class, and reading achievement. Unpublished study, University of Rhode Island.

Easterbrooks, M. A., & Goldberg, W. A. (1984). Toddler development in the family: Impact of father involvement and parenting characteristics. *Child Development, 55*, 740–752.

Easterbrooks, M. A., & Goldberg, W. A. (1985). Effects of early maternal employment on toddlers, mothers, and fathers. *Developmental Psychology, 21*, 774–783.

Easterbrooks, M. A., & Goldberg, W. A. (1990). Security of toddler-parent attachment: Relation to children's sociopersonality functioning during kindergarten. In M. T. Greenberg, D. Cicchetti, and E. M. Cummings (Eds.), *Attachment in the preschool years: Theory, research and intervention* (pp. 221–244). Chicago: University of Chicago Press.

Easterbrooks, M. A., & Lamb, M. E. (1979). The relationship between quality of infant-mother attachment and infant competence in initial encounters with peers. *Child Development, 50*, 380–387.

Eccles, J. S. (1987). Gender roles and achievement patterns: An expectancy value perspective. In J. M. Reinisch, L. A. Rosenblum, & S. A. Sanders (Eds.), *Masculinity/Femininity*. New York: Oxford University Press.

Eccles, J. S., & Hoffman, L. W. (1984). Sex roles, socialization, and occupational behavior. In H. W. Stevenson & A. E. Siegel (Eds.), *Research in child development and public policy* (Vol. 1). Chicago: University of Chicago Press.

Egeland, B., & Farber, E. A. (1984). Infant-mother attachment: Factors related to development and changes over time. *Child Development, 55*, 753–771.

Egeland, B., Jacobvitz, D., & Papatola, K. (1988). Intergenerational continuity of parental abuse. In J. Lancaster & R. Gelles (Eds.), *Biosocial aspects of child abuse*. New York: Jossey-Bass.

Egeland, B., Jacobvitz, D., & Sroufe, L. A. (1987). *Breaking the cycle of abuse: Relationship predictors*. Minneapolis: University of Minnesota Press.

Eiger, M. S., & Olds, S. W. (1987). *The complete book of breastfeeding*. New York: Bantam.

Einstein, E. (1982). *The stepfamily: Living, loving and learning*. Boston: Macmillan.

Eisenberg, N. (1987). The relation of altruism and other moral behaviors to moral cognition: Methodological and conceptual issues. In N. Eisenberg (Ed.), *Contemporary topics in developmental psychology*. New York: Wiley.

Eisenberg, N., Lennon, R., & Roth, K. (1983). Prosocial development: A longitudinal study. *Developmental Psychology, 19*, 846–855.

Eisenstadt, J. M. (1978). Parental loss and genius. *American Psychologist, 33*, 211–223.

Eitzen, D. S. (1975). Athletics in the status system of male adolescents: A replication of Coleman's "The Adolescent Society." *Adolescence, 10*, 267–276.

Elder, G. H. (1974). *Children of the Great Depression*. Chicago: University of Chicago Press.

Elder, G. H. (1979). Historical change in life patterns and personality. In P. Baltes & O. Brim (Eds.), *Life-span development and behavior* (Vol. 2, pp. 117–159). New York: Academic Press.

Elder, G. H. (1983). Families, kin, and the life course. In R. Parke (Ed.), *The family*. Chicago: University of Chicago Press.

Elder, G. H., Caspi, A., & Nguyen, T. (1986). Resourceful and vulnerable children: Family influence in hard times. In R. K. Silbereisen, K. Eyferth, & G. Rudinger (Eds.), *Development as action in context* (pp. 167–186). New York: Springer-Verlag.

Elder, G. H., Nguyen, T., & Caspi, A. (1985). Linking family hardship to children's lives. *Child Development, 56*, 361–375.

Elizur, J. (1986). The stress of school entry: Parental coping behaviors and children's adjustment to school. *Journal of Child Psychology and Psychiatry, 27*, 625–638.

Elkin, M. (1984). *Families under the influence: Changing alcoholic patterns*. New York: Norton.

Elkind, D. (1981). *The hurried child: Growing up too fast too soon*. Reading, MA: Addison-Wesley.

Elkind, D. (1984). *All grown up and no place to go: Teenagers in crisis*. Reading, MA: Addison-Wesley.

Elkind, D. (1987). *Miseducation: Preschoolers at risk*. New York: Knopf.

Elliot, F. A. (1988). Neurological factors. In V. B. Van Hasselt, R. L. Morrison, A. S.

Bellack, & M. Herson (Eds.), *Handbook of family violence* (pp. 359–382). New York: Plenum.

Elster, A. B., & Lamb, M. E. (Eds.). (1986). *Adolescent fatherhood*. Hillsdale, NJ: Erlbaum.

Emery, R. E. (1988). *Marriage, divorce, and children's adjustment*. Beverly Hills, CA: Sage.

Emery, R. E. (1989). Family violence. *American Psychologist, 44*, 321–328.

Epstein, A. S., & Radin, N. (1975). Motivational components related to father behavior and cognitive functioning in preschoolers. *Child Development, 46*, 831–839.

Erikson, E. H. (1963). *Childhood and society* (rev. ed.). New York: Norton.

Erikson, E. H. (1968). *Identity: Youth and crisis*. New York: Norton.

Erikson, E. H. (1980). *Identity and the life cycle*. New York: Norton.

Erikson, E. H. (1982). *The life cycle completed*. New York: Norton.

Erikson, E. H., Erikson, J. M., & Kivnick, H. Q. (1986). *Vital involvement in old age*. New York: Norton.

Evans, R. B. (1969). Childhood parental relationships of homosexual men. *Journal of Consulting and Clinical Psychology, 33*, 129–135.

Faber, A., & Mazlish, E. (1974). *Liberated parents, liberated children*. New York: Grosset & Dunlap.

Faber, A., & Mazlish, E. (1980). *How to talk so kids will listen and listen so kids will talk*. New York: Avon.

Faber, A., & Mazlish, E. (1987). *Siblings without rivalry*. New York: Norton.

Fagot, B. I. (1975, April). *Teacher reinforcement of feminine-preferred behavior revisited*. Paper presented at the biennial meeting of the Society for Research in Child Development, Denver.

Fagot, B. I. (1978). The influence of sex of child on parental reactions to toddler children. *Child Development, 49*, 459–465.

Fagot, B. I., & Patterson, G. R. (1969). An in vivo analysis of reinforcing contingencies for sex-role behaviors in the preschool child. *Developmental Psychology, 1*, 563–568.

Falbo, T. (1982). Only children in America. In M. E. Lamb & B. N. Sutton-Smith (Eds.), *Sibling relationships: Their nature across the lifespan*. Hillsdale, NJ: Erlbaum.

Faretra, G. (1981). A profile of aggression from adolescence to adulthood: An 18-year follow-up of psychiatrically disturbed and violent adolescents. *American Journal of Orthopsychiatry, 51*, 439–453.

Farley, G. K., & Werkman, S. (1986). Overseas fathers: Vulnerabilities and treatment strategies. In M. E. Lamb (Ed.), *The father's role: Applied perspectives* (pp. 277–292). New York: Wiley.

Farrell, W. (1986). *Why men are the way they are*. New York: McGraw-Hill.

Feingold, A. (1988). Cognitive gender differences are disappearing. *American Psychologist, 43*, 95–103.

Feldman, S. S., & Nash, S. C. (1972). The effect of family formation on sex-stereotypic behavior: A study of responsiveness to babies. In W. Miller & L. Newman (Eds.), *The first child and family formation*. Chapel Hill: University of North Carolina Press.

Feldman, S. S., & Nash, S. C. (1978). Interest in babies during young adulthood. *Child Development, 49*, 617–622.

Feldman, S. S., Nash, S. C., & Aschenbrenner, B. G. (1983). Antecedents of fathering. *Child Development, 54*, 1628–1636.

Ferholt, J. B., & Gurwitt, A. R. (1982). Involving fathers in treatment. In S. H. Cath, A. R. Gurwitt, & J. M. Ross (Eds.), *Father and child: Developmental and clinical perspectives* (pp. 547–568). Boston: Little, Brown.

Ferrante, R. J., & Biller, H. B. (1986). School-based counseling for children of divorce. Unpublished manuscript, University of Rhode Island.

Field, T. M. (1978). Interaction behaviors of primary versus secondary caretaker fathers. *Developmental Psychology, 14*, 183–184.

Field, T. M., Cohen, D., Garcia, R., & Greenberg, R. (1984). Mother-stranger face discrimination by the newborn. *Infant Behavior and Development, 7*, 19–25.

Field, T. M., Sandberg, D., Garcia, R., Vega-Lahr, N., Goldstein, S., & Guy, L. (1985). Pregnancy problems, postpartum depression, and early mother-infant interactions. *Developmental Psychology, 21*, 1152–1156.

Field, T. M., & Widmayer, S. M. (1982). Motherhood. In B. B. Wolman (Ed.), *Handbook of developmental psychology* (pp. 681–701). Englewood Cliffs, NJ: Prentice-Hall.

Finkelhor, D. (1984). *Child sexual abuse.* New York: Free Press.

Fish, K. D., & Biller, H. B. (1973). Perceived childhood paternal relationships and college females' personal adjustment. *Adolescence, 8*, 415–420.

Fisher, S. F. (1973). *The female orgasm: Psychology, physiology, fantasy.* New York: Basic Books.

Fisher, S. F. (1986). *Development and structure of the body image* (Vols. 1 & 2). Hillsdale, NJ: Erlbaum.

Flavell, J. H. (1985). *Cognitive development* (2nd ed.). Englewood Cliffs, NJ: Prentice-Hall.

Fleck, J. R., Fuller, C. C., Malin, S. Z., Miller, D. H., & Acheson, K. R. (1980). Father psychological absence and heterosexual behavior, personal adjustment, and sex-typing in adolescent girls. *Adolescence, 15*, 847–860.

Florin, P. R., & Dokecki, P. R. (1983). Changing families through parent and family education: Review and analysis. In I. E. Sigel & L. M. Laosa (Eds.), *Changing families.* New York: Plenum.

Forehand, R., Long, N., Brody, G. H., and Fauber, R. (1986). Home predictors of young adolescents' school behavior and academic performance. *Child Development, 57*, 1528–1533.

Forward, S., & Buck, C. (1978). *Betrayal of innocence: Incest and its devastation.* New York: Penguin Books.

Francoeur, R. (1987). Human sexuality. In M. B. Sussman & S. K. Steinmetz (Eds.), *Handbook of marriage and the family* (pp. 509–534). New York: Plenum.

Franz, C. E., McClelland, D. C., and Weinberger, J. (1991). Childhood antecedents of conventional social accomplishment in midlife adults: A 35-year prospective study. *Journal of Personality and Social Psychology, 60*, 586–595.

Freud, S. (1950). Some psychological consequences of the anatomical distinction between the sexes (1939). In J. Rivers (Ed.), *Collected papers of Sigmund Freud* (Vol. 5). London: Hogarth.

Freud, S. (1962). *Three essays on the theory of sexuality.* New York: Dutton. (Original work published 1905)

Friedan, B. (1981). *The second stage.* New York: Summit Books.

Friedman, S. L., & Jacobs, B. S. (1981). Sex differences in neonates' behavioral responsiveness to repeated auditory stimulation. *Infant Behavior and Development, 4,* 175–183.

Frodi, A. M., & Lamb, M. E. (1978). Sex differences in responsiveness to infants: A developmental study of psychophysiological and behavioral responses. *Child Development, 49,* 1182–1188.

Frodi, A. M., & Lamb, M. E. (1980). Infants at risk for child abuse. *Infant Mental Health Journal, 1,* 240–247.

Fry, P. S., & Scher, A. (1984). The effect of father-absence on children's achievement motivation, ego-strength, and locus of control orientation: A five-year longitudinal assessment. *British Journal of Developmental Psychology, 2,* 167–178.

Fullmer, R. (1988). Lower-income and professional families: A comparison of structure and lifecycle processes. In B. Carter & M. McGoldrick (Eds.), *The changing family life cycle: A framework for family therapy* (pp. 545–578). New York: Gardner Press.

Furstenberg, F. F., Jr. (1988). Child care after divorce and remarriage. In E. M. Hetherington & J. Arasteh (Eds.), *Impact of divorce, single parenting, and stepparenting on children* (pp. 245–261). Hillsdale, NJ: Erlbaum.

Furstenberg, F. F., Jr., Brooks-Gunn, J., & Chase-Lansdale, L. (1989). Teenaged pregnancy and childbearing. *American Psychologist, 44,* 313–320.

Furstenberg, F. F., Jr., Brooks-Gunn, J., & Morgan, S. P. (1987). *Adolescent mothers in later life.* New York: Cambridge University Press.

Furstenberg, F. F., Jr., & Harris, K. T. (1992). When fathers matter/why fathers matter: The impact of paternal involvement on the offspring of adolescent mothers. In R. Lerman and T. Ooms (Eds.), *Young unwed fathers.* Philadelphia: Temple University Press.

Furstenberg, F. F., Jr., Morgan, S. P., & Allison, P. D. (1987). Paternal participation and child's well-being after marital dissolution. *American Sociological Review, 52,* 697–701.

Furstenberg, F. F., Jr., & Nord, C. W. (1985). Parenting apart: Patterns of child rearing after marital disruption. *Journal of Marriage and the Family, 47,* 893–904.

Galinsky, E. (1981). *Between generations: The six stages of parenthood.* New York: Times Books. (Reprinted as *The six stages of parenthood.* Reading, MA: Addison-Wesley, 1987.)

Galinsky, E. (1986). Family life and corporate policies. In M. Yogman & T. B. Brazelton (Eds.), *In support of families* (pp. 109–145). Cambridge, MA: Harvard University Press.

Galinsky, E., & David, J. (1988). *The preschool years.* New York: Times Books.

Galinsky, E., & Hooks, W. H. (1977). *The new extended family: Day care that works.* Boston: Houghton Mifflin.

Gallagher, J. J., Cross, A. H., & Scharfman, W. (1981). Parental adaptation to a young handicapped child: The father's role. *Journal of the Division for Early Childhood, 3,* 3–14.

Gamong, L., & Coleman, M. (1984). The effects of parent remarriage on children: A review of the empirical literature. *Family Relations, 33,* 398–406.

Garbarino, J. (1981). An ecological approach to child maltreatment. In L. H. Pelton (Ed.), *The social context of child abuse and neglect.* New York: Human Sciences Press.

Garbarino, J., Guttman, E., & Seeley, J. W. (1988). *The psychologically battered child.* San Francisco: Jossey-Bass.

Garbarino, J., Sebes, J., & Schellenbach, C. (1984). Families at risk for destructive parent-child relations in adolescence. *Child Development, 55*, 174–183.

Gardner, H. (1983). *Frames of mind: The theory of multiple intelligences*. New York: Basic Books.

Garmezy, N., & Rutter, M. (Eds.). (1988). *Stress, coping, and development in children*. Baltimore, MD: Johns Hopkins University Press.

Gasser, S., & Murray, E. J. (1969). Dominance and conflict in the interactions between parents of normal and neurotic children. *Journal of Abnormal Psychology, 74*, 33–41.

Gelles, R. J., & Strauss, M. A. (1988). *Intimate violence: The definitive study of the causes and consequences of abuse in the American family*. New York: Simon & Schuster.

Gelman, R. (1979). Preschool thought. *American Psychologist, 34*, 900–905.

Genevie, L., & Margolies, E. (1987). *The motherhood report*. New York: Macmillan.

Gershon, M., & Biller, H. B. (1977). *The other helpers: Paraprofessionals and non-professionals in mental health*. Lexington, MA: Lexington Books, D.C. Heath.

Gerson, K. (1986). *Hard choices: How women decide about work, career, and motherhood*. Berkeley: University of California Press.

Gesell, A., Ilg, F. L., & Ames, L. B. (1977). *The child from five to ten* (rev. ed.). New York: Harper & Row.

Gibbs, J. (1984). Black adolescents and youth: An endangered species. *American Journal of Orthopsychiatry, 54*, 6–21.

Gibson, E. J., & Spelke, E. S. (1983). The development of perception. In P. H. Mussen (Ed.), *Handbook of child psychology* (4th ed., Vol. 3), New York: Wiley.

Gilan, L. (1984). *The adoption resource book: A comprehensive guide to all the things you need to know about creating an adoptive family*. New York: Harper & Row.

Gilbert, L., Hanson, G., & Davis, B. (1982). Perceptions of parental role responsibilities: Differences between mothers and fathers. *Family Relations, 31*, 261–268.

Gill, S., Stockard, J., Johnson, M., & Williams, S. (1987). Measuring gender differences: The expressive dimension and critique of the androgyny scales. *Sex Roles, 17*, 375–400.

Gilligan, C. (1982). *In a different voice*. Cambridge, MA: Harvard University Press.

Ginott, H. (1969). *Between parent and child*. New York: Macmillan.

Giveans, D. L. (1986a). Speaking out. *Nurturing News, 8*(2), 1.

Giveans, D. L. (1986b). Today's spectrum of fathering examined through film. In R. A. Lewis & M. B. Sussman (Eds.), *Men's changing roles in the family* (pp. 255–272). New York: Haworth.

Gleason, J. B. (1988). Language and socialization. In F. Kessel (Ed.), *The development of language and language researchers*. Hillsdale, NJ: Erlbaum.

Glenn, N. D., & Hoppe, S. K. (1984). Only children as adults: Psychological well-being. *Journal of Family Issues, 3*, 363–382.

Glennon, L. M., & Butsch, R. (1983). The family U.S. portrayed on television 1946–1978. In J. C. Wright & A. C. Huston (Eds.), *Children and television*. (3rd ed.,) Lexington, MA: Ginn.

Glick, P. G., & Norton, A. J. (1978). Marrying, divorcing, and living together in the U.S. today. *Population Bulletin, 32*, 3–38.

Glover, B., & Shepherd, J. (1989). *The family fitness handbook*. New York: Penguin.

Goertzel, V., & Goertzel, M. (1978). *Cradles of eminence*. Boston: Little, Brown.

Goffman, E. (1956). *Stigma*. Englewood Cliffs, NJ: Prentice-Hall.

Gold, D., & Reis, M. (1982). Male teacher effects on young children: A theoretical and empirical consideration. *Sex Roles, 8*, 493–513.

Goldberg, S., & Lewis, M. (1969). Play behavior in the year-old infant: Early sex differences. *Child Development, 40*, 21–31.

Goldberg, W. A., & Easterbrooks, M. A. (1984). Role of marital quality in toddler development. *Developmental Psychology, 20*, 504–514.

Goldman, J. D. G., & Goldman, R. J. (1983). Children's perceptions of parents and their roles: A cross-national study in Australia, England, North America, and Sweden. *Sex Roles, 9*, 791–812.

Goldman, R. J., & Goldman, J. D. G. (1982). How children perceive the origin of babies and the roles of mothers and fathers in procreation: A cross-national study. *Child Development, 53*, 491–504.

Goldstein, J., Freud, A., & Solnit, A. (1973). *Beyond the best interests of the child.* New York: Free Press.

Gongla, P. A., & Thompson, E. H., Jr. (1987). Single-parent families. In M. B. Sussman & S. K. Steinmetz (Eds.), *Handbook of marriage and the family* (pp. 397–418). New York: Plenum.

Gordon, E., & Braithwaite, A. (1986). *Defiers of negative prediction.* Washington, DC: Howard University Press.

Gordon, T. (1970). *Parent effectiveness training: P.E.T.* New York: Wyden.

Gordon, T. (1974). *Teacher effectiveness training: T.E.T.* New York: Wyden.

Gordon, T. (1989). *Teaching children self-discipline.* New York: Times Books.

Gottfried, A. E., Gottfried, A. W., & Bathurst, K. (1988). Maternal employment, family environment, and children's development: Infancy through the school years. In A. E. Gottfried & A. W. Gottfried (Eds.), *Maternal employment and children's development: Longitudinal research* (pp. 11–58). New York: Plenum.

Gould, D. (1984). Psychosocial development and children's sport. In J. R. Thomas (Ed.), *Motor development during childhood and adolescence.* Minneapolis, MN: Burgess.

Gould, R. L. (1978). *Transformations: Growth and change in adult life.* New York: Simon & Schuster.

Gould, R. L. (1980). Transformations during early and middle adult years. In N. J. Smelser & E. H. Erikson (Eds.), *Themes of work and love in adulthood.* Cambridge, MA: Harvard University Press.

Grebstein, L. C. (1986). An eclectic family therapy. In J. Norcross (Ed.), *Handbook of eclectic therapy.* New York: Brunner/Mazel.

Green, R. (1974). *Sexual identity conflict in children and adults.* New York: Basic Books.

Green, R. (1976). One hundred ten feminine and masculine boys: Behavioral contrasts and demographic similarities. *Archives of Sexual Behavior, 5*, 425–446.

Green, R. (1978). Sexual identity of 37 children raised by homosexual or transsexual parents. *American Journal of Psychiatry, 6*, 692–697.

Green, R. (1987). *The "sissy boy syndrome" and the development of homosexuality.* New Haven, CT: Yale University Press.

Green, R., Williams, K., & Goodman, M. (1985). Masculine or feminine gender identity in boys: Developmental differences between two diverse groups. *Sex Roles, 12*, 1155–1171.

Greenberg, M. (1985). *The birth of a father.* New York: Continuum.

Greenberg, M., & Morris, N. (1974). Engrossment: The newborn's impact upon the father. *American Journal of Orthopsychiatry, 44*, 520–531.

Greenberger, E., & Steinberg, L. (1986). *When teenagers work: The psychological and social costs of adolescent employment*. New York: Basic Books.

Greeno, I. G. (1989). A perspective on thinking. *American Psychologist, 44*, 134–141.

Greif, J. B. (1985). *Single fathers*. Lexington, MA: Lexington Books, D.C. Heath.

Grollman, E. A., & Sweder, G. L. (1986). *The working parent dilemma: How to balance the responsibilities of children and careers*. Boston: Beacon Press.

Grossman, F. K., Pollack, W. S., & Golding, E. (1988). Fathers and children: Predicting the quality and quantity of fathering. *Developmental Psychology, 24*, 82–91.

Grotevant, H. D., & Cooper, C. R. (1986). Individuation in family relationships. *Human Development, 29*, 82–100.

Guidubaldi, J. (1983). The impact of parental divorce on children: Report of the nationwide NASP study. *School Psychology Review, 12*, 300–323.

Guidubaldi, J., & Cleminshaw, H. K. (1985). Divorce, family health, and child adjustment. *Family Relations, 34*, 35–41.

Guidubaldi, J., Cleminshaw, H. K., Perry, J. D., Nastasi, B. K., & Lightel, J. (1986). The role of selected family environment factors in children's post-divorce adjustment. *Family Relations, 35*, 141–151.

Guidubaldi, J., & Perry, J. D. (1984). Divorce, socioeconomic status, and children's cognitive-social competence at school entry. *American Journal of Orthopsychiatry, 54*, 459–468.

Guidubaldi, J., & Perry, J. D. (1985). Divorce and mental health sequelae for children: A two-year follow-up of a national sample. *Journal of the American Academy of Child Psychiatry, 24*, 531–537.

Guilford, J. P. (1967). *The structure of intellect*. New York: McGraw-Hill.

Gunnar, M. R., & Donahue, M. (1980). Sex differences in social responsiveness between six and twelve months. *Child Development, 51*, 262–265.

Gurman, A. S., & Kniskeon, D. P. (Eds.). (1981). *Handbook of family therapy*. New York: Brunner/Mazel.

Gurwitt, A. R. (1982). Aspects of prospective fatherhood. In S. H. Cath, A. R. Gurwitt, & J. M. Ross (Eds.), *Father and child: Developmental and clinical perspectives* (pp. 275–299). Boston: Little, Brown.

Haggerson, N. (1981). Birth rites: Grandson and grandfather. In R. A. Lewis (Ed.), *Men in difficult times: Masculinity today and tomorrow*. Englewood Cliffs, NJ: Prentice-Hall.

Halpern, D. F. (1986). *Sex differences in cognitive abilities*. Hillsdale, NJ: Erlbaum.

Halpern, D. F. (1989). The disappearance of cognitive gender differences: What you see depends on where you look. *American Psychologist, 44*, 1156–1158.

Hansen, M., & Biller, H. B. (1992). Intergenerational perceptions of paternal nurturance and personality adjustment among young adult sons and daughters. Unpublished study, University of Rhode Island.

Hanson, S. M. H. (1988). Divorced fathers with custody. In P. Bronstein & C. P. Cowan (Eds.), *Fatherhood today: Men's changing role in the family* (pp. 166–194). New York: Wiley.

Harkins, E. B. (1978). Effects of empty nest transition on self-report of psychological and physical well-being. *Journal of Marriage and the Family, 40*, 549–556.

Harriman, L. C. (1986). Marital adjustment as related to personal and marital changes accompanying parenthood. *Family Relations, 34*, 233–239.

Harter, S. (1983). Developmental perspectives on the self system. In P. H. Mussen (Ed.), *Handbook of child psychology* (4th ed., Vol. 4), New York: Wiley.

Harter, S., Alexander, P. C., & Neimeyer, R. A. (1988). Long-term effects of incestuous child abuse in college women: Social adjustment, social cognition, and family characteristics. *Journal of Consulting and Clinical Psychology, 56*, 5–8.

Hartl, E. M., Monnelly, E. P., & Elderkin, R. D. (1982). *Physique and delinquent behavior*. New York: Academic Press.

Hartman, A., & Nicolay, R. (1966). Sexually deviant behavior in expectant fathers. *Journal of Abnormal and Social Psychology, 71*, 232–234.

Hartup, W. W. (1989). Social relationships and their developmental significance. *American Psychologist, 44*, 120–126.

Hatfield, A. B., & Lefley, H. P. (1987). *Families of the mentally ill: Coping and adaptation*. New York: Guilford.

Hatfield, E., & Sprecher, S. (1986). *Mirror, mirror . . . The importance of looks in everyday life*. Albany: State University of New York Press.

Hattie, J., & Rogers, H. J. (1986). Factor models for assessing the relation between creativity and intelligence. *Journal of Educational Psychology, 78*, 482–485.

Havinghurst, R. J. (1982). The world of work. In B. B. Wolman (Ed.), *Handbook of developmental psychology* (pp. 771–787). Englewood Cliffs, NJ: Prentice-Hall.

Hay, D. F. (1985). Learning to form relationships in infancy: Parallel attachments with parents and peers. *Developmental Review, 8*, 122–161.

Heath, D. H. (1976). Competent fathers: Their personalities and marriages. *Human Development, 19*, 26–39.

Heath, D. H. (1977). Some possible effects of occupation on the maturing of professional men. *Journal of Vocational Behavior, 11*, 263–281.

Heath, D. H. (1978). What meaning and what effects does fatherhood have on the maturing of professional men? *Merrill-Palmer Quarterly, 24*, 265–278.

Heath, D. H., & Heath, H. E. (1991). *Fulfilling lives: Paths to maturity and success*. San Francisco: Jossey-Bass.

Heckhausen, H. (1986). Achievement and motivation through the lifespan. In A. B. Sorensen, F. E. Weinert, & L. R. Sherrod (Eds.), *Human development and the life course*. Hillsdale, NJ: Erlbaum.

Heilbrun, A. B., Jr. (1973). *Aversive maternal control*. New York: Wiley.

Heilbrun, A. B., Jr. (1974). Parent identification and filial sex-role behavior: The importance of biological context. In J. C. Cole & R. Dienstbier (Eds.), *Nebraska Symposium on Motivation, 1973* (pp. 125–194). Lincoln: University of Nebraska Press.

Heilbrun, A. B., Jr. (1976). Identification with the father and sex-role development of the daughter. *Family Coordinator, 25*, 411–416.

Heinicke, C. M., Diskin, S. D., Ramsey-Klee, D. M., & Given, K. (1983). Pre-birth parent characteristics and family development in the first year of life. *Child Development, 54*, 194–208.

Helson, R. (1971). Women mathematicians and the creative personality. *Journal of Consulting and Clinical Psychology, 36*, 210–220.

Helson, R., & Moane, G. (1987). Personality change in women from college to midlife. *Journal of Personality and Social Psychology, 53*, 176–186.

Helson, R., & Wink, P. (1987). Two conceptions of maturity examined in the findings of a longitudinal study. *Journal of Personality and Social Psychology, 53*, 531–541.

Henderson, N. (1982). Human behavior genetics. *Annual Review of Psychology, 33*, 403–440.

Henker, B., & Whalen, C. K. (1989). Hyperactivity and attention deficits. *American Psychologist, 44*, 216–223.

Henneborn, W. J., & Cogan, R. (1975). The effect of husband participation on reported pain and probability of medication during labor and birth. *Journal of Psychosomatic Research, 29*, 215–222.

Herman, J. L. (1981). *Father-daughter incest.* Cambridge, MA: Harvard University Press.

Herzog, J. M. (1982). On father hunger: The father's role in the modulation of aggressive drive and fantasy. In S. Cath, A. R. Gurwitt, & J. M. Ross (Eds.), *Father and child: Developmental and clinical perspectives* (pp. 163–174). Boston: Little, Brown.

Hess, R. D., & Camara, K. A. (1979). Post-divorce family relationships as mediating factors in the consequences of divorce for children. *Journal of Social Issues, 35*, 79–96.

Hetherington, E. M. (1965). A developmental study of the effects of sex of the dominant parent on sex-role preference, identification, and imitation in children. *Journal of Personality and Social Psychology, 2*, 188–194.

Hetherington, E. M. (1966). Effects of paternal absence on sex-typed behaviors in Negro and white preadolescent males. *Journal of Personality and Social Psychology, 4*, 87–91.

Hetherington, E. M. (1972). Effects of father-absence on personality development in adolescent daughters. *Developmental Psychology, 7*, 313–326.

Hetherington, E. M. (1977, November). *My heart belongs to Daddy: A study of the marriages of daughters of divorcees and widows.* Paper presented at the meeting of the National Association for the Education of Young Children, Washington, DC.

Hetherington, E. M. (1987). Family relations six years after divorce. In K. Palsey & M. Ihinger-Tollman (Eds.), *Remarriage and stepparenting today: Current research and theory* (pp. 185–205). New York: Guilford.

Hetherington, E. M. (1989). Coping with family transitions: Winners, losers, and survivors. *Child Development, 60*, 1–14.

Hetherington, E. M. (1991). Presidential address: Families, lies, and video-tapes. *Journal of Research on Adolescence, 1*, 323–348.

Hetherington, E. M., & Arasteh, J. (Eds.). (1988). *Impact of divorce, single-parenting and stepparenting on children.* Hillsdale, NJ: Erlbaum.

Hetherington, E. M., Cox, M., & Cox, R. (1976). Divorced fathers. *Family Coordinator, 25*, 417–428.

Hetherington, E. M., Cox, M., & Cox, R. (1978). Family interaction and the social, emotional, and cognitive development of children following divorce. In V. Vaughn & B. Brazelton (Eds.), *The family: Setting priorities.* New York: Science and Medicine Publishing.

Hetherington, E. M., Cox, M., & Cox, R. (1982). Effects of divorce on parents and children. In M. E. Lamb (Ed.), *Nontraditional families* (pp. 233–288). Hillsdale, NJ: Erlbaum.

Hetherington, E. M., Cox, M. & Cox, R. (1985). Long-term effects of divorce and remarriage on the adjustment of children. *Journal of the Academy of Psychiatry, 24*, 518–530.

Hetherington, E. M., & Frankie, G. (1967). Effects of parental dominance, warmth, and conflict on imitation in children. *Journal of Personality and Social Psychology*, 6, 119–125.

Hetherington, E. M., & Parke, R. D. (1986). *Child psychology: A contemporary viewpoint* (3rd ed.). New York: McGraw-Hill.

Hetherington, E. M., & Stanley-Hagan, M. (1986). Divorced fathers: Stress, coping, and adjustment. In M. E. Lamb (Ed.), *The father's role: Applied perspectives* (pp. 103–134). New York: Wiley.

Hetherington, E. M., Stanley-Hagan, M., & Anderson, E. R. (1989). Marital transitions: A child's perspective. *American Psychologist, 44*, 303–312.

Hill, C. R., & Stafford, F. P. (1980). Parental care of children: Time diary estimate of quantity, predictability, and variety. *Journal of Human Resources, 15*, 219–239.

Hill, J. P., Holmbeck, G. N., Marlow, I., Green, T. M., & Lynch, M. E. (1985). Pubertal status and parent-child relations in families of seventh-grade boys. *Journal of Early Adolescence, 5*, 31–44.

Hill, R. (1986). Life-cycle stages for types of single-parent families: On family development theory. *Family Relations, 35*, 19–29.

Hillenbrand, E. D. (1976). Father-absence in military families. *Family Coordinator, 25*, 451–458.

Hines, P. M. (1988). The family life cycle of poor black families. In B. Carter & M. McGoldrick (Eds.), *The changing family life cycle: A framework for family therapy* (pp. 513–544). New York: Gardner Press.

Hobart, C. (1987). Parent-child relations in remarried families. *Journal of Family Issues, 8*, 259–277.

Hochschild, A., & Machung, A. (1989). *The second shift: Working parents and the revolution at home*. New York: Viking.

Hodges, W. F. (1986). *Interventions for children of divorce*. New York: Wiley.

Hoffman, L. W. (1972). Early childhood experiences and women's achievement motives. *Journal of Social Issues, 28*, 129–155.

Hoffman, L. W. (1977). Changes in family roles, socialization, and sex differences. *American Psychologist, 32*, 644–657.

Hoffman, L. W. (1983). Increased fathering: Effects on the mother. In M. E. Lamb & A. Sagi (Eds.), *Fatherhood and family policy*. Hillsdale, NJ: Erlbaum.

Hoffman, L. W. (1984). Maternal employment and the young child. In M. Perlmutter (Ed.), *Parent-child interaction and parent-child relations in child development*. Hillsdale, NJ: Erlbaum.

Hoffman, L. W. (1987). The value of children to parents and childrearing patterns. *Social Behavior, 2*, 123–141.

Hoffman, L. W. (1989). Effects of maternal employment in the two-parent family. *American Psychologist, 44*, 283–292.

Hoffman, M. L. (1971a). Father-absence and conscience development. *Child Development, 42*, 400–406.

Hoffman, M. L. (1971b). Identification and conscience development. *Child Development, 42*, 1071–1082.

Hoffman, M. L. (1975). Altruistic behavior and the parent-child relationship. *Journal of Personality and Social Psychology, 31*, 937–943.

Hoffman, M. L. (1976). Empathy, role-taking, guilt, and development of altruistic motives. In T. Lickona (Ed.), *Moral development and behavior: Theory, research and social issues*. New York: Holt, Rinehart & Winston.

Hoffman, M. L. (1981). The role of the father in moral internalization. In M. E. Lamb

(Ed.), *The role of the father in child development* (2nd ed., pp. 359–378). New York: Wiley.

Hoffman, M. L., & Saltzstein, H. D. (1967). Parent discipline and the child's moral development. *Journal of Personality and Social Psychology, 5*, 45–57.

Hogan, J., & Quigley, A. M. (1986). Physical standards for employment and the courts. *American Psychologist, 41*, 1193–1217.

Holden, C. (1980). Identical twins reared apart. *Science, 207*, 1323–1328.

Holmes, D. L., Reich, J. N., & Pasternak, J. A. (1983). *The psychological development of infants born at risk*. Hillsdale, NJ: Erlbaum.

Holstein, C. E. (1972). The relation of children's moral judgment level to that of their parents and to communication patterns in the family. In R. C. Smart & M. S. Smart (Eds.), *Readings in child development and relationships*. New York: Macmillan.

Hopkins, J., Marcus, M., & Campbell, S. B. (1984). Postpartum depression: A critical review. *Psychological Bulletin, 95*, 498–515.

Horn, J. (1983). The Texas Adoption Project: Adopted children and their intellectual resemblance to biological and adoptive parents. *Child Development, 54*, 268–275.

Horner, M. S. (1972). Femininity and successful achievement: A basic inconsistency. In J. M. Bardwick, E. Douvan, M. S. Horner, & D. Guttman (Eds.), *Feminine personality and conflict*. Monterey, CA: Brooks/Cole.

Horner, M. S. (1978). The measurement and behavioral implications of fear of success in women. In J. W. Atkinson & J. O. Raynor (Eds.), *Personality, motivation and achievement* (pp. 41–70). Washington, DC: Hemisphere.

Houseknecht, S. K. (1987). Voluntary childlessness. In M. B. Sussman & S. K. Steinmetz (Eds.), *Handbook of marriage and the family* (pp. 369–395). New York: Plenum.

Houston, B., & Vevak, C. (1991). Cynical hostility: Developmental factors, psychosocial correlates and health factors. *Health Psychology, 10*, 9–17.

Huckel, L. H. (1984). Personality correlates of parental maltreatment. (Doctoral dissertation, University of Rhode Island). *Dissertation Abstracts International, 44*, 3592B.

Huebeck, B., Watson, J., & Russell, G. (1986). Father involvement and responsibility in family therapy. In M. E. Lamb (Ed.), *The father's role: Applied perspectives* (pp. 191–226). New York: Wiley.

Hughes, D., & Galinsky, E. (1988). Balancing work and family life: Researched corporate applications. In A. E. Gottfried & A. W. Gottfried (Eds.), *Maternal employment and children's development*. New York: Plenum.

Humphrey, L. L. (1986). Structural analysis of parent-child relationships in eating disorders. *Journal of Abnormal Psychology, 95*, 395–402.

Humphrey, M. (1977). Sex differences in attitude toward parenthood. *Human Relations, 30*, 737–749.

Hunter, E. J. (Ed.). (1978). *A report on the military family research conference*. San Diego, CA: Family Studies Branch, Naval Health Research Center.

Hunter, E. J. (Ed.). (1982). *Families under the flag*. New York: Praeger.

Hutchings, B., & Mednick, S. A. (1977). Criminality in adoptees and their adoptive and biological parents: A pilot study. In S. A. Mednick & K. O. Christiansen (Eds.), *Biosocial bases of criminal behavior* (pp. 127–141). New York: Gardner Press.

Huttunen, M. O., & Niskanen, P. (1978). Prenatal loss of father and psychiatric disorders. *Archives of General Psychiatry, 35*, 429–436.

Iannotti, R. J. (1985). Naturalistic and structured assessment of prosocial behavior in preschool children: The influence of empathy and perspective taking. *Developmental Psychology, 21*, 46–55.

Ilg, F. L., Ames, L. B., & Baker, S. M. (1981). *Child behavior*. New York: Harper & Row.

Inazu, J. K., & Fox, G. L. (1980). Maternal influence on the sexual behavior of teenage daughters. *Journal of Family Issues, 1*, 81–102.

Jacklin, C. N. (1989). Female and male: Issues of gender. *American Psychologist, 44*, 127–133.

Jacklin, C. N., Maccoby, E. E., & Doering, C. (1983). Neonatal sex-steroid hormones and timidity in 6–18 month old boys and girls. *Developmental Psychology, 16*, 163–168.

Jacklin, C. N., Maccoby, E. E., & Doering, C. (1984). Neonatal sex-steroid hormones and muscular strength of boys and girls in the first three years. *Developmental Psychobiology, 17*, 301–310.

Jaffe, E. D. (1983). Fathers and child welfare services: The forgotten client? In M. E. Lamb & A. Sagi (Eds.), *Fatherhood and family policy*. Hillsdale, NJ: Erlbaum.

John-Steiner, V. (1986). *Notebooks of the mind: Explorations of thinking*. Albuquerque: University of New Mexico Press.

Jones, M. C. (1957). The later careers of boys who were early or late maturers. *Child Development, 28*, 113–128.

Jones, M. C., & Mussen, P. H. (1957). Self-conceptions, motivations, and interpersonal attitudes of early and late maturing girls. *Child Development, 28*, 243–256.

Julian, T. W., McKenry, P. C., & Arnold, K. (1990). Psychosocial predictors of stress associated with the male midlife transition. *Sex Roles, 22*, 707–722.

Kagan, J. (1969). Sex typing during the preschool and early school years. In I. Janis, G. Mahl, J. Kagan, & R. Holt (Eds.), *Personality: Dynamics, development, and assessment*. New York: Brace & World.

Kagan, J. (1984). *The nature of the child*. New York: Basic Books.

Kagan, J. (1989). *Unstable ideas: Temperament, cognition, and self*. Cambridge, MA: Harvard University Press.

Kagan, J., & Moss, H. (1962). *Birth to maturity*. New York: Wiley. (Reprinted, New Haven: Yale University Press, 1983).

Kaliski, J., & Biller, H. B. (1978). The sex-role development of children with liberated parents. Unpublished manuscript, University of Rhode Island.

Kalter, N. (1990). *Growing up with divorce*. New York: Free Press.

Kaslow, F. W. (1981). Involving the peripheral father. In A. Gurman (Ed.), *Questions and answers in the practice of family therapy* (Vol. 1). New York: Brunner/Mazel.

Katchadourian, H. A. (1985). *Fundamentals of sexuality* (4th ed.). New York: Holt, Rinehart & Winston.

Katz, I. (1967). Socialization of academic motivation in minority group children. In D. Levine (Ed.), *Nebraska Symposium on Motivation, 1967* (pp. 133–191). Lincoln: University of Nebraska Press.

Katz, M. N., & Konner, M. J. (1981). The role of the father: An anthropological perspective. In M. E. Lamb (Ed.), *The role of the father in child development* (pp. 155–186). New York: Wiley.

Kaye, H. E., et al. (1967). Homosexuality in women. *Archives of General Psychiatry, 17*, 626–634.

Kayton, R., & Biller, H. B. (1971). Perception of parental sex-role behavior and psychopathology in adult males. *Journal of Consulting and Clinical Psychology, 36,* 235–237.

Kayton, R., & Biller, H. B. (1972). Sex-role development and psychopathology in adult males. *Journal of Consulting and Clinical Psychology, 38,* 308–310.

Kazdin, A. E. (1987). *Conduct disorder in childhood and adolescence.* Newbury Park, CA: Sage.

Kazdin, A. E. (1988a). Childhood depression. In E. J. Mach & L. Terdal (Eds.), *Behavioral assessment of childhood disorders* (2nd ed., pp. 157–196). New York: Guilford.

Kazdin, A. E. (1988b). *Child psychotherapy: Developing and identifying effective treatments.* New York: Pergamon.

Kazdin, A. E. (1989). Developmental psychopathology: Current research, issues, and directions. *American Psychologist, 44,* 180–187.

Keen, S. (1991). *Fire in the belly.* New York: Bantam.

Kellam, S. G., Ensminger, M. E., & Turner, R. J. (1977). Family structure and the mental health of children. *Archives of General Psychiatry, 34,* 1012–1022.

Keller, S., & Seraganian, P. (1984). Physical fitness and autonomic reactivity to psychosocial stress. *Journal of Psychosomatic Medicine, 28,* 279–287.

Kelly, F. J., & Baer, D. J. (1969). Age of male delinquents when father left home and recidivism. *Psychological Reports, 25,* 1010.

Kelly, J. A., & Worell, J. (1976). Parent behaviors related to masculine, feminine, and androgynous sex-role orientation. *Journal of Consulting and Clinical Psychology, 44,* 843–851.

Kelly, J. A., & Worell, J. (1977). New formulations of sex roles and androgyny: A critical review. *Journal of Consulting and Clinical Psychology, 45,* 1101–1115.

Kempe, C. H., Silverman, F. N., Steele, B. F., Droegemueller, W., & Silver, H. K. (1962). The battered child syndrome. *Journal of the American Medical Association, 181,* 17–24.

Kerschner, J. R., & Ledger, G. (1985). Effect of sex, intelligence, and style of thinking on creativity: A comparison of gifted and average I.Q. children. *Journal of Personality and Social Psychology, 48,* 1033–1040.

Keshet, H., & Rosenthal, R. (1978). Fathering after marital separation. *Social Work, 25,* 14–18.

Keyes, R. (1980). *The height of your life.* New York: Warner Books.

Kiernen, D. K., & Monro, B. (1987). Following the leaders: Parents' influence on adolescent religious activity. *Journal for the Scientific Study of Religion, 26,* 249–255.

Kimbal, K. K., & McCabe, M. E. (1981). Should we have children? A decision-making group for couples. *Personnel & Guidance Journal, 2,* 153–159.

Klaus, M. H., & Kennell, J. H. (1976). *Maternal-infant bonding.* St. Louis, MO: Mosby.

Klesges, R. C., Eck, L. H., Hanson, C. L., Haddock, C. K., & Klesges, L. M. (1990). Effects of obesity, social interactions, and physical environment on physical activity in preschoolers. *Health Psychology, 9,* 35–49.

Klinman, D. G. (1986). Fathers and the educational system. In M. E. Lamb (Ed.), *The father's role: Applied perspectives* (pp. 413–428). New York: Wiley.

Klinman, D. G., & Kohl, R. (1984). *Fatherhood U.S.A.: The first national guide to programs, services, and resources for and about fathers.* New York: Garland.

Kobasa, S. C., Maddi, S., & Kahn, S. (1982). Hardiness and health: A prospective study. *Journal of Personality and Social Psychology, 42,* 168–177.

Kobasa, S. C., Maddi, S., Puccetti, M. C., & Zola, M. (1985). Relative effectiveness of hardiness, exercise, and social support as resources against illness. *Journal of Psychosomatic Research, 29*, 525–533.

Koestner, R., Franz, C., & Weinberger, J. (1990). The family origins of empathic concerns: A 26-year longitudinal study. *Journal of Personality and Social Psychology, 58*, 709–717.

Koestner, R., Zuroff, D. C., & Powers, T. A. (1991). Family origins of adolescent self-criticism and its continuity into adulthood. *Journal of Abnormal Psychology, 100*, 191–197.

Kohlberg, L. (1966). A cognitive-developmental analysis of children's sex-role concepts and attitudes. In E. E. Maccoby (Ed.), *The development of sex differences* (pp. 81–173). Stanford, CA: Stanford University Press.

Kohlberg, L. (1969). *Stages in the development of moral thought and action*. New York: Holt, Rinehart & Winston.

Kohlberg, L. (1976). Moral stages and moralization: The cognitive-developmental approach. In T. Lickona (Ed.), *Moral development and behavior*. New York: Holt, Rinehart & Winston.

Kohlberg, L. (1981). *The philosophy of moral development*. New York: Harper & Row.

Kohlberg, L., & Zigler, E. (1967). The impact of cognitive maturity on the development of sex-role attitudes in the years four-eight. *Genetic Psychology Monographs, 75*, 89–165.

Kohn, M. L. (1979). The effects of social class on parental values and practices. In D. Reiss & H. A. Hoffman (Eds.), *The American family: Dying or developing* (pp. 45–68). New York: Plenum.

Kohn, M. L., & Schooler, C. (1978). The reciprocal effects of substantive complexity of work and intellectual flexibility: A longitudinal assessment. *American Journal of Sociology, 84*, 29–52.

Kopp, C. B., & Kaler, S. R. (1989). Risk in infancy: Origins and implications. *American Psychologist, 44*, 220–230.

Kornhaber, A. (1987). *Between parents and grandparents*. New York: Berkley Books.

Kornhaber, A., & Woodward, K. L. (1981). *Grandparents/grandchildren: The vital connection*. New York: Doubleday Anchor Books.

Kotelchuck, M. (1976). The infant's relationship to his father: Experimental evidence. In M. E. Lamb (Ed.), *The role of the father in child development* (pp. 329–344). New York: Wiley.

Kotelchuck, M., Zelazo, P., Kagan, J., & Spelke, E. (1975). Infant reaction to parental separations when left with familiar and unfamiliar adults. *Journal of Genetic Psychology, 126*, 255–260.

Kovacs, M. (1989). Affective disorders in children and adolescents. *American Psychologist, 44*, 209–215.

Krestan, J., & Bepko, C. (1988). Alcohol problems and the family life cycle. In B. Carter & M. McGoldrick (Eds.), *The changing family life cycle: A framework for family therapy* (pp. 483–511). New York: Gardner Press.

Lamaze, F. (1970). *Painless childbirth: The Lamaze method*. Chicago: Henry Renery.

Lamb, M. E. (1976). Interactions between eight-month-old children and their fathers and mothers. In M. E. Lamb (Ed.), *The role of the father in child development* (pp. 307–327). New York: Wiley.

Lamb, M. E. (1977). Father-infant and mother-infant interaction in the first year of life. *Child Development, 48*, 167–181.

Lamb, M. E. (1981a). The development of father-infant relationships. In M. E. Lamb (Ed.), *The role of the father in child development* (2nd ed., pp. 459–478). New York: Wiley.

Lamb, M. E. (Ed.). (1981b). *The role of the father in child development* (2nd ed.). New York: Wiley.

Lamb, M. E. (Ed.). (1982). *Nontraditional families: Parenting and child development.* Hillsdale, NJ: Erlbaum.

Lamb, M. E. (1983). Fathers of exceptional children. In M. Seligman (Ed.), *The family with a handicapped child: Understanding and treatment.* New York: Grune and Stratton.

Lamb, M. E. (1984). The father-child relationship. In G. Miller et al. (Eds.), *Paternal absence and fathers' roles* (pp. 85–90). Hearing before the Select Committee on Children, Youth and Families, House of Representatives, 98th Congress, 1st Session. Washington, DC: U.S. Government Printing Office.

Lamb, M. E. (Ed.). (1986). *The father's role: Applied perspectives.* New York: Wiley.

Lamb, M. E. (Ed.). (1987). *The father's role: Cross-cultural perspectives.* Hillsdale, NJ: Erlbaum.

Lamb, M. E., & Elster, A. B. (1985). Adolescent mother-father relationships. *Developmental Psychology, 21,* 768–773.

Lamb, M. E., & Sagi, A. (Eds.). (1983). *Fatherhood and family policy.* Hillsdale, NJ: Erlbaum.

Lamb, M. E., & Sutton-Smith, B. (Eds.). (1982). *Sibling relationships: Their nature and significance across the lifespan.* Hillsdale, NJ: Erlbaum.

Lamborn, S. D., Mants, N. S., Steinberg, L., & Dornbusch, S. M. (1991). Patterns of competence and adjustment among adolescents from authoritative, authoritarian, indulgent, and neglectful families. *Child Development, 62,* 1049–1065.

Lamke, L. K. (1989). Marital adjustment among rural couples: The role of expressiveness. *Sex roles, 21,* 579–590.

Landy, F. J. (1989). *Psychology of work behavior* (4th ed.). Chicago: Dorsey Press.

Larzelere, R. E., & Klein, D. M. (1987). Methodology. In M. B. Sussman & S. K. Steinmetz (Eds.), *Handbook of marriage and the family* (pp. 125–155). New York: Plenum.

Lasser, V., & Snarey, J. (1989). Ego development and perceptions of parent behavior in adolescent girls: A qualitative study of the transition from high school to college. *Journal of Adolescent Research, 4,* 319–355.

Leboyer, F. (1975). *Birth without violence.* New York: Knopf.

Lee, P. C. (1973). Male and female teachers in elementary schools: An ecological analysis. *Teachers College Record, 75,* 79–98.

Lee, P. C., & Wolinsky, A. L. (1973). Male teachers of young children: A preliminary empirical study. *Young Children, 28,* 342–352.

Lefkowitz, M. M., & Tesiny, E. P. (1984). Rejection and depression: Prospective and contemporaneous analyses. *Developmental Psychology 20,* 776–785.

Lefley, H. P. (1989). Family burden and family stigma in mental illness. *American Psychologist, 44,* 556–560.

LeMasters, E. E., & DeFrain, J. (1983). *Parents in contemporary America: A sympathetic view.* Homewood, IL: Dorsey.

Lepper, M. R., & Gurtner, J. (1989). Children and computers: Approaching the twenty-first century. *American Psychologist, 34,* 170–178.

Lerner, R. M., Karagenick, S. A., & Stuart, J. L. (1973). Relations among physical attractiveness, body attitudes, and self-concepts in male and female college students. *Journal of Psychology, 85,* 119–129.

Lerner, R. M., Orlos, T. R., & Knapp, J. R. (1976). Physical attractiveness, physical effectiveness, and self-concept in later adolescence. *Adolescence, 11,* 313–306.

Lerner, R. M., & Spanier, G. B. (Eds.). (1978). *Child influences on marital and family interaction: A life-span perspective.* New York: Academic Press.

Lessing, E. E., Zagorin, S. W., & Nelson, D. (1970). WISC subtest and IQ score correlates of father absence. *Journal of Genetic Psychology, 67,* 181–195.

Levant, R. F. (1987). Client-centered skills training for families. In R. F. Levant (Ed.), *Psychoeducational approaches to family therapy and counseling.* New York: Springer.

Levant, R. F. (1990). Psychological services designed for men: A psychoeducational approach. *Psychotherapy, 27,* 309–315.

Levant, R. F., & Doyle, G. F. (1983). An evaluation of a parent education program for fathers of school-aged children. *Family Relations, 32,* 29–37.

Levant, R. F., & Kelly, J. (1989). *Between father and child.* New York: Viking.

Levine, J. A. (1976). *Who will raise the children.* Philadelphia: Lippincott.

Levine, J. A., & Klinman, D. (1984). The Fatherhood Project. In D. Miller et al. (Eds.), *Paternal absence and fathers' roles* (pp. 115–121). Hearing before the Select Committee on Children, Youth and Families, House of Representatives, 98th Congress, 1st Session. Washington, DC: U.S. Government Printing Office.

Levine, J. A., Pleck, J. H., & Lamb, M. E. (1983). The Fatherhood Project. In M. E. Lamb & A. Sagi (Eds.), *Fatherhood and family policy.* Hillsdale, NJ: Erlbaum.

Levinson, D. (1988). Family violence in cross-cultural perspective. In V. B. Van Hasselt, R. L. Morrison, A. S. Bellack, & M. Hersen (Eds.), *Handbook of family violence* (pp. 435–455). New York: Plenum.

Levinson, D. J. (1978). *The seasons of a man's life.* New York: Ballantine.

Levinson, D. J. (1986). A conception of adult development. *American Psychologist, 41,* 3–13.

Levinson, H. N. (1984). *Smart but feeling dumb.* New York: Warner Books.

Levy-Shiff, R. (1982). The effects of father absence on young children in mother-headed families. *Child Development, 53,* 1400–1405.

Lewis, C., & O'Brien, M. (Eds.). (1987). *Reassessing fatherhood: New observations on fathers and the modern family.* London: Sage.

Lewis, K. (1978). Single-father families: Who they are and how they fare. *Child Welfare, 57,* 643–651.

Lewis, M., Feiring, C., & Weinraub, M. (1981). The father as a member of the child's social network. In M. E. Lamb (Ed.), *The role of the father in child development* (2nd ed., pp. 259–294). New York: Wiley.

Lewis, M., & Rosenblum, L. A. (Eds.). (1974). *The effect of the infant on its caregiver.* New York: Wiley.

Lewis, M., & Weinraub, M. (1976). The father's role in the infant's social network. In M. E. Lamb (Ed.), *The role of the father in child development.* New York: Wiley.

Lewis, R., & Roberts, C. (1982). Post-parental fathers in distress. In K. Solomon & N. Levy (Eds.), *Men in transition.* New York: Plenum.

Lickona, T. (1985). *Raising good children: From birth through adolescence.* New York: Bantam Books.

Liebert, R. M., & Spratkin, J. N. (1988). *The early window: Effects of television on children and youth* (3rd ed.). Elmsford, NY: Pergamon.

Lifshitz, M. (1976). Long-range effects of father's loss: The cognitive complexity of bereaved children and their school adjustment. *British Journal of Medical Psychology, 49*, 189–197.

Lips, H. M. (1983). Attitudes toward childbearing among women and men expecting their first child. *International Journal of Women's Studies, 6*, 119–129.

Lips, H. M. (1988). *Sex and gender: An introduction*. Mountain View, CA: Mayfield.

Liss, L. (1987). Families and the law. In M. B. Sussman & S. K. Steinmetz (Eds.), *Handbook of marriage and the family* (pp. 767–793). New York: Plenum.

Litton-Fox, G., & Inazu, J. K. (1980). Patterns and outcomes of mother-daughter communication about sexuality. *Journal of Social Issues, 36*, 45–63.

Lock, R. D. (1988). *Job search and taking care of your career direction*. Pacific Grove, CA: Brooks/Cole.

Lockheed, M. E. (1985). Women, girls, and computers: A first look at the evidence. *Sex Roles, 13*, 115–122.

Loehlin, J. C., & Nichols, R. C. (1976). *Heredity, environment, and personality: A study of 850 sets of twins*. Austin: University of Texas Press.

Loman, K. (1984). *Of cradles and careers: A guide to reshaping your job to include a child in your life*. Philadelphia: Franklin Press/LaLeche League International.

Lott, B. E. (1981). *Becoming a woman: The socialization of gender*. Springfield, IL: C.C. Thomas.

Lott, B. E. (1987). *Women's lives: Themes and variations in gender learning*. Belmont, CA: Brooks/Cole.

Lozoff, B. (1989). Nutrition and behavior. *American Psychologist, 44*, 231–236.

Lozoff, M. M. (1974). Fathers and autonomy in women. In R. B. Kundsin (Ed.), *Women and success* (pp. 103–109). New York: Morrow.

Lynn, D. B. (1974). *The father: His role in child development*. Belmont, CA: Brooks/Cole.

Lynn, D. B. (1979). *Daughters and parents: Past, present, and future*. Belmont, CA: Brooks/Cole.

Lytton, H. (1976). The socialization of two-year-old boys: Ecological findings. *Journal of Child Psychology and Psychiatry, 17*, 287–304.

Lytton, H. (1979). Disciplinary encounters between young boys and their mothers and fathers: Is there a contingency system? *Developmental Psychology, 15*, 256–268.

Lytton, H. (1990a). Child and parent effects in boys' conduct disorder: A reinterpretation. *Developmental Psychology, 26*, 683–697.

Lytton, H. (1990b). Child effects—still unwelcome: Response to Dodge and Wahler. *Developmental Psychology, 26*, 703–709.

Maccoby, E. E. (1984). Middle childhood in the context of the family. In W. A. Collins (Ed.), *Development during middle childhood* (pp. 184–239). Washington, DC: National Academy Press.

Maccoby, E. E. (1987). The varied meanings of "masculine" and "feminine." In J. M. Reinisch, L. A. Rosenblum, & S. A. Sanders (Eds.), *Masculinity/femininity*. New York: Oxford University Press.

Maccoby, E. E., Doering, C. H., Jacklin, C. N., & Kraemer, H. (1979). Concentrations of sex hormones in umbilical cord blood: Their relation to sex and birth order. *Child Development, 50*, 632–640.

Maccoby, E. E., & Jacklin, C. N. (1973). Stress activity and proximity seeking: Sex differences in the year-old child. *Child Development, 40*, 34–42.

Maccoby, E. E., & Jacklin, C. N. (Eds.) (1974a). *The development of sex differences.* Stanford, CA: Stanford University Press.

Maccoby, E. E., & Jacklin, C. N. (1974b). *The psychology of sex differences.* Stanford, CA: Stanford University Press.

Maccoby, E. E., & Martin, J. A. (1983). Socialization in the context of the family: Parent-child interaction. In P. H. Mussen (Ed.), *Handbook of child psychology* (4th ed., Vol. 4), New York: Wiley.

MacDonald, K. (1987). Parent-child physical play with rejected, neglected, and popular boys. *Developmental Psychology, 23,* 705–711.

Machtlinger, V. T. (1981). The father in psychoanalytic theory. In M. E. Lamb (Ed.), *The role of the father in child development* (pp. 113–153). New York: Wiley.

Mackey, W. C. (1985). *Fathering behaviors: The dynamics of the man-child bond.* New York: Plenum.

Mackey, W. C., & Day, R. D. (1979). Some indicators of fathering behaviors in the United States: A cross-cultural examination of adult male-child interaction. *Journal of Marriage and the Family, 41,* 287–299.

Main, M., & Cassidy, J. (1988). Categories of response in reunion with the parent at age 6: Predictable from infant attachment-classifications and stable over a 1-month period. *Developmental Psychology, 24,* 415–426.

Main, M., & Weston, D. R. (1981). The quality of the toddler's relationship to mother and to father: Related to conflict behavior and the readiness to establish new relationships. *Child Development, 52,* 932–940.

Maklan, D. M. (1977). *The four-day workweek.* New York: Praeger.

Margalit, M. (1985). Perceptions of parents' behavior, familial satisfaction, and sense of coherence in hyperactive children. *Journal of School Psychology, 23,* 355–364.

Marone, N. (1988). *How to father a successful daughter.* New York: McGraw-Hill.

Martel, L. F., & Biller, H. B. (1987). *Stature and stigma: The biopsychosocial development of short males.* Lexington, MA: Lexington Books, D.C. Heath.

Martin, H. P. (1980). The consequences of being abused and neglected: How the child fares. In C. H. Kempe & R. E. Helfer (Eds.), *The battered child* (3rd ed.). Chicago: University of Chicago Press.

Maslow, A. H. (1971). *The father reaches of human nature.* New York: Viking.

Masters, W. H., & Johnson, V. E. (1966). *Human sexual response.* Boston: Little, Brown.

Masters, W. H. & Johnson, V. E. (1970). *Human sexual inadequacy.* Boston: Little, Brown.

Mattessich, P., & Hill, R. (1987). Lifecycle and family development. In M. B. Sussman & S. K. Steinmetz (Eds.), *Handbook of marriage and the family* (pp. 437–469). New York: Plenum.

McAdoo, H. P. (1978). Factors related to stability in upwardly mobile black families. *Journal of Marriage and the Family, 40,* 761–776.

McAdoo, H. P. (Ed.). (1981). *Black families.* Beverly Hills, CA: Sage.

McClelland, D. C., Constantian, C. A., Regalado, D., & Stone, C. (1978, June). Making it to maturity. *Psychology Today, 12,* pp. 42–46.

McCord, J. (1979). Some child-rearing antecedents of criminal behavior in adult men. *Journal of Personality and Social Psychology, 37,* 1470–1486.

McCord, J., McCord, W., & Thurber, E. (1962). Some effects of paternal absence on male children. *Journal of Abnormal and Social Psychology, 64,* 361–369.

McCullough, P., & Rutenberg, S. (1988). Launching children and moving on. In B. Carter & M. McGoldrick (Eds.), *The changing family life cycle: A framework for family therapy* (pp. 285–309). New York: Gardner Press.

McDonald, G. W. (1980). Parental power and adolescent-parental identification: A reexamination. *Journal of Marriage and the Family, 42*, 289–296.

McEvan, K. L., Costello, C. G., & Taylor, P. J. (1987). Adjustment to infertility. *Journal of Abnormal Psychology, 96*, 108–116.

McGlaughlin, P., & Micklin, M. (1983). The timing of the first birth and changes in personal efficacy. *Journal of Marriage and the Family, 45*, 47–55.

McGoldrick, M. (1988a). Ethnicity and the family life cycle. In B. Carter & M. McGoldrick (Eds.), *The changing family life cycle: A framework for family therapy* (pp. 69–90). New York: Gardner Press.

McGoldrick, M. (1988b). Women and the family life cycle. In B. Carter & M. McGoldrick (Eds.), *The changing family life cycle: A framework for family therapy* (pp. 29–68). New York: Gardner Press.

McGoldrick, M., & Carter, B. (1988). Forming a remarried family. In B. Carter & M. McGoldrick (Eds.), *The changing family life cycle: A framework for family therapy* (pp. 399–429). New York: Gardner Press.

McHale, S. M., & Huston, T. L. (1984). Men and women as parents: Sex-role orientations, employment, and parent roles with infants. *Child Development, 55*, 1349–1361.

McKenry, P., Arnold, K., Julian, T., & Kuo, J. (1987). Interpersonal influences on the well-being of men at mid-life. *Family Perspective, 21*, 225–233.

McLoyd, V. (1989). Socialization and development in a changing economy: The effects of paternal job and income loss on children. *American Psychologist, 44*, 293–302.

McNeil, J. D. (1964). Programmed instruction versus usual classroom procedures in teaching boys to read. *American Education Research Journal, 1*, 113–119.

Mednick, S. A. (1973). Breakdown in high-risk subjects: Familial and early environment factors. *Journal of Abnormal Psychology, 82*, 469–475.

Meichenbaum, D. (1977). *Cognitive-behavior modification: An integrative approach.* New York: Plenum.

Melina, L. R. (1986). *Raising adopted children.* New York: McGraw-Hill.

Meltzoff, A. N. (1988). Infant imitation and memory: Nine-month-olds in immediate and deferred tests. *Child Development, 59*, 217–225.

Meltzoff, A. N., & Moore, M. K. (1983). Newborn infants imitate adult facial gestures. *Child Development, 54*, 702–709.

Menken, J., Trussell, J., & Larsen, V. (1986). Age and infertility. *Science, 233*, 1389–1394.

Menning, B. (1975). The infertile couple: A plea for advocacy. *Child Welfare, 54*, 459–460.

Meyer, D. J. (1986). Fathers of children with mental handicaps. In M. E. Lamb (Ed.), *The father's role: Applied perspectives.* New York: Wiley.

Miller, B. C. (1987). Marriage, family, and fertility. In M. B. Sussman & S. K. Steinmetz (Eds.), *Handbook of marriage and the family* (pp. 565–595). New York: Plenum.

Miller, L., & Roll, R. (1977). Relationships between sons' feelings of being understood by their fathers and measures of sons' psychological functioning. *Journal of Genetic Psychology, 130*, 19–25.

Minnett, A. M., Vandell, D. L., & Santrock, J. W. (1983). The effects of sibling status on sibling interaction: Influence of birth order, age spacing, sex of the child, and sex of the sibling. *Child Development, 54*, 1064–1072.

Minuchin, S. (1974). *Families and family therapy.* Cambridge, MA: Harvard University Press.

Mischel, W. (1961a). Delay of gratification, need for achievement, and acquiescence in another culture. *Journal of Abnormal and Social Psychology, 62*, 543–552.

Mischel, W. (1961b). Father-absence and delay of gratification. *Journal of Abnormal and Social Psychology, 62*, 116–124.

Mishler, E. G., & Waxler, N. E. (1968). *Interaction in families.* New York: Wiley.

Moen, P., & Dempster-McClain, D. I. (1987). Employed parents: Role strain, work time, and preferences for working less. *Journal of Marriage and the Family, 49*, 579–590.

Money, J. (1987). Sin, sickness, or status. Homosexual gender identity and psychoendocrinology. *American Psychologist, 42*, 384–399.

Money, J., & Ehrhardt, A. (1972). *Man and woman: Boy and girl.* Baltimore, MD: Johns Hopkins University Press.

Money, J., & Tucker, P. (1975). *Sexual signatures.* Boston: Little, Brown.

Monroe, R. (1988). *Creative brainstorms.* New York: Irvington.

Montemayor, R., & Brownle, J. R. (1987). Fathers, mothers, and adolescents: Gender-based differences in parental roles during adolescence. *Journal of Youth and Adolescence, 16*, 281–292.

Moore, M. L. (1992). The family as portrayed on prime-time television, 1947–1990: Structure and characteristics. *Sex Roles, 26*, 41–61.

Moran, P., & Barclay, A. (1988). Effect of fathers' absence on delinquent boys: Dependency and hypermasculinity. *Psychological Reports, 62*, 115–121.

Moreland, J., & Schwebel, A. (1981). A gender-role transcendent perspective on fathering. *The Counseling Psychologist, 9*, 45–54.

Moynihan, D. P. (1965). *The Negro family: The case for national action.* Washington, DC: U.S. Department of Labor.

Murstein, B. I. (1982). Marital choice. In B. B. Wolman (Ed.), *Handbook of developmental psychology* (pp. 652–666). Englewood Cliffs, NJ: Prentice-Hall.

Murstein, B. I., & Williams, P. (1983). Sex roles and marital adjustment. *Small Group Behavior, 14*, 77–93.

Mussen, P. H., Bouterline-Young, H., Gaddini, R., & Morante, L. (1963). The influences of father-son relationships on adolescent personality and attitudes. *Journal of Child Psychology and Psychiatry, 4*, 3–16.

Nash, J. (1965). The father in contemporary culture and current psychological literature. *Child Development, 36*, 261–297.

Nash, J. (1978). *Developmental psychology: A psychobiological approach* (2nd ed.). Englewood Cliffs, NJ: Prentice-Hall.

Nelsen, E. A., & Vangen, P. M. (1971). The impact of father-absence upon heterosexual behaviors and social development of preadolescent girls in a ghetto environment. *Proceedings of the 79th Annual Convention of the American Psychological Association, 6*, 165–166.

Nelson, M., & Nelson, G. K. (1982). Problems of equity in the reconstituted family: A social exchange analysis. *Family Relations, 31*, 223–231.

Neugarten, B. L., & Neugarten, D. A. (1987, May). The changing meanings of age. *Psychology Today, 21*, pp. 29–33.

Newcomer, S., & Udry, J. R. (1987). Parental marital status effects in adolescent sexual behavior. *Journal of Marriage and the Family, 49*, 235–240.

Nicholls, J. G. (Ed.). (1983). *The development of achievement motivation.* Greenwich, CT: JAI Press.

Nicholls, J. G., & Miller, A. J. (Eds.). (1983). *Children's achievement motivation.* Greenwich, CT: Guilford Press.

Nichols, M. P. (1984). *Family therapy: Concepts and methods.* New York: Gardner Press.

Nida, P. C. (1983). *Families on the move: Human factors in relocation.* Dubuque, IA: Kendal-Hunt.

Novak, W. (1981). *The great American man shortage.* New York: Basic Books.

Offer, D. (1981). *The adolescent.* New York: Basic Books.

O'Hanlon, W., & Weiner-Davis, M. (1989). *In search of solutions: A new direction in psychotherapy.* New York: Norton.

Olds, S. W. (1989). *Working parents' survival guide.* Rocklin, CA: Prima Publishing.

Olweus, D. (1980). Familial and temperamental determinants of aggressive behavior in adolescent boys: A causal analysis. *Developmental Psychology, 16*, 644–666.

Osherson, S. (1986). *Finding our fathers: The unfinished business of manhood.* New York: Free Press.

Osherson, S. (1992). *Wrestling with love: How men struggle with intimacy, with women, children, parents and each other.* New York: Fawcett.

Oshman, H. P., & Manosevitz, N. (1976). Father absence: Effect of stepfathers upon psychosocial development in males. *Developmental Psychology, 12*, 479–480.

Osofsky, J. D., & O'Connell, E. J. (1972). Parent-child interaction: Daughters' effects upon mothers' and fathers' behaviors. *Developmental Psychology, 1*, 157–168.

Osofsky, H. J., Osofsky, J. D., Culp, R., Krantz, K., & Tobiasen, J. (1985). Transition to parenthood: Risk factors for parents and infants. *Journal of Psychosomatic Obstetrics & Gynecology, 4*, 303–315.

Palkovitz, R. (1985). Fathers' birth attendance, early contact, and extended contact with their newborn. *Child Development, 36*, 392–406.

Parish, T. S., & Copeland, T. (1980). Locus of control and father loss. *Journal of Genetic Psychology, 136*, 147–148.

Parish, T. S., & Dostal, J. W. (1980a). Evaluations of self and parent figures by children from intact, divorced, and reconstituted families. *Journal of Youth and Adolescence, 9*, 347–351.

Parish, T. S., & Dostal, J. W. (1980b). Relationships between evaluations of self and parents by children from intact and divorced families. *Journal of Psychology, 104*, 35–38.

Parke, R. D. (1979). Perspectives on father-infant interaction. In J. D. Osofsky (Ed.), *The handbook of infant development* (pp. 549–590). New York: Wiley.

Parke, R. D. (1981). *Fathers.* Cambridge, MA: Harvard University Press.

Parke, R. D. (1982). Theoretical models of child abuse: Their implications for prediction, prevention, and modification. In R. Starr (Ed.), *Prediction of abuse.* New York: Ballinger.

Parke, R. D. (1985). Fathers, families, and children: New perspectives. In M. Green (Ed.), *The psychosocial aspects of the family: The new pediatrics.* Lexington, MA: Lexington Books, D.C. Heath.

Parke, R. D. (1986). Fathers: An intrafamilial perspective. In M. W. Yogman & T. B.

Brazelton (Eds.), *In support of families* (pp. 59–68). Cambridge, MA: Harvard University Press.

Parke, R. D., & Beitel, A. (1986). Hospital-based intervention for fathers. In M. E. Lamb (Ed.), *The father's role: Applied perspectives* (pp. 293–323). New York: Wiley.

Parke, R. D., MacDonald, K. D., Beitel, A., & Bhavnagri, N. (1988). The role of the family in the development of peer relationships. In R. D. Peters & R. J. McMahan (Eds.), *Marriages and families: Behavioral treatments and processes*. New York: Brunner/Mazel.

Parke, R. D., & Sawin, D. B. (1980). The family in early infancy: Social interactional and attitudinal analysis. In F. A. Pedersen (Ed.), *The father-infant relationship: Observational studies in the family setting*. New York: Praeger.

Parke, R. D., & Tinsley, B. R. (1981). The father's role in infancy: Determinants of involvement in caregiving and play. In M. E. Lamb (Ed.), *The role of the father in child development* (pp. 429–459). New York: Wiley.

Parker, G. (1983). *Parental overprotection: A risk factor in psychosocial development*. New York: Grune & Stratton.

Parker, H., & Parker, S. (1986). Father-daughter sexual abuse: An emerging perspective. *American Journal of Orthopsychiatry, 56*, 531–549.

Parsons, T. (1955). Family structure and socialization of the child. In T. Parsons and R. F. Bales (Eds.), *Family, socialization, and interaction process* (pp. 25–131). Glencoe, IL: Free Press.

Pasley, K., & Ihinger-Tallman, M. (Eds.). (1987). *Remarriage and step-parenting*. New York: Guilford.

Pastor, D. L. (1981). The quality of mother-infant attachment and its relationship to toddlers' initial sociability with peers. *Developmental Psychology, 17*, 326–335.

Patterson, G. R., DeBaryshe, B. D., & Ramsey, F. (1989). A developmental perspective on antisocial behavior. *American Psychologist, 44*, 325–329.

Patterson, G. R., & Stouthamer-Loeber, M. (1984). The correlation of family management practices and delinquency. *Child Development, 55*, 1299–1307.

Pawson, M., & Morris, N. (1972). The role of the father in pregnancy and labor. In N. Morris (Ed.), *Psychological medicine in obstetrics and gynecology*. Basel: Karger.

Peck, E. (1971). *The baby trap*. New York: Bernard Geis.

Pedersen, F. A. (1966). Relationships between father-absence and emotional disturbance in male military dependents. *Merrill-Palmer Quarterly, 12*, 321–331.

Pedersen, F. A. (1976). Does research on children reared in father-absent homes yield information on father influences? *Family Coordinator, 25*, 458–466.

Pedersen, F. A. (Ed.). (1980). *The father-infant relationship: Observational studies in the family setting*. New York: Praeger.

Pedersen, F. A. (1981). Father influences viewed in family context. In M. E. Lamb (Ed.), *The role of the father in child development* (pp. 295–317). New York: Wiley.

Pedersen, F. A., Anderson, B. J., & Cain, R. L. (1980). Parent-infant and husband-wife interactions observed at age five months. In F. Pedersen (Ed.), *The father-infant relationship: Observational studies in the family setting*. New York: Praeger.

Pedersen, F. A., Cain, R., Zaslow, M., & Anderson, P. (1983). Variation in infant expectancy associated with alternative family role organization. In L. Laosa & I. Sigel (Eds.), *Families as learning environments for children*. New York: Plenum.

Pedersen, F. A., & Robson, K. S. (1969). Father participation in infancy. *American Journal of Orthopsychiatry, 39*, 466–472.

Pedersen, F. A., Rubinstein, J., & Yarrow, L. J. (1979). Infant development in father-absent families. *Journal of Genetic Psychology, 135*, 51–61.

Pedersen, F. A., Suwalsky, J. T. D., Cain, R. L., Zaslow, M. J., & Rabinovich, B. A. (1987). Paternal care of infants during maternal separations: Associations with father-infant interaction at one year. *Psychiatry, 60*, 193–205.

Pelton, L. (Ed.) (1981). *The social context of child abuse and neglect.* New York: Human Sciences Press.

Peterson, G. H., Mehl, L. E., & Leiderman, P. H. (1979). The role of some birth-related variables in father attachment. *American Journal of Orthopsychiatry, 49*, 330–338.

Peterson, G. W., & Rollins, B. C. (1987). Parent-child socialization. In M. B. Sussman & S. K. Steinmetz (Eds.), *Handbook of marriage and the family* (pp. 471–507). New York: Plenum.

Peterson, J. L., & Zill, N. (1986). Marital disruption, parent-child relationships, and behavior problems in children. *Journal of Marriage and the Family, 46*, 295–307.

Peterson, L., Farmer, J., & Kashani, H. (1990). Parental injury prevention endeavors: A function of health beliefs? *Health Psychology, 9*, 177–191.

Peterson, P. L. (1977). Interactive effects of student anxiety, achievement orientation, and teacher behavior on student achievement and attitude. *Journal of Educational Psychology, 69*, 779–792.

Peterson, S. L. (1979). *Self-defense for women: The West Point way.* New York: Simon & Schuster.

Peterson, S. L. (1984). *Self-defense for women: How to stay safe and fight back.* New York: Leisure Press.

Pettigrew, T. F. (1964). *A profile of the Negro American.* Princeton, NJ: Van Nostrand.

Pettit, G. S., Dodge, K. A., & Brown, M. M. (1988). Early family experience, social problem-solving patterns, and children's social competence. *Child Development, 59*, 107–120.

Phares, V. (1992). Where's Poppa?: The relative lack of attention to the role of fathers in child and adolescent psychotherapy. *American Psychologist, 47*, 656–664.

Phares, V., & Compas, B. E. (1992). The role of fathers in child and adolescent psychopathology: Make room for daddy. *Psychological Bulletin, 111*, 387–412.

Piaget, J. (1954). *The construction of reality in the child.* New York: Basic Books.

Piaget, J. (1967). *The child's construction of the world.* Totowa, NJ: Littlefield, Adams.

Piotrowski, C. S. (1979). *Work and the family system: A naturalistic study of working-class and lower middle-class families.* New York: Free Press.

Piotrowski, C. S., & Crits-Christoph, P. C. (1982). Women's jobs and family adjustment. In J. Aldous (Ed.), *Two paychecks: Life in dual-earner families.* Beverly Hills, CA: Sage.

Piotrowski, C. S., Rapoport, R. N., & Rapoport, R. (1987). Families and work. In M. B. Sussman & S. K. Steinmetz (Eds.), *Handbook of marriage and the family* (pp. 251–283). New York: Plenum.

Pipes, P. (1988). Nutrition in childhood. In S. R. Williams & B. S. Worthington-Roberts (Eds.), *Nutritition throughout the life cycle.* St. Louis, MO: Times Mirror/Mosby.

Pleck, J. H. (1981). *The myth of masculinity.* Cambridge, MA: MIT Press.

Pleck, J. H. (1984). *Working wives and family well-being.* Beverly Hills, CA: Sage.

Pleck, J. H. (1985). *Working wives, working husbands*. Beverly Hills, CA: Sage.

Pleck, J. H. (1986). Employment and fatherhood. In M. E. Lamb (Ed.), *The father's role: Applied perspectives* (pp. 384–412). New York: Wiley.

Pleck, J. H., & Staines, G. L. (1985). Work schedules and family life in two-earner couples. *Journal of Family Issues, 6*, 61–82.

Plomin, R. (1987). Developmental behavioral genetics and infancy. In J. D. Osofsky (Ed.), *Handbook of infant development*. New York: Wiley.

Plomin, R. (1989). Environment and genes: Determinants of behavior. *American Psychologist, 44*, 103–111.

Plomin, R., & Thompson, L. (1987). Life-span developmental behavioral genetics. In P. B. Baltes, D. L. Featherman, & R. M. Lerner (Eds.), *Life-span development and behavior* (Vol. 7). Hillsdale, NJ: Erlbaum.

Pogrebin, L. C. (1983). *Family politics: Love and power on an intimate frontier*. New York: McGraw-Hill.

Portnoy, S. M., Biller, H. B., & Davids, A. (1972). The influence of the child-care worker in residential treatment. *American Journal of Orthopsychiatry, 42*, 719–722.

Power, R. G. (1985). Mother- and father-infant play: A developmental analysis. *Child Development, 56*, 1514–1524.

Pratt, L. (1973). Child-rearing methods and children's health behavior. *Journal of Health and Social Behavior, 14*, 61–69.

Preston, R. (1962). Reading achievement of German and American children. *School and Society, 90*, 350–354.

Prochaska, J. O. (1984). *Systems of psychotherapy: A transtheoretical analysis* (2nd ed.). Homewood, IL: Dorsey Press.

Pruett, K. D. (1987). *The nurturing father*. New York: Warner Books.

Pruett, K. D., & Litzenberger, B. (1992). Latency development in children of primary nurturant fathers: Eight year follow-up. *Psychoanalytic Study of the Child, 47*, 85–101.

Purves, A. L. (1973). *Literature education in ten countries*. New York: Wiley.

Radin, N. (1972). Father-child interaction and the intellectual functioning of four-year-old boys. *Developmental Psychology, 6*, 353–361.

Radin, N. (1973). Observed paternal behaviors as antecedents of intellectual functioning in young boys. *Developmental Psychology, 8*, 369–376.

Radin, N. (1976). The role of the father in cognitive, academic, and intellectual development. In M. E. Lamb (Ed.), *The role of the father in child development* (pp. 237–276). New York: Wiley.

Radin, N. (1981). The role of the father in cognitive, academic, and intellectual development. In M. E. Lamb (Ed.), *The role of the father in child development* (2nd ed., pp. 379–427). New York: Wiley.

Radin, N. (1982). Primary caregiving and role-sharing fathers of preschoolers. In M. E. Lamb (Ed.). *Nontraditional families: Parenting and child development*. Hillsdale, NJ: Erlbaum.

Radin, N., & Goldsmith, R. (1985). Caregiving fathers of preschoolers: Four years later. *Merrill-Palmer Quarterly, 31*, 375–383.

Radin, N., Oyserman, D., & Benn, R. (1991). Grandfathers, teen mothers, and children under two. In P. K. Smith (Ed.), *The psychology of grandparenthood: An international perspective* (pp. 85–89). London: Routledge.

Radin, N., & Russell, G. (1983). Increased father participation and child development outcomes. In M. E. Lamb & A. Sagi (Eds.), *Fatherhood and family policy.* Hillsdale, NJ: Erlbaum.

Rainwater, L., & Yancey, W. L. (1967). *The Moynihan Report and the politics of controversy.* Cambridge, MA: MIT Press.

Rapoport, R., Rapoport, R. N., Strelitz, Z., & Kew, S. (1977). *Fathers, mothers, and society: Towards new alliances.* New York: Basic Books.

Raschke, H. J. (1987). Divorce. In M. B. Sussman & S. K. Steinmetz (Eds.), *Handbook of marriage and the family* (pp. 597–624). New York: Plenum.

Raschke, H. J., & Raschke, V. J. (1979). Family conflict and children's self-concepts: A comparison of intact and single-parent families. *Journal of Marriage and the Family, 41,* 367–374.

Ray, S. A., & McLoyd, V. C. (1986). Fathers in hard times: The impact of unemployment and poverty on paternal and marital relations. In M. E. Lamb (Ed.), *The father's role: Applied perspectives* (pp. 339–383). New York: Wiley.

Rebelsky, R., & Hanks, C. (1971). Fathers' verbal interaction with infants in the first three months of life. *Child Development, 42,* 63–68.

Redican, W. K., & Taub, D. M. (1981). Male parental care in monkeys and apes. In M. E. Lamb (Ed.), *The role of the father in child development* (2nd ed., pp. 203–258). New York: Wiley.

Reis, M., & Gold, D. (1977). Relation of paternal availability to problem solving and sex-role orientation in young boys. *Psychological Reports, 40,* 823–829.

Rendina, I., & Dickerscheid, J. D. (1976). Father involvement with first-born infants. *Family Coordinator, 25,* 373–379.

Resnick, J. L., Resnick, M. B., Parker, A. B., & Wilson, J. (1978). Fathering classes: A psychoeducational model. *The Counseling Psychologist, 7,* 56–60.

Reuter, M. W., & Biller, H. B. (1973). Perceived paternal nurturance-availability and personality adjustment among college males. *Journal of Consulting and Clinical Psychology, 40,* 339–342.

Rice, M. L. (1989). Children's language acquisition. *American Psychologist, 44,* 149–156.

Roberts, G. C. (1983). Children's achievement motivation in sports. In J. Nicholls (Ed.), *The development of achievement motivation.* Greenwich, CT: JAI Press.

Roberts, P., & Newton, P. M. (1987). Levinsonian studies of women's adult development. *Psychology and Aging, 2,* 154–163.

Robinson, B. E. (1984). The contemporary American stepfather: A review of the literature. *Family Relations, 33,* 381–388.

Robinson, B. E., & Barrett, R. L. (1986). *The developing father: Emerging roles in contemporary society.* New York: Guilford.

Rogers, C. R. (1980). *A way of being.* Boston: Houghton Mifflin.

Rose, S. A., & Ruff, H. A. (1987). Cross-modal abilities in human infants. In J. D. Osofsky (Ed.), *Handbook of infant development* (2nd ed.). New York: Wiley.

Rosen, R., & Hall, E. (1984). *Sexuality.* New York: Random House.

Rosenberg, M. (1965). *Society and the adolescent self-image.* Princeton, NJ: Princeton University Press.

Rosenberg, M. S., & Repucci, N. D. (1985). Primary prevention of child abuse. *Journal of Consulting and Clinical Psychology, 53,* 576–585.

Rosenfield, A., & Stark, E. (1987, May). The prime of our lives. *Psychology Today, 21,* pp. 62–70.

Rosenthal, K., & Keshet, H. F. (1981). *Fathers without partners: A study of fathers and the family after marital separation*. Totowa, NJ: Rowman & Littlefield.

Ross, G., Kagan, J., Zelazo, P., & Kotelchuck, M. (1975). Separation protest in infants in home and laboratory. *Developmental Psychology, 11*, 256–257.

Ross, J. M. (1982a). From mother to father: The boys' search for a generative identity and the oedipal era. In S. H. Cath, A. R. Gurwitt, & J. M. Ross (Eds.), *Father and child: Developmental and clinical perspectives* (pp. 189–204). Boston: Little, Brown.

Ross, J. M. (1982b). In search of fathering: A review. In S. H. Cath, A. R. Gurwitt, & J. M. Ross (Eds.), *Father and child: Developmental and clinical perspectives* (pp. 21–33). Boston: Little, Brown.

Rothbart, M. K., & Maccoby, E. E. (1966). Parents' differential reactions to sons and daughters. *Journal of Personality and Social Psychology, 4*, 237–243.

Rubenstein, C. (1980, January). The children of divorce as adults. *Psychology Today, 14*, pp. 74–75.

Rubin, J., & Rubin, C. (1989). *When families fight: How to handle conflict with those you love*. New York: Morrow.

Rubin, J. Z., Provenzano, E. J., & Luria, Z. (1974). The eye of the beholder: Parental views on sex of newborns. *American Journal of Orthopsychiatry, 43*, 720–731.

Rubin, Z. (1982, May). Fathers and sons. The search for reunion. *Psychology Today, 16*, pp. 23–27.

Russell, G. (1978). The father role and its relation to masculinity, femininity, and androgyny. *Child Development, 49*, 1174–1181.

Russell, G. (1982). Shared-caregiving families: An Australian study. In M. E. Lamb (Ed.), *Nontraditional families: Parenting and child development*. Hillsdale, NJ: Erlbaum.

Russell, G. (1983). *The changing role of fathers?* St. Lucia, Queensland: University of Queensland Press.

Russell, G. (1986). Primary caretaking and role-sharing fathers. In M. E. Lamb (Ed.), *The father's role: Applied perspectives* (pp. 29–57). New York: Wiley.

Russell, G., & Radin, N. (1983). Increased paternal participation: The father's perspective. In M. E. Lamb & A. Sagi (Eds.), *Fatherhood and family policy*. Hillsdale, NJ: Erlbaum.

Rutherford, E. E., & Mussen, P. H. (1968). Generosity in nursery school boys. *Child Development, 39*, 755–765.

Rutter, M. (1979). Maternal deprivation, 1972–1978: New findings, new concepts, new approaches. *Child Development, 50*, 283–305.

Rutter, M. (1983). School effects on pupil progress: Research findings and policy implications. *Child Development, 54*, 1–29.

Rutter, M. (1986). The developmental psychopathology of depression: Issues and perspectives. In M. Rutter, C. E. Izard, & P. B. Read (Eds.), *Depression in young people: Developmental and clinical perspectives* (pp. 3–30). New York: Guilford.

Rutter, M., & Madge, N. (1976). *Cycles of disadvantage: A review of research*. London: Heinemann.

Rutter, M., Maugham, B., Mortimer, P., & Ouston, J. (1979). *Fifteen thousand hours*. London: Open Books.

Rypma, C., & Kolarik, G. (1981). A training project for fathers. In R. A. Lewis (Ed.), *Men in difficult times*. Englewood Cliffs, NJ: Prentice-Hall.

Saghir, M. T., & Robbins, F. (1973). *Male and female homosexuality*. Baltimore: Williams & Wilkins.

Sagi, A. (1982). Antecedents and consequences of various degrees of paternal involvement in child rearing: The Israeli project. In M. E. Lamb (Ed.), *Nontraditional families: Parenting and child development*. Hillsdale, NJ: Erlbaum.

Santrock, J. W. (1972). Relation of type and onset of father-absence to cognitive development. *Child Development, 43*, 455–469.

Santrock, J. W. (1975). Father-absence, perceived maternal behavior, and moral development in boys. *Child Development, 46*, 753–757.

Santrock, J. W. (1989). *Life-span development* (3rd ed.). Dubuque, IA: Wm. C. Brown.

Santrock, J. W., & Sitterle, K. A. (1987). Parent-child relationships in stepmother families. In K. Pasley & M. Ihinger-Tallman (Eds.), *Remarriage and stepparenting* (pp. 135–154). New York: Guilford.

Santrock, J. W., Sitterle, K. A., & Warshak, R. A. (1988). Parent-child relationships in stepfather families. In P. Bronstein & C. Cowan (Eds.), *The father's role today: Men's changing roles in the family*. New York: Wiley.

Santrock, J. W., & Warshak, R. A. (1979). Father custody and social development in boys and girls. *Journal of Social Issues, 35*, 112–125.

Santrock, J. W., & Warshak, R. A. (1986). Development, relationships, and legal/clinical considerations in father custody families. In M. E. Lamb (Ed.), *The father's role: Applied perspectives* (pp. 135–163). New York: Wiley.

Santrock, J. W., Warshak, R. A., & Elliot, G. L. (1982). Social development and parent-child interaction in father-custody and stepmother families. In M. E. Lamb (Ed.), *Nontraditional families: Parenting and child development*. Hillsdale, NJ: Erlbaum.

Santrock, J. W., Warshak, R. A., Lindbergh, C., & Meadows, L. (1982). Children's and parents' observed social behavior in stepfather families. *Child Development, 53*, 472–480.

Sarason, I. (1976). *A guide for foster parents*. New York: Human Sciences Press.

Scarf, M. (1987). *Intimate partners: Patterns in love and marriage*. New York: Random House.

Scarr, S. (1984). *Mother care/other care*. New York: Basic Books.

Scarr, S., & Kidd, K. K. (1983). Developmental behavior genetics. In P. H. Mussen (Ed.), *Handbook of child psychology* (4th ed., Vol. 2). New York: Wiley.

Scarr, S., & Weinberg, R. A. (1976). IQ test performance of Black children adopted by white parents. *American Psychologist, 31*, 726–739.

Scarr, S., & Weinberg, R. A. (1980). Calling all camps! The war is over. *American Sociological Review, 45*, 859–865.

Schaffer, H. R., & Emerson, R. E. (1964). The development of social attachments in infancy. *Monographs of the Society for Research in Child Development, 29* (Serial No. 94).

Schaffer, J., & Lindstrom, C. (1989). *How to raise an adopted child*. New York: Crown.

Schiff, R., & Biller, H. B. (1976). Psychological adjustment among the elderly. Unpublished manuscript, University of Rhode Island.

Schufeit, L. J., & Wurster, S. J. (1976). Frequency of divorce among parents of handicapped children. *Resources in Education, 11*, 71–78.

Schulenberg, J. E., Vondracek, E. W., & Crouter, A. C. (1984). The influence of the family on vocational development. *Journal of Marriage and the Family, 40*, 129–143.

Schulman, M., & Mekler, E. (1985). *Bringing up a moral child*. Reading, MA: Addison-Wesley.

Sciara, F. J. (1975). Effects of father-absence on the educational achievement of urban black children. *Child Study Journal, 5*, 45–55.

Sears, R. R. (1970). Relations of early socialization experiences to self-concepts and gender role in middle childhood. *Child Development, 41*, 267–289.

Sears, R. R. (1977). Sources of life satisfaction of the Terman gifted men. *American Psychologist, 32*, 119–128.

Sears, R. R., Maccoby, E. E., & Levin, H. (1957). *Patterns of child rearing*. New York: Harper & Row.

Sears, R. R., Rau, L., & Alpert, R. (1965). *Identification and child rearing*. Stanford, CA: Stanford University Press.

Seefeldt, V. D. (Ed.). (1987). *Handbook for youth sports coaches*. Reuston, VA: American Alliance for Health, Physical Education, Recreation, and Dance.

Seefeldt, V. D., Smoll, F. L., Smith, R. E., & Gould, D. (1981). *A winning philosophy for youth sports programs*. East Lansing: Michigan Institute for the Study of Youth Sports.

Seeman, J. (1989). Toward a model of positive health. *American Psychologist, 44*, 1099–1109.

Segal, M., & Adcock, D. (1981). *Just pretending: Ways to help children grow through imaginative play*. Englewood Cliffs, NJ: Prentice-Hall.

Seligman, M. E. P. (1975). *Helplessness*. San Francisco: Freeman.

Sexton, P. C. (1969). *The feminized male: Classrooms, white collars, and the decline of manliness*. New York: Random House.

Sgroi, S. M. (1981). *Handbook of clinical intervention in child sexual abuse*. Lexington, MA: Lexington Books, D.C. Heath.

Sheehy, G. (1976). *Passages: Predictable crises of adult life*. New York: Dutton.

Sheldon, W. H. (1940). *The varieties of human physique: An introduction to constitutional psychology*. New York: Harper & Row.

Sheldon, W. H., & Stevens, S. S. (1970). *The varieties of temperament: A psychology of constitutional differences* (Rev. ed.). New York: Hafner.

Shinn, M. (1978). Father absence and children's cognitive development. *Psychological Bulletin, 85*, 295–324.

Shneidman, E. (1989). The indian summer of life. *American Psychologist, 44*, 685–694.

Shortell, J. R., & Biller, H. B. (1970). Aggression in children as a function of sex of subject and sex of opponent. *Developmental Psychology, 3*, 143–144.

Siegal, M. (1984). Economic deprivation and the quality of parent-child relations: A trickle-down framework. *Journal of Applied Developmental Psychology, 5*, 127–144.

Silber, S. J. (1980). *How to get pregnant*. New York: Warner Books.

Silver, L. B. (1984). *The misunderstood child: A guide for parents of learning disabled children*. New York: McGraw-Hill.

Silverstein, L. B. (1991). Transforming the debate about child care and maternal employment. *American Psychologist, 46*, 1025–1032.

Simonton, D. K. (1984). *Genius, creativity, and leadership*. Cambridge, MA: Harvard University Press.

Singer, D. G., & Singer, J. L. (1977). *Partners in play*. New York: Harper & Row.

Singer, D. G., & Singer, J. L. (1987). Practical suggestions for controlling television. *Journal of Early Adolescence, 7*, 365–369.

Slavin, R. E. (1987). Developmental and motivational perspectives on cooperative learn-
    ing: A reconciliation. *Child Development, 58*, 1161–1167.
Slobin, D. (1972, July). Children and language: They learn the same all around the world.
    Psychology Today, 6, pp. 71–76.
Smith, M. T. (1989). Research in developmental sociobiology: Parenting and family
    behavior. In K. B. MacDonald (Ed.), *Sociobiological perspectives on human
    development* (pp. 271–292). New York: Springer-Verlag.
Smith, N. J., Smith, R. E., & Smoll, F. L. (1983). *Kidsports: A survival guide for
    parents*. Reading, MA: Addison-Wesley.
Smoll, F. L., & Smith, R. E. (1979). *Improving relationship skills in youth sport coaches*.
    East Lansing: Michigan Institute for the Study of Youth Sports.
Smoll, F. L., & Smith, R. E. (1984). Improving the quality of coach-player interaction.
    In J. R. Thomas (Ed.), *Motor development during childhood and adolescence*.
    Minneapolis, MN: Burgess.
Snarey, J. R. (1992). *Child rearing fathers: A four decade study of paternal generativity*.
    Cambridge, MA: Harvard University Press.
Snarey, J. R. (1985). Cross-cultural universality of social-moral development: A critical
    review of Kohlbergian research. *Psychological Bulletin, 97*, 202–232.
Snarey, J., Kuehne, V. S., Son, L., Hauser, S., & Vaillant, G. (1987). The role of
    parenting in men's psychosocial development: A longitudinal study of early adult-
    hood infertility and midlife generativity. *Developmental Psychology, 23*, 593–
    603.
Snarey, J., Maier, A., & Pleck, J. (1988, August). *Longitudinal consequences of father's
    participation in childrearing: Fathers' midlife outcomes and their children's early
    adult outcomes*. Paper presented at 96th Annual Convention of the American
    Psychological Association, Atlanta, GA.
Sokoloff, B. Z. (1983). Adoption and foster care. In M. D. Levine, W. B. Carey, A.
    C. Crocker, & R. T. Gross (Eds.), *Developmental-behavioral pediatrics*. Phila-
    delphia: Saunders.
Solomon, D. (1969). The generality of children's achievement-related behavior. *Journal
    of Genetic Psychology, 114*, 393–409.
Spanier, G. B., & Furstenberg, F. F., Jr. (1987). Remarriage and reconstituted families.
    In M. B. Sussman & S. K. Steinmetz (Eds.), *Handbook of marriage and the
    family* (pp. 419–434). New York: Plenum.
Spelke, E., Zelazo, P., Kagan, J., & Kotelchuck, M. (1973). Father interaction and
    separation protest. *Developmental Psychology, 9*, 83–90.
Sroufe, L. A. (1985). Attachment classification from the perspective of infant-caregiver
    relationships and infant temperament. *Child Development, 56*, 1–14.
Staffieri, J. R. (1967). A study of social stereotypes of body image in children. *Journal
    of Personality and Social Psychology, 7*, 101–104.
Starr, R. H., Jr. (1988). Physical abuse of children. In V. B. Van Hasselt, R. L. Morrison,
    A. S. Bellack, & M. Hersen (Eds.), *Handbook of family violence* (pp. 119–155).
    New York: Plenum.
Stechler, G., & Halton, A. (1982). Prenatal influences on human development. In B. B.
    Wolman (Ed.). *Handbook of developmental psychology* (pp. 175–189). Engle-
    wood Cliffs, NJ: Prentice-Hall.
Stein, A. H. (1971). The effects of sex-role standards for achievement and sex-role
    preference on three determinants of achievement motivation. *Developmental Psy-
    chology, 4*, 219–231.

Stein, A. H., & Bailey, M. M. (1973). The socialization of achievement orientation in females. *Psychological Bulletin, 80*, 345–366.

Stein, S. B. (1983). *Girls and boys: The limits of nonsexist childrearing*. New York: Scribner's.

Steinberg, L. (1981). Transformations in family relations at puberty. *Developmental Psychology, 17*, 833–840.

Steinberg, L. (1987a). Impact of puberty on family relations: Effects of pubertal status and pubertal timing. *Developmental Psychology, 23*, 451–460.

Steinberg, L. (1987b). Recent research on the family at adolescence: The extent and nature of sex differences. *Journal of Youth and Adolescence, 16*, 191–198.

Steinberg, L. (1988). Reciprocal relation between parent-child distance and pubertal maturation. *Developmental Psychology, 24*, 451–460.

Steinberg, L., Mants, N., Lamborn, S., & Dornbusch, S. (1991). Authoritative parenting and adolescent adjustment across varied ecological niches. *Journal of Research on Adolescence, 1*, 19–36.

Steinberg, L. D., Catalano, R., & Dooley, D. (1981). Economic antecedents of child abuse and neglect. *Child Development, 52*, 975–985.

Steinman, S. B. (1981). The experience of children in a joint-custody arrangement: A report of a study. *American Journal of Orthopsychiatry, 51*, 403–414.

Steinman, S. B., Zemmelman, S. E., & Knoblauch, T. M. (1985). A study of parents who sought joint custody following divorce: Who reaches agreement and sustains joint custody and who returns to court. *Journal of the American Academy of Child Psychiatry, 24*, 545–554.

Steinmetz, S. K. (1987). Family violence: Past, present, and future. In M. B. Sussman & S. K. Steinmetz (Eds.), *Handbook of family violence* (pp. 725–765). New York: Plenum.

Stern, D. N. (1985). *The interpersonal world of the infant: A view from psychoanalysis and developmental psychology*. New York: Basic Books.

Stern, M., Northman, J. E., & Van Slyk, M. R. (1984). Father-absence and adolescent "problem behaviors": Alcohol consumption, drug use, and sexual activity. *Adolescence, 19*, 301–312.

Sternberg, R. J. (1985). *Beyond IQ*. New York: Cambridge University Press.

Sternberg, R. J. (1986a). *Intelligence applied*. San Diego, CA: Harcourt Brace Jovanovich.

Sternberg, R. J. (1986b). A triangular theory of love. *Psychological Review, 93*, 119–135.

Stevenson, M. R., & Black, K. W. (1988). Paternal absence and sex-role development: A meta-analysis. *Child Development, 59*, 793–814.

Stewart, A. (1984). *Child proofing your home*. Reading, MA: Addison-Wesley.

Stipek, D., & McCroskey, J. (1989). Investing in children: Government and workplace policies for parents. *American Psychologist, 44*, 416–423.

Stoller, R. J. (1968). *Sex and gender*. New York: Science House.

Strickland, B. R. (1987). Menopause. In E. A. Blechaman & K. D. Brownell (Eds.), *Handbook of behavioral medicine for women*. Elmsford, NY: Pergamon.

Stull, D. E., & Hatch, L. R. (1984). Unravelling the effects of multiple life changes. *Research on Aging, 6*, 560–571.

Sutton-Smith, B. N. (Ed.). (1979). *Play and learning*. New York: Gardner Press.

Sutton-Smith, B. N. (1985, October). The child at play. *Psychology Today, 19*, pp. 64–65.

Sutton-Smith, B. N., & Rosenberg, B. G. (1970). *The sibling*. New York: Holt, Rinehart & Winston.

Szinovacz, M. E. (1987). Family power. In M. B. Sussman & S. K. Steinmetz (Eds.), *Handbook of marriage and the family* (pp. 651–693). New York: Plenum.

Talovic, S. A., Mednick, S. A., Schulsinger, F., & Faloon, I. R. H. (1981). Schizophrenia in high-risk subjects: Prognostic maternal characteristics. *Journal of Abnormal Psychology, 89*, 501–504.

Tannen, D. (1990). *You just don't understand: Women and men in conversation*. New York: Morrow.

Taylor, M. K., & Kogan, K. L. (1973). Effects of birth of a sibling on mother-child interactions. *Child Psychiatry and Human Development, 4*, 53–58.

Taylor, S. E. (1986). *Health psychology*. New York: Random House.

Telford, C. W., & Sawrey, J. M. (1986). *The exceptional individual*. Englewood Cliffs, NJ: Prentice-Hall.

Tegner, B. (1975). *Bruce Tegner's complete book on self-defense*. Ventura, CA: Thor.

Terman, L. M., & Oden, M. H. (1959). *Genetic studies of genius: The gifted group at midlife*. Stanford, CA: Stanford University Press.

Tharp, R. G. (1989). Psychocultural variables and constants: Effects on teaching and learning in schools. *American Psychologist, 44*, 349–359.

Thomas, A., & Chess, S. (1977). *Temperament and development*. New York: Brunner/ Mazel.

Thomas, J. L. (1986). Gender differences in satisfaction with grandparenting. *Psychology and Aging, 1*, 215–219.

Thomas, J. R. (1984). Children's motor skill development. In J. R. Thomas (Ed.), *Motor skill development during childhood and adolescence*. Minneapolis, MN: Burgess.

Thomas, J. R., & French, K. E. (1985). Gender differences across age in motor performance: A meta-analysis. *Psychological Bulletin, 98*, 260–282.

Thompson, N. L., & McCandless, B. R. (1976). The homosexual orientation and its antecedents. In A. Davids (Ed.), *Child personality and psychopathology: Volume 3* (pp. 157–197). New York: Wiley.

Thompson, N. L., Schwartz, D. M., McCandless, B. R., & Edwards, D. A. (1973). Parent-child relationships and sexual identity in male and female homosexuals and heterosexuals. *Journal of Consulting and Clinical Psychology, 41*, 120–127.

Thompson, R. A. (1983). The father's case in child custody disputes: The contributions of psychological research. In M. E. Lamb & A. Sagi (Eds.), *Fatherhood and family policy*. Hillsdale, NJ: Erlbaum.

Thompson, R. A. (1986). Fathers and the child's best interests: Judicial decision-making in custody disputes. In M. E. Lamb (Ed.), *The father's role: Applied perspectives* (pp. 61–102). New York: Wiley.

Troll, L. E., & Bengston, V. L. (1982). Intergenerational relations through the life span. In B. B. Wolman (Ed.), *Handbook of developmental psychology* (pp. 890–911). Englewood Cliffs, NJ: Prentice-Hall.

Trotter, R. J. (1987, December). Project Day-Care. *Psychology Today, 21*, pp. 32–38.

Tuck, S. (1971). Working with black fathers. *American Journal of Orthopsychiatry, 41*, 465–472.

Tuma, J. M. (1989). Mental health services for children: The state of the art. *American Psychologist, 44*, 188–199.

Turner, B. F. (1982). Sex-related differences in aging. In B. B. Wolman (Ed.), *Handbook of developmental psychology* (pp. 912–936). Englewood Cliffs, NJ: Prentice-Hall.

Tyler, A. H. (1986). The abusing father. In M. E. Lamb (Ed.), *The father's role: Applied perspectives* (pp. 255–275). New York: Wiley.

Tyler, L. E. (1983). *Thinking creatively*. San Francisco: Jossey-Bass.

Vadasy, P. F., Fewell, R. R., Meyer, D. J., & Greenberg, M. T. (1985). Supporting fathers of handicapped young children: Preliminary findings of program effects. *Analysis Intervention in Developmental Disabilities, 5*, 151–163.

Vaillant, G. E. (1977). *Adaptation to life*. Boston: Little, Brown.

Vaillant, G. E. (1978). Natural history of male psychological health, VI: Correlates of successful marriage and fatherhood. *American Journal of Psychiatry, 135*, 653–659.

Vaillant, G. E., & Vaillant, C. O. (1981). Natural history of male psychological health, X: Work as a predictor of positive mental health. *American Journal of Psychiatry, 138*, 1433–1440.

Vander Zanden, J. W. (1989). *Human development* (4th ed.). New York: Knopf.

Van Hasselt, V. B., Morrison, R. L., Bellack, A. S., & Hersen, M. (Eds.). (1988). *Handbook of family violence*. New York: Plenum.

Veevers, J. E. (1982). Researching voluntary childlessness: A critical assessment of current strategies and findings. In E. Macklin & R. Rubin (Eds.), *Contemporary families and alternative lifestyles*. Beverly Hills, CA: Sage.

Viorst, J. (1986). *Necessary losses*. New York: Simon & Schuster.

Visher, E. B., & Visher, J. (1982). *How to win as a stepfamily*. New York: Dembner Books.

Vondracek, E. W., & Lerner, R. M. (1982). Vocational role development in adolescence. In B. B. Wolman (Ed.), *Handbook of developmental psychology* (pp. 602–614). Englewood Cliffs, NJ: Prentice-Hall.

Vorhees, C. V., & Mollnow, E. (1987). Behavioral teratogenesis: Long-term influences in behavior from early exposure to environmental agents. In J. D. Osofsky (Ed.), *Handbook of infant development*. New York: Wiley.

Voydanoff, P. (1983). Unemployment and family stress. In H. Lopata (Ed.), *Research in the interweave of social roles: Jobs and families* (Vol. 3, pp. 239–250). Greenwich, CT: JAI Press.

Waite, L. J., Haggstrom, G. W., & Kanouse, D. E. (1985). The consequence of parenthood for the marital stability of young adults. *American Sociological Review, 50*, 850–857.

Walker, R. N. (1962). Body-build and behavior in young children: I. Body-build and nursery school teachers' ratings. *Monograph of the Society for Research in Child Development, 27*(3, Serial No. 84).

Walker, R. N. (1963). Body-build and behavior in young children: II. Body-build and parents' ratings. *Child Development, 34*, 1–23.

Wallach, M. A., & Kogan, N. (1965). *Modes of thinking in young children*. New York: Holt, Rinehart & Winston.

Wallerstein, J. S., & Blakeslee, S. (1989). *Second chances: Men, women, and children a decade after divorce*. New York: Ticknor & Fields.

Wallerstein, J. S., & Kelly, J. B. (1980a, January) California's children of divorce. *Psychology Today, 14*, pp. 67–76.

Wallerstein, J. S., & Kelly, J. B. (1980b). *Surviving the breakup: How children actually cope with divorce*. New York: Basic Books.

Wallerstein, J. S., & Kelly, J. B. (1982). The father-child relationship: Changes after divorce. In S. H. Cath, R. A. Gurwitt, & J. M. Ross (Eds.), *Father and child: Developmental and clinical perspectives* (pp. 451–466). Boston: Little, Brown.

Warshak, R. A. (1992). *The custody revolution: The fatherhood factor and the motherhood mystique*. New York: Poseidon Press.

Warshak, R. A., & Santrock, J. W. (1983). The impact of divorce in father-custody and mother-custody cases: The child's perspective. In A. Kurdek (Ed.), *Children and divorce: New directions for child development*. San Francisco: Jossey-Bass.

Washburn, W. E. (1962). The effects of physique and intrafamily tension on self-concept in adolescent males. *Journal of Consulting Psychology, 26,* 460–466.

Weiner-Davis, M. S. (1992). *Divorce busting: A revolutionary and rapid program for staying together*. New York: Summit Books.

Weinstein, G. W. (1987). *Children and money: A parent's guide*. New York: New American Library.

Weintraub, M., & Frankel, J. (1977). Sex differences in parent-infant interaction during free play, departure, and separation. *Child Development, 48,* 1240–1249.

Weintraub, M., & Lewis, M. (1977). The determinants of children's response to separation. *Monographs of the Society for Research in Child Development, 42* (4, Serial No. 172).

Weisberg, P. S., & Springer, K. J. (1961). Environment factors in creative function: A study of gifted children. *Archives of General Psychiatry, 5,* 554–564.

Weiss, R. S. (1975). *Marital separation*. New York: Basic Books.

Weiss, R. S. (1979a). *Going it alone: The family life and social situation of the single parent*. New York: Basic Books.

Weiss, R. S. (1979b). Growing up a little faster: The experience of growing up in a single-parent household. *Journal of Social Issues, 35,* 97–111.

Weitzman, L. J. (1985). *The divorce revolution: The unexpected social and economic consequences for women and children in America*. New York: Free Press.

Wellborn, S. N. (1987, April 13). How genes shape personality. *U.S. News & World Report*, pp. 58–62.

Wender, P. H., Kety, S. S., Rosenthal, D., Schulsinger, F., Ortmann, J., & Lunde, I. (1986). Psychiatric disorders in the biological and adoptive families of adopted individuals with affective disorders. *Archives of General Psychiatry, 43,* 923–929.

Wente, A. S., & Crockenberg, S. B. (1976). Transition to fatherhood: Lamaze preparation, adjustment difficulty, and the husband-wife relationship. *Family Coordinator, 25,* 351–357.

Werner, E. E. (1979). *Cross-cultural child development: A view from planet earth*. Monterey, CA: Brooks/Cole.

Werner, E. E., & Smith, R. S. (1982). *Vulnerable but invincible: A longitudinal study of resilient children and youth*. New York: McGraw-Hill.

Werts, C. E., & Watley, D. J. (1972). Paternal influence on talent development. *Journal of Counseling Psychology, 19,* 367–373.

Westley, W. A., & Epstein, N. B. (1970). *The silent majority*. San Francisco: Jossey-Bass.

White, B. L. (1986). *The first three years of life* (rev. ed.). New York: Prentice-Hall.

White, B. L. (1988). *Educating the infant and toddler*. Lexington, MA: Lexington Books.

White, B. L., & Watts, J. C. (Eds.). (1973). *Experience and environment*. Englewood Cliffs, NJ: Prentice-Hall.

White, R. W. (1960). Competence and the psychosexual stages of development. In M.

R. Jones (Ed.), *Nebraska Symposium on Motivation* (pp. 174–195). Lincoln: University of Nebraska Press.

Whiting, B., & Whiting, J. W. M. (1975). *Children in six cultures.* New York: Wiley.

Wilkie, J. (1981). The trend toward delayed parenthood. *Journal of Marriage and the Family, 43,* 583–591.

Willemsen, E., Flaherty, D., Heaton, C., & Ritchey, G. (1974). Attachment behavior of one-year-olds as a function of mother vs. father, sex of child, session, and toys. *Genetic Psychology Monographs, 90,* 305–324.

Willoughby, A. (1979). The alcohol troubled person. Chicago: Nelson-Hall.

Wilson, M. N. (1989). Child development in the context of the Black extended family. *American Psychologist, 44,* 380–385.

Wishard, L., & Wishard, W. (1979). *Adoption: The grafted tree.* New York: Avon.

Wiswell, R. A. (1980). Relaxation, exercise, and aging. In J. E. Birren & R. B. Sloane (Eds.), *Handbook of mental health and aging.* Englewood Cliffs, NJ: Prentice-Hall.

Witkin, H. A., & Goodenough, D. R. (1981). *Cognitive styles: Essence and origins.* New York: International Universities Press.

Wohlford, P., & Liberman, D. (1970). Effects of father-absence on personal time, field independence, and anxiety. *Proceedings of the 78th Annual Convention of the American Psychological Association, 5,* 263–264.

Wolins, M. (1983). The gender dilemma in social welfare: Who cares for children? In M. E. Lamb and A. Sagi (Eds.), *Fatherhood and family policy.* Hillsdale, NJ: Erlbaum.

Wolman, B. B. (Ed.). (1982). *Handbook of developmental psychology.* Englewood Cliffs, NJ: Prentice-Hall.

Wright, B. (1983). *Physical disability: A psychological approach* (2nd ed.). New York: Harper & Row.

Wylie, R. C. (1979). *The self-concept, Vol 2.* Lincoln: University of Nebraska Press.

Yablonsky, L. (1982). *Fathers and sons.* New York: Simon & Schuster.

Yogman, M. W. (1981). Development of the father-infant relationship. In H. Fitzgerald, B. Lester, & M. W. Yogman (Eds.), *Theory and research in behavioral pediatrics* (Vol. 1, pp. 221–279). New York: Plenum.

Yogman, M. W. (1982). Observations on the father-infant relationship. In S. H. Cath, A. R. Gurwitt, & J. M. Ross. (Eds.), *Father and child: Developmental and clinical perspectives* (pp. 101–122). Boston: Little, Brown.

Yogman, M. W. (1984). Father's roles with infants and children. In G. Miller et al. (Eds.), *Paternal absence and fathers' roles* (pp. 3–12). Hearing before the Select Committee on Children, Youth and Families, House of Representatives, 98th Congress, 1st session. Washington, DC: U.S. Government Printing Office.

Zahn-Waxler, C., Radkle-Yarrow, M., & King, R. M. (1979). Child rearing and children's prosocial initiations toward victims of distress. *Child Development, 50,* 319–330.

Zajonc, R. B. (1983). Validating the confluence model. *Psychological Bulletin, 93,* 457–480.

Zeits, C. R., & Prince, R. M. (1982). Child effects on parents. In B. B. Wolman (Ed.), *Handbook of developmental psychology* (pp. 751–770). Englewood Cliffs, NJ: Prentice-Hall.

Zigler, E. F. (1985). Assessing Head Start at 20: An invited commentary. *American Journal of Orthopsychiatry, 55,* 603–609.

Zigler, E. F. (1987). Formal schooling for four-year-olds? No. *American Psychologist, 42*, 254–260.

Zigler, E. F., & Gordon, E. W. (Eds.). (1982). *Day care: Scientific and social policy issues*. Boston: Auburn House.

Zigler, E. F., & Muenchow, S. (1984). How to influence social policy affecting children and families. *American Psychologist, 59*, 415–420.

Zill, N. (1985). *Happy, healthy, and insecure: A portrait of middle childhood in the United States*. New York: Cambridge University Press.

Zill, N. (1988). Behavior, achievement, and health problems among children in step-families: Findings from a national survey of child health. In E. M. Hetherington & J. D. Arasteh (Eds.), *Impact of divorce, single-parenting, and stepparenting on children*. Hillsdale, NJ: Erlbaum.

Zimbardo, P. G., & Radl, S. L. (1981). *The shy child: A parent's guide to preventing and overcoming shyness from infancy to adulthood*. New York: McGraw-Hill.

Author Index

Subject Index

About the Author

HENRY B. BILLER is Professor of Psychology at the University of Rhode Island, where he has taught since 1970. As a developmental clinical psychologist, he is a consultant to the John E. Fogarty Center and the Elmwood Community Center. He has also worked with a variety of other organizations serving parents and children. He was a Phi Beta Kappa, Magna Cum Laude graduate from Brown University and received his Ph.D. from Duke University in 1967. He is a consulting editor to *Archives of Sexual Behavior and Sex Roles* and is a fellow of the American Psychological Association and the American Psychological Society. He has contributed to *Annual Progress in Child Psychiatry and Child-Development* and *The Handbook of Developmental Psychology*, and he is the author and co-author of many books including *Father Power* and *Child Maltreatment and Paternal Deprivation*.